How to Do Public Policy

How to Do Public Policy

Anke Hassel
Kai Wegrich

OXFORD

UNIVERSITY PRESS

OXFORD
UNIVERSITY PRESS

Great Clarendon Street, Oxford, OX2 6DP,
United Kingdom

Oxford University Press is a department of the University of Oxford.
It furthers the University's objective of excellence in research, scholarship,
and education by publishing worldwide. Oxford is a registered trade mark of
Oxford University Press in the UK and in certain other countries

Impression: 1

Published in the United States of America by Oxford University Press
198 Madison Avenue, New York, NY 10016, United States of America

British Library Cataloguing in Publication Data
Data available

Library of Congress Control Number: 2021944566

ISBN 978-0-19-874700-0(Hbk)
ISBN 978-0-19-874719-2(Pbk)

DOI: 10.1093/oso/9780198747000.001.0001

Printed and bound by
CPI Group (UK) Ltd, Croydon, CR0 4YY

Preface

This book is a textbook for students in Master's programmes of public policy. The authors combine more than a decade of teaching public policy and public administration to the students of the Hertie School, Berlin, with a re-evaluation of the current tools and concepts of policy research. We want to equip students of public policy with a toolbox to navigate their professional roles and make their work more effective. When teaching public policy, we are often confronted with the gap between the policy knowledge among many experts and the quality of decision-making by policy-makers. On the one hand, academic researchers and policy experts know a great deal about how to address policy problems. On the other hand, decision-making by policy-makers often fails to reflect the evidence and follows different logics. We argue that students need to understand the different dynamics among those who are policy experts (acting in the 'engine room' of policy-making) and those who are in charge (the superstructure actors). These dynamics structure policy decisions to a large extent. While this insight is not new in policy research, we think that addressing the interaction between evidence and politics systematically is crucial for teaching public policy.

This book is also a mission. While we fully embrace the trend towards evidence-based policy-making and the role of knowledge in the policy process, we think how evidence is conceived in policy analysis and the practice of policy-making could and should be improved. We currently witness that, with the rise of big data and the use of new data sets in research, many policy problems are understood more quickly and could be addressed more thoroughly. For instance, in recent years there have been many studies on the importance of distinguishing between men and women when it comes to policy and product design. Women are more likely to be injured in car accidents than men are, respond differently to drugs and health care, and generally suffer from the fact that most products are designed for men (for instance the size of smartphones). These facts have always been objectively true, but it required the work of many to make them visible and turn them into usable knowledge, i.e. evidence for policy-making. However, this evidence has not yet had an impact on the regulation of drugs, health care, or product standards. To translate evidence into policy is a distinct process, which includes the politics of representation (influence of women on the policy process) and political power plays.

We think that we can do better when engaging with these issues. We aim to systematically introduce the political nature of policy-making into the teaching of public policy, but also to promote a policy research agenda that reconnects analysis for policy with policy process research. To discuss the role of capacity—in the form of stakeholders, coordination, and institutions—next to the process of policy design, implementation, and evaluation helps to broaden our understanding of problem-solving. Often policy problems are not solved because standard solutions (for instance, financial incentives or regulation) do not match the policy or political context. Actors (stakeholders), institutions (rules, norms, and mental maps) and coordination (responsibilities and adjustment) are necessary to make policies effective. A mere change in formal rules does not suffice. The context of policy is crucial. This insight has profound implications: for instance, for national or international league tables and best practice models, as well as for controlled experiments (randomized controlled trials) that feed into policy design, even though they usually do not pay much attention to the wider policy context in which experiments are set. If we want to exploit the opportunities created by more and better data, we must not only control for policy context but also understand and make use of it.

This becomes even more important given the fast-moving world of the 2020s. The impact of global changes—from climate change to digital tools—requires on the one hand a more global and coordinated policy approach. On the other hand, it also demands better, more adaptable, and intelligent policies at the local level. The problem of CO_2 emissions takes many different forms in different places. Reducing emissions cannot be addressed by a general policy toolbox, but has to be tailored to context and capacity. Many governments have tried but failed to copy successful policies from each other, due to a lack of understanding of the circumstances under which the success occurred. While learning from others is a vital part of improving policy, such learning has to be embedded in a clear understanding of the logics of context.

Basic assumptions on rationality and politics

Very often, the popular view of politics is that it is irrational and random. We do not agree with this interpretation. While the result of decision-making on policy matters is often inadequate, contradictory, and half-hearted, it is almost always the result of the interaction of rational actors. Pressing policy problems are frequently not addressed simply because it does not make sense for those in charge to invest political capital in the issue (for instance, on homelessness). Policies are inadequate because the costs of a more stringent policy are too high politically (for instance, on climate change). Policies are half-hearted because they serve the majority of citizens and do not take into account the minority (on diversity issues, but also education).

Political science research has shown that decision-making procedures structure policies. Electoral rules, federalism, and the role of independent agencies matter for policy decisions. Similarly, research in public administration and organizational studies shows that organizational forms and processes shape organizational behaviour. We think it is important to underline that policy-makers are rational actors who act in the framework of their organizational and institutional norms. Policy-makers are also individuals who simultaneously strive for their personal wellbeing and seek to fill their professional roles as policy-makers or experts.

It is not easy to make assumptions about the preferences of policy-makers. While politicians have to maintain power and pay attention to the power context to remain effective, it is less clear how this translates into policy decisions. Some policy decisions change the power context of policy-making, for instance when they redistribute resources. Some policy decisions are driven by normative or value judgements, for instance when they refer to morality issues (sex work, cannabis).

What the book offers to graduate and executive students

Master of Public Policy programmes usually aim to attract students with at least some work experience so that they can become better at their jobs. Students taking part in executive programmes arrive in public policy courses with a set of problems they face at work—either in a management role or as policy experts. Our approach is to use their considerable knowledge about their own policy experience to reflect on the underlying issues of policy design and implementation. When taking a course in public policy or the policy process, students often write insightful papers applying the concepts of the course to their own work experience. For policy students with limited work experience, the risk of falling into a 'technocratic trap', by focusing one's intellectual energy on good policy design and considering matters of political decision-making and implementation as secondary, is even higher. This book therefore offers students an interactive approach to policy analysis that includes the political and administrative process that drives policy-making in the real world.

The fields of application for these approaches are almost universal, and not confined to the rich world of OECD countries—rather the opposite. While not claiming to be experts in development issues, we contend that many problems of policy-making in the context of developing countries could and should be addressed not through simple policy design but through the analysis of capacity. Strengthening institutions is a key theme in development, alongside the role of private actors (stakeholders) and coordination.

Acknowledgements

As always, this book is built on the shoulders of many people. We would like to mention our intellectual role models, in particular Fritz W. Scharpf and Renate Mayntz, who laid the foundations for interactive policy research. Anke spent her formative academic years at the Max Planck Institute for the Study of Societies in Cologne, where both were directors. It goes without saying that they don't bear any responsibility for our take on their approach. Kai was first introduced to policy analysis by Göttrik Wewer and Werner Jann. Werner Jann became his mentor and collaborator. Ralf Clasen was an essential companion on the journey.

We are also indebted to the students at the Hertie School, who endured our teaching, gave us feedback, and were engaged in our courses and programmes. We had feedback sessions with many students who gave us useful hints and criticism. Among students offering comments and feedback were Shevaun Fitzmyers, Dunja Nofal, Diego Salazar Morales, and Renato Ventocilla Franco.

We also had a lot of help researching the case studies of the book. In particular, we would like to thank Rachel Griffin, Jessica Leong Cohen (who also edited early draft chapters), Julia Melzer, Julia Seefeld, and Milan Thies. Amanda Slater helped us with editing, referencing, and formatting the manuscript with a lot of patience. Daavid and his colleagues at bitteschoen.tv showed a lot of understanding for our particular requests for illustrations for figures and tables.

Our colleagues at the Hertie School created the environment to develop our courses and gave us advice on the material. Sonja Wälti, Gregor Walter, and Stein Kuhnle helped to initially design the course on the Policy Process. Lukas Graf, Christian Flachsland, and Thurid Hustedt used chapters in their courses; Luciana Cingolani offered very helpful and encouraging feedback on draft chapters. Cesar Zucco from FGV in Rio de Janeiro also offered excellent comments on draft chapters. We are grateful for funding from faculty activity funds and for the support from the school leadership for the project. Andrea Römmele boosted our motivation with phone calls, text messages, and by taking us for dinner. Cocomat in Bad

Belzig, Motel One Berlin Upper-West, and Gleisdreieckpark hosted us for fruitful retreats.

A very special thanks goes to Regina List, who edited the entire book with a lot of attention to detail. She challenged our thinking in numerous ways, which improved the book tremendously.

Finally, we would like to thank our partners and children for hanging in there as it took us six years to complete the book. Many weekends and holidays were spent on the manuscript, which could have been spent in other ways. We appreciate your understanding!

We dedicate this book to Henrik Enderlein, long-standing colleague at the Hertie School and an exceptional president of the School (2018–21), who left this world much too soon. A tribute to a friend.

Anke Hassel and Kai Wegrich
Berlin
April 2021

Contents

List of Figures

List of Tables

List of Boxes

Roadmap of the Book

Part I of this book presents the basic analytical concepts needed to understand the policy process and the structures and dynamics involved in it, as well as to understand how and why actors behave the way they do—and how to engage with different types of actors. But good policy-making is not only about working the seams of the policy process. Part II moves further into the nuts and bolts of making policies, including policy design, implementation, and evaluation. While engaging with the toolbox of policy-making, these chapters also show how politics and capacities influence the use of tools. Readers will learn about choices and strategies available when designing, implementing, and evaluating policies, and how politics and capacities make these strategies viable, or undermine them.

Part III introduces and explores three key aspects of the capacity to make good policies: engagement with stakeholders, the process of policy coordination in a context of interdependence, and the role of institutions. While policy analysis is mostly concerned with policy designs that should achieve effects, we consider the capacity embodied in the actors and institutions—in the state domain but also in civil society—as the critical precondition for deploying policy tools successfully.

PART I

PROCESS

Understanding the Policy Process

We live in an age of data. Big data analysis has become the dominant innovative path in policy analysis since the beginning of the twenty-first century. The exponential rise of computational power makes the use of better data compelling and very exciting.

We have been in a similar place before. Robert McNamara, former Secretary of Defense of the United States, was a strong believer in data-driven policy-making and explained in 1967:

> It is true enough that not every conceivable complex human situation can be fully reduced to the lines on a graph, or to percentage points on a chart, or to figures on a balance sheet. But all reality can be reasoned about. And not to quantify what can be quantified is only to be content with something less than the full range of reason.
>
> (cited in Danielsson 2018)

Quantification has been at the heart of policy science in the post-World War II period. Most training for policy analysts has consisted of statistics and economics, with little substantive knowledge of policy fields.

The original conception of policy analysis was moreover hierarchical or asymmetrical: knowledge was to be produced through professional re-search, and the policy-making world should use and utilize this knowledge for improving the practice of policy-making. The vision of the founder of the 'policy sciences'—Harold Lasswell—was the development of a multi-disciplinary field of science that produces knowledge for application in practice. The professional schools for public policy that opened in the 1960s, starting in the US, had the mission to train future policy-makers in the tools of policy analysis (in particular, applied economics, operations research, and management tools) in order to turn them into better users and, in part, producers of such knowledge.

The result of highly quantified policy analysis and its application to the political world is not necessarily better policy. Under McNamara, the US lost the Vietnam War despite its overpowering military command, and he later regretted his involvement in it. In policy science we have seen that, 'despite the sophisticated methods of inquiry, policy analysis has not had a major substantive impact on policy-making. Policy analysts have remained distant from power centers where policy decisions are made.... In this envi-ronment, the values of analytical rigor and logic have given way to political necessities' (Heinemann et al. 1990, 1, 9).

The project of providing public policy with a firmer scientific foundation was a 'successful failure'. It was a failure because the ambition was never realized; the use of more knowledge and state-of-the-art tools of policy analysis has not solved all political issues and problems, and indeed many of the social reforms initiated with the help of policy analysis failed. Am-bitious social reform policies designed by policy analysts did not show the expected results, and the use of policy analysis tools in government was sidelined, politicized, or neglected. But it was also a great success because policy analysis learnt from these experiences, started to study the politics of policy-making (i.e. the policy process), and invented new research fields such as implementation research and later the study of policy networks. The bottom line of much of this research is that knowledge and policy tools matter, but actors and institutions that create, adapt, and implement these policies matter more.

Fast forward forty years and look at the dominant themes of policy analysis in the early twenty-first century. Evidence-based policy-making became the dominant approach of policy analysis practised by govern-ments across the world (and not only in the Global North). Economic policy analysis is still among the most influential tools bringing knowledge and analysis to policy practice—now packaged in internal rules, proce-dures, and checklists, and supervised by watchdogs in systems of 'impact assessment'. In addition, policy experiments in the form of randomized controlled trials (RCTs) using randomly selected treatment and control groups became popular and—combined with the rise of big data and artifi-cial intelligence—promised a new level of knowledge, control, and change. With better methods, more knowledge about how to use them, more data, and multiplying computational power, it is possible to avoid the failures from the childhood of policy analysis—and unleash the potential of evi-dence. Of course, political leaders must still use data and knowledge, but the quality of the input they get is much higher.

While not seeking to quash anyone's enthusiasm for working with data, knowledge, and information, the starting point and conviction of this book is that data are neither neutral inputs that only need to be used, nor are they apolitical and independent from the world of politics (which includes the highly visible policy-making 'on deck' of the political ship and the 'bureaucratic' policy-making in the engine room). Indeed, we might have to be more mindful of using data because the increased methodologi-cal firepower, the availability of data, and the enhanced computational capacities make the use of data more consequential—for example, when automated systems make decisions about social benefits, paroles, or fines. Over-confidence in the superior power of data and modelling—and the apolitical framing of their use—can have far-reaching consequences.

In short, policy analysis needs to bring politics, actors, and institutions back into the centre of 'how to do public policy'. Tools are important as tools, and they should be used for a purpose without becoming the purpose. Good policy analysis needs to work with politics, and not try to replace it (Wildavsky 1979). Our aim with this book is to bring an understanding of politics to improve policy-making.

Politics is fundamental to policy, and we introduce our conceptual map for navigating this world in the three chapters of this first part of the book. Chapter 1 discusses the three branches of policy analysis and how we seek to reconnect them. Chapter 2 introduces our fundamental model of how to think about the political structure of policy-making, namely the vis-ible high politics of executive leaders and their publicly staged struggle for power and influence, on one level, and the more specialized working level consisting of experts, bureaucrats, and stakeholders. We call the vis-ible part the 'superstructure', which consists of all the political actors on deck and the institutions structuring their interactions. The more hidden policy work happens in what we call the 'engine room'. Chapter 2 shows that policy-making is driven by the different logics and structures of the superstructure and engine room and discusses how exchange between the two levels is organized.

Chapter 3 then focuses on the dynamics of the policy process. Successful policy-making is inherently linked to change, since new problems call for new or adapted solutions. But as we argue in Chapter 3, such change is not easily achieved when political forces are in an equilibrium. Policy change is strongly associated with the dynamics of agenda-setting, i.e. which policy issues enter the agenda of policy-making institutions, when, and how, and which issues are not seriously considered or are actively suppressed. Understanding the dynamics of agenda-setting is key for understanding the policy process and policy change. The chapter captures this dynamic by showing how different types of actors in the superstructure and engine room pursue different agenda-setting strategies, and how these strategies interact and shape policy development.

1
Public Policy

Key concepts

- Public policy
- Policy analysis
- Evidence-based policy-making
- Process, policies, capacity
- Policy process and decision-making

This introductory chapter gives an overview of the essential components of public policy. Starting from the quest for evidence-based policy-making in twenty-first-century states, the chapter introduces this book's fundamental understanding of 'how to do (good) public policy'. The core argument is that doing public policy requires the skills and capacities to understand the policy problem at hand and expertise regarding past and present policies related to this problem—what has been tried and tested, what failed, and what worked. But policy-makers and supporting analysts also need an understanding of the political process of getting to good policies. On the basis of a brief survey of the intellectual foundations of policy analysis, the chapter introduces an 'interactive' approach to policy analysis and how it relates to other branches of policy analysis. Finally, the chapter identifies the constituent components of how to do public policy which structure the book: process, policies, and capacity.

1.1 Public Policy in the Twenty-First Century

Throughout 2019, fierce protests by the *gilets jaunes* (yellow vests) dominated French politics. There were weekly demonstrations for forty-five weeks. Almost 3,000 protesters and police were injured, almost 100 had serious injuries, and at least ten protesters died (Gautier 2020). The *gilets jaunes* were initially prompted to protest by tax increases on fuel (see Box 1.1). As President Macron pointed out: taxing non-renewable fuel

How to Do Public Policy. Anke Hassel and Kai Wegrich, Oxford University Press.
© Anke Hassel and Kai Wegrich (2022). DOI: 10.1093/oso/9780198747000.003.0001

to pay for investments in renewable energy was on the list of policy instruments available to combat climate change. Nonetheless, the introduction of this particular policy instrument backfired badly.

Box 1.1 The gilets jaunes

The *gilets jaunes* movement began as a protest against a rise in duties on diesel, the fuel most commonly used by French motorists, which has long been less heavily taxed than other types of fuel. The original group of *gilets jaunes* consisted mainly of working- and middle-class people, who had little choice but to commute to work by car.

The price of diesel rose by more than 23% between 2017 and 2018, to an average of €1.51 (£1.32/$1.71) per litre, higher than it had been in the early 2000s. President Emmanuel Macron blamed world oil prices for the majority of the price increase, but insisted that higher taxes on fossil fuels were needed to fund renewable energy investments. The prospect of a further increase in the fuel tax, of 6.5 cents on diesel from 1 January 2019, was the spark that sent the *gilet jaunes* into the streets in November 2018 (BBC News 2018). In terms of policy substance, the purpose of the transport fuel tax is to reduce the miles travelled by making it more expensive and to provide incentives for the purchase and manufacturing of vehicles with lower CO_2 emissions.

We often think of public policies today as an exercise in problem-solving that should be separate from the world of politics, with its ideologies, emotions, and power plays. Experts argue that good tools and regulations can help governments respond to major global challenges, such as climate change: surely, as Macron and his administration must have thought, a tax on non-renewable fuel will make drivers shift to electric cars or public transport and will raise money needed for investment. At the same time, many policy tools backfire—as evidenced by the expanding protests of the *gilets jaunes*—or are ineffective because the political context is not taken into account.

Modern public policy-making aims to square effective problem-solving with the reality of the political context in which policy-making takes place. This includes not only an assessment of which parts of policies are contentious but also the necessary actions to mobilize political support for a policy. While problems are becoming more complex and intertwined, the

inherent nature of politics continues to be seen in the conflict between societal groups and their aspirations. This is also expressed in the symbols
of policy and politics. More complex legislation running into thousands of
pages is passed by old-fashioned parliamentary rules under which members of parliament are subjected to ancient rituals. The Queen, as the head
of state of the United Kingdom, presides over a government which has to
deal with exceptionally complicated policy issues, such as financial regulation. The national budget which affects millions of jobs, livelihoods, and
the health of the British people is still paraded through the ancient halls
of Westminster in a red leather box. There is a stark contrast between the
rituals of power in established democracies and the complexity of policy
tools available to them.

The aim of this book is to offer guidance on how to do public policy
under these changing conditions. Such guidance has to take into account
complex and numerous policy problems, while offering analytical clues for
dealing with new policy tools and for exploring the role of policy analysis in the context of multi-actor decision-making. While our ambition
is unashamedly applied, we argue for a way of thinking about the making of public policy that aims to complement the offerings of other public
policy textbooks (Howlett et al. 2020; Knill and Tosun 2020; Bardach and
Patashnik 2019; Bekkers et al. 2017).

The tools and recommendations from the typical policy analysis and
problem-solving literature are too often oblivious to the reality of the
policy-making process, which is shaped by political conflicts at various
levels—from public contestation to bureaucratic in-fights. We do not deny
the value of, and need for, policy analysis tools, such as the many variations of cost–benefit analysis, stakeholder mapping, and ex post evaluation.
However, we aim at a more realistic and politically astute take on how to use
them and on how to think about policy-making more generally. In particular, we stress the limited value of thinking in terms of 'best practice' or 'what
works', the crucial role of context and institutions, and the importance of
critical thinking and judgement. Effective solutions, in other words, have
to be seen in the societal context and that of administrative and political
capacity.

In order to better explain what that means, we will first briefly introduce the role of evidence-based policy, the dominant catchword in policy
analysis circles of the twenty-first century. Then we explain the field of
policy analysis and explore the core characteristics of policy analysis that
have developed since the field's inception in the early 1950s. We simplify

the multifaceted realm of policy analysis by distinguishing between three branches—substantive, tools-oriented, and interactive—and their underlying assumptions and understandings of policy-making. In doing so, we also introduce some fundamental definitions, concepts, and models on which we draw in the subsequent chapters. In the concluding section, we outline our own understanding of what policy analysis for the real world today can, and should, deliver. As our aim is to make the accumulated knowledge in public policy research useful for policy analysts, we use policy cases throughout the book as illustrations.

1.2 Evidence-Based Policy-Making

Evidence-based policy-making has become the gold standard of modern public policy. The approach has been applied more often in some policy fields, such as health and environmental studies, but it primarily grew out of the ambitions of certain governments to deploy modern tools in public administration. In 1999, the British government published the white paper *Modernising Government* and launched a substantial drive towards better policy-making. The white paper states:

> People are becoming more demanding, whether as consumers of goods and services in the market place, as citizens or as businesses affected by the policies and services which government provides. To meet these demands, government must be willing constantly to re-evaluate what it is doing so as to produce policies that really deal with problems; that are forward-looking and shaped by the evidence rather than a response to short-term pressures; that tackle causes not symptoms; that are measured by results rather than activity; that are flexible and innovative rather than closed and bureaucratic; and that promote compliance rather than avoidance or fraud. To meet people's rising expectations, policy making must also be a process of continuous learning and improvement.
>
> (Cabinet Office 1999, 8)

Since then, many governments around the world have increasingly pursued an evidence-based policy agenda. Evidence-based policy aims to apply scientific knowledge to policy problems. The Secretariat-General of the European Commission includes evidence-based policy in its mission statement: the secretariat 'coordinates, facilitates, advises and arbitrates, so as to ensure the coherence, quality and delivery of policy, legislation and operations across policy areas and Commission departments, in line with the better regulation principles and evidence-based policy making' (European Commission n.d.-a).

International organizations, such as the Organization for Economic Cooperation and Development (OECD) and the World Bank, also see the use of evidence and knowledge as essential for improving policy and addressing critical issues, such as poverty. 'Policymakers need evidence of what works to reduce poverty and improve people's lives. The World Bank is working to generate and disseminate knowledge on effective policies and programs that can raise living standards and give people the opportunity to escape poverty and raise healthy and productive children' (World Bank 2012).

However, evidence-based policy is not as easy as it sounds. Studies have shown that evidence only partially enters the policy-making process and that evidence cannot take the place of politics in public policy-making. Often the resulting policy is based on many implicit assumptions about the distribution of costs and benefits, as well as risks, among different groups in society. Furthermore, such a policy might violate other competing goals or the normative orientations of many citizens. Evidence-based policy might also be perverted when governments seek to capture and control knowledge production—a process that might be called the making of 'policy-based evidence' (Boden and Epstein 2006). Governments might thus commission research that provides results supportive of their preferred policy, or they might cherry-pick particular evidence. Evidence-based policy-making can also be used as a way to politicize the research community, with the promise of earmarked research funding, university positions, or government advisory roles.

Pointing to the potential for unduly politicized evidence should, however, not be confused with the technocratic claim that evidence is already 'out there' and only needs to be 'used' by policy-makers in an objective and unbiased way to arrive at good policy. Evidence is not simply 'out there'. Instead:

- Research, even applied research dedicated to addressing policy problems, often does not provide conclusive answers to 'what to do' questions. This requires interpretation, the weighing of different aspects and dimensions, and the like (Lindblom and Cohen 1979). Indeed, research becomes 'evidence' in the sense that lawyers use the word: as pieces of information that are used to support an argument of one stakeholder in the policy process (Majone 1989).

- The policy process is an integral part of evidence creation in the first place. Prominent examples are the OECD's Programme for International Student Assessment (PISA) studies on student achievement (see Chapter 6), data generated by so-called smart city technologies, poverty and race-related data, and even crime statistics. The categories used and technologies deployed not only reflect choices already made about what is important or should be done, but also ultimately influence how a policy is implemented. For example, in the 1950s and 1960s, the newly created crime statistics recorded steeply rising crime rates in cities in the United States as a result of 'over-policing' black youth and 'measuring' crime at the same time. 'The fact that segregated urban neighborhoods received a disproportionate amount of police attention led to an increased number of reported arrests and continued to skew the national crime rate accordingly' (Hinton 2016, 84–5).

While good policy-making entails an honest effort to use available evidence or to generate it during the policy process, it remains a technocratic illusion that an increased use of evidence will solve policy problems, reduce the level of political conflict, or eliminate the need to take political decisions.

In short, evidence-based policy is by no means a panacea that results in 'neutral' or strictly scientific policy-making. Even in circles promoting the use of evidence, the language has shifted from 'evidence-based' to 'evidence-informed' policy-making (Mair et al. 2019, Zubaşcu 2019). While evidence-based policy-making remains the most promising path to improve public policy, it has its own problems (Parkhurst 2017).

The Paris Agreement illustrates some of the current challenges of making public policy (see Box 1.2). The reduction of greenhouse gas emissions appears to be a fundamentally technical challenge as it requires, for example, the adoption of renewable energy technologies, a move from combustion engines to electric cars, the insulation of buildings, and the like. At the same time, reducing emissions has wide implications for the lives of people whose mobility might be restricted, for whom the cost of living might rise, and whose livelihoods are endangered. These same climate change policies have winners too: for instance, when non-arable land can be used for windfarms or new technologies create jobs. Implementation of the treaty involves policy decisions that have distributive effects. These decisions are heavily contested and can potentially undermine the political legitimacy of governments. In France, in November 2018, the *gilet jaunes* movement started to protest against higher petrol prices, which were partly the result of higher taxes enacted to reduce CO_2 emissions from car traffic (see Box 1.1). The Paris Agreement and the reaction by the *gilet jaunes* to efforts to implement it in France illustrate how evidence-informed policy-making can lead to backlash if it is not situated in a broader policy strategy that identifies a policy's winners and losers and provides the means to compensate the losers.

Even when a broader strategy is well thought through and the underlying evidence is scientifically sound, other factors can hinder implementation. For example, even the large number of well-respected scientists who work on climate issues cannot provide the necessary trust and political support which enable governments to take sufficient action. Indeed, they face pushback from 'merchants of doubt', a politically and economically motivated campaign intended to undermine the case for far-reaching climate change policy, which uses unproven or pseudoscientific 'evidence' to sow seeds of doubt about the facts (Oreskes and Conway 2010).

Box 1.2   Excerpts from the 2015 Paris Agreement

Article 2

1. This Agreement, in enhancing the implementation of the [United Nations Framework] Convention [on Climate Change], including its objective, aims to strengthen the global response to the threat of climate change, in the context of sustainable development and efforts to eradicate poverty, including by:

    (a) Holding the increase in the global average temperature to well below $2\,°C$ above pre-industrial levels and pursuing efforts to limit the temperature increase to $1.5\,°C$ above pre-industrial levels, recognizing that this would significantly reduce the risks and impacts of climate change;

    (b) Increasing the ability to adapt to the adverse impacts of climate change and foster climate resilience and low greenhouse gas emissions development, in a manner that does not threaten food production; and

    (c) Making finance flows consistent with a pathway towards low greenhouse gas emissions and climate-resilient development.

continued

Box 1.2 *continued*

---

2. This Agreement will be implemented to reflect equity and the principle of common but differentiated responsibilities and respective capabilities, in the light of different national circumstances.

Article 4

1. In order to achieve the long-term temperature goal set out in Article 2, Parties aim to reach global peaking of greenhouse gas emissions as soon as possible, recognizing that peaking will take longer for developing country Parties, and to undertake rapid reductions thereafter in accordance with best available science, so as to achieve a balance between anthropogenic emissions by sources and removals by sinks of greenhouse gases in the second half of this century, on the basis of equity, and in the context of sustainable development and efforts to eradicate poverty.

2. Each Party shall prepare, communicate and maintain successive nationally determined contributions that it intends to achieve. Parties shall pursue domestic mitigation measures, with the aim of achieving the objectives of such contributions.

3. Each Party's successive nationally determined contribution will represent a progression beyond the Party's then current nationally determined contribution and reflect its highest possible ambition, reflecting its common but differentiated responsibilities and respective capabilities, in the light of different national circumstances.

(United Nations 2015)

1.3 What is Policy Analysis?

Policy analysis was launched as a problem-oriented and interdisciplinary field of study that should inform decision-making. Originating from the optimistic can-do attitude of the post-World War II age of technological advancement, the idea was to introduce scientific research methods and findings into the political decision-making process, and thereby improve the practice of policy-making and, ultimately, policy outcomes. Policy research institutions and think tanks acted as intellectual driving forces for this agenda, and by the 1960s the tools of policy analysis had taken centre stage in government efforts to enhance the policy-making capacity of their departments and agencies, first in the US and later across countries of the Western world. Since that time, policy analysis has become a growth industry, and the 'policy analyst' has approached the status of a distinct profession (Radin 2013).

Policy analysis is usually defined as the field of study and practice dealing with the development, implementation, and evaluation of public policies and their outcomes. In the title of his primer on the topic, Thomas Dye (1976) defined policy analysis as 'what governments do, why they do it and what difference it makes'. *Public policies* are considered courses of action, rather than just individual case-by-case decisions, that governments deploy in order to address societal problems that have entered the political agenda with the mandate and expectation to do something about them. Hence, the term policy includes a strong element of intention, of purposeful action in response to a perceived societal problem. Paradoxically, that also includes purposeful inaction, which could result in the upholding of the status quo or change brought about by doing nothing. For example, welfare policies for the poor in many countries include not enforcing property laws and instead tolerating informal housing on public or private land (Holland 2017).

This also implies that policy is not the same as a programme: while a *programme*—a government action to address a particular issue by deploying the resources of government (authority, monetary resources, information, or personnel and organizational resources)—is the materialization of a policy. A policy can also be to not adopt a (new) programme. Finally, the focus on intent does not presume that the policy-maker's primary motivation is to address a societal problem. Rather, policy analysis explores political action by asking how it addresses such a problem.

This *policy* dimension—the substantive aspect of political action, i.e. the programmes, laws, and agency activities in policy domains, such as agriculture, defence, energy, and the environment—defines the field of policy analysis. The other two dimensions of the threefold understanding of 'the political' in the English language are *polity*, referring to the institutional system or regime and its formal and informal rules, norms, and standard operating procedures, and *politics,* referring to the political games being played between the various actors that are, or want to be, involved.

Policy analysis is in particular concerned with how policies are made—the *policy-making* or *policy process*—and what difference that makes in terms of addressing societal problems. The basic understanding of *policy-making* entails the following: an actor or organization with the legitimacy to deploy public policies does so by deciding on a course of action, or *intervention*, from among different *policy instruments* or *tools*—such as regulations, incentives, or information—to influence the behaviour of a defined *target group*. For example, a speed limit employs regulation to influence the behaviour of motorists (how fast they drive). The activities of these implementing agencies (which could include non-governmental organizations charged with policy implementation) are called the policy *output*. The behaviour change triggered by the intervention (compliance with the speed limit), called the *outcome*, should help to address the perceived problem by reducing the number of road accidents and hence improving road safety (the policy's *impact*) (see Box 1.3).

Policy-making, therefore, entails identifying a problem and putting it on the agenda in order to develop a course of action; formulating and adopting a particular intervention (a policy, programme, or instrument); implementing this decision, and evaluating its impact, possibly leading to its termination or adaptation. This ideal-typical model of policy-making has been called the *policy cycle*, a term which emphasizes the continuous nature of policy-making, in which the outputs, impacts, and outcomes of one policy-making process become the input, or starting point, of another cycle (Jann and Wegrich 2007). While this depiction of the policy cycle is often criticized for its simple assumptions, it is frequently used because it can structure diverse literature and answer important questions about the nature of the policy process (Fischer et al. 2007, xx–xxi).

Box 1.3   Basic terms of policy analysis

Public policy: any measure by governments to address a problem

Polity: the institutional system or regime and its formal and informal rules, norms, and standard operating procedures

Politics: the way to establish power structures and order within societies; the interaction between actors involved

Policy input: knowledge and evidence for solving problems; resources (budget, personnel); demands and support for policy change

Policy instrument or tool: the type of policy intervention used to influence the target population to achieve desired policy objectives

Programme: a concrete policy intervention, not necessarily, but often, relying on a combination of policy instruments

Policy output: activities carried out by implementing agencies

Policy outcome: effect of policies on behaviour of target population
Policy impact: overall effect of measures on policy problem

Policy analysis was established as an applied field of study with the aim of informing, influencing, and improving public policy. Recent times have seen an increased demand for such an interdisciplinary field, which can improve how governments, international organizations, and, increasingly, non-governmental organisations (NGOs) go about debating, designing, adopting, and implementing policies to address perceived societal problems.

Following a first wave in the late 1960s and early 1970s, starting in the US and then diffusing globally, the late twentieth and early twenty-first centuries saw a second wave of professional schools and programmes for public policy established across the globe. These courses are intended to train future policy-makers in the art and craft of policy-making, in particular by equipping them with the analytical tools and skills to formulate better (policy) solutions and to devise the right means and ways to implement policies successfully. The ambition of the field of policy analysis and these professional schools is to contribute towards solving pertinent challenges confronting societies and, hence, governments. However, though professional schools became increasingly specialized and policy analysis became more established, the contribution of public policy schools to solving the 'wicked' problems of our times remained disappointing (cf. Piereson and Riley 2013; Anheier 2019). We highlight three central developments that present challenges for the practical world of policy-making.

The first fundamental challenge relates to the increasing complexity of the policy problems at hand. Major issues in many policy fields—including climate change, development, poverty, and public health—remain unsolved, and all of these call for persistent efforts to improve how policies are designed and implemented. At the same time, new problems have populated the agenda which are no less challenging. The global financial crisis, which began in 2007, exposed the vulnerability of the global model of economic governance, which is also under siege today from renewed populism and nationalism. 2020 saw the global spread of an airborne disease (COVID-19, caused by a coronavirus variation), and this pandemic has again shown both the essential relevance of good public policy and the pivotal role of process, policies, and capacity in managing the crisis. Containing pandemic diseases, regulating financial industries, fighting tax avoidance, or limiting the online circulation of hate speech and disinformation in an interdependent world are major endeavours, which have to be addressed while simultaneously engaging in efforts to maintain and enhance the capacity of political institutions that develop and deliver policies. This includes efforts to strengthen the regulatory, implementation, coordination, and analytical capacities of government organizations, as well as efforts to limit corruption and improve accountability and transparency, i.e. maintain a sufficient level of trust in political institutions (Lodge and Wegrich 2014a).

But it is not only the problem side of policy-making that has evolved. The government toolbox to address these problems has also changed at an increasing pace since the turn of the twenty-first century. The tools of government, i.e. the means or instruments that governments have at their disposal to influence a target population, have diversified from the basic types—regulations, incentives, information, and direct provision of services—to a range of hybrids and combinations: for example, various forms of self- and co-regulation. New policy tools such as 'nudges' (tweaks of the design of programmes to influence people's choices, such as changing the default option for organ donation to opting out) have begun to change how policies are conceptualized, placing additional demands on the analytical capacity of policy-makers. In policy delivery, private sector organizations and NGOs play more prominent roles, even up to the point of 'co-production'. While one should not overestimate the novelty of some policy fashions, the menu from which policy-makers can choose has surely become longer. At the same time, the analytical tools that policy-makers are expected to use in developing and justifying policy proposals have also become more ambitious and diverse. While many variations of cost–benefit analysis and related tools for economic analysis remain at the core, others have been added—not only experimental methods for running trials to test nudges, 'behavioural insights', and 'big data analytics', but also tools to engage with other actors, such as stakeholder mapping and consultation.

The third development making public policy a more challenging business today is the policy-making system itself. Since the inception of policy analysis, the architecture of modern governance has changed, as has the underlying political economy shaping decision-making. In the past, policy analysis and advice was about 'speaking truth to power' (Wildavsky 1979). Today the question is often about who the powerful decision-makers actually are: are they government leaders, international organizations, philanthropic organizations, or industry associations and private sector firms? Dispersion of power upwards to the transnational level, downwards to regional and local governments, and in particular sideways to a range of societal actors has changed the way policies are made—but without making government superfluous or less important, as the debate about the decline of the state sometimes suggests.

No less significant than the developments in policy-making itself are changes in the wider environment of policy-makers: long-standing political cleavages between business and labour and the constituencies of conservative and progressive political parties have been changing for decades. The white working class have abandoned their support for progressive parties and started voting for conservative and right-wing parties in many countries. Political coalitions have broken up, and new alliances are in the making. In addition, communication and public discourses have been transformed through social media (Stockmann and Luo 2018). They have a profound impact on how policies are debated and evaluated, how actors mobilize support or resistance, how issues are launched or dropped from political agendas, and how blame games are played. Even our understanding of what constitutes an 'actor' in policy-making needs to be updated, given the new political role of crowds (or mobs).

1.4 Three Branches of Policy Analysis

Policy analysis as a field of study has developed into three different branches (cf. Heclo 1972; Scharpf 1997), each of which comes with its own understandings about policy-making and how it should work. In Table 1.1, we sketch a rough outline of these three main branches: substantive and tools-oriented policy analysis, both of which are more directly applied, and interactive policy analysis, which is less instrumental but nonetheless critically relevant for policy-makers.

The field of public policy research developed with a clear emphasis on the first two branches, which are also related. The birth of policy analysis is usually associated with the work of Harold Lasswell, who aimed to establish the 'policy sciences' as a social science meta-discipline intended to provide decision-makers with objective solutions to policy problems. In 'The Policy Orientation', published as part of *The Policy Sciences,* co-edited with Daniel Lerner, Lasswell (1951) introduced policy analysis as the study of the role of knowledge both 'in and of the policy process'. Problems were

Table 1.1 The three branches of policy analysis

BRANCH	PRIMARY CONCERN	MAIN ACTIVITY	OVERALL AIM
Substantive	The substance of policies, i.e. what difference policies make for society and the problem at hand	Acquiring and using (expert) knowledge to provide the best solutions to policy problems; evaluating the effectiveness of policies	To find optimal policy solutions to address particular policy problems
Tools-oriented	The tools of policy-making, i.e. how to use methods of policy analysis to improve policy-making	Providing tools, methods, and procedures to governments (and NGOs) for planning, designing, and implementing the best policy solutions	To make the policy-making process more intelligent and rational through tools and procedures of planning and decision-making
Interactive	The political process of policy-making, i.e. how to achieve good policies under conditions of contested politics	Explaining policy processes and their outcomes, often with an emphasis on cross-national and cross-sectoral comparison	To understand policy-making as the result of actors' aims to influence decisions that allocate values and resources under institutional constraints

considered (already then) too complex for standard modes of democratic decision-making to suffice, not least because of the limited capacity of the lay citizen to judge what should be done to address complicated policy issues. The conceived role of the policy sciences was to mediate between the academic domain, political decision-makers, and citizens and to reduce the need for political conflicts and politics in general by providing dispassionate, impartial solutions.

1.4.1 Substantive policy analysis

Substantive policy analysis is concerned with the question of 'what should be done' to address societal problems (hence Fritz W. Scharpf (1997) refers to this branch as 'problem-oriented policy research'). Given the multitude of policy issues being dealt with at any given point in time, substantive policy analysis can only be multidisciplinary or, better yet, interdisciplinary. For example, climate scientists are as relevant as engineers for energy policy, public health experts are as relevant as urban planners in developing water policy, and virologists and epidemiologists for pandemic diseases. The substantive branch of policy analysis is also the most sector- or topic-specific branch—becoming an expert in energy policy, for example, naturally entails specialization, and the lessons from climate science are relevant for climate policy, but not necessarily for labour market policy (which makes learning across fields difficult). Even for more generalist policy analysts working in the other branches and for policy practitioners, it is essential to develop some expertise in a specific policy field (Herrera and Post 2019).

This branch of policy analysis gained major influence in the mid-1960s, during the 'Great Society' and 'War on Poverty' programmes of US President Lyndon B. Johnson, whose ambitious social policy reforms addressed civil rights, poverty, inequality, urban development, health care, and education. Much of the input for policy design came from various academic experts and government advisers. Ideally, figuring out what a good policy solution should look like, on the basis of expert input, should be the first step in the policy process on which the two other branches can build (see Scharpf 1997).

Substantive policy analysis is of critical importance, and policy analysts and policy-makers need a fair degree of expertise in the respective subfield. Networks and interaction between experts, government policy-makers, and politicians are essential for overcoming barriers to communication shaped by the different logics of science and policy/politics. The COVID-19 pandemic crisis that began in 2020 has shown just how critical scientific capacity and expertise are for problem-solving, but it has also revealed the kind of communication problems that might hinder a fruitful relationship (van Dooren and Nordegraaf 2020). Virologists and epidemiologists became important government advisers for formulating policy responses to contain the spread of the virus. As the pandemic developed, science-based government advice moved from social distancing and mask-wearing (which was questioned early on) to more specific recommendations with regard to the risks of opening (and closing again) public schools or organizing mass events.

At the same time, knowledge of which policy could address a problem is seldom enough. That expert input and knowledge are not sufficient for solving policy problems was one major lesson from the disappointing track record of the War on Poverty programmes in the US (cf. Nelson 1977).

While limits of available knowledge for solving complex problems were seen as a major factor accounting for policy failure, attention increasingly turned to how the ways in which policies were developed and implemented could create bottlenecks for 'knowledge utilization'.

1.4.2 Tools-oriented policy analysis

From the perspective of tools-oriented policy analysis, the availability of substantive knowledge is not enough to address policy problems. To improve policies, tools and processes are needed that allow knowledge to be infused into the policy-making process, thereby improving political or bureaucratic decision-making. Already in 1956, Lasswell had introduced a linear model of how policy should be formulated and executed, which later developed into the policy cycle mentioned earlier in this chapter (Lasswell 1956). Lasswell's model consisted of seven stages: intelligence, promotion, prescription, invocation, application, appraisal, and termination. While later variations also served descriptive and analytical purposes, Lasswell's stages model was clearly more prescriptive in its outlook: good policy-making should go through this linear sequence of stages in order to address a problem rationally.

This rational model of problem-solving—and the idea that policy-making is a process that can, and should, be structured in a way to maximize the use of knowledge and analysis in the process of decision-making—lies at the heart of the tools-oriented branch of policy analysis. Rational planning frameworks and economic decision modelling became the hallmarks of this branch of policy analysis. Based on early experiences in the fields of (water) infrastructure planning and weapons procurement in defence, applied quantitative fields, such as operations research, systems analysis, and cost–benefit analysis, provided models for decision-making tools with the ambition of a wider application to any policy issue (cf. Nelson 1977). These models were developed and tested in think tanks, like the RAND Corporation and Brookings Institution, and then imported to (US) government practice in the late 1960s. Heclo (1972, 98) captured the common logic of these models: 'Information and analysis is organised around comparisons of alternative courses of action aimed at reaching some objective or set of objectives.' The aim of policy analysis is thus to aid the selection of the most efficient option to address a pre-established, politically mandated objective ('logic of choice', Nelson

1977). While sharing this general logic, operations research, systems analysis, and cost–benefit analysis differ in terms of the specificity of the decisional situation, with operations research targeting very specific situations and systems analysis targeting broader decisions about strategic priorities, including objectives. Cost–benefit analysis as the middle ground (fairly clear but more general objectives) has been the most influential variation in practice.

Once considered the ultimate cost–benefit analysis scheme, the Planning, Programming, and Budgeting System (PPBS) was introduced in the US Department of Defense in 1961 and then across all federal departments. It sought to establish rational decisions for allocating resources between alternative programmes by linking each programme to performance information and budgetary costs. The case for PPBS was compelling: it promised to provide more informed political decisions about priorities. However, the practice of PPBS in the US government revealed more than that: the information-processing capacities of government were overwhelmed by the demands of PPBS. In effect, comparing the costs and benefits of different programmes in different policy areas in an 'objective' way remained an illusion. As William Gorham (at that time Assistant Secretary at the Department of Health, Education, and Welfare, a key department pushing cost–benefit analysis and other tools of economic policy analysis in government) put it during a Congressional hearing in 1967:

> No amount of analysis is going to tell us whether the Nation benefits more from sending a slum child to pre-school, providing medical care to an old man or enabling a disabled housewife to resume her normal activities. The 'grand decisions'—how much health, how much education, how much welfare, and which groups in the population shall benefit—are questions of value judgments and politics. The analyst cannot make much contribution to their resolution.
>
> (cited in Wildavsky 1969, 195)

While PPBS was quickly abandoned in the US, as it was in other countries that experimented with the model, the push to use analytical tools and methods to inform and change the policy-making process continued, and in particular to guide the choice between different programmes or policy options. Cost–benefit analysis was introduced as a tool to aid policy design in the form of regulatory impact assessment (or analysis), and variations of performance budgeting have remained widely used. Since the 1990s, these analytical tools—plus new ones, such as policy experiments (RCTs)—have been integrated in the evidence-based policy-making agenda. Neverthe-less, in the early 1970s, disappointment with both the outcomes of (welfare) reform programmes and the analytical tools of rational decision-making provided a tailwind for the development of the third branch of policy analysis, namely the interactive branch.

1.4.3 Interactive policy analysis

In general, research influenced by interactive policy analysis is interested in explaining policy outputs and outcomes, i.e. which policy choices gov-ernments make and how they influence the targeted problem area. It often links to the substantive branch of policy analysis by asking why a (good) policy solution has, or has not, been adopted in one context (i.e. a coun-try) or has been poorly implemented. In the 1960s, comparative analyses of policy outcomes between US states had already become a fruitful area of research, but the experience with the reform period of the late 1960s and early 1970s shifted attention more to the politics of the policy process by exploring the question of why well-designed policies, which had been adopted with broad political support and sufficient resources, still failed to deliver the intended results. As policy-oriented research built on a num-ber of case studies that used decision-making as an analytical focus to study the distribution of political power and its impact on policy in the 1960s (cf. Lowi 1970; Heclo 1972), Theodore Lowi became a key figure in advancing this agenda.

At the core of studying public policy-making, in Lowi's view, was the analysis of decisions about how the power of the state is applied in the de-sign of public policies. One way of conducting such an analysis is to study the use of coercion, as well as positive and negative incentives in the adop-tion and implementation of public policies. Policy problems, objectives, and intentions are of secondary relevance in this view. Instead, emphasis is placed on exploring how different actors—government organizations, politicians, interest organizations, and others—seek to influence policy de-cisions, successfully or not. In short, interactive policy analysis explores the politics of policy-making as a process of conflict and consensus-building among interdependent actors. Both how these processes play out and their results are influenced by the actors' preferences and strategies, on the one hand, and the institutional context providing the rules of the game, on the other (Scharpf 1997). In fact, the interactive perspective is the least applied branch of policy analysis, at least in a direct and instrumental way. It be-comes relevant for problem-solving when one considers that potentially effective policies only truly become effective when adopted and imple-mented in practice—and this is shaped by the politics of the policy process, which the interactive branch explores.

Among the most important themes of interactive policy analysis are the study of decision-making within networks of governmental and non-governmental (including private sector) organizations and the exploration of the implementation stage of the policy process. In both areas, prevailing images of how the policy-making process works have been brought into question. In substantive and tools-oriented policy analysis, there is usu-ally the image of a 'benevolent dictator', who will adopt and implement the best policy instrument. Interactive policy analysis assumes that there is no 'right' policy solution because the decision to adopt a policy is not under the control of a single actor nor is there one unique point in the decision-making process that would allow the infusion of the 'right' solution into the process (cf. Cairney 2016). Instead, different actors and organizations com-pete over what the right policy response is and shape the outcome across all stages of the policy process. Hence, implementation is reconsidered as an extended stage of the political process rather than a purely adminis-trative activity of putting fixed programmes and laws into practice. This makes it important to think in terms of alternatives and multiple 'good' policy solutions depending on different criteria, such as political feasibility, effectiveness, and distributional effects.

From the 1970s onwards, interactive policy analysis has been character-ized by a gradual deviation from the linear model of policy-making as cap-tured in Lasswell's stages model. First, stages of the policy-making process beyond decision-making have come into focus. Implementation research, for example, developed into the most productive field of interactive policy analysis in the 1970s. What was initially a narrow exploration of adminis-trative programme implementation developed into a multifaceted research area. It challenged conventional assumptions about policy-making as a lin-ear process, beginning with a decision about a particular policy at the top and ending with street-level programme delivery. Second, the discovery of agenda-setting as a stage of the policy process questioned assumptions about linear policy-making that started invariably with a sober analysis of the nature of a problem and what could be done about it. The rise and decline of policy issues and the way they are framed were uncovered as major factors driving policy change. Indeed, models of agenda-setting became, and still remain, highly influential as models of the policy process in general, and we will rely on these theories in the rest of the book.

Box 1.4   Climate policy from the perspective of the three branches of policy analysis

The three branches of policy analysis have different takes on how climate change policies are (to be) formulated and implemented.

Substantive policy analysis: Climate change experts would make forecasts about the trajectory of rising global temperatures, analyse the underlying interaction between greenhouse gases and global temperatures, and develop models, which can potentially predict the causes and effects of climate change. As of 2020, the Intergovernmental Panel on Climate Change (IPCC), a UN body, assesses available scientific evidence relating to climate change and prepares comprehensive assessment reports outlining the drivers of climate change and its risks. On its website (www.ipcc.ch), the IPCC states that its reports are 'neutral, policy-relevant but not policy-prescriptive', the ideal kind of input the substantive policy analysis perspective would expect.

Tools-oriented policy analysis: From this perspective, the design and implementation of climate change policy instruments, such as carbon taxes, would be rethought using policy analysis tools, such as cost–benefit analysis. Environmental impact assessment would be used to model the likely impact of a policy on the natural environment. A design thinking-inspired approach would call for a process of co-designing new mobility concepts in order to reduce CO_2 emissions from individual mobility and expand public infrastructure.

Interactive policy analysis: Climate change policies would have to be designed and implemented in each country in the context of the existing energy mix, its CO_2 emissions, and its population density, industries, and employment structure. These contextual factors would lead to different country-specific policy solutions that reflect political and administrative as well as economic and social factors. Vested interests (in particular industries, such as mining, nuclear energy, or renewable energy) as well as individuals affected by interventions (as in the case of the *gilets jaunes* in France) could shape policy choices at any point in the policy process.

1.5 Balancing Different Understandings of Policy Analysis

This short run-through of the three branches of policy analysis shows that very different understandings of policy analysis coexist (see Box 1.4 for an illustration of how each plays out in the field of climate policy). The major difference relevant for our purpose lies in the understanding of evidence in the policy process, in particular between the substantive and tools-oriented branches, on the one hand, and the interactive perspective, on the other. While advocates of the former approaches will readily admit that the reality of policy-making is characterized by all kinds of irrationalities and the limited use of evidence and analysis, they still hold on to the general possibility of enhancing the rationality of decision-making through the use of analytical tools and methods of policy analysis. This kind of policy analysis aims at a model of comprehensive rationality that maximizes the use of information and assessments in the search for the single best possible policy option.

In addition to assuming that policy-making is, or can be, based on (somewhat) rational choices, the 'how to' advice coming from the substantive and tools-oriented branches of policy analysis often implies that decision-making is under the control of a single actor—the proverbial decision-maker—and that it takes place at a particular moment in time. Interactive policy analysis, on the other hand, considers policy-making to be a political choice, i.e. the result of conflict and consensus among more than one individual or corporate actor (Windhoff-Héritier and Czada 1991, 9). Policy-making is hence both a result of interaction and an ongoing process, in which all stages of the ideal-typical policy process contribute to decision-making. This implies that different actors with different preferences, resources, and worldviews carry their own beliefs about what is right and wrong and what should be done about a particular problem. In other words, policy-making according to interactive policy analysis is fundamentally shaped by plural rationalities, and decision-making is about accommodating these different rationalities.

Policy analysis in the early twenty-first century is characterized by a further divergence of the three branches. Interactive policy analysis has developed into numerous subfields that are often related to specific policy domains, such as welfare, economic governance, and environmental policy. While these subfields engage in specific debates and use specialized concepts, one commonality is their rightful critique of the linear model of policy-making (Sabatier and Weible 2014)—and, as a result, their disengagement with the practical issues of policy design, implementation, agenda-setting, and so on. How to design and implement public policy, the key topics of earlier debates, has shifted out of focus. While revivals of perspectives focusing on policy design, i.e. the choice of policy instruments, have been attempted at various times, the connection to the dominant stream of policy process studies has remained limited.

The disengagement between the three branches of policy analysis is mutual. Tools-oriented policy analysis has established a strong foothold in governmental reform programmes and organizations, increasingly so since the late 1990s. Frontrunners like the UK, the US, and the European Commission have launched various initiatives to establish evidence-based policy-making, and a professional discourse has emerged which is again (like in the 1960s and 1970s) concerned with increasing the use of evidence in policy design and implementation. In the twenty-first century, this agenda is no longer limited to the Global North; initiatives promoting evidence-based policy-making can be found across the globe, also encouraged by the World Bank and global philanthropic initiatives. These attempts often cite the advancements in social science methods that can be brought to bear in policy-making. Experiments (in particular RCTs) have become the latest method to provide evidence, and governments across the world are engaged in related reforms to improve policy-making (see Chapter 4).[1] A number of more or less authoritative guides and manuals advise decision-makers, analysts, and other bureaucrats on how to use evidence.[2] These guidelines do not ignore the insights of interactive policy analysis. Often, the limits of rationality, the non-linear nature of the policy process, and its political character are readily admitted. However, concrete 'how to' advice often reverts to the ideas and tools of rational policy-making—not least because of the lack of a developed alternative of politically informed advice on how to do public policy. This is where we come in.

---

[1] Some governments and city administrations have installed so-called 'behavioural insights teams' or 'nudge units', which promote and support the use of RCTs to test the small-scale policy interventions we introduced earlier as nudges. The original behavioural insights team was established in 2010 in the UK government's Cabinet Office (John 2018).

[2] E.g. the UK government's *The Green Book: Appraisal and Evaluation in Central Government* (HM Treasury and Government Finance Function 2020), which was updated in 2020. Alternatively, see the EU Commission's *Better Regulation: Guidelines and Toolbox'* (European Commission n.d.-b).

1.6 How to Do Public Policy: Understanding Process, Policies, and Capacity

Public policy today needs to integrate the three branches of policy analysis. It is not sufficient, and generally not helpful, to follow only the advice of the two branches of applied policy analysis literature, which provide analytical tools for the search for optimal solutions in a politics-free world. Too often, the reality of the politics of policy-making will overrule attempts to deploy 'objective' analytical tools to inherently political issues. Moreover, the analytical mindset accompanying many tools and methods under the umbrella of tools-oriented policy analysis creates problematic expectations regarding 'what works' and how to find out what works. In particular, as we noted earlier, conceptualizing policy-making as a linear process under the control of a single governmental actor, devising strategies for intervention in response to perceived societal problems, is a simplification at best. Without taking the multiplicity of actors and the political economy that are part of any policy-making process into account, the tools of policy analysis will continue to disappoint and will actually reinforce apolitical, if not technocratic, assumptions about how the policy process can, and should, work. To that end, it is crucial to integrate concepts and knowledge from interactive policy analysis research about the policy process into the debate about the tools of policy analysis and our understanding of their role in policy-making.

At the same time, we acknowledge the increasing significance of analytical tools and methods in the practice of policy-making. We argue, however, that the interactive policy analysis literature has latent potential to develop a more realistic—and useful—understanding of the role of policy analysis tools and methods in the policy process. We hope that systematically drawing on these insights for a 'how to do public policy' perspective will move the policy analysis debate beyond the somewhat rigid perspectives on all sides.

Our ambition, however, goes beyond didactics. In confronting policy analysis tools and recommendations with interactive policy analysis concepts and findings about the policy process, we also seek to instil some fundamentals about how policy-making works and what makes policy successful. Our main argument is that recent developments in policy analysis have shifted attention back to the optimization of individual policy interventions at the expense of comprehending the key roles of institutional context, interaction between actors, and more complex combinations of policies in shaping the policy process and its outcomes. Decades of comparative policy research from the interactive perspective have identified all those factors as critical for policy processes and outcomes.

Therefore, we argue that for policy-makers and policy analysts all three branches together form the foundation for good policy-making. They lead us to the crucial ingredients for effective public policy, namely *Process*, *Policies*, and *Capacity* (Figure 1.1). Policy-makers, policy analysts, and everyone else who strives to influence the policy process have to be concerned with mobilization and organization of these three components and make sure that they complement each other. Understanding all three is a precondition for effective policy-making.

- **Process:** Despite comprehensive scientific knowledge on many policy problems, policy responses have often been ill-guided and ineffective. The political nature of the policy process, key institutions that shape decision-making (Chapter 2), and patterns of agenda-setting (Chapter 3) influence the general approach of policy-makers. In modern policy processes, addressing policy problems starts with assessing available knowledge and understanding causal inference and linkages—not just within a policy field, but also between different fields. More importantly, process is not only a constraint but also an opportunity. Political support can be mobilized during the policy process and provide legitimacy for controversial (e.g. costly or intrusive) policy measures. If French President Macron's administration had consulted regional constituencies and local politicians more thoroughly before introducing the fuel tax, options might have been discussed to help rural villages and peri-urban communities cope with new transportation systems and other emissions-reducing measures.
- **Policies:** There is a wide variety of policy instruments that policy actors can employ, ranging from information-based tools to regulation and financial tools (see Chapters 4 and 5). These instruments vary with underlying assumptions, and the type of problem to be addressed. Each policy instrument poses different challenges during implementation. Understanding the logics of bureaucracies and the target population is critical for a policy's success. Policy-makers need to have a good command of the toolbox available and should not apply the same type of instruments for all types of problems. Though the fuel tax was only the starting point for the *gilets jaunes* protests, one wonders whether use of different emissions-reducing instruments might have prevented the

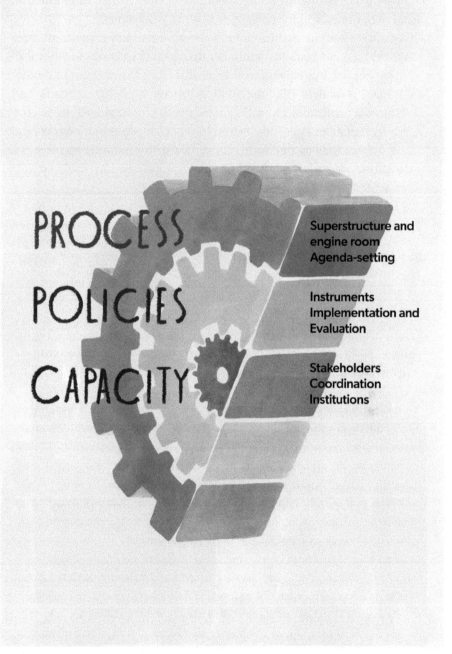

Fig. 1.1 Three components of policy-making

demonstrations in the first place. Policy-makers also need to know the challenges of evaluating policies, both in terms of evaluation techniques and the political implications of evaluation (Chapter 6).

- **Capacity**: Capacity is the ability to conceive and implement measures. It includes state capacity, administrative capacity (Lodge and Wegrich 2014a, 2014b), but also the role of civil society, the organization of the business community, and the political process itself (see Chapters 7–9). Many potentially effective policy tools cannot be implemented because of a lack of state and administrative capacity. Moreover, capacity can vary between policy problems, policy fields, and national and other jurisdictions. Being aware of and compensating for limitations in capacity is essential for effective policy-making.

We can understand the issues of climate change policies better when addressing them through the categories of process, policies, and capacity (Box 1.5).

Box 1.5 Process, policies, and capacity when addressing climate change

Countries have very diverse positions in the climate debate, depending on their greenhouse gas emissions, energy mixes, and vulnerabilities. They have to address different aspects of climate change and face different challenges. Though climate change is a global phenomenon, it threatens developing countries more because their livelihoods are typically more adversely affected by rising temperatures. Poorer countries find it more difficult to develop evidence-based policy tools to either respond to or mitigate climate change. Finally, developing countries tend to have less state capacity to implement policies.

At the same time, the research community in the field of climate change is well organized, and knowledge on climate change is widespread. Due to the global epistemic community on climate change and the Paris Agreement, the policy *process* is already far advanced in terms of understanding the causes and effects of, as well as responses to, climate change (despite vocal deniers). Many of the most appropriate *policies* and related instruments for combating climate change are well-known in the policy community, even if differences and debates continue over policy design and choice.

However, implementation of the known policy responses remains difficult be-cause rising energy and fuel prices, among other consequences, affect the pop-ulation and many businesses, creating conflict about the distribution of costs and resources, not only within a given country but also between countries. Governments hesitate to intervene too quickly and too massively because they fear political backlash. It is therefore the *capacity* issue—with regard to stake-holder involvement, coordination, and institutional changes—that needs to be addressed in the climate debate. However, it has so far received much less atten-tion than the technical and scientific debate.

To be in command of process, policies, and capacity also reduces the need to use general statements about 'what works' or suggestions of 'best prac-tice'. General assessments of how particular policy instruments (should) work, which abound in the public policy literature, are often of little use. If there is one general lesson from decades of policy research, it is that the effects and effectiveness of a particular policy intervention are dependent on political, societal, and institutional contexts, as well as the specific situ-ation with which the policy-maker is confronted. We believe in the ability of the policy-maker to develop the capacities of analysis and judgement, which require skills in the use of policy analysis tools and awareness of the policy process and ways to influence it.

2

The Dual Structure of Policy-Making

Key concepts

- Superstructure
- Engine room
- Channels linking superstructure and engine room
- Policy networks

2.1 The Superstructure and the Engine Room

Industrial action swept across British universities between 2018 and 2020. University staff complained about precarious work, rising salaries for university administrators, and proposed changes to university pensions. They claimed that changes in the pension system could leave each member of university staff up to £240,000 worse off in pensions (see Box 2.1, Weale 2019). The dispute particularly centred around the methodologies used to value the liabilities and assets of the Universities Superannuation Scheme (USS), which is used to pay out defined benefit pensions to university staff. The scheme had reported an official deficit of around £5bn, following its 2017 actuarial valuation, but other calculations put the shortfall as high as £12bn–£17bn. Proposals to close the defined benefit section of the scheme led to weeks of strike action from university staff. The conflict played out between the university employers, University UK (UUK), and the university staff union, University and College Union (UCU). In order to forge a compromise, both sides appointed a joint panel to scrutinize university pension funding and to make recommendations for its reform (Reeve 2018). Solving the dispute regarding the actuarial valuation of university pensions is not an easy task. The panel report introduced a joint method for making the calculations.

The bulk of the policy world deals with very concrete problems and a plethora of actors who are tasked to resolve them. In the case of the university pension conflict in the United Kingdom (see Box 2.1), university

How to Do Public Policy. Anke Hassel and Kai Wegrich, Oxford University Press.
© Anke Hassel and Kai Wegrich (2022). DOI: 10.1093/oso/9780198747000.003.0002

employers feared that the university pension scheme would soon face a massive deficit, while staff and their trade unions disputed the figures and resisted proposed cuts to pension payouts and increases in contributions. University leaders aim to keep their budgets sound and prevent ever higher contribution rates to pension schemes, but staff legitimately want to protect their pension entitlements. Solving the conflict of interest crucially depends on the preparation and calculation of data, which informs decision-makers during the decisive steps of conflict resolution.

Box 2.1   University pension conflict in the UK

University workers in the UK receive an occupational pension, which is organized in the University Superannuation Scheme (USS), one of the largest private pension schemes in the country. The scheme covers more than 350 employers (universities and higher education organizations). The USS corporate trustee has the responsibility of ensuring the scheme is adequately funded, has an appropriate investment strategy, and is well run. For this, the USS trustee is required by law to carry out an assessment of the scheme's assets and liabilities every three years and, on this basis, recommends changes in order to ensure the scheme's viability. The actual change is decided by the Joint Negotiating Committee (JNC), a panel of union and employer representatives.

In 2017, the USS announced that the scheme had a deficit, which needed to be addressed. The employers, University UK (UUK), proposed a move to a defined benefit system and a cap on contributions. Throughout the year, the JNC could not agree on a solution, but at the end of 2017, the committee voted in favour of the USS proposal. The university workers' trade union, University and College Union (UCU), launched an industrial action strike ballot and 88 per cent of its members voted for strike action. By law, the 2017 valuation had to be completed by June 2018. UCU and UUK negotiated a compromise in the first half of 2018, which was rejected by the union members. As a consequence, a Joint Expert Panel (JEP) was set up to review the USS valuation and agree on a joint approach to future USS valuations. The JEP delivered a recommendation in September 2018, which, however, did not overcome the deadlock in the JNC. Throughout 2019, the trustee made new proposals to increase contributions and reduce benefits, while the trade union UCU threatened more strike action. In December 2019, the JEP issued a second report on the valuation. At the core of the dispute were different types of calculations of the expected costs of the scheme and disagreements on the sharing out of those costs. The workers complained about higher contributions and lower pensions, which affected them negatively, while university leaders were not prepared to contribute sufficiently.

The conflict continued in 2020 with discussions on the JEP report. In February and March 2020, UCU organized further strikes. While the support for the strikes was stronger than in earlier strike waves, they came to a sudden end with the lockdown of universities due to the coronavirus pandemic. Moreover, the fear over funding shortages and a lack of international students meant that the USS reported itself to the regulators after it triggered a sustainability metric. In April 2020, the employers and union issued a joint statement and voiced concern over the state of the USS. After the USS announced in early 2021 the raising of contribution rates to up to 56 per cent of payroll, universities and unions called the increase 'unrealistic' and condemned the move (Adams 2021).

Sources: Weale (2019); Reeve (2018); Grove (2020) Universities UK (2018); University of Kent (2021); Huskisson et al. (2020); Adams (2021).

This chapter introduces the 'superstructure' and the 'engine room' as key arenas of the policy process to understand how public policies are made. This perspective emphasizes the institutional and political context in which policy-making takes place and explores the interdependencies between political interaction and policy work. Because of the complex and multifaceted relationship between the superstructure and the engine room, we maintain that there are many policy choices that might address a policy problem, but not all of these choices will be feasible or effective in any given context and at any given time. Hence, the search for good policies has to be contextualized in the real policy process. This is not trivial, as the world of policy analysis puts a high premium on general solutions to specific problems. In reality, good public policy needs to work within a given context and with key stakeholders in order to align political opportunities with policy needs.

Our approach to policy-making is grounded in the assertion that the relation and interaction between the political sphere of decision-making, which we liken to the superstructure of a ship, and the policy sphere, the engine room of the same vessel, are in fact the most crucial factors for successful policy-making (Figure 2.1). On ships and large boats, the *superstructure* is everything on view above deck (with the exception of masts, sails, and weaponry). Superstructures are the most visible element of such vessels, and their size and make-up have a significant impact on mobility and speed. We use this metaphor to refer to the mostly visible political

Fig. 2.1 The superstructure and engine room of the policy process

actors and institutions that are associated with politics and major policy decisions in a given polity, i.e. top politicians, the legislature, powerful interest organizations, and powerful corporate actors. This superstructure is distinct from the mostly invisible *engine room* of policy-making, where bureaucrats work with other stakeholders, such as interest organizations, experts, and non-governmental organizations (NGOs), to develop and implement policy.

The superstructure consists of more than just structural aspects, such as the system of government and core institutions of the political economy of a particular jurisdiction. It also entails the political context and power dimensions, coalitions of political actors, and normative orientations that cut across individual policy problems and shape how they are perceived in the engine room. In the case of pensions, for example, related policies are highly salient in the superstructure because of the importance of pensioners as part of the electorate (see Box 2.2). How the superstructure influences and structures the policy process varies across polities and is essential for understanding and influencing policy-making. Moreover, the superstructure of policy-making—the political sphere—shapes and determines the kinds of choices policy-makers have and the pathways and likely roadblocks ahead. Attempting to develop policies in ignorance of the political superstructure often ends in frustration and policy failure.

At the same time, much of the more detailed policy work—the choice of policy instruments, their implementation, and their evaluation—takes place in the policy sphere: the engine room of policy-making. In the engine room, one finds policy analysts, bureaucrats, think tankers, and experts, as well as interest groups. They form a network of specialists dealing with policy formulation, maintenance, delivery, and enforcement on a day-to-day basis, often outside the limelight of national media attention and with only limited involvement from major actors in the superstructure. For example, in the field of pension policy, experts in ministries, employers, and trade unions, but also pension funds, liaise about the need for, financing, and distribution of pension contributions and benefits.

While the superstructure engages in the 'bigger issues' of higher political significance, relations with the engine room are not simply unidirectional, with the superstructure providing a broad framework and the engine room filling in the details. The superstructure is better conceived as structuring the policy work of the engine room, and the relationship works both ways. Practical policy issues can lead to the reframing of political power structures, while political decisions are necessary for policies to be adopted.

A government has little to no effect on policy if it does not know how to use the toolbox at its disposal. Political leaders can be ineffective or make very costly decisions if they do not know their instruments. This became evident during the global COVID-19 pandemic that began in 2020, when some governments responded to the health threats half-heartedly and this may have led to higher rates of infection and death. By the same token, those in the engine room in charge of the toolbox cannot use it if the decision-makers deprive them of resources or other means. A better fit between the superstructure and the engine room leads to better policy outcomes.

As was made clear in Chapter 1, policy-making is a political and so-cial process. As such, the policy process and its outcomes are shaped by the interactions of intentionally rational actors pursuing their own interests and following their norms and values in institutional contexts

---

Box 2.2   The importance of pensions

Pensions have become one of the core policy fields of nation states. To provide social protection for the elderly was one of the very first social policy measures undertaken by the modern state. Social spending for the elderly represents the largest share of national governments' budgets among OECD member countries, with public pensions accounting for 18.4 per cent of GDP on average in 2015 (OECD 2019a, Chapter 8).

Historically, pension policies have been at the core of the evolution of the welfare state—and therefore also at the centre of conflicts between employers and trade unions. Both the business sector and organized labour have sought to influence pension decisions through lobbying, as pensions are understood by both sides as a form of deferred compensation. Pensions are also a lucrative market for the financial services industry: pension privatization has opened up new business opportunities. Also, pension contributions are part of non-wage labour costs and an important factor in labour taxation. They are therefore also relevant for other policy fields, such as labour market and economic policy-making.

Moreover, pensioners are hugely important in electoral terms, as their share of the electorate grows and their voter turnout is generally higher. The pension-ers' vote is highly attentive to changes in pension policy. Given these diverse dimensions of pension policies, we can identify different primary concerns of su-perstructure and engine room actors (note that the focus can change and issues shift from the engine room to the superstructure and vice versa; see also Box 2.4).

that provide the 'rules of the game'. But, as Heclo (1974) famously put it, actors are not only 'powering', i.e. achieving and maintaining power, they are also 'puzzling', i.e. seeking solutions to challenging policy problems. This dual character applies not only to the political superstructure: issues of power and influence are also important to the engine room of policy-making.

Our aim in this chapter is to explore how attempts at problem-solving are shaped by a political context in which powering plays an important role. The distinction between the political-institutional superstructure and the engine room of policy-making allows us to explore how policy-making (problem-solving) is constrained and enabled by politics and institutions. After introducing the logics of the superstructure and engine room separately, we explore three major channels linking the two levels of policy-making and then discuss the implications for how to do public policy.

2.2 The Superstructure of Policy-Making

In every political system, the superstructure is where power is structured and allocated. The primary concern of any system of government, whether democratic or authoritarian or something in between, is to provide a stable distribution and division of power between competing societal groups. Policies and policy-making are conceived in terms of achieving, defending, or improving power positions.

Superstructure actors engage in policy-making by setting policy guidelines, trying to control the policy agenda, and initiating sometimes far-reaching policy changes. But the normative orientation of superstructure actors is as much about problem-solving as it is about maintaining and improving one's own position in the political power play. This is most apparent when incumbent governments introduce new affordable housing programmes, hikes in social benefits, or lower taxes just ahead of crucial elections, as the literature on the electoral budget cycle shows (Alesina and Paradisi 2014). Some might argue that Obamacare (the Patient Protection and Affordable Care Act of 2010) did as much for the Democratic Party in the US, by bolstering support in African-American communities, as it did for poor and working-class households. In day-to-day politics, policies are also perceived by superstructure actors as a means to expand or protect their power bases, either electorally or through fundraising. Pierson (2015) argues that policies are used by actors in power to hardwire their positions, through changes in the 'mini constitutions' of individual policy areas that favour the allies of those in political power positions.

Powering and power politics are at the heart of the political super-structure, and policy-making often affects the underlying power structure. Policy change in general is contested, not only because it might alter who gets what in society, but also because it is likely to shift the power positions of key actors. Changes in tax policy can give some groups in society more resources, which they might use to back politicians of the political parties that promise (more) tax cuts. In developing countries, access to land and electricity is often used during election campaigns to strengthen the pop-ularity of candidates among the poor. Among member countries of the Organization for Economic Co-operation and Development (OECD), we can also observe a political budget cycle in which government consump-tion increases or changes at the end of an electoral cycle, that is, in the run-up to elections (Rogoff 1990; for a different view see Klomp and de Haan 2013). In welfare states, the state regulates the rights and obligations of diverse organized interests (such as organized labour and employers' organizations; or health insurers and care providers). Actors in the super-structure arguably care at least as much about their relative power gains and losses as about good policy-making. But this does not imply a cynical worldview—influence is a precondition for policy work.

At the same time, superstructure actors seldom work out policies with-out the involvement of the engine room. Oftentimes, substantial discretion is delegated to bureaucratic agencies and even to street-level bureaucra-cies, because only general compromises (often masking disagreements on underlying aims and objectives) are feasible within the superstructure. Politicians face opportunity costs: they cannot always engage in all the details of a policy because they lack expertise and because this would eat up time needed for more 'political' work, such as forging political al-liances and attending publicity-generating ceremonies to showcase, for example, new bike lanes (Majone 2001; Epstein and O'Halloran 1999; Calvert et al. 1989). Another motivation for delegating policy-making capacity to the engine room is that blame can be shifted to those bu-reaucratic actors (with the politician claiming 'my hands are tied') in the event that something goes wrong (Moe 2012). Before we continue discussing how the superstructure and the engine room interact, we shall take a closer look at what goes on in each sphere of the policy process.

2.2.1 Power and policy: the politics of the superstructure

Systems of government determine how power is allocated and structured. In democracies, power is usually limited by checks and balances provided by different institutions (legislature, executive, judiciary, administrative levels of government); and electoral competition holds executive politicians and legislators accountable. In authoritarian and semi-authoritarian systems of government, power is captured by groups of actors who exert substantial influence over political decision-making via their ties to the military and/or important business groups as well as leading media outlets and are, therefore, difficult to challenge. Electoral competition is muted and replaced by direct control. But even authoritarian governments, except for the most repressive regimes, depend on some degree of citizen approval. All governments, therefore, aim to shape and determine the policy space primarily to solidify their own legitimacy. Improving economic growth and the quality of life for citizens, but also addressing urgent societal problems, are essential government goals. These objectives can only be achieved by policies.

That policies matter for power does not mean that policy-making straightforwardly corresponds to the preferences of large parts of society. Political science research in OECD countries has unearthed a pattern of selective responsiveness, in which the interests of low- and median-income groups are mostly ignored when they differ from those of higher income groups (Gilens 2005; Gilens 2015). Analysts of the policy-making process in the US argue that governments are dependent on private donations to political parties and electoral campaigns and, therefore, follow the preferences of donors and the wealthy in general (Gilens 2015). In contrast, governments are relatively inattentive to the concerns of lower income citizens (Jacobs and Skocpol 2005; see also Bhatti and Erikson 2011, who find this pattern to be less pronounced). However, even in European and other countries, where money plays a much weaker role in campaigning, a similar pattern is discernible, where governments are unresponsive to the will of poorer voters (Schäfer et al. 2017). On the other hand, politicians observe public opinion very closely and tend to follow it, particularly when it does not conflict with their own priorities. For instance, high incarceration rates in the US are in line with public opinion, which became increasingly 'punitive', beginning in the 1950s, and can been seen as responding to a general preference for strict sentencing among large segments of society (Enns 2016)—although the tide might be changing, especially with the legalization of marijuana. Top politicians seeking to stay in power—or aspiring to gain positions of power—need to balance the pressures from the general public, the demands of client groups—or 'the base'—of a particular party, and their own interests.

Donors and lobby groups provide politicians with the resources they need to gain or maintain office. Resources can be financial, but they can also take the form of crucial information on policy issues, influence over the citizens or member organizations they represent, or control over investments or jobs. On the other hand, high spending by lobby groups and donations to campaigns do not always yield effects. The tobacco industry has worked hard to influence research and policy-makers around the world, in an effort to deflect attention from the harmful effects of smoking. The industry was successful in delaying regulation, even decades after the link between smoking and cancer was made, but eventually could not stop policies that banned smoking in most public places (Cairney 2019 on the case of the UK). Similarly, business groups have been far more successful when lobbying for lower taxes than when pushing to reduce the welfare state. Research on the US confirms that there is no direct link between resources and policy outcomes, i.e. between campaign contributions and votes in Congress (Schlozmann et al. 2012).

On the other hand, as Paul Pierson (2015) points out, power structures are enshrined in the political process in a way that dominating groups can reap rents without much political lobbying or conflict. Here, power and dominance by business groups vary by policy areas. The business community is particularly powerful on policy issues that receive low media attention and are decided in informal settings. The higher the salience of an issue, and the more formal the institutional arena governing it, the greater the likelihood will be that business will be defeated and that it will have to build alliances with other actors (Culpepper 2010; Naczyk and Hassel 2019).

2.2.2 Superstructure actors and their power resources

For the observer of superstructure politics, the behaviour of key actors 'on deck'—such as heads of governments, ministers, leaders of parliamentary parties, and subnational elected officials or political executives in government (such as junior ministers)—can appear puzzling. The concern with power and their position within the party, the government, their public image—all this sometimes seems to matter more than the substance of policy and their actual jobs, i.e. improving the lives of people and steering the ship in the right direction. Understanding the rationale of superstructure actors is important because political leaders possess resources of power that are critical for policy-making, in particular for changing the distribution of resources (such as budgets, jurisdiction, major policy directions). Political leaders (and aspiring leaders) need to build and maintain these resources of power if they are to be able to implement policies, because their position is precarious—it needs to be constantly defended against (potential) competitors.

The strength of leading politicians is based on mobilizing political support, access to funds, and an organizational infrastructure to win elections. They have invested heavily in their political careers. They need electoral campaign strategies and a constituency. To mobilize this support takes most of their time and attention. A (positive) public image, name recognition, and attention on television and social media are key resources of politicians in the superstructure. This is true for getting into power but remains the case when in power. To stay ahead of the game, top decision-makers have to defend their position against competitors from within their own support network and from outside. There is always a successor at their heels, as other people want their jobs. Political leaders and executives devote substantial amounts of their daily time to coordination meetings with allies and information-gathering about the potential moves of others (e.g. MPs) (cf. Rhodes 2005 and 2011 for an ethnographic study on the daily lives of top officials in the UK). Political work also includes delivering material benefits to voters and important organized interests. Channelling public investments or other resources to constituents is a key concern for members of the legislature in any country. Research on the US and Europe has shown the prevalence of 'pork barrel politics' and 'bringing home the bacon', i.e. the distribution of federal funds to home states or regions (Golden and Min 2013 for a global overview; Golden and Picci 2008 for Italy; Lancaster and Patterson 1990 for Germany). The same mechanisms work in other contexts: Auerbach (2020) has shown that the variation in public goods provision—paved roads, piped water, and trash removal—in Indian slum settlements is driven by a variation in political activity, especially the distribution of party workers, within these settlements.

This logic of political actors' behaviour has implications for policy-making. When top politicians in the superstructure engage in policy debates, their key job is to forge compromises, build coalitions, and generate enough political support for their preferred options. This sometimes includes side payments for political support and rewards for loyalty. Forging coalitions often means compromising on other policy decisions and might weaken policies. In order to gain support from a particular parliamentary group for one policy, the government might have to compromise on unrelated policies. Sometimes these compromises are painful for party loyalists and supporters and have to be defended against criticism, especially when policy purists find the result of such political negotiations difficult to accept.

Their expertise in staying in power often comes at the expense of policy knowledge. That decision-makers in the superstructure are not always on top of the substance of major policy issues should, therefore, not surprise the policy analysts. They need support from the engine room and have to trust in its work to find good solutions. Leaders are usually specialists in powering, not experts in policy substance. On the other hand, experts often lack sufficient power resources and do not make successful leaders. There is sometimes the idea that technocratic governments or expert-led governments will lead to better policy-making, especially when the politics going on in the superstructure creates quagmire or even chaos. Yet, as in the case of the technocratic government under Mario Monti, put in place in Italy in the midst of its sovereign debt crisis in 2011, policies enacted by technocratic leaders carry political implications and hence will become politically contested. In other countries, there are sometimes attempts to appoint technocratic ministers to enhance the image of expertise. This often fails as ministers find it difficult to build support for their expert-led policies.

Top politicians rely on trusted staff to understand the policies for which they are responsible. Loyal junior ministers or division heads are appointed because they are trustworthy and prepare policy decisions. In many government systems, advisory positions directly supporting the political executive, such as 'special advisors' or ministers' 'cabinets', have become increasingly important (cf. Hustedt et al. 2017; Craft and Halligan 2020). These advisers are personal confidants and have played an increasingly strong role in many countries' governments. Their task is to vet policy proposals (from the experts in the ministries and elsewhere) with regard to their political implications.

2.3 The Engine Room of Policy-Making

Most policy-making takes place in the engine room—in ministries, agencies, and parliamentary committees in which bureaucrats work with specialized interest groups on specific, sectorally confined policy issues. As Page and Jenkins (2005) have pointed out, the making of public policy happens 'with a cast of thousands'; it is the (mid-ranking) 'policy bureaucrats' that actually draft legislative proposals and policy programmes, liaise with stakeholders on a routine basis, commission research, policy advice, and evaluations, and engage in professional networks. The engine room is where actual policy work gets done, and the superstructure cannot function without the engine room; the workings of the engine room are also shaped by what happens in the superstructure. While there are always many different engine rooms working in parallel on different policy issues, interactive policy research has identified common patterns of how policy-making works at that level. We highlight specialization, informality, and horizontal relations as three of these key patterns and discuss rivalry between sectors as an important motivational driver of policy specialists' behaviour.

2.3.1 The territory of specialists

In order to formulate policies with a level of expertise that does justice to the complexity of the field at hand, specialization is crucial. As has been observed many times in policy research (Heclo 1978; Jordan 1981; Börzel 1998), specialists in ministerial departments and agencies form enduring relationships with their counterparts in broader society, i.e. the sectors they are engaged in (e.g. in energy or agricultural policy). State and non-state actors from one policy domain usually interact more with each other than with their counterparts in other policy domains. Specialized legislators in committees can also be members of such networks.

Since neither executive leaders nor the general public can give each policy issue the same level of attention, these policy networks of specialists enjoy a substantial degree of autonomy in dealing with routine policy issues in their domains. When specialized actors from the bureaucracy, the legislature, and interest organizations form a closed shop, preventing other actors with different preferences and beliefs from joining in, such networks are called 'iron triangles' (Heclo 1978). More open networks with broader participation are called 'issue networks'. Whether and when a policy network becomes an iron triangle or an issue network depends on the interaction of the engine room with the superstructure, as we discuss later in this chapter.

2.3.2 The importance of informal pre-planning stages

A second key feature of the engine room concerns the process of policy development (or formulation), in which the 'pre-planning stages' of decision-making are critical. The formal, 'official' stage of decision-making is usually preceded by an informal process of policy formulation that is dominated by actors in the engine room. When it comes to shaping final policy decisions, this informal pre-planning stage is often even more influential than formal policy adoption by top executives and legislators.

The pre-planning stage of policy development matters because political and bureaucratic actors—who aim to support successful policy initiatives—invest political and bureaucratic capital into the process of developing policies (Bach and Wegrich 2020). A successful policy bureaucrat and departmental leader is one who oversees policy initiatives that will eventually be enacted, and scarce resources—including administrative capacities and political capital, such as trust from the upper echelons—need to be used with care. Blame for failed policy initiatives should be avoided, in particular since the political sphere (i.e. the superstructure) tends towards negativity bias, meaning bad news matters more than good (Weaver 1986). Hence, minimizing risks and avoiding blame are normal behaviours of policy bureaucrats in the engine room. Building support and seeking compromises in order to ensure backing from key actors when a policy proposal enters the formal decision-making arena is also routine practice in policy work. By the time formal decisions are made, sufficient support for the adoption of certain initiatives has likely already been generated.

Launching potentially controversial reforms without previously secured support can be self-defeating. The informal pre-planning stage can involve attempts to test public sentiment on a particular initiative, for example, by having a backbencher make a statement to the press. But, just like important meetings in any organization are preceded by informal, often bilateral get-togethers and agreements, policy-making also happens largely outside the arenas of the legislature and cabinet. That cabinet decisions are often (e.g. in the European Union (EU) Commission's college of commissioners) taken by unanimous votes does not indicate an absence of conflict, but simply shows that any conflicts were dealt with long before (as otherwise, the policy proposal would have been taken off the agenda).

2.3.3 The logic of horizontal relations

Most policy-making takes place as a more or less cooperative and often horizontal exchange between public and private sector actors—not as a hierarchical exercise of power by the state. Indeed, most policy-making is delegated to the specialized policy networks that we introduced earlier, and programmes are often adopted on the basis of their demands. Specialized actors in policy networks often have complementary interests. While the private and non-profit sectors seek policy decisions in their favour, policy-makers in government rely on these external actors for information during policy formulation and for support during policy implementation. In times of normal policy-making—meaning the absence of a surge in attention from top politicians and the public—policy-making resembles a bargaining system more than a unilateral activity directed at a target population by the government (Scharpf 1997).

This does *not* mean that that all actors in a policy network have similar interests or that all policy activity is captured by regulated entities. For example, different actors in the pension policy network—insurance companies, employers' groups, trade unions, regulators, the public pension fund, and social policy specialists in the legislature or the executive (see Box 2.4)—have partly complementary and partly opposing interests. But policies must be coordinated with all of those actors, and the lion's share of public policies is self-regulated, i.e. negotiated between societal actors in a bargaining system sanctioned by state regulation (see the example of the pension scheme for university workers in the UK, described in Box 2.1). Changing the inherent status quo bias of self-regulated policy networks requires substantial effort from top politicians to intervene in these networks. Oftentimes, conflict in the engine room is as much about which actors deserve a seat at the table and which forum is the right one for decision-making as it is about policy substance.

2.3.4 Inter-sectoral rivalry

A key implication derived from these insights is that politics does play a major role in the inner workings of the engine room, but in a different guise than in the superstructure. While party politics, institutions, and general ideas of governance contribute to structuring the politics of policy-making in the superstructure, other mechanisms are specific to the politics of (and in) the engine room.

We mentioned earlier that the engine room of policy-making is actually composed of many different but connected engine rooms, dealing with distinct policy areas and representing diverse societal interests. As a consequence, there is often conflict between the preferences, goals, and worldviews of representatives of different policy fields in government and society. While some policy fields might not have many overlaps, and hence ministries and respective interest groups can coexist in mutual ignorance, there is always competition for resources from the budget, which introduces some degree of rivalry. But many policy fields do overlap substantively, particularly in our current era of multidimensional problems. For example, agricultural and environmental policies have many overlaps, with at least partly conflicting goals and objectives. In the face of the COVID-19 pandemic, it became clear that the goals of economic and public health policies could not always be easily reconciled. In short, government departments and agencies representing different sectors sometimes find themselves in a situation of subtle rivalry for resources and jurisdiction, and sometimes direct conflict over policy decisions.

As a consequence of this competition, policy work is shaped by more than the substantive preferences and views of different actors from different organizations (and by more than the evidence that might be available or sought). Organizational self-interests and their maintenance also play an important role. In other words, government departments not only seek to achieve their substantive aims but also to maintain their positions in the decision-making system (Scharpf 1986). It is a widespread stereotype that bureaucrats and managers of public agencies instinctively defend their turf (or autonomy of jurisdiction; Wilson 1989), generating silo mentality as an obstacle to cross-sectoral collaboration in policy formulation and implementation. Organizational (or bureaucratic) culture and socialization may play a part in developing silo mentalities. But at the core of bureaucrats' turf-conscious behaviour is the inherent risk of losing capacity for effective policy work, including implementation, when overlapping juris-dictions and limited resources create (inevitable) competition. Defending one's turf is a managerial task of 'organizational maintenance', i.e. sustain-ing as much autonomy and capacity as possible in a political environment shaped by competing values and demands.

2.4 Three Channels Linking the Superstructure and the Engine Room

Where are policies actually made? In the superstructure, or in the engine room? On the one hand, as noted earlier, most actual policy work—communicating with stakeholders; commissioning and analysing research and consultancy; drafting programmes, laws, and by-laws; and writing evaluation reports—takes place in the engine room. On the other hand, key policies are usually initiated and launched by members of the govern-ment, including both the executive and legislature. Party manifestos and coalition agreements have also developed into important agenda-setting devices for governments' legislative terms in parliamentary systems. Then again, there is solid evidence that many of the decisions made at the top (including those about legislation) often remain general, with lingering dis-agreements between actors shrouded in formal compromises and sweeping statements. In addition, the task of filling in the details is often delegated to the engine room, with the settling of political conflicts shifted to the domain of implementation.

To understand decision-making, we need to focus on the question of how the political and policy spheres interact. Our approach to policy analysis stresses the distinct logics of both the superstructure and the engine room, but it also emphasizes that anyone who wants to shape the policy-making process needs to be aware of the links between the two. Political support and powering in the superstructure without spe-cialized policy work in the engine room is bound to fail—as is highly ambitious, systematic, and rational policy work in the engine room that is disconnected from, and ill-suited to, the superstructure. Politics and poli-cies interact, as we illustrate in Table 2.1 using the example of pension policies.

The remainder of this section explores three channels—structural, sit-uational, and procedural—that link the superstructure and the engine room. These channels, which overlap and are not mutually exclusive,

Table 2.1 Politics and policy issues in superstructure and engine room regarding pensions

SUPERSTRUCTURE	ENGINE ROOM
o Pensioners' votes vis-à-vis younger electorates	o Demographic change (longevity) and sustainability of pension spending
o Pressure from producer groups regarding cost burden through social insurance (tax wedge) particularly from services and manufacturing industries and trade unions	o Old-age poverty
o Pressure from financial services industries	o Effect of pensions on inequality and social cohesion
o Budgetary impact of pension spending (crowding-out of other policy fields)	o Impact of tax wedge on labour markets and economic growth
	o Risk allocation of private–public pension mix
	o Portability of pensions

capture important ways in which the two levels of policy-making are linked. Understanding—and exploiting—those links is a critical precondition for successful policy-making. Table 2.2 provides a brief overview of the three channels and examples of how they play out in practice more generally, while Box 2.3 illustrates the dynamic interaction between the superstructure and engine room through these channels in the field of pensions.

2.4.1 The structural channel

The structural channel links the superstructure to the engine room of policy-making via superstructure institutions and superstructure politics. In general, the design and operation of the engine room follows key elements of the superstructure. For one, national policy styles (Howlett and Tosun 2021) are shaped by their respective country's superstructure. For example, the superstructure of countries such as the US, Germany, and Belgium is characterized by federalism, a strong emphasis on the rule of law, and a strong judiciary. The superstructure of the UK and Sweden is that of a unitary state with a strong emphasis on informal and trust relations and, more recently, on managerial and quasi-market tools. The

Table 2.2 Three channels linking the superstructure and the engine room

	STRUCTURAL	SITUATIONAL	PROCEDURAL
Summary	Laws and rules structuring the relation between legislative and executive bodies, structuring ministries, and agencies (for example regarding the autonomy of ministries or the independence of agencies)	Shifting of attention to issues between superstructure and engine room in response to crises and peaking media attention	Shaping engine room policy-making through procedural rules and regulations and government-wide reforms
Example	Transparency rules of lobby organisations in parliament	Government task forces for crisis management	Impact assessment; administrative procedures

managerial revolution of the 1980s and 1990s resulted in a change towards more formal relations in the UK, with strong emphasis on performance management and quantitative targets (Boswell 2018). These differences between the countries' superstructures result in differences in their policy styles, especially in terms of their preferred policy instruments. While Germany tends towards detailed regulation and prescription, the UK, at least until the 1980s, relied more on flexible regulatory norms (cf. Richardson 2013).

The relations between politicians (in the superstructure) and bureaucrats (in the engine room) are also shaped by the superstructure. In this case, a more autonomous bureaucracy with a dominance of legal professionals in Germany is the result of constitutional rules protecting the civil service as well as an engrained culture. The UK, on the other hand, is home to a more instrumental administration with few limits to political interference in the administration and a strong reliance on generalist bureaucrats (Knill 1999). These characteristics allow executive leaders to direct substantial changes in the administrative machinery of the engine room in the UK, while tight constraints would be placed on such attempts in Germany.

Box 2.3   Three channels linking superstructure and engine room dynamics in the field of pension policies

---

Structural: Public pension administrations are institutionalized in very different ways: from divisions in the Department for Work and Pensions in the UK to a semi-autonomous, tripartite administrative body in Germany (German pension insurance). In Germany, the participation of so-called social partners (employers' groups and workers' unions) in pension policies gives them access to the policy process and a privileged position in the superstructure. In many countries, a large share of pensions is allocated to privately run pension funds, which are regulated by financial market authorities independent of public pension authorities.

Situational: Pension policies are shifted on and off the policy agenda, and therefore back and forth between superstructure and engine room, through the following mechanisms: studies of (looming) old-age poverty; bankruptcy of major private pension providers (particularly pension funds); studies of underfunded occupational pension schemes; or government attempts to tax, raise, or level pensions.

Procedural: Pension administrators at the level of the engine room are required by law to provide realistic data on future pension expenditures based on mortality tables and actuarial models. These models are complex and based on many assumptions, which are dependent on policy decisions, such as pension level, family, and immigration policies.

The structural channel also shapes many other aspects of the engine room, including the position of the bureaucracy, legislature–bureaucracy relations, and also the power of ministries and the core executive. To give another example, the relatively high number of federal ministries in Brazil (more than twenty, most of the time) is the result of the multi-party presidential system: ministerial positions are a bargaining chip for the president's party, which is dependent on support from various mid-sized and smaller parties, in the forging of multi-party coalitions in the National Congress. Policy-making in this system is driven by a strong president, who is, however, forced to find support in the legislature among a large number of (smaller) parties because they cannot rely on a majority of their own (cf. Melo and Pereira 2012). This results in an engine room that is fairly fragmented, with many ministries led by politicians from the different coalition partners, but also a strong centre, i.e. the president's office (Ministro da Casa Civil do Brasil).

2.4.2 The situational channel

The second channel linking the superstructure and the engine room is the situational channel. Most routine policy-making takes place in the engine room without much *direct* involvement from the superstructure. However, the nature of politics involves shifting public agendas and hence shifting priorities at the top. While some policy areas and issues tend to be generally more important than others, basically any issue has the potential to be shifted into the limelight and thus attract the involvement of the political superstructure.

As we discuss further in Chapter 3 on agenda-setting, the problem for actors in both the superstructure and—at a different level—the engine room is one of setting priorities under conditions of uncertainty; top politicians simply cannot predict which issues will emerge as salient on the public agenda. For example, migration policy in Europe was, for a long time, an issue that attracted some notice but seldom involved top politicians or sustained public attention. But at different times since the 1990s, issues of immigration and integration and questions of 'naturalization' have attracted spiking media attention (following attacks on migrants by right-wing extremists or violent crimes by migrants), calling top politicians into the ring. The latest of these episodes has evolved since 2015, as large numbers of refugees have sought to settle in the EU. Since then, certain engine rooms have been subjected to continuous involvement and interference from the superstructure, as evidenced in Germany by the direct involvement of Chancellor Merkel and her chief of staff in the coordination of refugee policies, the rapid growth of the federal agency dealing with immigration, and the centralization of decision-making at the federal level.

In the model suggested by Baumgartner and Jones (2009), the shifting of issues from the engine room to the superstructure is only temporary but still leads to lasting changes in the former. For example, actors previously excluded from the policy-making process (outside the 'iron triangle') may become part of the inner circle in the engine room. Baumgartner and Jones speak of an 'equilibrium' that can eventually be 'punctuated', with equilibrium referring to widely autonomous policy-making in the policy subsystem (our engine room) and punctuation being rapid policy change following a build-up in sustained public and superstructure attention to a certain topic (see also Chapters 3 and 9).

In times of crisis, the relationship between superstructure and engine room is particularly important for formulating and implementing adequate policy interventions.

Of course, incident-driven media attention is not the only trigger for the involvement of the superstructure. Some issues might simply be deliberate priorities for top politicians, for example, when digitalization is defined as a key strategy for future-proofing an economy and society. A bottleneck is created when the superstructure seeks to directly engage in the specifics of particular policy fields, and executive leaders have only limited capacity to process information and resolve conflicts (Scharpf 1997). Not everything can be a top priority, and the more issues being dealt with at the top, the higher the likelihood that information gets lost or distorted in its transmission from the engine room to the superstructure. Moreover, top politicians are keenly aware of the potential for them to be blamed if things go wrong (and that the potential for credit is limited even if things work out). For example, Chancellor Merkel's party lost a significant share of votes in the 2017 general election following the refugee crisis. Hence, politicians will cautiously weigh the potential risks and benefits of getting involved in too many substantive policy issues.

Times of crisis are situations in which executive politicians move into the centre of day-to-day policy-making. Crises are characterized as serious threats to the fundamental values and norms of a system (Rosenthal et al. 1989, 10), but their effects can be addressed by political action. These political actions have to be conceived and carried out under conditions of high time pressure and uncertainty (cf. Boin et al. 2017). As crisis management often requires far-reaching interventions (such as bank bailouts in the financial crisis or lockdowns in the coronavirus pandemic), they require the authority and legitimacy of leading politicians, who are often directly involved. Crisis management is therefore highly political and requires strong political leadership, which can create tensions with engine room experts (see Box 2.4).

Box 2.4 Public policy in times of public health crises

When COVID-19 hit the world in the first half of 2020, governments responded remarkably differently despite very similar health threats. In Spain, families were locked in their homes and children were not allowed to go outside for six weeks, and in Italy, residents of northern cities had to carry forms with them when going shopping. In France, jogging was only allowed after sunset, while, at the same time, Swedish schools remained open, universities moved to distance learning, and only very large gatherings were banned. Germany introduced a milder version of a lockdown that allowed for walks and bike rides but forbade locals from going to the beaches of the Baltic Sea, and in the UK, social distancing was strictly monitored in parks. This was, of course, in even starker contrast to measures in China and South Korea, where digital tracking was swiftly enforced, or to policies in the US, which were uneven and, unlike in authoritarian China, politically contested.

In the pandemic, the relationship between superstructure decision-makers, on the one hand, and the engine room, on the other, has become particularly important because of the severity and complexity of the situation. Leadership on the part of the top executives was certainly critical, but so was the way the executives worked with the engine room in order to respond rapidly under conditions of very high uncertainty. The virus was novel, and it was the first time in roughly a century that a pandemic hit Western developed countries. Moreover, social distancing was an entirely new concept of behaviour in public and in private and had new repercussions for businesses, families, and public services. The diverse ways governments dealt with the pandemic up to the middle of 2020 reveal several key features.

Cooperation between experts and decision-makers can increase legitimacy in decision-making in hard times. Legitimacy, on the other hand, facilitates compliance with government policies. Rules are followed voluntarily if citizens trust the decision-makers and are convinced that the rules are appropriate and fair. Enforcement remains relevant, also as a signal to those who comply voluntarily that others do not get away with a lack of compliance. Most governments have relied on key experts in virology, epidemiology, and related sciences or heads of public health institutes to formulate and justify policy decisions. These experts have independent knowledge and cannot easily be drawn into political considerations. In cases in which experts were taken for granted or forced to follow a government line, it tended to reflect badly on decision-makers and undermine trust in the quality of the decisions made. The ambiguity of the role of Dr Anthony Fauci, an immunologist and Director of the US National Institute of Allergy and Infectious Diseases, in the US administration's response under then President Donald Trump contributed to falling levels of support for the government's strategy. His role was basically subordinated to political games about blame and credit, while the administration ignored or misrepresented expert advice throughout much of the crisis. Already as President-elect, Joe Biden aimed at changing this by publicly

continued

Box 2.4 *continued*

---

signalling his trust in Dr Fauci and in science more broadly; for example, Biden said he would take a coronavirus vaccine as soon as Fauci said it was safe to take one.

Experience shows that there is no perfect or right answer to the COVID-19 crisis, but variations of weighing up and deciding on the options. Complex situations that affect public health, families, education, and businesses call for well-balanced answers. The exceptional level of uncertainty requires a rapid, but step-by-step search and—where possible—test of solutions. The need to adapt policies on the go places very high demands on political actors, who need to leave their comfort zone, and on experts, who have to give recommendations on the basis of limited and rapidly changing evidence (and who are being drawn into political gaming because they 'change their mind' in light of new findings).

In times of crisis, the relationship between decision-makers—the superstructure—and the experts—the engine room—determines, in large part, whether responses are 'right' or even adequate. Populist politicians tend to campaign against experts to sharpen their profile as 'representatives of the people' against technocrats. In a crisis situation, this is a particularly dangerous approach as complex situations require expertise. A breakdown of trust and cooperation between governments and experts can lead to damaging policy responses, which, in turn, can fuel populist responses even further. In contrast, cooperation between experts and politicians might have lasting effects on the standing of expertise in politics and policy. In the end, the COVID-19 crisis has also shown that no amount of expertise can replace political judgement in times of high uncertainty.

2.4.3 The procedural channel

The procedural channel refers to the regulation of policy work in the engine room by the superstructure. It includes all kinds of government-wide regulations and policies that seek to influence policy-making in ministries and agencies: think of the internal rules and procedures that guide how departments draft legislative proposals, liaise with interest groups and other stakeholders (see Chapter 7), and coordinate with other departments and levels of governments (see Chapter 8). Since the 1970s, procedural channels have been used to influence and change the ways in which policies are conceived in the engine room, not least in light of the rise of (tools-oriented) policy analysis. Cost–benefit analysis has become mandatory during policy formulation in many countries and, since the 1980s and even more so 1990s, has been integrated into comprehensive impact assessment systems along with other impact tests, such as environmental impact and social impact assessments. For example, the European Commission's (2018) impact assessment system demands that assessments are carried out for all 'initiatives expected to have significant economic, social or environmental impacts' and hence covers these three dimensions in one assessment procedure.

While the stated goal of these meta-policies is to enhance the capacities of departments to develop sound, balanced policies, these procedures can also be seen as a way to keep policy-makers in the engine room under some level of control—not only from actors in the superstructure but also from societal stakeholders and other interested parties. To that end, in many countries and other policy jurisdictions such as the EU, draft laws and regulations are subjected to public consultation (see for instance European Commission, n.d.-c).

Other examples of procedural channels or meta-policies are managerial tools such as performance management and budgeting. While performance management (see Chapter 6) differs substantially from impact assessment, it shares the broader aim of keeping the engine room in check, whether by avoiding bureaucratic slack and increasing accountability for results or by overcoming resistance against policy and organizational innovations. Indeed, in countries with a strong emphasis on management reform policies, the engine room has substantially if not fundamentally changed due to the implementation of managerial tools. Again, the UK is a fitting example: the introduction of performance management, combined with structural changes (namely, the creation of so-called executive agencies) and the flexibilization of the civil service labour market, has fundamentally altered the structure and working style of the engine room. Performance-related pay and new career opportunities such as fast track careers have made the civil service a more competitive place to work, with the upside of more dynamics and the downside of a loss of classic bureaucratic virtues such as institutional memory, longer term orientation, and impartiality.

There are, however, limits to such strategies for controlling the engine room. In the UK, attempts by former Prime Minister Tony Blair to deliver public service reform against departmental (engine room) resistance by way of ongoing personal involvement could not be sustained over time; pressing issues of international politics crowded out domestic issues of public service reform (Barber 2007). In general, the implementation of procedural rules intended to regulate the engine room is not unproblematic. Policy-making bureaucrats may not embrace procedural rules prescribing that the drafting of policies and regulations need to be combined with extensive analytical procedures, such as cost–benefit analysis and impact assessment, because these procedures increase the workload and reduce the autonomy of policy-making bureaucrats. And engine room actors can deploy all kinds of coping strategies to deal with and therefore potentially undermine the effectiveness of central regulation of the policy process (cf. Lodge and Wegrich 2012).

2.5 So What? Implications for How to Do Public Policy

This chapter presents our view of the policy-making process as shaped by the relationships and interactions between two distinct, if overlapping, spheres of action in public policy: the political superstructure of politicians, political power and coalitions, and political institutions, on the one hand, and the engine room of policy-making populated by experts within and outside government, on the other hand. This perspective highlights that the way policies are made and how they work depend on the interaction of the three dimensions of the political—policy, politics, and polity—introduced in Chapter 1. These three dimensions feature in both the superstructure and the engine room, although with different weights and in different guises.

The image of the superstructure and the engine room illustrates how the political and institutional aspects of governance shape policy-making. While the remaining chapters in this book put stronger emphasis on the engine room, the influence of the superstructure and how that influence translates into political logics within the engine room will be a recurring theme. Placing the links and interactions between the superstructure and the engine room at the core of how policy-making works—and fails—should not only help in grasping seemingly erratic or outright irrational episodes of policy-making. It should also support smart practitioners as they explore policy approaches, solutions, and processes that have some chance to work in their favour. Because policy-making is so context-dependent, it is hard to generalize about the link between political logics and policy-making. However, the mechanisms that guide the policy process can be generally identified.

But before moving on to the various duties of the policy-maker in the engine room, some general points concerning the role of policy analysis need to be reiterated. Today, policy-makers are confronted with a vast array of analytical tools and techniques, suggesting that their use will yield better policy outputs and outcomes. We highlight three critical, and connected, points in this regard.

First, the limited impact of evidence-based (or -informed) policy-making in practice is often attributed to either politicians' lack of willing-ness or ability to make use of available evidence, or the communication deficits of academics and researchers, who lack the political sensitivity to infuse knowledge at the right time and in the right dosage. However, 'politicians' are a diverse group of actors, from opposition members of parliament to executive leaders, all with very different relations to the en-gine room of policy-making. Moreover, the policy-making bureaucracy is a larger and overall more important target (or consumer) audience for policy analysis. The staffers of executive departments and interest groups do not live in a world completely detached from that of knowledge production. Instead, individual units in the engine room have routine working rela-tions with various stakeholders, who offer relevant information, feedback, demands, and support for policies (see Chapter 7 for more on stakeholder engagement). These stakeholders are not limited to, but definitely include, experts and knowledge production organizations. Framing 'politicians' as the biggest hindrance to better use of evidence misses the point, and any attempts to improve the relation between the worlds of analysis and prac-tice, by improving the communication skills of academics and experts, will have limited effect. Far more critical is understanding that most of the 'con-sumers' of expertise, also a diverse group of actors, are, in fact, located in the engine room, which is in itself an all but politics-free context.

Second, policy analysis tools target the formal, later stages of the decision-making process, but, as noted earlier in this chapter, key features of policies are actually decided during the informal, pre-planning stages of policy-making. The discussion about the use and non-use of tools and ev-idence widely ignores these informal, pre-planning stages and the strong political incentive structure to use evidence to confirm decisions that have already been made informally. For the development of policy analysis, it is critical to understand this variant of confirmation bias and the resulting coping strategies of engine room actors in dealing with demands to use evidence-creating tools.

Third, the emphasis of tools-oriented policy analysis on policy (instrument) design and discrete moments of decision-making is based on a dated and, at best, partially valid image of how policy-making truly works. Policy design and the choice of policy instruments are certainly part of the work that takes place in the engine room (if heavily constrained by the superstructure). But picturing policy-making as a design process with the proverbial policy-maker taking centre stage (implicitly) builds on images of the policy process that have been debunked by interactive policy research since the 1980s. As described earlier in this chapter, policy development takes place in a network of actors, who are linked horizontally in a bargaining system, and the image of state executives or legislators designing policies on their own volition is misleading.

Moreover, and related to this, policy analysis often implicitly assumes that the goal of a policy is, or can be, set at the beginning of a process, leading to some kind of concrete policy or programme. The key question policy analysis seems to ask, and the one its tools are designed to answer, is how to best achieve a predefined goal. However, not only are goals often stated in vague or inconsistent ways that barely conceal disagreements between the actors involved, but goals also evolve during the process of adopting and implementing a policy. The engine room and the street-level bureaucracy are often left to take inherently political decisions, such as defining who is a more or less deserving beneficiary of social programmes. If policy analysis wants to solve problems through the better analysis of options to achieve fixed goals, it ignores a reality of the politics of policy-making that will not change fundamentally, no matter how many tools of policy analysis are instituted in the engine room.

This leads directly to one key contribution of our approach of how to do public policy, which seeks to make insights and concepts from interactive policy research more useful for policy workers in the engine room. While analysing and evaluating policy options and their costs, benefits, and side effects is an essential building block of our understanding of good policy-making, the 'relational' components of the policy process are just as, if not even more, important. This includes relations with other stakeholders (in the engine room and eventually the superstructure) as well as understandings of how institutions at both levels shape the policy process by empowering certain actors, how the framing of a policy issue influences different actors' opportunities and willingness to engage, and how networks of specialists allow and inhibit coordination and collaboration. A good policy-maker should have an eye on forging coalitions and alliances that support the adoption and implementation of a policy. In doing so, one should be able to learn what makes other actors and organizations tick; for example, how and why they would respond to a particular policy initiative. Policy-makers should also be capable of foreseeing challenges for institutional reform and change—for example, understanding how a reform might invade an organization's turf and hence create resistance—and take these likely responses into account when devising a reform strategy. In short, those wanting to actually make policy need to be trained to think in terms of processes and organizational logics, not only the hard analytical tools of policy analysis.

3

How to Set the Agenda

Key concepts

- Problem stream
- Garbage can model of policy-making
- Window of opportunity
- Framing
- Venue-shopping

At the core of policy-making are decisions taken (or not) by governments or legislatures. But these decisions arise because problems emerge, and political actors choose to address them. An important part, and a precondition for other parts, of the policy process is hence the selection and definition of problems, and how they find their way onto a government's to-do list.

Governments' agendas are often driven by events. Conflicts break out, disasters occur, a social problem makes the headlines, and parliamentary or international timetables dominate everyday decision-making. Also, governments are elected on a platform of policies and will aim to implement them. In addition, many actors and stakeholders in the engine room, who might be part of the government or not, try to influence government agendas. They aim to draw attention to policy problems in order to induce measures to deal with them by providing evidence or organizing campaigns or protests. But sometimes, actors in the engine room might also seek to avoid broadening attention to 'their' issue because they benefit from the status quo.

In this chapter, we explore when and how policy problems catch the attention of policy-makers and who takes on responsibility for their solution. We also analyse how the different modes of agenda-setting have implications for the policy process itself and for problem definition. Exploring the logic of agenda-setting as a process of selecting and framing some issues

How to Do Public Policy. Anke Hassel and Kai Wegrich, Oxford University Press.
© Anke Hassel and Kai Wegrich (2022). DOI: 10.1093/oso/9780198747000.003.0003

for heightened attention while keeping others in the background provides a key to understanding and influencing the policy process.

3.1 Attracting Attention

Agenda-setting is the selection of problems demanding action. The agenda is understood as 'the list of subjects or problems to which government officials, and people outside government closely associated with those officials, are paying some serious attention at any given time' (Kingdon 1995, 3). This governmental (or 'systemic') agenda is distinct from the media (or 'public') agenda, and a key concern is the relationship between the two. While some policy areas will almost always be more important than others (Jennings et al. 2011)—say, foreign compared to cultural policy, or finance compared to family policy—'low politics' issues can also attract amplified attention when scandals and crises make the headlines. For the policy-maker, setting the (governmental) agenda represents a balancing act between responding quickly to issues high on the media agenda and maintaining a more strategic, longer term orientation.

The challenge presented by agenda-setting is that not all problems and issues can receive similar amounts of attention at a given time—neither from individuals nor from the government or society. A government leader, for example, cannot pay personal attention to more than a handful of issues and problems at a time. Ministries and government agencies can handle many more issues and prioritize these, but even here the list is limited. Given the infinite number of problems that any government could potentially deal with, and considering limited resources in terms of time, capacity, and finances, the process of agenda-setting is essentially about setting priorities.

However, the issue at stake is not so much an 'either–or' question of whether a government deals with a particular issue. For sure, some issues are completely suppressed from consideration, and the exercise of *negative* agenda-setting power is an important way in which power is exercised, for example by parliamentary leaders who determine what should be discussed and voted on during the legislative session (McConnel and 't Hart 2019). But more often the question is *who* in government deals with the issue and *how much* political and other capital is invested in solving it.

Agenda-setting takes place both in the superstructure and in the engine room. In the superstructure, it is often driven by external events. In 2017, seventy-two people were killed as a result of a fire in London's Grenfell Tower (Rice-Oxley 2018). Subsequently, the concerns that had been growing for many years from residents, experts, and public agencies about fire-related risks (from a common type of cladding) in apartment towers caught the attention of the public and the government. Only then did the United Kingdom's government step in by launching an independent inquiry, initiating more thorough fire safety checks in other tower blocks, and arranging for tests of cladding samples from buildings around the country. But the agenda is also influenced and shaped by powerful actors. Dominant political actors, ministers, political entrepreneurs, or corporations might be able to push issues on the agenda single-handedly. Governments are elected on the basis of electoral platforms and promises and are measured at least to some extent by those promises.

In the engine room agenda-setting occurs through external events but also through the reframing of existing issues. Existing practices turn into problems, and the unintended side-effects of policies adopted earlier become 'their own cause' (Wildavsky 1979). For instance, the use of fertilizers and pesticides in agriculture led to high productivity increases in agriculture but has also had negative effects on biodiversity, causing actors in the environmental protection engine room to start to address farming as an environmental problem. Many issues remain entirely under the control of the specialists in the engine room and are approached incrementally without any public discussion. Whether the actors from the network in the engine room have an interest in keeping an issue off the public agenda or whether, alternatively, they seek to draw greater attention and participation depends on how satisfied they are with the status quo. Actors that assess the status quo as generally beneficial overall will not seek to arouse the interest of outsiders or the superstructure; those who consider the status quo as problematic will often seek to expand participation in and attract wider attention to the issue.

Powerful actors in the superstructure and experts in the engine room need to be able to communicate their issues in a convincing way. Power and persuasion are the two pillars of agenda-setting and should be employed in a complementary fashion. The less powerful the actors and the less salient the issue, the more important the storytelling, framing, and evidence become in winning support from more powerful actors. Vice versa, very powerful actors need to exert less persuasion to get their items on the agenda. However, even the most powerful actors must tell a story. Agenda-setters therefore have to engage in the crafting of stories in order to appeal to the electorate as well as to others in their network. In short, agenda-setting combines issue-framing and power exertion to gain the attention of decision-makers for these issues. But this process takes place in an arena where others will push competing frames or seek to keep the issue from entering the agenda altogether.

In the next sections, we discuss how problems attract the attention of governments. For this we will need to look at the policy process more closely and establish the essentials for policy change. We identify the role of problem definition in agenda-setting and discuss the role of evidence. We look at the task of agenda-setting in greater detail and discuss different mechanisms and modes of agenda-setting from the perspectives of both advocates of particular policy issues and government leaders. Finally, we end the chapter with five recommendations on how to set the agenda effectively.

Box 3.1 How 'golden visas' moved onto the agenda of the European Commission

---

Over twenty countries or territories currently offer so-called 'golden visa' programmes by which citizenship or residence rights are granted to foreign nationals in exchange for sizeable investments. It is estimated that the European golden visa schemes—exercised by thirteen EU member states—globally generate US$13 billion (€11.15 billion) a year, of which citizenship-by-investment schemes represent about US$3 billion (Citizenship by Investment 2018).

Civil society groups such as Transparency International (TI) started to draw attention to the issue using individual cases prepared by investigative journalists that connected individuals buying entry into the EU to corruption and criminal activity, above all the laundering of ill-gotten gains into real estate in the countries selling them safe havens. They used key messages that golden visa and passport programmes provide safe havens inside the EU for corrupt and other criminal actors and opportunities to launder illicit wealth, and thereby contribute to corruption in the EU.

The European Parliament had already expressed its concerns about these golden visa programmes in a January 2014 joint resolution expressing concern about the sale of EU citizenship and calling on the Commission to assess the practice (European Parliament 2014). In 2017, not waiting for the Commission's assessment, investigative journalists at the Organized Crime and Corruption Reporting Project (OCCRP) noted that a high number of Russians connected with transnational money-laundering were settling in Cyprus. The network of journalists decided that an editor would work with some ten national journalists across Europe to look into these schemes to profile some of the individuals taking advantage of the visa-free travel into the EU.

In September 2017, *The Guardian* newspaper began publishing articles resulting from the investigation. First came reports based on a leaked list of the names of hundreds of those who have benefited from Cyprus's sale of passports, including prominent Russian businesspeople and individuals with considerable political influence (Farolfi et al. 2017). The OCCRP cooperated with TI under the auspices of the Global Anti-Corruption Consortium. TI held a press conference in March 2018, which coincided with a series of investigative articles published by the OCCRP that showed how citizenship- and residence-by-investment schemes are vulnerable to abuse and undermine the fight against corruption in the EU and neighbouring countries (Transparency International 2018).

The European Commission urged member states in August 2018 to restrict issuing investor visas to non-nationals and announced plans to publish new regulations. EU Justice Commissioner Vera Jourova called the golden visa programmes a 'serious security risk' (Wright 2018).

TI and the human rights advocacy group Global Witness published a report *European Getaway—Inside the Murky World of Golden Visas* in October 2018 to provide analysis of the corruption risks inherent with the golden visa programmes (Transparency International n.d.). In January 2019, the European Commission published a study that recognized that golden visa schemes present 'inherent' risks to the EU's collective integrity and security (European Commission 2019a). By November 2019, after the new members of the European Parliament were elected, the European Economic and Social Committee (EESC) demanded an end to all investor citizenship and residence schemes in the EU (European Economic and Social Committee 2019).

In December 2019, the group of experts convened by the Commission in 2018 met for the fourth time but the anticipated proposal for minimum security and due diligence checks for investor schemes had stalled (European Commission n.d.-d). Almost two years after the launch of the joint campaign, in February 2020, Global Witness published an evaluation briefing showing that the passports and visas industry was still going strong in the EU (Global Witness 2020).

In April 2020, one year after the European Parliament's Committee on Civil Liberties, Justice, and Home Affairs (LIBE) expressed serious concerns about the citizenship-by-investment programmes in Cyprus and Malta, the new EU Justice Commissioner Didier Reynders reassured the committee that the Commission had entered into a dialogue with the governments of Bulgaria, Cyprus, and Malta

continued

Box 3.1 *continued*

---

to recommend the phasing out of their citizenship programmes and to convince them to not 'go too far with these schemes' (Transparency International 2020a). Six months later, the European Commission launched infringement procedures against Cyprus and Malta regarding their investor citizenship schemes (European Commission 2020a).

Contributing author: Casey Kelso

3.2. Understanding Policy Change and Stability

The policy science literature of the 1950s and 1960s introduced an idealized version of the policy process. As highlighted in Chapter 1, Harold Lasswell (1956) conceived of the policy process in seven stages: intelligence, promotion, prescription, invocation, application, appraisal, and termination. In many public policy textbooks, the policy process is presented as a policy cycle (Jann and Wegrich 2007): policy problems emerge, they find their way onto the agenda, and policy instruments are adopted and implemented leading to new policy problems, which again find their way onto the agenda.

The ideal-typical policy cycle narrative—though convenient and somewhat logical—distorts everyone's understanding of the policy process by implying a sequence which does not exist, because the order of different steps in the policy process varies. That narrative also implies a particular role for policy analysis as a depoliticized space in which new policy solutions are researched and subsequently brought seamlessly into the policy process. Like the ideal-typical policy cycle, such a depoliticized space is hard to find.

The starting point for understanding the policy process is the power constellation of actors in the superstructure whose aims are stability and dominance; in other words, they seek to remain in power. Despite a huge increase in legislative activism in terms of laws passed, we find a rather stable status quo when it comes to most policy questions, and not wildly fluctuating decisions (Baumgartner and Jones 2009). This reflects an overall state of equilibrium, or a steady state of modern-day policy-making.

The situation is less surprising when you think about it: Different political forces have different views about policies. Policy-makers operate in a system in which an entire range of vested interests watch over the state of play. Each country's existing system has resulted from previous decisions but also reflects a constellation of political forces, not only at the time of decision-making but also in the past. The continuity of an existing system is evidence of dependence on a path once taken and of the political forces that hold onto that path (see Chapter 9 regarding path dependence).

This gives us a key insight into the logic of steady-state policy-making: wherever you are, the existing system shapes any policy proposal on the table. The status quo presents us with a scenario in which we are more oriented to what we know than to alternative ideas. This is because we know what the pay-off is in an existing system but can make only vague calculations as to what new systems might bring. Existing systems of policies and institutions constitute a cognitive map that guides how actors think about policy (change).

This status quo bias exists in both the superstructure and the engine room but for different reasons. In the superstructure, the political forces tend to be in equilibrium for longer periods of time. As politics consists of coalitions of actors in the superstructure, these coalitions forge agreements on particular policies and tend to control these policies. This does not mean that the majority of political actors in a country favours the system. Even if everyone in, for example, France were to oppose the public pension scheme, the political groupings that could do something about it have either reached a consensus as to why it is preferable to keep the system or backed each other into a corner in which the status quo is preserved even though it is in no one's interest.

In the engine room, the dominance of the status quo is often based on the constellation of experts, civil servants, and organized interests who also control access to the inner world of engine room policy-making. Communities of experts, civil servants, and activists in the engine room tend to be closed networks as participants make it hard for newcomers to come in. The degree of openness of the policy field (see section 5.4 on modes of agenda-setting later in this chapter) gives different actors different kinds of access to participate in policy-making and agenda-setting.

Besides power constellations and access to the engine room, the underlying belief system and cognitive orientation of the actors also determines the overall opportunity for change. Many policy fields develop particular images of policies. When policy-makers agree on a particular framing, actors achieve a policy monopoly, which can survive over long periods of time. The monopoly shapes the framing of an issue and the policy solutions (not) considered. There might be institutional backing for policy monopolies, for example, by defining the type of expertise admissible to the network of experts in a policy field (Baumgartner and Jones 2009). Similarly, as Sabatier and Weible (2007) argue, a particular deeply held belief might be the foundation of the policy field. For instance, there are a number of deeply held beliefs that are the basis for education policies, such as the role of schools and teachers and the relative importance of different subjects (such as mathematics versus physical education). These beliefs are shared by nearly all participants in the policy field and are hard to shake.

The main forces favouring policy change are shifts in the power distribution through a new situation (an external event), a competing coalition of actors that gains influence on the policy issue, or a window of opportunity (a moment in which the policy issue is not guarded sufficiently) (see Box 3.2). But also, medium- to long-term changes in societal values and understanding of issues drive change. In short, agenda-setting needs to overcome the status quo orientation of policy-making by urging policy-makers to act. This includes the definition of problems and the various techniques for placing issues on the agenda.

Box 3.2 The garbage can model of organizational and policy change

---

The garbage can model of organizational choice was originally developed with reference to decision-making in universities. It argued that a decision is 'an outcome or interpretation of several relatively independent streams within an organization' (Cohen, March, and Olsen 1972, 3–4). Problems, solutions, and participants come to the decision process independently of each other and coincide at choice opportunities, which are decision-making moments (such as meetings or contracts). The resulting outcome is based on chance, timing, and who happens to be present.

Kingdon (1995) applied the garbage can model to agenda-setting in public policy-making and developed today's 'multiple streams' framework. These two models capture the fluid and contingent, if not random, dynamics of agenda-setting. Kingdon distinguishes three 'streams' that develop independently from one other. The *problem stream* is about the (media) attention given to a particular issue. The *policy stream* refers to the available—or at least fashionable—solutions in the pipeline. Within the policy stream, particular solutions to problems are discussed. Consider for example the wave of 'behavioural insights' influencing many current policy debates: nudges and related interventions are one type of policy solution being advanced within the policy stream (see Chapter 4). The key point is that the policy stream develops independent of the problem stream, i.e. particular solutions tend to be most strongly advocated by those who have a stake in their application regardless of the problem at hand. The *political stream* is about the motivation of and opportunity for politicians to enact a policy.

A 'window of opportunity' for pushing a topic high(er) up on the government's agenda arises when there is a conjunction between the three different streams, for example, through a focusing event. Attention to a problem is combined with a feasible policy option and a political motive to adopt this option.

3.3 How to Define Policy Problems

Is it really a problem when governments sell residence rights and citizenships to investors? Many governments have no problem justifying it as a win–win situation: Rich businesspeople want to invest in the country and expect residence in exchange. They do not accept that 'golden visa' programmes (Box 3.2) might be implicated in money-laundering, tax evasion, and other forms of corruption and crime. For activists, the task of defining standard practice as a problem is therefore an important step in the agenda-setting process.

Although the standard textbook approach suggests that the two should be separated—agenda-setting is not considered as an integral part of policy analysis that usually is supposed to start with the definition of the problem and then moves to the collection of evidence for constructing alternative policy options (see the overview of various 'five-step models' of how to do policy analysis in Cairney 2021, 11–15)—the reality is less clearly structured. Problem definition takes place during the process of agenda-setting and is shaped by it. Changing the definition of a problem can help to put it on the agenda as it addresses different actors.

A problem is best understood as a social, political, or economic ill that from the perspective of policy-makers needs remedy and improvement. Therefore, it often comes in the form of too much or too little of a social or other phenomenon: 'too much' poverty, homelessness, or pollution on the one hand, 'too little' high-quality schools or well-functioning public infrastructure on the other (Bardach and Patashnik 2019, 1). Unemployment, inflation, poverty, drug addiction, and pollution are universal policy problems that have plagued modern societies since at least the Industrial Revolution.

In the real world, problem definition often already includes policy so-lutions as many policy actors enter the scene with certain solutions in mind, coming from different branches of policy analysis (as described in Chapter 1). In the superstructure, many policy problems derive from election platforms as promises to the electorate. Centre-left parties might promise to raise the minimum wage. Other politicians in the superstruc-ture pledge to lower taxes, reduce costs in public administration, or build new highways. These pledges do not necessarily aim to solve problems, but rather to attract voters who potentially benefit from those measures. Once the problem has been taken up by the superstructure, it is often too late to define it through an evidence-based policy-making process.

In contrast, in the engine room problem definitions are based on a deeper understanding of the issue (Baumgartner and Jones 2015). As pol-icy experts puzzle over effective solutions for certain problems and have a clearer understanding of the policy trade-offs, they are potentially more open to various definitions than are those in the superstructure. The core question that is asked in the engine room is how to frame the problem definition so as to come to solutions that are manageable and actually ad-dress the problem. This requires knowledge of problem boundaries and the universe of potential solutions. In other words, policy analysis and policy instruments are already part of the problem definition and the agenda-setting process. If problems do not lend themselves to problem-solving strategies or have solutions that are either too complex or too expensive for policy-makers to propose or pursue, they are unlikely to become part of the agenda-setting process. Stated somewhat differently, in the practice of policy-making, it is unlikely that problem definition will be decoupled from the selection of policy instruments.

Problem boundaries describe the context in which policy problems are addressed. For instance, instead of addressing global security issues broadly, problem definition would target the problem of ISIS strongholds in Syria. Similarly, while reducing the number of homeless people in big cities across the world (or even in one city) might be the policy target, the problem definition might benefit from clearer specifications such as tar-geting specifically vulnerable groups (young homeless people) or during specific periods.

But even when problems are identified within narrow boundaries, the complexity of many policy issues makes attempts to define them difficult if not intractable. As Rittel and Weber (1973, 160) argue, public policy prob-lems, especially social problems, are ill-defined, and their resolution relies on political judgement. In contrast to problems encountered by engineers, for whom the mission is clear, policy problems are characterized by the fact that the definition of the problem depends on one's idea for solving it. These are, in the words of Rittel and Weber (1973, 161), wicked problems: 'Problem understanding and problem resolution are concomitant to each other.'

For instance, many policy problems that touch upon human misery, poverty, and illness come with value judgements concerning the role of responsibility and self-reliance, as well as redistribution and social infrastructure. Often, they become part of the electoral competition between policy-makers. For some, the issue of unemployment is an expression of wages that are too high (thus preventing employers from hiring), for some an expression of wages that are too low (thus making jobs unattractive for the unemployed). Unemployment, in particular long-term unemployment, is closely connected to health, housing, childcare, and skills, each of which in turn can be defined as an individual's responsibility or as a broader public policy problem. The wider public policy issues range from the lack of jobs for the long-term unemployed to a host of other policy problems which are in turn affected by the nature of the labour market. In view of this obvious complexity, defining the problem of homelessness in terms of 'there are too many homeless people in the United States', as Bardach and Patashnik (2019, 2) recommend, is therefore too simplistic. The definition of wicked problems has to take into account the complexity of the issue, the repercussions and side-effects of different solutions, the close entanglement with other policy issues, and the value judgements entailed.

Alternatively, especially when many different and difficult problems are intertwined, a particular problem can be highlighted as the starting point, as in the case of 'housing first', an approach to address homelessness by prioritizing access to housing over other often coexisting issues, such as drug or alcohol abuse.

Defining the problem therefore requires understanding the degree of wickedness of the policy issue as well as the political controversies that might surround it. Because many of these issues are long-standing problems of modern societies, we should not naively start with a problem definition from scratch. Instead, we should first look to the experience of policy-makers over the last decades and situate the issue in the context of contemporary policy change and policy discourse. Rather than stating merely that there are 'too many unemployed', one could start with partial problems such as 'current welfare-to-work programmes do not get the

unemployed into jobs'. In most cases policy change will build on existing policies (in this case welfare-to-work policies) and only rarely aim at
a radical departure from those policies. A narrower problem statement in-
corporates existing knowledge about the policy's history and starts with
a clear expectation with regard to policy instruments (see Chapter 4).
Moreover, debating policy solutions between stakeholders—be it in organized deliberations, for example in commissions, or in a less structured
way—can serve as an effective way to develop a common understanding of key issues surrounding a complex problem such as poverty or
unemployment.

How a problem is defined and described for action purposes depends
significantly on the type of policy problem it is (see Table 3.1). Morality
issues, for example, are frequently very divisive as they rest on normative
foundations and belief systems. Since there is generally no consensus on

Table 3.1 Four basic types of policy problems, solutions, and their attributes

PROBLEM TYPE	SOLUTION TYPE	ATTRIBUTE	EXAMPLES
Morality	Moral and criminal code	Highly normative, controversial	Sex work, drug use
Equity	Taxation, spending, social insurance	Win–lose constellation, distribution conflicts	Basic income, inheritance tax, climate change
General welfare	Social investment, public infrastructure	Potentially win–win, but different degrees of salience	Education, social insurance
Regulating the commons	Regulation of economic and other activities	Enforcement-intensive	Pollution, climate change

morality within societies, a clear problem definition is very difficult to formulate. There will be some who do not see sex work or drug use, to name two prominent issues, as a problem per se and would not engage in policy discussions to ban them. Here problem definition is in itself a value judgement.

With regard to equity and (re)distribution issues, there are by definition winners and losers who will have particular views on what a just society should look like. Wealth taxes are at the heart of these discussions, but there is also discussion of deserving versus non-deserving poor, unemployed, or sick. The distribution of wealth, income, and other resources cannot be determined without political conflict.

General welfare problems are those which governments take on in order to increase economic growth or the general wealth and well-being of societies. In modern societies these often affect investment in education, research, and public infrastructure for innovation. While there is a win–win situation deriving from economic growth, the benefits of these policies are distributed unevenly. Some will benefit the most from public spending on education, while others prefer subsidies for investment in research and development. Problem definitions have to take into account these different perspectives.

Finally, there is a set of policy problems which can generally be described by the 'tragedy of the commons' (Hardin 1968) of overuse of common goods. These can be environmental problems such as ocean pollution or the overuse of public infrastructure (for instance public litter bins). The nature of common pool resources entails that the pursuit of pure individual self-interest results in overuse and depletion of resources; fishing grounds are a typical example. Here, regulation is usually the first solution offered, but it tends to require intensive enforcement efforts and presents many trade-offs with regard to the preferences of those affected. Ostrom (1990) developed her research around the potential of alternative solutions lying between top–down state regulation and private property rights, i.e. self-regulatory schemes of multiple stakeholders (see also Chapter 8 on coordinating policies).

Defining policy problems is based on 'thick descriptions' of the problem and analysis of data that reveal the possible causes and interdependences across issues. Addressing golden visa work as a problem needs to show that granting visas for investment commitments has significant impact. Here problem definition links up with the use of evidence, as we show in the next section.

3.4 How to Use Evidence to Set the Agenda

Evidence is crucial for agenda-setting. In Chapter 1 we explained that evidence-based policy-making strives to use the best available knowledge to come up with the best policy response to a policy problem. In fact, the best available knowledge is necessary (but not sufficient) to bring a problem to the agenda and to frame the issue as a policy problem in the first place. In the case of golden visa programmes, investigative reporting by a network of journalists highlighted how many convicted criminals had obtained residence visas or passports in the EU (see Box 3.1). The reporting, combined with advocacy work on the part of TI and Global Witness, was used to strengthen the case for putting such golden visa programmes back on the agenda of the European Commission.

The policy world is bursting with reports and studies monitoring how problems develop. Often such reports are created to institutionalize attention towards a particular problem. Thereby, evidence and analysis become part of political strategy and framing contests in agenda-setting, rather than replacing politics or taking centre stage after the agenda has already been set.

Indeed studies, reports, green and white papers, as well as other 'products' of policy research, point to problems that should be addressed and often link them to particular solutions. The key point, however, is that forecasts, rankings, indicators, and so on are not independent from the political process of allocating attention between different policy issues and different ways of framing those issues. Instead, analysis is part and parcel of the tug of war between actors seeking to keep issues within the closed shop of the engine room and those trying to raise attention amongst a wider set of actors, including, via the public, superstructure actors. Indeed, many analyses are created at least in part with the purpose of increasing attention to a particular issue, such as the World Bank Doing Business ranking or the OECD's Programme for International Student Assessment (PISA) studies comparing school students' performance across countries.

Indicators in particular have the potential to focus attention on certain issues. Quantitative indicators can summarize complex affairs into single numbers, such as the gross domestic product (GDP) indicating the health of an economy, the GINI coefficient measuring economic inequality in society, or *The Economist*'s Big Mac index calculating the purchasing power of national currencies. Particularly when presented in a comparative way, allowing for a ranking of units (e.g. countries or cities), indicators can have a powerful, attention-grabbing effect.

Consider the question of the quality of education systems, a key concern for policy-makers, parents, the taxpaying public, and the education engine room actors: what could be more complex? But when 15-year-old students are assessed by a tool such as the OECD's PISA standardized test that measures scholastic performance in exactly the same way in nearly sixty countries, the comparison of vastly different school systems becomes possible. More than that, the results of hundreds of thousands of tested school children can be aggregated to create relative rankings of countries' school systems. The mediocre position of Germany in the first edition of the PISA ranking pushed the issue high on the agenda; the resulting 'PISA shock' triggered all kinds of reforms in schooling. Each new edition of PISA is eagerly awaited, and educational experts are quick to interpret results in terms of the successes and limitations of earlier reforms (showing that agenda-setting also entails the evaluation of earlier policies).

Governments, international organizations, think tanks, and advocacy groups are aware of the agenda-setting potential of indicators and rankings. For organizations in the 'indicators industry' (Lehtonen 2015), gaining attention for such studies can be the primary goal, and hence indicators and indexes are usually designed to do exactly that. Studies with quantifiable results have greater chances of being recognized. However, policy-makers and policy analysts need to be able to critically review the design and construction of indicators. For example, PISA is in general perceived as following high methodological standards. But of course choices in the design of any study can be debated. Possibly the most striking design choice when it comes to PISA is that foreign language skills are not assessed (though they are scheduled to be in future rounds). We come back to this example in Chapter 6 on how to evaluate policies.

Similar questions can be asked regarding any set of indicators. The World Bank's (2017) Doing Business project, for example, includes as indicators relatively uncontested issues such as the number of agencies to be contacted when opening a business and the days needed to do so (World Bank 2019). But the study also includes the ease of laying off workers, a highly contested indicator that says more about the underlying politics of the World Bank than about how easy it is to conduct business in a particular location.[1] The

---

[1] The 'employing workers' indicator set is not included in the ease of doing business ranking in the 2020 report (World Bank 2019), which might be a sign that the World Bank has responded to the criticism.

inclusion of such an indicator not only invites debate on moral grounds (whether making the sacking of workers easy is good regulation) but also ignores that labour regulation and relations play distinctively different roles within each country's specific form of capitalism.

As indexes and similar data projects become increasingly widely promulgated, used, and referred to, today's policy-makers and policy analysts need to be able to critically assess (the design of) indicators and other data products just as much as they need to be equipped to respond to such publications (Anheier et al. 2018). But from an agenda-setting perspective, as we shall see later in the discussion of agenda-setting modes, having the right indicator or other evidence at hand to support a particular narrative and policy frame is an important element for successful agenda-setting strategies.

3.5 Mechanisms and Modes of Agenda-Setting

Governments are structured by policy fields (e.g. defence, finance, health), and ministers have responsibility for particular areas. Within these areas several themes continue to flow in the public discussion: security, poverty, (un)employment, energy, and the environment. Within these themes new aspects emerge and become pressing: health risks, energy crisis, or biodiversity loss. Policy-makers in the engine room usually have worked on the policy issue at hand for a very long time. Actors with vested interests in some of these issues aim to push to get their preferred policies on the agenda or suppress them. They often engage in coalitions with others who have similar interests against others who push back. These coalitions can be more or less stable: farmers battle against environmentalists and engage in coalitions with retailers for looser environmental protection. Farmers, environmentalists, and retailers organize in lobby groups, interest organizations, and think tanks to provide evidence in support of their preferred policies.

When working the policy process and developing strategies to pursue their aims, policy actors need to take into account three general factors of agenda-setting—timing, framing, and venue choice—that apply to all actors involved or affected (see also Annex 2 on 'How to Design an Advocacy Campaign').

3.5.1 Timing: windows of opportunity

Timing refers to the question of when to invest in efforts to mobilize a wider audience for the concern of a particular group. Timing is often crucial, even if no coalition of actors can afford to completely pause their efforts. Limited resources have to be used with care, and in a (media) context that seems unfavourable to a group's cause, it might be advisable to wait. Of course, whether and when winds will change is always a matter of uncertainty.

In the case of the golden visa programmes (Box 3.1), timing mattered as the impending end of the legislative period of the European Parliament meant that any further action by the EP was time constrained. The journalists' reporting and the release of the report by TI and Global Witness had to be synchronized to leave enough time for parliamentarians to raise the issue with the responsible EU Commissioner. Campaigning for the EP election, to be held in May 2019, and the subsequent selection of a new team of EU Commissioners diverted energy from the process (Transparency International n.d.).

The 'multiple streams framework' argues that policy-makers generally have a drawer full of policy proposals, which they can pull out when the opportunity arises (see Box 3.2 and Kingdon 1995). A major terrorist attack is likely to be used as a window of opportunity for those within and outside government advocating tighter monitoring and surveillance—for example, of electronic communications—to kick off a policy initiative to that end. In other words, policy initiatives need to be ready for a public launch within days, and hence need to be pre-emptively prepared by the policy bureaucrats in government and the advocacy groups outside it.

Note that from the perspective of top politicians such as heads of government, the decision problem is often about waiting for the right moment to advance a project. Top politicians make use of windows of opportunity in order to introduce major policy changes. Bureaucratic blunders or critical evaluation reports of existing policies might be used as a springboard to engage in major policy reforms. The German welfare reforms of the early 2000s (Hartz reforms) were launched on the basis of such a critical report (Hartz 2002). In some situations, governments tend to watch how a policy discourse develops and allow the involved actors from the engine room to play out their game. Only when it becomes clear where the chips will fall, will governments take over the policy issue and present the engine room's initiatives as either successes or failures. And while this often results in successful blame avoidance, it backfired in the case of the 2015 refugee crisis, when the issue was left to the engine room for a long time before German Chancellor Merkel chose to engage, at a point when the media and the populace demanded such involvement (see Jugl 2020 for a comparison of the crisis management in Germany with the more proactive Luxembourg).

3.5.2 Framing: images and contests

The framing of policy issues and policy problems shapes their perception in the policy process. Framing aims to attach particular images to a problem by way of categorizing or linking the problem to wider concepts or values. It can be understood as a conceptual way of looking at the world and hence is associated with particular interpretations of problems. Framing is important, and powerful, because of the same underlying capacity limits that drive agenda-setting: we cannot grasp all potential aspects of a complex policy problem and instead rely on frames or images that give us ways to connect particular problems to already familiar ideas and widely shared values.

As Jones and Baumgartner (2005) have demonstrated, organizational systems such as systems of government do not respond to incoming information in a balanced, proportional way. New information that does not fit neatly into dominant, pre-existing frames is mostly disregarded. Only after a long period of persistent challenges to existing frames by new information will a system react, often in a similarly disproportionate way, that is, by overemphasizing the 'newly discovered' problem. Framing efforts play an important role in shifting attention to new, or alternative, information in general. The reframing of the golden visa programmes—from a minor issue that was entirely the responsibility of individual member states to a security risk threatening the entire EU—directed attention to other information, namely the extent of the problem and the sometimes shady dealings between governments and businesspeople.

The 'policy image' constructed via framing can be more technical or left open to wider societal engagement, more positive or more negative. Actors will attempt to shape policy images by various means, such as selectively presenting facts, constructing simplified narratives, and making emotional appeals. It makes a difference for the dynamics of agenda-setting whether smoking is considered a health risk that a rational adult can assess on their own behalf or a public health problem that links to the financing of the healthcare system or the protection of non-smokers, including children, from passive smoking. Even the naming of a problem contributes to its frame. The 'golden visa' frame aimed to highlight an unfair part of the system. Though many European countries had programmes in place to facilitate 'investment-based migration', including so-called start-up visas, the 'golden visa' moniker served to highlight those countries' citizenship- and residence-by-investment programmes that deliberately sought to attract the super-rich and implied an element of favouritism.

In short, framing is an essential element of any agenda-setting strategy, and it is critical to identify the frame that will engage key actors in support of the pursued ends. In the case of the golden visa programmes, those buying residence or citizenship rights, mainly Chinese and Russian, were first depicted as dubious and often as using illicit money. As might have been expected, governments denied knowledge of deliberate wrongdoing. After extensive reporting and campaigning, however, TI and Global Witness, among others, were able to successfully frame golden visa programmes, which in effect give holders access to the privileges such as freedom of movement enjoyed throughout the EU and the Schengen area, as security risks.

In general, when a new policy image gains acceptance, the information highlighted by its frame will receive more attention and may eventually lead to substantial policy change. Hence framing strategies are an important tool for policy-makers and stakeholders to gain or preserve influence. As we mentioned earlier, those actors with an established position in the engine room will try to preserve the existing policy image in order to maintain that position and influence over engine room policy-making. As noted earlier in the chapter, a 'policy monopoly' exists when a singular, dominant policy image (or frame) is particularly 'locked in' in the engine room, so actors carrying that interpretation of the policy problem dominate the engine room.

The literature on agenda-setting argues that pro-status quo groups are likely to have a strong comparative advantage over 'status quo challengers' (Varone et al. 2017). While challengers need to increase the salience of issues and expand conflicts, pro-status quo groups can act defensively, drawing on the resources of their policy monopoly to fend off challengers' attempts to expand conflict with responses that point out the costs, feasibility, and side-effects of new initiatives (Varone et al. 2017). But as numerous cases show—Baumgartner and Jones (2009) highlight the attitude reversal towards nuclear energy in the US in the 1970s and, more gradually, the

surprising decline in support (and legal provision for) the death penalty—
even some of the strongest policy monopolies can be broken up when
an outsider group challenges the insiders, unleashing opportunities for
revising the agenda and eventually also policy change.

3.5.3 Location: venue-shopping

The third important component of an agenda-setting strategy is the selection of the location, or venue, for conducting agenda-setting activities.
Change in a policy image usually occurs in tandem with a change in the
institutional 'policy venue' in which the policy is handled. When the key
engine room actors are resistant to changes in the status quo, those actors
pursuing policy change by challenging a prevailing policy image are often
forced to test the waters elsewhere. This strategy of searching for an institutional location receptive to a new (and competing) policy image is referred
to as venue-shopping (Baumgartner and Jones 2009).

The choice of venue is not entirely voluntary but more the result of difficulties faced by actors attempting to refocus attention to a new policy
image within the network of actors dominating engine room politics. As
mentioned earlier, any new policy image will be considered inherently
risky for those actors in the engine room controlling the image that best
serves their interests. So, the challengers need to find other ways to raise
attention and search for a more receptive audience. Often this results in
simply appealing to the public, but it need not be limited to raising general
awareness. In the case of the golden visa programmes, the initial venue
for highlighting the danger of selling residence rights could have been the
individual EU member states. However, since all EU member states are affected by new citizens because of freedom of movement within the EU, the
EU institutions seemed to be a better target location for advocacy efforts.
Though the Commission, the EP, and some member state governments
became increasingly concerned about the use of golden visa programmes,
policy change was still on hold as of early 2021 as the member states
had not yet agreed on a common policy. In October 2020, however, the
EU opened infringement proceedings against Malta and Cyprus for their
golden passport programmes (EU Commission 2020a).

Especially in federal systems, lower levels of government—in particular
cities and states—should be considered as alternate venues. The diffusion
of same-sex marriage rights from one to thirty-six states in the US between

2004 and 2015 (at which time same-sex marriage was established in all fifty states, based on a Supreme Court ruling) is one example of an effective venue-change strategy. In this case, state legislatures, state courts, and federal courts served as some of the alternative locations enabling successful policy change at the subnational level. Taking the field of climate change policy as another example, both the transnational and the subnational levels are considered to be alternative venues when the road towards more active climate change policies is blocked at the national level. After the Trump administration in 2017 announced its intent to withdraw the US from the Paris Agreement, state and local governments as well as businesses, churches, and other organizations pledged their continued commitment and actions to reduce greenhouse gas emissions as originally promised.

While we believe that these three strategic considerations—of timing, framing, and venue—are essential for effective agenda-setting, there is of course no guarantee of success when applying them in real-world contexts. Not only is agenda-setting to a large extent shaped by forces outside the control of any one actor; also, other actors and organizations will be similarly as politically smart and will apply the same strategies from the agenda-setting playbook. As Baumgartner et al. (2009) show, most attempts to (re)frame an issue remain unsuccessful, not least because counter-framing strategies are simultaneously applied by other actors. Matters are further complicated today by the increasingly prominent role of social media, including the rise of coordinated online campaigning for the purpose of spreading false information.

3.5.4 Modes of agenda-setting

There are many actors who aim to set or influence the policy agenda from different positions in the policy process. Political leaders can dominate the agenda of the day by choosing to respond to problems, even though they do not control them exclusively. Other actors, insiders and outsiders, usually need to battle to make their voices heard. Depending on the actor seeking to set the agenda, the task is pursued differently (Cobb and Elder 1971). We highlight four modes of agenda-setting that vary with regard to their degrees of openness. Openness in this case refers to the access of large numbers of policy actors to opportunities to engage in agenda-setting. While executive agenda-setting is the most controlled and closed,

Table 3.2 Mechanisms and modes of agenda-setting

DEGREE OF OPENNESS			TIMING	FRAMING	VENUE	USE OF EVIDENCE
CLOSED		EXECUTIVE	Manipulated	Controlled	Controlled	Legitimation
		BARGAINING	Negotiated	Negotiated	Organised	Negotiation
OPEN		NETWORK COMPETITION	Orchestrated	Competitive	Organised	Policy-informing
		ADVOCACY	Event-driven	Competitive	Multiple	Persuasion

the subsequent modes are increasingly open and therefore accessible to more actors. Table 3.2 combines these modes with the previously discussed mechanisms.

> **Executive** agenda-setting refers to the ability of a government to control the agenda for its own ends. Governments can suppress issues they do not want to have on the agenda, but they can also use external events in order to put on the agenda issues that they wanted to pursue anyway. Executive agenda-setting relies on the power of political leaders. In this mode of agenda-setting, venues can be chosen freely, and the political leadership has strong influence over framing and timing. Evidence is used to legitimize government's actions. Indeed, timing is often manipulated by attaching policy issues to external events. For instance, the nuclear power accident following the earthquake and tsunami in Fukushima, Japan, in 2011 was used by the German government to announce that it would move forward the target for phasing out nuclear power, an action that was already on the agenda.
>
> Executives are also in a position to keep issues off the agenda. Pierson (2015) argues that studying the development of governmental agendas over time allows one to observe such tendencies of agenda suppression and suggests that the political analysis of policy-making has an important job to fulfil in detecting such patterns. For instance,

Crenson's (1971) comparative case study of the 'unpolitics of air pollution' in two neighbouring US cities brought to light that, even when air pollution was an actual and severe problem, it was not always addressed.

Bargaining takes place when political leaders are themselves part of wider coalitions (Sabatier and Weible 2007), either formally in government or informally with their financial or political supporters, and have to negotiate priorities. Bargaining frameworks can be more or less institutionalized and regulated. In some settings, for instance, in the context of the EU, priorities of member states determine the bargaining dynamics which help to shift policy issues on the agenda. In bargaining environments policy actors have a high level of influence over timing and location, but framing will be subject of negotiations between different policy-makers. They use different statistics and reports in order to argue their case. This evidence becomes part of the bargaining process and the value of information is negotiated. For instance, highly contentious policy issues among member states of the EU are often framed in different ways by different members and other actors. During the refugee crisis in 2015, some member states framed the matter as a human rights issue while others pushed back with arguments that the refugees posed a threat to security within the EU.

Network competition recognizes that there are potentially different coalitions of actors who compete to influence the policy process. Different interpretations of policy problems can lead to various coalitions or networks of policy-makers in different venues. Such coalitions seek to reframe policy problems. In network competition both the framing and the venue of agenda-setting are open for variation rather than fixed beforehand by the most powerful. Evidence is provided by participants in coalitions in order to inform and convince actors of the urgency and type of policy problem.

Advocacy is the strategy pursued by political outsiders who seek access to the policy process. They are neither part of the government executive nor of established bargaining constellations. These outsiders might be part of a policy network, but framing, timing, and venues are in flux and often driven by events. For an advocacy strategy, evidence is of particular importance because policy outsiders have to argue a convincing case that their cause is worth the attention of policy-makers. They often research and present carefully argued reports as to why the topic is important or violates existing norms. Many international NGOs, including human rights organizations such as Transparency International and Global Witness (see Box 3.1), work on the basis of evidence-gathering and reframing of issues (see also Annex 2).

Different modes of agenda-setting have advantages and disadvantages. For example, being part of an advocacy campaign allows actors to be highly flexible and autonomous, but also less politically influential, because those who engage in advocacy campaigns typically remain outsiders to the policy process. In the next section we discuss the implications of the different modes for agenda-setting strategies.

3.6 How to Set the Agenda

Given the political nature of agenda-setting and the plurality of interests and voices involved, we can identify several criteria for successful, politically smart agenda-setting and thus derive a number of recommendations for both policy actors and analysts (see Table 3.3).

First, timing matters! Exploiting windows of opportunity is essential, especially for all those who do not control the agenda. Executives aim to control the agenda and are very often in a position to keep certain issues off of it. However, dealing with unexpected events, media frenzies,

Table 3.3 Politically smart agenda-setting

	TIMING	FRAMING	VENUE
ROLE	Shifting public/media attention and de-coupling problem, political and policy streams	Framing problem as an important driver of attention and support, and eventually for policy change	Institutional locations of policy-making differ in their receptiveness to new (framing of) problems
STRATEGY	Exploit windows of opportunity	Framing strategies to expand or limit participation	Strategic choice of venue ('venue-shopping')

and scandals can lead to unwanted policy decisions, which are driven by uncontrolled developments.

Policy actors might make use of such events for their own advantage. After a terrorist attack, both government and other policy-makers in the superstructure are tempted to present new security measures that might have been politically unacceptable in the past. Exploiting windows of opportunity is even more important for non-executives and outsiders to the policy process. When a fire broke out in the refugee camp on the Greek island of Lesbos in 2020, humanitarian NGOs used the media attention to criticize inhumane living conditions of asylum-seekers in Greece. Similarly, natural disasters are often an opportunity to discuss long-standing problems relating to environmental degradation, building safety, and the like. Even annual remembrance days are useful occasions to launch agenda-setting activities, through reports, events, or press releases.

Second, ideas, framing, and attention-grabbing information (such as indicators) play an important role in actors' strategies to raise awareness, (re)focus attention, and establish dominant interpretations of policy problems (policy images) in the public perception. In other words and as argued earlier in this chapter, problem definition is an integral part of the political contestation between actors and groups to shape whether and how a problem becomes an issue for governmental action. The analytical tools that are employed for policy design (Chapter 4) have to be brought to bear to inform strategies of agenda-setting. An evidence-based approach to agenda-setting—leveraging green and white papers, or one of the many other tools at hand—remains critical. Problem definition (framing), problem solution (instrument), and targeting of venue and timing must be complementary to make agenda-setting effective. How the case or argument is presented depends on whether policy insiders or outsiders do it.

Framing strategies can target the use of particular language. Activists in the field of sexual identity and transgender issues as well as those fighting against racism put a lot of emphasis on introducing anti-discriminatory language in order to raise awareness. Many trans- and intersexual activists insist on different personal pronouns for themselves in order to underline the legitimacy of their quest for public recognition, if not acceptance.

Third, the venue for agenda-setting is an important strategic decision. Many activists who are not strong enough to leverage their concern at the location where the policy problem is usually addressed (or should be addressed) move their activism to a different venue, where they might receive more attention. For instance, many human rights groups target international organizations for their agenda-setting strategies as these are often more receptive to human rights arguments than national governments are.

Finally, the distinction between policy outsiders (NGOs or lobby groups) and insiders is crucial for agenda-setting. Outsiders have to spend more time and energy to tell the story of why the problem is important, whereas policy insiders must focus more on how it should be solved.

PART II
POLICIES

Understanding Policies

Policies are the instruments for solving societal problems. The design and implementation of policies are crucial for effective problem-solving, and their evaluation is essential for providing feedback for learning and for adapting policies based on how they fared in practice. Policy interventions use a limited set of instruments—or tools—to influence the target population. While varying in detail, legal basis, and a number of issue-related specifics, these policy instruments rely on mechanisms that have the potential to change the behaviour of citizens or companies. One way to change behaviour is through 'sticks': setting a rule and punishing non-compliance. Another way is to offer 'carrots': offering monetary rewards or other kinds of benefits to induce a particular behaviour. A third approach is 'sermons': to use information and moral persuasion to influence what target actors want to do (Bemelmans-Videcet al. 1998). The direct provision of services is a fourth basic type of policy instrument.

Policy analysis is concerned with finding out which of these policy instruments works best for which problem—and how exactly a policy instrument needs to be designed to be effective in addressing a problem. For example, what is the best level of a fuel tax to change the behaviour of car drivers, and which other instruments are needed to make the tax effective (e.g. information about fuel efficiency of cars, subsidies for electric cars, or provision of alternative modes of transport). But good policy design is not enough: good policy implementation is as important. Policy implementation entails that policies are adapted in light of experiences gained during the implementation, including the responses of the target population.

Take the issue of vaccination against the novel coronavirus, spreading across the globe since 2020. Governments started their mass vaccination campaigns when the first vaccine became available in the latter part of 2020. Once the first vaccines were determined to be safe and effective, production, distribution, and delivery were the foremost concerns—and the state acted as a direct provider of services in many countries. Parts of the population worried about the safety of the vaccine, and rumours about potential side effects spread on social media. For example, a substantial share of the British population (at least initially) was unsure or did not want to get vaccinated (Paul et al. 2020). Scepticism was widespread even among healthcare workers, that is, those working with people who have the highest risk of dying from COVID-19. Many governments hence faced the question of how to respond to sceptics or even so-called anti-vaxxers. Information provision including public communication by top politicians is critical but might not reach the sceptics. Direct engagement with people, who have doubts about their decision to get vaccinated or are influenced by misinformation, might be more effective. Incentives were considered in some places: for example, offering a relaxation of restrictions for those who had received the vaccine. However, such measures might indeed have further alienated those who were already cynical about politicians' motives.

The example illustrates that policy design needs to be based on more than technical expertise. Policy-making is complex and often requires the combination of different policy measures. Such policy combinations are challenging to design and implement, as more actors are involved in both tasks. Policy-making also has to take implementation seriously as a core pillar of policy work. Implementation is more than the administrative delivery of a fixed policy design; rather, it means working with a living system, in which those at the receiving end of policy might seek to evade attempts at being controlled and try to 'game' the system. Those delivering policies and services, the 'street level bureaucrats' (Lipsky 2010), often have substantial discretion during implementation—and their own ways to deal with the pressures of demanding work at the front line of policy.

While the application of innovative approaches to policy design—such as interventions informed by 'behavioural insights' and 'design thinking'— can help the policy-maker to better take into account the motivations of target actors, the social context for policy-making seems to become more challenging. Longer term trends such as individualization (Beck and Beck-Gernsheim 2001) and—in the twenty-first century—digitalization, the rise of social media, and political polarization have changed the behaviour of many people. This makes it harder for governments to understand those towards whom the policies are directed (the target populations).

Policy-makers have to deal with these challenges in a political context. Most policies are contested by diverging interests, power games in the superstructure, and bureaucratic politics in the engine room. While policy analysts and policy-makers in the engine room should know their policies and their tools, they also need to be mindful of the political aspect of their work. Even policy evaluation, sometimes seen mainly as a research activity to objectively assess the merits of a policy, is deeply influenced by the diverse perspectives, interests, and ideologies that different stakeholders have.

The three chapters of Part II of this book delve into these issues at the core of policy work. Chapter 4 explores the choice and design of policy instruments. Starting from the task of matching policy instruments to the problem at hand ('tools to get the job done'), we stress the importance of reflecting on the 'programme theory'—the assumptions about how the implementation of a policy instrument will change the behaviour of the target population, which in turn leads to the intended impact, that is, change in the state of the targeted problem. To take into account complexity, policy-makers should consider how new policies fit into the existing set of policies and into the institutional context. They should also consider the (availability of) resources and administrative capacities needed to implement policies. Beyond the heuristics related to the problem-solving potential of new policies, policy-makers also have to be mindful of the political implications of policies which they consider submitting to the superstructure for validation. Will such a policy contribute to enhancing the standing of the policy-makers' organization in the policy subsystem? Is there a potential for scaling-up the new policy or using it as a stepping stone for future initiatives?

Chapter 5 explores five recurring challenges to be met in order to successfully implement policies. Two of these challenges (vertical follow-through and horizontal coordination) relate to the authorities who carry out the policy, and three of them (enforcement, activation, and conflict management) relate to the behaviour of the target population. We discuss the underlying rationales of the actors and organizations involved which create these implementation problems. These include the different logics and interests of implementing (street-level) and higher level bureaucracies for vertical follow-through, and the attention leaders of bureaucratic agencies pay to autonomy ('turf'), which makes horizontal coordination difficult. Enforcement, activation, and conflict management are challenges that arise from the motivations of norm-takers. It is important for policymakers to recognize the diverse nature of implementation problems in order to develop targeted strategies for improvement. It is just as important that they are aware of the root causes of these problems, so that they can spot potential roadblocks when applying these strategies.

In exploring evaluation as the third core pillar of policy work in Chapter 6, we point to the dual nature of policy evaluation. On the one hand, evaluation is conceived as an objective study of the impacts and outcomes of policies. This understanding calls for the application of the standards of professional knowledge production to policy evaluation. On the other hand, evaluation is an activity that involves many, if not all, stakeholders in the policy process. We argue that professional standards for evaluation practices are important, but we also emphasize that evaluations will in most cases not end political debates and contestation, because different stakeholders will invariably evaluate policies from different standpoints and push for different evaluation criteria. The chapter offers a discussion of different options in designing evaluation studies that reflect these tensions, explores the trend towards holding policy-implementing organizations accountable for performance, and presents models of knowledge utilization (Weiss 1979) that go beyond the instrumental use of research findings for policy design.

4

How to Choose and Design Policy Instruments

Key concepts

- Policy design
- Policy formulation
- Policy instruments (also: tools of government)
- Programme theory (also: theory of change)
- Administrative capacities

Policy design—finding the right policy instrument for a given problem—is at the core of policy-making. This chapter argues that policy design includes the assessment of costs, benefits, and potential unintended side-effects of different policy options, but also the consideration of the fit of a new policy to the social, institutional, and policy context to which it will be added. We maintain that policy-makers should critically review whether the programme theory of a particular policy instrument is valid in a given context. The chapter develops a set of guiding questions that policy-makers can use for assessing goodness of fit to the relevant context. But smart policy design also considers the task's political aspect, and the chapter points to four ways in which policy choices may affect policy processes in the future and the position of a policy-making organization therein. Again, these four mechanisms can serve as heuristics for policy-makers to take into account when designing policies.

4.1 Policy Problems and Policy Instruments

Today's policy problems are increasingly complex along many dimensions. Addressing them requires changing the ingrained behaviour of individuals and organizations, in the case of a range of health and consumer policies;

How to Do Public Policy. Anke Hassel and Kai Wegrich, Oxford University Press.
© Anke Hassel and Kai Wegrich (2022). DOI: 10.1093/oso/9780198747000.003.0004

making decisions with long-term implications under conditions of competing and incomplete knowledge; and often imposing immediate costs to achieve uncertain future benefits—think of climate change policies or pension schemes. As outlined in Chapter 1, not only have policy problems become more complex, but governments' means to address these problems and the context of policy-making also have changed.

Until several decades ago, these means or *tools of government* (Hood 1983) or *policy instruments* (the term we will use the most) were limited to the basic arsenal of regulation, incentives, information provision, and direct provision of services and goods. Today, governments have at their disposal new policy instruments, such as nudges (see Box 4.1), and new ways to deliver and finance services, such as public–private partnerships and social impact bonds. Variations and hybrids of the basic tools of government, such as ways of combining state regulation with societal self-regulation, have also emerged. At the same time, traditional tools may be less effective under today's conditions, for example, when the target population tends to be more critical in general due to political polarization, and mass organizations cannot credibly commit to the implementation of policies in their domain due to declining membership and loyalty. Finding the 'right' policy tool to address a problem, that is, an intervention that is not only feasible but also maximizes chances for effectiveness while limiting unintended side-effects, has become a key challenge for policy-makers: the task of *policy design*.

We start this chapter with a discussion of what policy design is and how policy analysis has conceptualized policy design, including concepts of 'design thinking' that gained sway in the 2010s. A core element of policy design is understanding the formulation of a policy—or combination of policies—in terms of matching policy instruments or tools to the policy problem on the agenda of the policy-maker. This is followed by a discussion of the role of evidence in policy design. Section 4.4 of this chapter introduces the basic toolbox—the set of policy instrument types—from which governments can choose a particular intervention (policy instrument) to address a problem that has been put on the agenda. How should policy-makers decide which policy instrument to use, and which criteria should guide them in their choice and the detailed design of the policy? Section 4.5 suggests four heuristics to guide policy instrument choice and design. Section 4.6 changes the perspective by discussing political aspects of instrument choice; in particular we discuss how instrument choice can affect the political standing of the main policy-making body (such as a department or an agency). Throughout this chapter, we refer to a key health policy challenge—how to reduce preventable health risks (mainly obesity, but also smoking and drinking and driving)—to explore how, and why, policy-makers select certain interventions over others.

Box 4.1   Behavioural insights and the nudge agenda

Information-based policies nowadays often use 'behavioural insights' (cf. Hallsworth and Kirkman 2020) to influence individuals' behaviours and de-cisions. The application of behavioural economics to public policy has, for some, become nearly synonymous with the use of 'nudges', a term coined by Richard Thaler and Cass Sunstein in their 2008 book of the same name. Nudges claim to effectively address a recurring policy challenge: how to shape the types of impulse-driven decisions made by individuals when not thinking much beforehand or reflecting much afterwards, for example, over-consumption of unhealthy food or not participating in voluntary pension schemes. Through the use of smart design strategies intended to gently steer target populations in the 'right' direction by altering the 'choice architecture', nudges aim to overcome the (perceived) limitations and biases of individuals' decision-making. For instance, rather than offering information about the health effects of various food choices, the policy-maker should instead think about the most effective way to present menu options in cafeterias in order to nudge consumers to choose health-ier options, say, by placing the healthiest foods at eye level while obscuring junk food from view. Another option would be to present health-related information about food in a way that directly influences choices, for example, by using traffic light symbols. Further examples of nudges include 'default-setting' (example: organ donations, where the opt-out model declares all adults as potential organ donors unless they actively decline) and 'social nudges' (example: information about the compliance behaviour in the social environment, such as 70 per cent of citizens in your neighbourhood have already submitted their tax declaration').

Thaler and Sunstein (2008) introduced the concept of nudges to depict an alternative that avoids overly intrusive or coercive government interventions but nevertheless moves beyond the do-nothing option. Nudges are supposed to be less intrusive than regulatory standards as they preserve the free choice of targeted individuals. Hence, they called the approach 'libertarian paternal-ism'. Critics pointed to the potential of nudges to border on manipulation and

continued

Box 4.1 *continued*

---

the possible lack of transparency in their implementation. Another point raised is the strong reliance on experts designing nudges and running experiments to test their effectiveness (cf. Lodge and Wegrich 2016; see also Chapter 6 on policy experiments).

4.2　What is Policy Design?

Policy design is the key activity during the policy formulation stage of the ideal-typical policy cycle (Jann and Wegrich 2007). In an ideal-typical scenario, *policy formulation*, and hence policy design, starts once a policy problem has been put on the governmental agenda, with the aim to respond with a new policy or the adaptation of an existing policy. The endpoint then in this ideal-typical model is when a draft policy, law, or regulation is on the table of the superstructure institutions (parliaments, cabinets) for decision. But note that this model hides that, even after formal adoption, policies and laws will be further specified, and sometimes also changed. The focus of this chapter—and the debate on policy design—is the stage when policy-makers and external stakeholders prepare the main policy choice, for example addressing obesity with a sugar tax or an incentive programme for exercises, or some combination of policies.

The task of policy design is to choose a policy instrument or package of policies—and detail its properties (for example, how stringent a regulatory standard should be)—that promises to have an effect on the behaviour of the groups, individuals, or organizations targeted (the target group or target population). Howlett (2019, 10) defines policy design as 'the deliberate and conscious attempt to define policy goals and to connect them to instruments or tools expected to realise those objectives'. He considers it to be a specific form of policy formulation, which is 'based on the gathering and application of knowledge of the effects of policy tool use on policy targets to the development and implementation of policies aimed at the attainment of desired policy ambitions'. In other words, to qualify as policy design, the policy formulation process needs to be more than an ad hoc, unstructured process of picking some policy response to a problem on the agenda; it is a more intelligent variation of policy formulation, a view widely shared in the research literature. We use the term policy design in a more neutral sense to describe the process of selecting and specifying policy instruments to address a policy problem on the agenda.

While the term policy design refers to the matching of tools to problems, policy formulation refers to the process of getting from the selection of a problem for government action (agenda-setting) to the formal adoption of a policy. Policy formulation entails the drafting of policies, regulations, and laws by government officials, and the coordination of those drafts within the policy-making engine room. Societal stakeholders are involved at various substages of the process, for example, informal consultation by government officials early on and public consultation in the parliamentary arena later. In the policy analysis literature, the formal adoption of a policy by the superstructure institutions is sometimes separated from the policy formulation stage and called decision-making (we do not follow that distinction here).

Policy designers are usually the responsible governmental actors in the engine room, but they can also be and often are societal actors, or superstructure actors who call for particular policies (in particular when media attention is high, for example after a scandal or in a crisis). The core question to be answered in the policy design process is how to influence the target population, those to whom a policy tool is addressed, in order to have an impact on the problem. In the case of obesity, for example, the target population could be the people already or at risk of becoming obese or the food production or marketing industries or organizations providing public or private services (schools, insurance companies, and the like). Whether and how effective policies are depends on the type of target population, and policy-makers should be mindful of the different logics and dispositions of individuals on the one hand and formal organizations (companies, non-government associations and groups, or other governmental entities) on the other hand.

Policy design seeks to conceptualize a chain of events from the introduction of a policy to the target population's behavioural change to that change's impact on the problem at hand. For example, a ban on sugary drinks (addressing beverage producers or restaurants and supermarkets as the immediate policy-takers) would be expected to lead to lower consumption of sugar among the entire population (the ultimate target population of the policy) and, as a result of changing consumption patterns, a reduced risk or prevalence of obesity. Note that, in this case, the chain from the introduction of the policy instrument to the desired outcome (reducing consumption) is long and includes first a direct policy target group (companies producing sugary drinks) and second the ultimate targeted group (the consumers). The task of policy design entails systematic consideration of this (sometimes long) chain. It also requires that the 'behavioural dispositions' (Offe 2014) of the actors (in the example, both companies and individuals) involved are well-understood and matched with a policy tool that promises to be effective in initiating the desired behavioural change. According to Offe (2014, 1), these dispositions include motivational drivers of behaviour (such as norms and interests) and cognitive beliefs about policies and their effects (for example, if wearing face masks is effective in limiting the spread of infectious diseases). A wrong assessment of these drivers of behaviour might lead to unintended consequences, for example, if consumers compensate for the ban on sugary drinks by consuming more sugar in their food.

We devote Chapter 5 to the implementation aspect of the chain of events that makes up the policy cycle and focus in this chapter on the policy design dimension. The aspects of policy formulation related to the interaction between actors play a crucial role in all three chapters of Part III of the book.

4.3 The Role of Evidence in Policy Design

As Howlett's (2019) definition emphasizes, policy design depends on the 'gathering and application of knowledge' or evidence. And, as we emphasized in Chapter 1, one of the main rationales behind policy analysis is the provision of knowledge and tools that should inform policy design. Indeed, tools of economic policy analysis have proliferated with the rise of policy analysis since the 1960s. Most governments in members countries of the Organization for Economic Co-operation and Development (OECD) and an increasing number in low and middle-income countries have introduced 'impact assessments' and other tools for testing policy designs during the process of policy formulation and decision-making.

Impact assessment is an umbrella term that captures the various methods of economic policy analysis used by policy-makers to consider policy options at the design stage, to explore their potential impact along different dimensions, and to determine which is most effective and efficient in achieving a set goal (cf. Dunlop and Radaelli 2019). For example, the guidelines of the European Commission (2017, 17) require responses to the following key questions, among others, as part of any impact assessment underpinning one of the Commission's policy drafts:

- What are the various options to achieve the objectives?
- What are their economic, social, and environmental impacts and who will be affected?
- How do the different options compare (in terms of effectiveness, efficiency, and coherence)?

Since the 2010s, and with the rise of behavioural economics and the nudge agenda (see Box 4.1), the conceptual thinking of behavioural insights has also informed governments' approaches to policy design. Behavioural insights draw on research from behavioural economics and cognitive psychology to develop a better understanding of how policy targets, mainly individuals, respond to policies. Through a better understanding of their 'behavioural dispositions' (Offe 2014), policy-makers gain clues as to why people do not submit their tax declarations on time, why they do not sign up as an organ donor, or why they do not reduce their consumption of sugary drinks (even though they might want to do all these things). Nudges are then designed and tested to change the behaviour of targeted individuals, without strict regulation or substantial incentives, but through changing the choice architecture (Thaler and Sunstein 2008), for example, by presenting healthy food and soft drinks more prominently in the layout of cafeterias or by sending reminders to submit tax declarations or to make appointments at the dentist (Altmann and Traxler 2014).

Many governments have set up behavioural insights units to advance that agenda. They also promote experimental trials of policy interventions as the preferred method of evidence-based policy-making. This trend is not confined to rich democracies but has been successfully promoted in the developing world by philanthropic organizations and research networks such as the Abdul Latif Jameel Poverty Action Lab (J-PAL) (povertyactionlab.org). Policy trials that apply an intervention to a randomly selected treatment group and observe the impact of the policy in comparison to a control group that has not received the intervention are seen as the most advanced way of isolating the effect of the intervention and controlling for the noise of other influencing factors (see also Chapter 6).

A third approach to policy design comes from a very different disciplinary background, namely 'design thinking' (cf. Junginger 2013; Bason 2017). Design thinking in the context of public policy was first applied to the design of public services, that is, how service provision processes and interactions were structured (Bason 2017). Since the 2010s, design thinking has been promoted as a tool to foster innovation in the public sector and also to change policy design processes. Despite a language that pitches design thinking in contrast to established ways of policy development, the approach broadly follows a logic of problem-solving that is rather similar to the policy cycle model of policy analysis (Clarke and Craft 2019). Design thinking puts emphasis on engaging (public service) users in the design process. Like in the development of a product, the problems from the user's perspective are the starting point of a process of brainstorming ('ideation') and then product development and testing. Advocates of design thinking stress the transformative potential of a more open and innovative form of public service and policy design (Bason 2017, 2018; cf. Clarke and Craft 2019; Iskander 2018 for more critical perspectives). Furthermore, the concept of 'agility' focusing on shorter and more rapid cycles of developing, testing, and adapting prototypes has made inroads in the design of government programmes, in particular in digitalization projects (Mergel et al. 2020; McBride et al. 2021).

All those approaches to using evidence for policy design have their merits. But they are rather oblivious to the political nature of policy formulation and policy design therein. Cost–benefit analysis zooms in to compare a few pre-selected options (see Box 4.2). The approach's emphasis on precision and quantitative measurement makes it hard to apply it to complex combinations of policy tools, and the approach cannot really take institutional capacities and actual implementation practices into account. The behavioural and experimental approach has been criticized for focusing exclusively on small-scale interventions, such as nudges, because only those interventions can be meaningfully tested in a randomized trial (De Souza Leão and Eyal 2019).

Box 4.2 Cost–benefit analysis (CBA)

Cost–benefit analysis (CBA; also benefit–cost analysis) is a technique to evaluate the costs and benefits of policies, regulations, or public investments. The basic logic is to convert all inputs and outcomes into monetary units and to compare the costs and negative outcomes with the expected positive outcomes (benefits). CBA is used to assess whether an intervention generates a net benefit at all and to compare different options (such as a bridge versus a ferry service as a river crossing). Related tools of economic evaluation such as cost-effectiveness or cost utility analysis are used when the outcomes of an intervention cannot be monetized, or even quantified. First applied in the planning of infrastructure projects, CBA became a key tool of economic policy analysis in the 1960s. Since then, many governments have used CBA (and variations of economic policy analysis) in impact assessments as well as evaluations. The US has been a frontrunner, where regulatory agencies have to demonstrate that the benefits of their regulations justify the costs. Among the challenges of applying CBA to policy-making are difficulties in monetizing all outcomes of a policy, either due to ethical concerns (monetizing lives saved) or because of the intangible nature of benefits (such as the value of wildlife), as well as including all intended (and unintended) outcomes.

Policy-makers in the real world cannot focus exclusively on the aspects emphasized by the dominant approaches to policy design (costs and benefits, rigorous experiments, and design thinking/user testing). They need to bear in mind the constraints and dynamics of the political process of policy-making, which most often plays out very differently than the notion of a 'design process' involving a single tool would suggest. In the practice of policy-making, the search for and design of policy instruments is also a political process characterized by coalition-building, strategic communication and action, bureaucratic politics, and lobbying. Policy instruments allocate values and distribute costs and benefits—and this is the core business of politics that does not follow the logic of economic policy analysis regardless of the approach used. As Theodore Lowi (1972: 299) put it, 'policies determine politics', which means that different types of policy instruments ignite different levels of conflict when put on the agenda for serious consideration. Redistributing resources from one societal group to another will stir up more conflict than would distributing resources to one group from the general pool of the government budget.

For the governmental policy-maker and for those outside government advocating particular solutions, this means that finding and designing policy instruments is a balancing act between a purely analytical task and a political task of assessing what can be done under the given (political, budgetary, legal, cognitive) constraints as well as how (and how far) these boundaries can be pushed. In practice, the analytical and the political aspects of instrument choice and policy design are mixed to the point of being almost indistinguishable. Indeed, the use of evidence in the selection of policy instruments is neither independent from nor untainted by political support and pressure for or against particular policy solutions. One might even question whether there is, in practice, a distinct and discrete phase of policy design in which policy-makers compare different options in order to select the most promising course of action. Instead, any final policy design is shaped by an ongoing process of policy development that is preceded by (often longer) phases of building support and political coalitions for a particular policy option. In other cases, particular policy instruments are suddenly moved to the top of the agenda by some external event, such as calls for tighter regulation in cases of food safety scandals (see Chapter 3 for more on agenda-setting). Nevertheless, being able to justify instrument choice with evidence and analysis is critical for advocating a particular policy, especially when an option is politically contested.

4.4 The Government's Toolbox

When a policy issue—existing or new—receives serious attention from government institutions, the key task for policy-makers is to find and select a policy that is both politically feasible and appropriate for addressing the perceived problem. This section offers some analytical clues to asking the right questions and prepares policy-makers to make a case in favour of, and also against, a particular policy option. As discussed in Chapter 3 on agenda-setting, how particular policy issues enter the agenda varies substantially depending on the issue, the public's attention at a given time, and the type of actors involved, among other factors. Regardless of how an issue reaches the policy-maker's desk, within government organizations, non-governmental organizations (NGOs), and the public, the debate remains centred upon the question of whether a particular instrument, versus one or more alternatives, will actually do the job.

Thus, within policy design, this is the challenge of instrument choice, of finding the right policy tool or combination of tools for the job. In order to do so, the policy-maker and supporting policy analysts should consider the available set of tools that governments normally have at their disposal. The literature on policy instruments or tools of government offers a number of different classifications of policy instruments, most of which distinguish between four basic types, as summarized in Table 4.1: regulatory instruments, financial instruments, information-based instruments, and direct provision of services and goods (cf. Hood 1983; Howlett 2019; Schneider and Ingram 1990).

Table 4.1 Four basic types of policy instruments

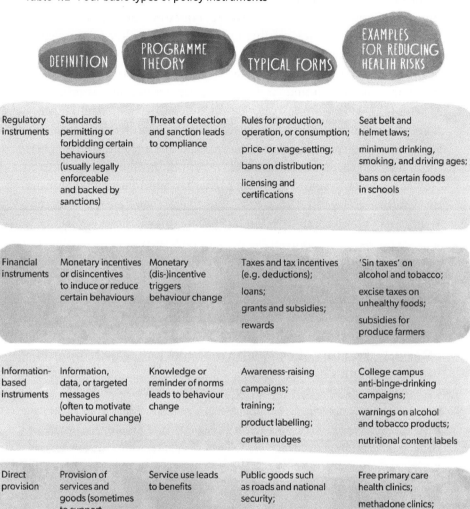

	DEFINITION	PROGRAMME THEORY	TYPICAL FORMS	EXAMPLES FOR REDUCING HEALTH RISKS
Regulatory instruments	Standards permitting or forbidding certain behaviours (usually legally enforceable and backed by sanctions)	Threat of detection and sanction leads to compliance	Rules for production, operation, or consumption; price- or wage-setting; bans on distribution; licensing and certifications	Seat belt and helmet laws; minimum drinking, smoking, and driving ages; bans on certain foods in schools
Financial instruments	Monetary incentives or disincentives to induce or reduce certain behaviours	Monetary (dis-)incentive triggers behaviour change	Taxes and tax incentives (e.g. deductions); loans; grants and subsidies; rewards	'Sin taxes' on alcohol and tobacco; excise taxes on unhealthy foods; subsidies for produce farmers
Information-based instruments	Information, data, or targeted messages (often to motivate behavioural change)	Knowledge or reminder of norms leads to behaviour change	Awareness-raising campaigns; training; product labelling; certain nudges	College campus anti-binge-drinking campaigns; warnings on alcohol and tobacco products; nutritional content labels
Direct provision	Provision of services and goods (sometimes to support behavioural change or maintenance)	Service use leads to benefits	Public goods such as roads and national security; essential services such as public schools and hospitals	Free primary care health clinics; methadone clinics; exercise equipment in public spaces

Beyond these instruments that seek to directly shape behaviour, scholars recognize various types of indirect policy tools, such as procedural instruments, which seek to influence relations between relevant actors and institutions in a particular policy subsystem by indirectly calibrating the context in which they interact. To deal with obesity, for example, a procedural policy instrument could establish joint task forces between schools, city planners, and health insurers with the aim of improving coordination of other more specific and direct policy instruments. (We discuss more extensively the role of this indirect type of policy instrument in Chapter 7 on how to liaise with stakeholders.)

Often, addressing policy problems requires the use of more than one policy instrument at a time. In Latin America, for example, surging rates of obesity and related non-communicable diseases have resulted from a combination of factors, not of all of which can be treated identically. Roughly two-thirds of all adults in Mexico and in Chile were overweight in 2016, with 28 per cent in Mexico and 29 per cent in Chile being obese. At least as concerning, some 15 per cent of children and adolescents in Mexico and Chile were obese in 2016, significantly higher than the 2 and 4 per cent, respectively, registered in 1975.[1] In Box 4.3, we present these two countries' approaches to preventing and reducing obesity. But, as we will explain in the next section, every policy instrument requires a series of careful considerations to ensure its appropriateness, and hence effectiveness, in a given context.

Box 4.3   Tackling obesity with multiple policy instruments in Mexico and Chile

Mexico's obesity prevention strategy is among the most comprehensive in the OECD world. After years of cross-sector consultations, the Ministry of Health introduced in 2010 the National Agreement for Health Nutrition. In 2013, Mexico formally launched its National Strategy for the Prevention and Control of Overweight, Obesity, and Diabetes, which included measures using all four instrument types:

- Regulatory instruments: Ban on advertising unhealthy foods on radio and television during certain times of day and during cinema screenings aimed at children; guidelines for schools that ban foods and beverages not complying with nutritional criteria and limit availability of snack foods;
- Financial instruments: 8 per cent tax on non-essential, excessively caloric food items; roughly 10 per cent tax on sugar-sweetened beverages (SSBs);
- Information-based instruments: Mandatory front-of-packaging (FOP) food labelling requirements; multi-platform, nationwide obesity prevention campaigns;

---

[1] Retrieved from http://www.who.int/gho/ncd/risk_factors/overweight/en/ (accessed 22 July 2020).

- Direct provision: the DiabetIMSS programme, including year-long, monthly health consultations plus education sessions for type-2 diabetes patients.

Some of Mexico's efforts seem to have begun to pay off, at least in the short term: the purchase of taxed food items declined by 4.8 per cent in 2014 and 7.8 per cent in 2015 (Tallie et al. 2017), the purchase of SSBs 5.5 per cent and 9.7 per cent (Colchero et al. 2017).

However, the impact of either of these measures on health outcomes remains uncertain. Evaluation mechanisms for information-based instruments and direct provision of services remain insufficient, and compliance with regulations has also been a challenge, with reports that some schools continue to sell prohibited foods. Individual policies, such as the tax on SSBs and the FOP labelling requirements, have been criticized as relatively weak, and lobbying from the private business sector has continued unabated: the SSB tax was very nearly reduced in 2015 after protracted industry pressure.

If Mexico has been noted for its comprehensiveness, then Chile has been lauded for its aggressiveness. Unlike in Mexico where the government issued guidelines, all high-calorie snack foods as well as sugar-sweetened beverages have been outright banned from Chilean schools. Similar to Mexico, marketing junk foods to children is prohibited across most media during waking hours. Chile has also outlawed promotional characters on, and toys in, packaged foods. And although food industry players still exert influence on obesity prevention policy in Chile, even an eventual compromise on FOP labelling (a black-and-white stop sign warning of unhealthy contents) appears to have had some effect. Early evaluations showed that more than one-third of consumers use the label to compare products and that the vast majority of those chose healthier items as a result (Ministerio de Salud 2017; Nakamura et al. 2018).

Contributing author: Jessica Leong Cohen.

4.5 Four Heuristics for Identifying and Designing the Right Tool for the Job

Each of the four broad types of instruments we have mentioned includes various subtypes, some of which are discussed later in the chapter. Here we highlight how this overall classification of policy instruments can be used to explore a set of analytical questions to guide the selection of policy instruments in the real world, that is, under conditions of limited resources, contested politics, and uncertainties about causes and effects.

1. Each type of policy instrument is associated with a specific under-lying *programme theory*, that is, assumptions about how the policy instrument could influence a target population and how this influ-ence could lead to a desired outcome and impact. The question for the policy-maker is whether the general programme theory of an instru-ment holds within a specific context and vis-à-vis a particular target population.

2. Each instrument type is based on one or more resources that govern-ments usually have at their disposal. Financial resources are only one type of these. A key analytical clue for the policy-maker is derived by assessing to what extent these resources are available and how rapidly they would deplete were a particular instrument to be used. A related concern is how capable the government engine room is in turning resources into actionable *administrative capacities*. These considera-tions are also linked to the selection of delivery model, or how the implementation of one or more policy instruments is organized (by a public agency, private organizations, or others).

3. Each policy instrument type is implemented in a particular insti-tutional context, which includes not only the governmental orga-nizations responsible for policy delivery but also the entire policy subsystem, that is, the engine room of policy-making. The key ques-tion here is whether the policy instrument under consideration fits the institutional context of the engine room at hand. A policy in-strument that has worked very effectively in one country's healthcare system might be ineffective or yield unintended consequences in another one.

4. Each tool is embedded in a particular *policy context* that includes the previous policies adopted in the issue area. Again, the main con-cern for the policy-maker is the fit of the policy instrument under consideration with existing policies, which will influence any newly introduced tool's effectiveness.

4.5.1 First consideration: matching programme theory and problem

The analytical task of the policy-maker is to consider how different pol-icy instruments could achieve a desired change in behaviour. This re-quires not only a good understanding of the underlying problem and its causes but also special attention to how different policy instruments might achieve the desired behavioural change within the target population. All policy instruments come with their own *programme theories*, which connect a diagnosed problem with a hypothesis as to how the instrument will influence behaviour within the target population so as to eventually help ameliorate the problem (Funnell and Rogers 2011). Those programme theories are usually implicit, that is, there will seldom be a chain of events spelled out in an official policy document describing how the intervention would lead to the desired outcome.[2] Often, they rely on widely shared assumptions, such as that people and organizations are susceptible to monetary incentives. Sometimes these programme theories, and the different elements of the chain of events from policy design to outcome, are spelled out in the form of *logic models* or 'logic frameworks' (for example, in evaluation reports of think tanks). The term *theory of change* is also used in the same way as we use 'programme theory' (Funnell and Rogers 2011).

The challenge for the policy analyst is that programme theories might not always be valid: an expected behavioural change might not materialize either because the theory's initial assumptions are incorrect or because the preconditions for the theory to work are not in place. And while much of the policy literature identifies the general logics behind policy instruments, whether a programme theory is actually valid depends on the specific context of a particular time and place. Using examples from each of the four families of policy instruments that are designed to prevent or reduce key risks to health, let's first discuss general programme logics and then look at some ways in which programme theories might get it wrong in certain contexts.

4.5.1.1 Basic programme theories of policy instruments

Regulatory instruments set standards that define what types of behaviour are and are not allowed from the target population, which could be very specific (e.g. a firm) or more general (e.g. the population). According to the programme theory of regulatory instruments, non-compliance with standards will lead to some kind of sanction, such as having to pay fines, having business licences revoked, or facing serious criminal charges. And since the target population wants to avoid these sanctions, they tend to comply—at least when there is a credible threat of sanctioning and, as a precondition,

---

[2] However, impact assessment documents do include explanations of how the policy intervention tries to achieve its goals.

some risk that non-compliance will in fact be detected. For example, in June 2018, a ban on the use of artificial trans fats (partially hydrogenated oils) in foods came into effect in the US; the World Health Organization called for a global elimination of the same ingredients by 2023.

Such instruments seem to be most appropriate when clear standards can be set and compliance with those standards can be consistently enforced. A body of literature in the field of regulation discusses when regulatory standards are appropriate—and also what types of standards are suitable for which situation (Lodge and Wegrich 2012, 63–9). A central topic has been motivation of target populations to adhere (or not) to regulations. Regulated entities—individuals, organizations such as companies, and even entire industries—often have complex, that is, mixed, motivations. For example, willingness to pay the fare on public transport depends not only on avoidance of penalties but also on whether riders value public transportation more generally and whether individuals believe that others comply as well.

Enforcing regulatory standards, which is more extensively discussed in Chapter 5 on implementation, is hence about more than just deterrence and punishment. It is also about motivating target populations to comply. In the field of regulation, this issue has given rise to debates about the proper design of regulatory standards. A key argument is that standards that allow regulated entities more flexibility in how they comply will lead to higher levels of compliance. Moreover, when regulated entities are invited to participate in the design of regulatory standards and the control of compliance, they should also be more strongly motivated to comply. Hence a wide variety of co- and self-regulatory schemes to (partly) delegate regulatory authority to the regulated entities have proliferated (cf. Gilad 2010). For example, since 2007, several food, beverage, and restaurant companies have signed up to the Children's Food and Beverage Advertising Initiative (CFBAI), pledging to change how they advertise to children in order to encourage healthier diet choices. Despite some positive developments over ten years, such advertising still predominantly promotes unhealthy products (Harris et al. 2017), highlighting the challenges of self-regulation. Despite their participation in the CFBAI, the majority of food or media companies did not voluntarily adopt the standards for marketing to youth (Harris et al. 2017, 90).

At times, direct regulation of behaviour might be politically unfeasible, legally impossible (as was the case with the New York City Board of Health's soda ban, which failed to hold up in state court: *Harvard Law Review* 2015), or a potential violation of rights. When a desired behaviour cannot be prescribed by regulatory standards, *financial instruments* may be an alternative. The basic premise is that individuals (and organizations) respond to financial incentives. According to this logic, if someone were to receive payment for exercising or for changing their diet, that person might actually change their behaviour.

This logic of incentives works both ways: positive incentives intend to induce behaviour change (exercising more), while negative incentives aim to reduce or deter some other behaviour (eating unhealthy foods). In the obesity case, health insurance providers in some countries—Germany and South Africa, among others—offer positive incentives in the form of bonus programmes that reward members' 'good' behaviour, such as attending regular fitness classes. On the flip side, a number of health-related excise taxes are in place in many countries, and while many may have been shown to generate significant government revenue, they are primarily used to drive behavioural change. 'Sin taxes' on products like alcohol and tobacco are designed to incentivize consumers to buy, and thus consume, fewer of these items. Taxes on sugar-sweetened beverages—thought to both discourage unhealthy diets and offset the economic costs of obesity—have been put into effect in numerous countries (Allcott et al. 2019 list thirty-nine countries, excluding the US, which have introduced taxes on sugary drinks), with mixed results in terms of actually reducing consumption (Marron et al. 2015; see also Box 4.4). For the US, Fletcher et al. (2010) argue that the reduction of soda consumption that was caused by sin taxes was completely offset by the consumption of other high-calorie drinks.

Importantly, for financial incentives to work, the level of incentive needs to be higher than the perceived costs of the incentivized behaviour. For example, if healthier foods such as fresh fruits and vegetables are more expensive than prepackaged junk foods, financial incentives such as offering food voucher recipients refunds on fresh produce purchases might help to even out that disadvantage. At the same time, incentives alone do not drive consumption behaviour. Routine behaviour patterns and psychological mechanisms might make behavioural change difficult, and we cannot assume that consumers behave in a fully rational way. When and under which conditions consumers change their behaviour in response to incentives (and which level of incentives) is still very much an open question.

The third family of policy tools, information-based instruments, work neither by coercing nor by incentivizing behaviour but rather by disseminating information to target populations in order to encourage or discourage certain behaviours. For example, food products and medicines are packaged with information concerning their ingredients and, for the latter, warnings of potential side-effects. In a number of countries, including all European Union member states, tobacco products must be labelled with not only text warnings but also graphic images of illnesses related to the use of tobacco.

More and more often, information-based instruments go beyond stating the facts and attempt to change behaviour by correcting underlying assumptions, emphasizing identities or social norms, or capitalizing on emotions. For example, rather than simply reminding students that excessive drinking is harmful to one's health, campaigns to reduce binge drinking at university have informed students that alcohol consumption can result in social risks (such as getting into fights or being compromised on social networks)—and also that such behaviour is not the norm, despite what many students might think (Watts 2018; Alcohol Awareness 2019; Immenkeppel 2020). This wider trend towards a more emotional and, at times, moralizing presentation of information is a result of changes to the underlying programme theory of information-based instruments. Whereas the majority of information-based instruments were once designed based on the assumption that more information would lead directly to 'better' (more rational) decision-making, policy-makers have increasingly adopted research findings from the fields of social psychology and behavioural economics that challenge that assumption (see Box 4.1).

The final basic policy instrument is the direct provision of services and goods by the government. This includes such diverse activities as running schools, hospitals, and armed forces; offering social services such as counselling for at-risk individuals; and providing public goods such as roads, rail tracks, and public parks. In the obesity example, the direct provision of services and goods plays a role in many different ways, ranging from attempts to change lunch menus in public schools (in the UK spearheaded by celebrity chef Jamie Oliver and in the US by former first lady Michelle Obama), offering consultation and advice, and providing exercise-friendly public infrastructure. While the programme theory varies with the specific subtype of service provision, direct provision of services and goods affords the opportunity for governments to both directly and visibly interact with, and shape the behaviour of, individuals.

4.5.1.2 How programme theories can be wrong

A policy analyst must be aware of potential mismatches between a particular programme theory (and therefore instrument) and the particular policy problem and social context to which it would be applied. While it makes sense to think about policy options from among the broad types of instruments and to assess whether the respective programme theories would elicit behavioural changes that eventually lead to the desired output, outcome, and impact, it is also reasonable to contemplate potential unintended effects. Take the example of regulatory instruments: does a particular sanction truly pose a significant deterrence for the target population? For instance, the UK government has addressed so-called anti-social behaviour, such as petty crimes and vandalism, with a relatively new legal tool: the anti-social behaviour order (ASBO). ASBOs are civil orders issued by courts against convicted individuals and come with various sanctions, including court-ordered community service, as well as methods of public naming and shaming such as requiring recipients to wear clothing identifying themselves as ASBO recipients. As later research found out, when the prevailing social norms in a given peer group actually value some degree of misbehaviour, the effect of an ASBO could be reversed, that is, work as a badge of honour (BBC News 2006).

Similar paradoxical effects have been observed in the context of (dis)incentives. In a classic example, small financial penalties for picking up children late from childcare facilities have been shown to backfire (Gneezy and Rustichini 2000). The fine was not only too low to act as an effective disincentive, but also undermined the norm of being on time; parents simply paid a price for their tardiness, which crowded out any previous moral obligation. Note that the claim here is not that such disincentives do not work at all, but that their effectiveness depends on the context, level of fines, and way they are implemented. The point is that the policy-maker must think through the potential failures as well as necessary conditions for such a programme to work.

Another example relates to controversial measures providing incentives for pregnant women to stop smoking. The crowding-out mechanism lies at the core of the controversy: under the assumption that pregnant women (and their partners) have the moral obligation to refrain from smoking and any other behaviours that may put their unborn children at risk, any financial or other incentives might undermine this moral obligation. However, as Jonathan Wolff (2015) argues, the theory behind such programmes is somewhat more complex. The behavioural motivation lies, again, in the relation to the peer group: if smoking is deemed normal by one's peers, to quit smoking would constitute a violation of that peer norm and hence incur the risk of sanctioning (for example, by exclusion). However, a monetary incentive might serve as an excuse to stop. Wolff does not claim that this mechanism will always work in this way, but he calls for a more open and reflective examination of potential interactions between incentives and peer norms. Programmes incentivizing children to read books (for instance, paying them to read) could in fact work towards a crowding-in effect (children learning to value the experience), and it may also give children in social contexts in which reading is not a peer norm an excuse to actually do so.

A final example of unintended effects refers to the direct provision of public services as a policy instrument. A widespread response to social concerns regarding educational achievement, such as the disadvantages of children from lower social strata, has been the expansion of childcare facilities. The implicit theory was that the expansion of public services would close or at least reduce that achievement gap, since children would begin participating in structured learning activities earlier. However, the concept known as the 'Matthew effect' could undermine the original intention: if the added childcare spots are taken by children from (upper) middle-class families, the achievement gap might actually be widened. Jessen et al. (2020) show that this effect materialized in Germany after the expansion of childcare offerings from the early 2000s onwards (cf. Pavolini and van Lancker 2018 and Bonoli and Liechti 2018 on the Matthew effect in childcare and in labour market policies).

Such considerations of mismatch between programme theory and context also need to be applied to the new instruments emerging from the behavioural insights agenda. While much of the debate focuses on the potentially manipulative character of non-transparent nudges and important questions of democratic accountability, the question of how well the overall programme theory fits a particular context and problem must also be addressed (cf. Traxler 2019). While a nudge might work at specific, decisive moments in time, it might not trigger more fundamental behavioural changes: one's addiction to chocolate bars might not prevail in a canteen stocked with salads and fresh fruit, but one's basic instincts will remain intact until the next easy opportunity to indulge. The issue of prevailing (peer) norms must also be taken into account here.

In short, policy-makers not only need to be mindful of the match between the problem at hand and the policy instrument that offers the right programme theory. They also need to be aware of the specific contextual conditions that shape the instruments' working mechanism—and be ready to update and adapt their theories as needed. Policy researchers should therefore avoid overgeneralizing how policy instruments work in practice, but offer insights into various effects that one intervention mechanism could generate (including null effects).

4.5.2 Second consideration: government resources and delivery model

The second key consideration in choosing and designing policy instruments concerns the question of whether a government possesses the resources to deliver a policy addressing the target population in the way envisaged by the programme theory. This refers not only to financial resources, which are often discussed as the major constraint on government action to do something about a particular problem. Hood (1983) distinguishes between four basic types of resources that governments need in order to influence behaviour:[3]

- the government's position within a network of information exchange ('Nodality'),
- power to adopt and enforce rules ('Authority'),
- financial capacity ('Treasure'), and
- organizational capacity to deliver policies ('Organization').

Although this so-called 'NATO scheme' is presented, and very often used, as a blueprint to classify basic types of policy instruments, it is important to note its key difference from many other classification schemes: it focuses on the resources at a government's disposal that enable it to do something to influence a target population, rather than the mechanisms that actually change behaviour. For example, when using Hood's classification, the task of taxation becomes a policy instrument that involves some combination of all four NATO resources, but especially authority (tax laws, including sanctions) and organization (tax collection agencies). Other schemes would classify taxation as a financial policy tool that works with either positive (tax breaks, subsidies) or negative (taxes) incentives.

---

[3] Hood also uses the typology for government tools to collect information.

The strength of Hood's classification scheme is that it points to ever-present mixes of policy instruments in any given programme or legislation. For example, a subsidy programme for companies to hire the long-term unemployed of course contains a financial incentive component—in this case, for the company to balance out the perceived risks of offering a job to someone who has been unemployed for some time. However, the programme or law will also include regulatory components, such as specifying which jobless people are eligible, how to determine if a person was indeed unemployed, and elements of enforcement and sanctioning in cases of violation of these standards. Finally, the programme might include an informational component to raise awareness among companies of the programme's existence. Another more general example is nudges: while they share the idea of altering choice architecture to correct for biases in individuals' decision-making (see Box 4.1), many nudges rely on a mix of regulation, financial instruments (incentives or disincentives), information, and direct provision of services and goods—with the weight of the different resources varying substantially between individual nudges.

The NATO scheme introduces an important second layer for the analysis leading to instrument choice. While the considerations about programme theory provide the first fundamental layer, this second layer introduces questions about the underlying resources of governments, their administrative capacities, and delivery models. The issue of resources is obvious in the case of financial subsidies, but the effective delivery of a subsidy programme also requires *administrative capacities* to effectively control eligibility criteria, manage programme payments, and collect and disseminate information concerning the uptake of the programme. While resources are the available input factors such as monetary and human resources, administrative capacities refer to the way these resources are used to solve problems (Wegrich 2021). Lodge and Wegrich (2014b, 27) define administrative capacities as 'the set of skills and competences that are expected of public bureaucracies so that they can facilitate and contribute to problem-solving', which includes both the 'structural and procedural provisions that enable bureaucracies to perform particular functions' and 'the individuals within these bureaucracies'. They distinguish between delivery, analytical, regulatory, and coordination capacity (on coordination capacity, see Chapter 8). Some nudges, for example, require analytical and regulatory capacity. Take the example of labelling schemes to signal the relative healthiness of food: analytical capacity is needed to identify the right design of the nudge (i.e. whether emojis, a traffic light system, or health warnings of over-consumption are more effective), and regulatory capacity is needed to effectively prescribe to the food industry the standard to actually put these labels on their products.

Exploring the capacities needed to make a particular policy instrument work in the real world can open doors to alternative delivery models, such as public–private partnerships or more novel approaches combining policy delivery by NGOs with funding from philanthropic investors (so-called social impact bonds). Such a delivery model might reduce the need for delivery capacity on the part of the government, but at the same time would require an increase in its regulatory capacity (to set standards and supervise delivery by third parties) and analytical capacity (to analyse and evaluate the quality of service delivery by third parties). One might also argue that more complex 'delivery networks' require more coordination capacity on the part of governmental actors (Lodge and Wegrich 2014b on capacity types).

4.5.3 Third consideration: fit to the institutional context

The third consideration of any search for a policy tool that is right for the job concerns institutional context, which is relevant in two ways. First, there are institutional limits to the application and use of policy instruments, and second, whether a policy instrument works in the way its programme theory intends it to work is dependent not only on social context, as we have just discussed, but also on institutional context.

Regarding the first point, institutions always constitute a constraining factor for what governments can do. In many instances, governments are limited by the division of responsibilities between levels of government, between different institutions at the same level of government, and between the government sphere and the economic and social spheres. Very often, such constraints are elements of constitutional regimes, such as limits to the central government's jurisdiction in federal systems. Independent central banks are designed to limit governments' powers to determine monetary policy. Independent regulatory agencies, established in most Western countries since the 1980s, are intended to limit direct political intervention in markets created in the wake of privatization of services such as telecommunications, electricity, and water. In the context of anti-obesity measures, the attempt to ban sugary drinks in New York City was reversed on the grounds that the boundary between state and local government power was overstepped. Furthermore, many potentially effective policy options cannot be applied because they would violate fundamental constitutional norms. For example, government mandates on dietary behaviours or exercise regimes are unlikely to be upheld in polities that place a high value on individual liberties.

In addition to constraining the decision-making capacity of governments, institutions also impact the effectiveness of the chosen policy instrument, even when it is a politically or legally feasible option. The same policy design might yield completely different results in different institutional contexts. One reason for this is unequal capacity, for example, when stringent regulations cannot be consistently enforced under conditions of low state enforcement capacity (see Chapter 5).

Beyond that, the institutional structures and logics in policy engine rooms also have an influence on the effectiveness of policy instruments, an insight which has especially been developed in the literature on economic governance, which shows that countries' economic systems are governed by institutional structures and logics at the political, associational, and firm levels. Banking systems, vocational training systems, and firms' innovation models and hence incentives for training workers are mutually reinforcing parts of a larger institutional system. The same incentive programme for further education and training might yield completely different results in countries such as Austria and Germany, on the one hand, and the UK and the US, on the other. In Austria and Germany, vocational training institutions provide high-quality training for school leavers who will not attend tertiary education. Because of the quality of the training, further incentives are often not necessary. In the UK and the US, where apprenticeships are not a strong part of the educational system, students will aim to attain costly tertiary education in order to secure a middle-class career (Busemeyer and Trampusch 2012; Crouch et al. 1999). In the area of obesity, incentive programmes for healthy lifestyles channelled through health insurance companies might not reach the most at-risk target groups in countries with a large proportion of uninsured people. We deepen the discussion of the role of institutions in Chapter 9.

4.5.4 Fourth consideration: place in the policy context

Policies are often responses to the perceived limits, limitations, unintended consequences, or ineffectiveness of existing policies (Wildavsky 1979,

62–85). Such responses do not necessarily even imply the adoption of new policies but often entail the maintenance or repair of existing ones. Given that policy-making takes place in a crowded policy space characterized by a multitude of laws, regulations, programmes, and organizations, policy researchers have suggested that 'policy succession' provides the most accurate image of what policy-making is truly about.

Hogwood and Peters (1982, 1983), for example, suggested the notion of policy succession to highlight that every new policy develops in a dense environment of pre-existing policies. Therefore, earlier policies form a central part of the context of policy-making, and these policies can either hinder or facilitate the adoption and implementation of a new measure. At the same time, policies generate side-effects and become the causes of later policy problems—both across sectors, such as when road construction leads to environmental problems, and within sectors, as when subsidies for agricultural products lead to overproduction. They hence lead new policies themselves, which Wildavsky (1979, 62) called 'policy as its own cause'.

The policy-maker must then ask whether a particular policy (instrument) under consideration fits into the fabric of existing programmes, rules, and laws. The literature on street-level bureaucracy (see Chapter 5) highlights the often contradictory rules and regulations that front-line public servants have to implement—for example, when social workers are responsible both for providing advice and support and for enforcing compliance with rules such as conditions for welfare benefits. Note that such an analysis would seldom feature in standard cost–benefit analysis tools since they consider only different alternative policy options and not how one policy options fits with or contradicts existing policies.

Useful advice for the combination of policy tools has been developed in the field of environmental regulation. The concept of 'smart regulation' has been introduced as a broad guideline for the combination of certain policy instruments (Gunningham 2010). According to this concept, classic command-and-control regulation should be used sparingly in order to not place excessive administrative burdens on companies who need to comply with regulatory standards. Regulatory norms should be combined with incentives and information-based instruments as well as self-regulatory schemes that positively facilitate company compliance. A combination of self-regulatory schemes with incentives (sin taxes) and nudge-type interventions (food labels with traffic lights) would go in the direction of smart regulation in addressing obesity.

4.5.5 Guiding questions for instrument choice

The impact of the best-intentioned interventions, even those backed by international recommendations as 'best practice', can be hampered by incomplete consideration of programme theories, government resources, institutional fit, and policy context (see Box 4.4 on how Mexico's and Chile's fight against obesity developed).

Box 4.4   Mixed results in addressing obesity in Mexico and Chile

---

Despite indications of at least short-term effects, the OECD (2017) has cautioned that Chile's obesity prevention policies need rigorous implementation, fine-tuning, and expansion and has recommended that more work be done to engage actors outside the public sector in obesity prevention. As in Mexico, adequate monitoring and evaluation is critical for success, yet still somewhat lacking. And certain counter-obesity measures may not affect, or even reach, all segments of the target population equally: not all consumers are primed to meaningfully interpret FOP labels or other information about nutritional content, and whether SSB and food taxes disproportionately harm poorer households remains heavily debated. Experts have also warned that the new taxes could incentivize the food and beverage industry to reformulate their products (as already reported in Chile; see Jacobs 2018), and not necessarily in a healthier fashion (Bonilla-Chacín et al. 2016).

Just as both countries have yet to determine whether any tool in place contributes to long-term behavioural or epidemiological change, Mexico and Chile could also benefit from addressing a more complete range of factors behind overweight and obesity. Much as increased incomes can catalyse significant changes in dietary habits, rapid urbanization, fewer labour-intensive jobs, and increased screen time (especially among children) have all contributed to more sedentary lifestyles in parts of Latin America. With the exception of a select number of information campaigns and in-school programmes, relatively little has been done to motivate behavioural change in this area. Lastly, overweight and obesity are only one half of the 'double burden' of disease in countries like Chile and Mexico, as well as in other low- and middle-income countries which also struggle with the problem of undernutrition. Obesity and undernutrition may coexist in the same communities and households and, as a result, require the careful adaptation and combination of policy instruments (WHO 2020).

Contributing author: Jessica Leong Cohen.

These four dimensions and related guiding questions, as well as the underlying factors to be considered when exploring these questions, are summarized in Table 4.2. Four key messages from the discussion thus far should be highlighted:

- First, the assessment of policy options as described in this chapter is much broader in scope than the standard cost–benefit analysis suggests. To capture the effectiveness of (a set of) policy instruments, the social, institutional, and policy context and the capacity conditions of the implementing bodies need to be included in an assessment.
- Second, such a widening of the perspective towards ex ante policy assessment necessarily comes at the expense of precision. It is very difficult to apply cost–benefit analysis or other tools of ex ante policy evaluation (such as experimental trials of policy interventions) to a combination of different policy tools. A precise (quantitative) analysis of all four dimensions of different policy options would result in an exercise that is too complex to be handled in real-life policy-making.
- Third, this is why we are not advocating for a new framework for the assessment of different policy options during the policy design process. We rather propose guiding questions: simplifying rules of thumb to be considered when policies are contemplated, negotiated, floated, and drafted.
- Fourth, while analysis is an important pillar of good policy design, interaction and communication within and across organizations involved in the engine room (and beyond) are just as important (see Chapters 7 and 8). It is during such interactions that we see the appropriate place for our guiding questions.

But before we explain in the next chapter how to implement the policies and programmes, the rest of this chapter will turn to critical aspects of the politics of tool choice.

Table 4.2 Guiding questions and factors to consider for instrument choice and design

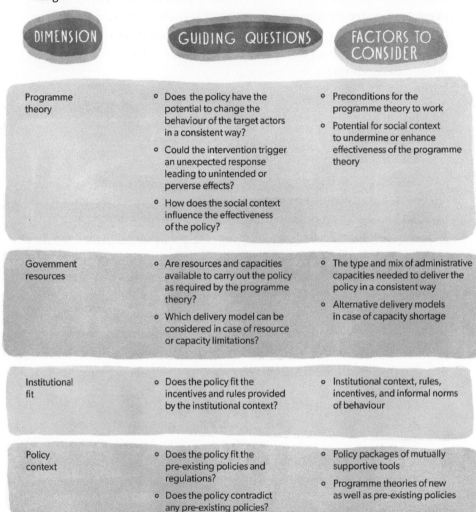

DIMENSION	GUIDING QUESTIONS	FACTORS TO CONSIDER
Programme theory	o Does the policy have the potential to change the behaviour of the target actors in a consistent way? o Could the intervention trigger an unexpected response leading to unintended or perverse effects? o How does the social context influence the effectiveness of the policy?	o Preconditions for the programme theory to work o Potential for social context to undermine or enhance effectiveness of the programme theory
Government resources	o Are resources and capacities available to carry out the policy as required by the programme theory? o Which delivery model can be considered in case of resource or capacity limitations?	o The type and mix of administrative capacities needed to deliver the policy in a consistent way o Alternative delivery models in case of capacity shortage
Institutional fit	o Does the policy fit the incentives and rules provided by the institutional context?	o Institutional context, rules, incentives, and informal norms of behaviour
Policy context	o Does the policy fit the pre-existing policies and regulations? o Does the policy contradict any pre-existing policies?	o Policy packages of mutually supportive tools o Programme theories of new as well as pre-existing policies

4.6 The Politics of Policy Instruments

Policy design is mostly conceived as a process of problem-solving. It is about matching the available policy instruments to the problem at hand by finding out 'what works'. But this 'puzzling' about finding out what works does not take place in a space where 'powering' (Heclo 1974) does not play a role. Of course, while some issues are very politicized and raise the attention of superstructure actors, other design processes are left to the engine room. But that does not mean that considerations of power and influence are muted when policy design is happening below deck. We argue that policy-makers in the engine room should be aware of the (potential) political impact of policy choices, for instance, how the adoption of policies influences the constellation of actors.

The foremost 'political' concern mentioned in debates about policy design is political feasibility, that is, whether a potential policy instrument is actually within the set of options that finds support in the policy superstructure. As we pointed out in Chapter 2, for those in the superstructure, the effectiveness of a policy in addressing a problem may be of secondary importance compared to the effect the policy will have on the (power) position of superstructure actors. But political feasibility is not the only aspect that policy-makers in the engine room need to assess when choosing policy instruments. As we just described in the discussion about policy context considerations, the adoption of any policy will have a downstream effect on future policy processes because enacted policy instruments allocate resources, influence the mandates, resources, and motivations of societal actors, and frame debates to come (Pierson 1993). We highlight four ways in which policy choices may affect policy processes in the future and the position of a policy-making organization therein. The first two points concern matters of bureaucratic politics within the engine room, and the latter two reflect features of interest group politics.

4.6.1 Bureaucratic politics

The first aspect of *bureaucratic politics* has at its core the policy-making organization, for example, a ministerial department or regulatory agency, that seeks to launch a policy. The key players from the engine room have, according to Scharpf (1986), two general organizational concerns (or interests) to take into account. One is the achievement of aims and objectives that define their mission, such as promoting public health for a ministry or agency of the same name. The other is the institutional interest of that organization. Wilson (1989) has discussed the task of 'organizational maintenance', which involves defending a bureaucratic agency's jurisdiction and autonomy (or turf) against other agencies that seek to exert influence within its domain (for example, a health ministry might seek to prevent a ministry for business affairs from intervening to shape public health legislation).

Note that defending the institutional self-interest of an organization is motivated by more than the selfish instincts of turf-conscious bureaucrats; a high level of autonomy is a precondition for bureaucratic agencies to fulfil their mission. Hence agency leaders have to reflect on how a particular policy measure will influence the position of their organization in relation to others. This includes deciding whether to *not* get involved in a new task that would perhaps increase an agency's budget but not contribute to achieving its core mission. For example, if there are calls for the regulation of food companies to provide transparent and simple (nudge-like) information on packages (such as traffic light labelling to signal the relative nutritional value of food products), the ministry responsible for agriculture needs to weigh its options: should it start an initiative taking up that policy idea, thereby possibly expanding its jurisdiction towards food safety? Could the regulation of information provision provide a first step towards a more comprehensive regulation of food from a consumer protection perspective that can be scaled up in future efforts? Or would this create what Wilson (1989) called 'divided constituencies' as the ministry would become responsible for both food production and consumer protection issues, which might increase the ministry's exposure to conflicts (see Chapter 5 for a more extensive discussion of divided constituencies and conflict management).

A second, and related, aspect of bureaucratic politics to be examined involves budgetary considerations. Budgetary limitations always play an important role in the choice of policy instrument. However, from the perspective of a single organization, or a subunit within an organization, getting an expenditure programme into the budget, even with a small overall budget amount, could turn out to be beneficial in the longer term: if the usefulness of the programme can be demonstrated, political demand for it may increase. Once this programme has been accepted as the part of the budget's 'base', which typically remains uncontested outside budget crisis situations, the seeds for further expansion will have been planted (see Wildavsky 1964 on the concepts of 'base' and 'fair share' in budgeting). Such strategic considerations are important for new policies and programmes. For instance, where it already exists, paid parental leave can be expanded to fathers but not at the expense of mothers because such leave has been established as a quasi-right that would be nearly impossible to withdraw.

4.6.2 Interest group politics

Beyond the concerns of bureaucratic politics, the role of interest groups and the wider population are another dimension of the political impact of policy choices. The first and most important way a policy (instrument) influences the world of interest groups is by creating or strengthening constituencies. Even in policy domains that lack strong representation by a specific interest group, the setting up of a programme that creates clear beneficiaries can eventually lead to the creation of such groups and thus to support for the programme. Efforts to dismantle the US Patient Protection and Affordable Care Act (Obamacare) throughout the administration of President Trump proved difficult despite Republican Party control over both chambers of the federal legislature (and despite such dismantling having been one of Trump's core campaign promises). Political scientist Paul Pierson has argued that Obamacare beneficiaries represent a political factor that cannot be ignored: 'People who are receiving benefits, they're going to react pretty strongly to that being taken away from them' (quoted in Matthews 2017). This argument relates to what psychologists call 'prospect theory', that is, that people attach more importance, and react more strongly, to potential losses than to potential gains.

However, the support of interest groups also hinges on an important condition pointed out by Mettler (2011): when policies are delivered through tax credits or third parties (such as NGOs), they become less visible even to the beneficiaries; or, more precisely, it becomes less obvious that the government is the one providing benefits. Mettler (2011) argues that strong reliance on such programmes results in a 'submerged state' that lacks political support for programmes, even from their beneficiaries.

This suggests that the way programmes are designed—in this case, their degree of visibility—matters for their downstream political effects. In other words, if you want credit for your programme and want to build a constituency for its continuation, make sure that the beneficiaries know about it. And of course, the reverse argument can be made as well: if you take something away from groups, make this as invisible as possible. Bezes (2007) has analysed this strategy of 'low visibility' in the context of budget cuts in France that were introduced with limited resistance.

The second way in which policies have implications for interest group politics relates to the creation of target groups through programmes. Schneider and Ingram (1993) have developed the theory of 'social construction of target populations', the key takeaway being that the ways in which target populations are defined and built up affects the perceptions of these groups in the political debate and shapes subsequent agenda-setting and policy formulation. Groups with little power, for example, can be defined as either 'dependents' or 'deviants'. Powerful target groups can also be labelled in a more positive ('advantaged') or a more negative ('contenders') way. Examples of dependent groups would be 'children', 'mothers', and 'disabled people'; examples of deviant groups include 'criminals' and 'drug addicts'. Target groups that are given the label of 'deserving' are more likely to be addressed with soft and supportive policy instruments such as incentives, information, and direct provision. In turn, deviants that are deemed 'undeserving' for whatever reason will be addressed with more regulatory and punitive policy instruments. Schneider and Ingram (1993) contend that the target groups mostly like to receive benefits through distributive policies are the powerful and positively constructed ones, such as 'the elderly' or 'business'. It does not require much imagination to see how these different ways of constructing target groups could be applied to the issue of obesity (are obese adolescents dependents or deviants, deserving or undeserving?). While this theory is mostly about explaining instrument choice, policy-makers can learn from it that the construction of target populations can make a difference in how the politics of policy formulation play out. In the interaction between engine room policy-makers, superstructure actors such as elected politicians, and the wider public, support for or resistance to policy proposals will hinge on the ways the policy's target population is defined and ultimately perceived.

4.7 How to Choose Policy Instruments

The choice and design of policy instruments is a process that combines seeking a solution that is effective in addressing the societal problem on the agenda and navigating this policy through the policy formulation process. Policy-makers and policy analysts need to be mindful of the dual nature of the task, which is both a design process and a political process. There can be some division of labour between different individuals engaged in the more analytical and the more political aspects of this task, but policy-makers should be aware that these two dimensions are entangled in practice—which means that the policy analysis dimension also serves strategic purposes, and the strategic aspects have an impact on the analytical aspects.

Analytical tools such as cost–benefit analysis can play an important role for very specific assessments of policy options, but the complexities of the policy process call for expanding the range of perspectives. We have introduced four heuristics that can guide policy-makers—considering whether the programme theory matches the problem, what (administrative) capacities for implementation are available, whether the solution fits the institutional context, and how it might work in the existing policy context. Together with the more focused approach of cost–benefit analysis and similar assessments, these perspectives should be applied in a pragmatic and context-sensitive way. Furthermore, approaches such as behavioural insights and design thinking can offer new angles, which allow for broadening the somewhat narrow view provided by cost–benefit analysis.

At the same time, policy-makers as well as policy analysts should be aware of the political implications of policy instrument choice and design. Basic political feasibility is important, but policy-makers should also be thinking about how the 'feasibility space' could be opened up, for example by initiating policies that can be expanded or increased in ambition in a next step. In other words, policy-makers need to be strategic about instrument choice and design, and think of policy design as a process that develops over time and not as a one-off event. This also includes considering how a new policy impacts the position, reputation, resources, and workload of the policy-making organization. Such considerations of 'organizational self-interest' are critical for maintaining high policy-making capacity.

An important aspect of all these considerations relates to the way policies could be implemented in theory and how they are implemented in practice. Thinking about implementation during policy design is critical, and the four heuristics (in particular the capacity heuristic) also serve that purpose. Hence understanding the challenges of implementing policies and ways to address those challenges is as essential for those who design policy as it is for those who are to implement them. We turn to implementation in the next chapter.

5

How to Implement Public Policy

Key concepts

- Vertical follow-through
- Horizontal coordination
- Enforcement
- Activation
- Conflict management
- Performance management

Implementation is what happens 'after a bill becomes a law' (Bardach 1977) and encompasses tasks ranging from the specification of programme details (budget, jurisdiction, personnel) to the street-level delivery or enforcement of a policy. Implementation is critical for policy success and failure, and policy research has identified the structure of the implementation field (including but not limited to the administrative structure of the engine room) and the motivation and behaviour of the target population as key factors (beyond the design of the policy itself, covered in Chapter 4). Based on these fundamental insights and a short reflection on the changing context for implementation in the twenty-first century, this chapter identifies five recurring problems or challenges impeding successful implementation and discusses solutions to these problems that are voiced in academic publications and in applied policy analysis work. The chapter provides analytical clues for assessing the appropriateness of these strategies in different contexts based on an understanding of the motivation of the actors involved. We highlight that implementation is a continuation of the political process at a different level, in which the interests and strategies of both superstructure and engine room actors matter.

How to Do Public Policy. Anke Hassel and Kai Wegrich, Oxford University Press.
© Anke Hassel and Kai Wegrich (2022). DOI: 10.1093/oso/9780198747000.003.0005

5.1 After a Bill Becomes a Law

Implementation is the stage of the policy process in which approved policies are executed, delivered, and enforced by the responsible organizations, which are typically, but not always, public sector organizations. Implementation is, as Bardach (1977) famously subtitled his book *The Implementation Game*, 'what happens after a bill becomes a law'. This includes specifying the details of a programme, allocating jurisdiction and resources to the implementing agencies, and case-by-case decision-making by front-line or street-level bureaucrats. While the scholarly usage of 'implementation' covers all these aspects and stresses the delivery of policy on the ground, some uses of the term in governments refer more narrowly to aspects of specifying the details of a programme after its adoption. Implementation in the sense of policy delivery mostly takes place in the engine room of policy-making, although superstructure actors can get involved at certain points, and, as we show in Chapter 2, superstructure institutions structure the implementation game.

Implementation is the process by which input—the previously adopted policy, the budgetary and other resources, and jurisdiction for implementation—is translated into action on the ground. This process produces outputs in the form of decisions taken or actions done by implementing agencies: building permits are issued, subsidies paid, or suspected criminals arrested. These outputs should help to address the targeted problem—uncontrolled urban development, stagnant economic growth, or high crime rates—by changing the behaviour of the target population in the intended way. These changes in the behaviour of the target population are called the outcome of the policy. How the changes in the behaviour of the target population influence the policy problem—urban development, economic growth, or crime—constitutes the impact of the policy (see Figure 5.1).

Policy analysis examines the chain leading from input to output, outcome, and impact, and implementation is the link connecting inputs (policy design, resources, jurisdiction) to outputs, which are expected to lead to the desired outcomes and impacts (cf. Chapter 4 on how programme theories conceptualize this chain). However, many environmental factors can influence outcomes and impacts, and hence the connection between implementation and outcomes and impacts is more indirect and uncertain than the policy designer might hope.

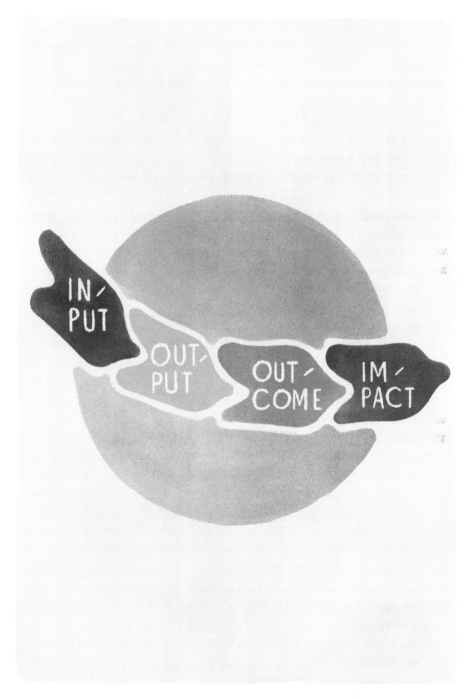

Fig. 5.1 The implementation process

The key questions for policy analysts and practitioners are what successful implementation entails and how typical implementation failures such as delays, cost overruns, unintended side-effects, and simply the lack of any visible effect of a policy on desired outcomes can be avoided. Implementation research has indeed identified three factors that shape the implementation process and hence determine success or failure, at least in terms of outputs (Mayntz 1983; Knill and Tosun 2020, 122–6).

The first factor is the design of the policy or programme itself. Every policy or programme has some implicit or explicit programme theory that connects the proposed activity with an expected outcome. Economic incentives such as subsidies, for example, should trigger investment by companies and lead to economic growth and more jobs. Higher sanctions for violating speed limits should lead to increased rates of compliance and safer roads. Educating children should make them more productive, social, and possibly happier people as adults. We have already discussed the role of programme theories in the context of choosing policy instruments (see Chapter 4): when this theory is wrong, a policy is bound to fail, even if the process of implementation is not significantly flawed.

The second factor is the politico-administrative machinery, or implementation field, which has to translate a policy into activities on the ground (output). If the administrative apparatus is under-resourced or fragmented, i.e. lacks coordination capacity between different agencies involved in policy delivery, implementation deficits are likely to occur (cf. Wegrich 2021).

The third factor relates to the character of the target population, which may be homogeneous or diverse and more or less hostile or cooperative in their response to the prescriptions of a policy. Wider social and peer norms shape a target population's predisposition towards compliance (Weaver 2014): the more people in one's social environment who comply, the higher one's own willingness to comply (Rothstein 2005; Bergmann 2009). The way in which the target population reacts to the policy depends on the objectives and tools of this policy: the offer to receive subsidies does not usually trigger resistance, while the enforcement of regulatory policies might do exactly that.

Against this background, this chapter explores (in section 5.3) five recurring challenges that delivery organizations and enforcement authorities have to manage. These challenges place rather different demands on policymakers and implementing agencies, and an important lesson for policymakers is to be aware of the most important implementation challenge or combination of challenges in each context. Implementation and public management research offer a number of strategies to address these challenges, which we will discuss throughout section 5.3 and summarize in section 5.4. However, these strategies are not silver bullets: they often call for unfeasible changes or do not fit the incentive structure of actors in the superstructure and the engine room. Each also entails trade-offs in addressing different challenges of policy implementation. Before moving to these issues, section 5.2 explores the changing context of implementation and how this links to the difficulty of evaluating implementation's success (on evaluation, see Chapter 6).

5.2 Policy Implementation in the Twenty-First Century

Since the late twentieth century, policy implementation has undergone major changes. With respect to policy design, a range of novel policy instruments such as nudges and social impact bonds have proliferated. They are more complex tools because they combine different basic instruments and involve non-governmental actors in delivery (especially social impact bonds). Also, the complexity of policy issues has increased due to internationalization, for example, in food safety, where production chains cut across national borders and undermine the effectiveness of inspections that are fragmented between jurisdictional boundaries.

Concerning the implementation field, decades of administrative reforms inspired by business management-oriented ideas have changed the architecture of the state. Today, implementation is less and less often the sole business of administrative agencies but often includes networks of organizations from the public, private, and non-profit sectors. Sometimes, these two trends are connected, as in the case of social impact bonds (Warner 2013; Fraser et al. 2018), which combine private sector or charity funding with delivery of public services by non-profits and social enterprises. Managerial reforms also have affected how implementation is monitored and governed, namely by increasingly relying on performance management (holding agencies accountable for achieving numerical targets) and benchmarking exercises (comparing agencies/governments across jurisdictions in search of best practices), arguably limiting the discretion of implementing agents and front-line bureaucrats in the engine room (cf. Hupe and Hill 2014).

Moreover, the target population is better informed about the activities and performance of implementation agencies, not only because of the introduction of performance management by governments but also as a result of technological advances allowing for real-time observation and comparison of indicators and performance results (for example, crime maps). Digital tools have also been used to evade enforcement, for example when social media warn of ticket inspections on public transport. At the same time, digital tools and artificial intelligence (AI) have also made substantial inroads in implementing agencies, for example in the field of policing ('predictive policing': Meijer and Wessels 2019) or social benefit regulation (using algorithms for fraud detection and classifying clients: Pencheva et al. 2020), often with the effect of limiting the discretion of implementing agents (Bullock 2019; Busch and Henriksen 2018). At the time of writing, the debate about the opportunities and risks of automation based on AI technologies is just taking off, but early evidence shows the substantial risk of biases and discrimination against particular groups (Eubanks 2018; Benjamin 2019; Crawford et al. 2019).

These trends certainly make implementation a more complicated business, which adds to a perennial evaluation problem that has troubled implementation research since its inception in the 1970s. This problem stems from the difficulty of clearly separating the process of implementation from that of policy formulation and isolating the effect of a particular intervention. As we know from a number of studies (for an excellent review, see Zacka 2017, 33–66), implementation is not just the stage of the policy cycle in which policies adopted at some higher level, i.e. the superstructure, are administratively processed and applied at the street level, i.e. the engine room. Instead, the political process continues throughout the implementation stage: policy conflicts from earlier stages of the policy cycle reappear, and the programme objectives and policy instruments are reassessed and renegotiated over time (Hacker et al. 2015).

Implementation can become an outright tool of political influence, for example in the sense of 'forbearance' (Holland 2017) when target populations are exempted from strict enforcement for social or economic policy reasons. Holland (2017) analyses 'forbearance' towards the poor, e.g. ignoring the questionable legality of street vending and informal housing, as an alternative to 'real' social policy at the local level. At the other end of the prosperity scale, lenient enforcement of the tax code has been observed as a reward for the politically and economically influential or as an instrument of economic policy-making (Dewey and Di Carlo 2021). Polarization and the rise of populist and aspiring autocratic leaders in a number of countries, including rich democracies, have shown that enforcement can also be used as a tool for punishing political opponents. In short, implementation is not always an activity exercised by benevolent state actors to achieve the best outcome in pursuit of a predefined objective.

But still, the people or entities that are in a policy's target population are not just fatalist subjects of intervention. Sometimes affected groups respond with 'counter-implementation from below' (Wollmann 1983) or 'entrepreneurial exit' (Gofen 2012) from what they perceive as overly intrusive implementation or poor quality of service delivery. Examples range from home or private rather than public schooling to urban and housing policies. While in the first examples, families have opted out of the existing public service systems, in the latter citizen initiatives have influenced local regulatory provisions (for example, tenant regulation). Whether and how such dynamics play out is highly contingent and context-dependent.

The continuation of politics and interest competition during implementation is not always problematic, since policies should be adapted to their context. But this does make it harder to evaluate success and failure in implementation, since the baseline, in the form of fixed objectives as well as the precise design of a policy, necessarily evolves with adaptation. Moreover, policies and programmes do not work in isolation but in conjunction with existing policies, rules, resources, and practices of organizations in the implementation field. Indeed, if we look at policy implementation from the perspective of those who have to do the work 'on the ground'—the frontline or street-level bureaucrats—implementation is not the execution of one particular programme or regulation but a process of coping with often conflicting demands imposed by a network of programmes, rules, and regulations (Lipsky 2010; Zacka 2017).

If we cannot draw a clear line between policy formulation and implementation, and if implementation is more accurately understood as an integral part of policy-making, then the evaluation of implementation becomes difficult because the yardstick for assessment—the policy, its intentions, and its design—cannot be fixed. How can an outcome of implementation be assessed when both the goals and instruments of policy are changing? How can the implementation of a policy be evaluated when one policy cannot be isolated from other policies already in place (see also Chapter 6 on policy evaluation)? Many have argued that implementation research needs to go beyond primarily focusing on how far original policies have been put into place.

Still, researchers and practitioners remain interested in how implementation works, what can go wrong, and what strategies can be used to deal with challenges that arise along the way. In the following, we introduce five recurring problems, which could also be seen as challenges, that need to be addressed for implementation to be successful. The significance of these problems depends on the policy to be implemented and a range of contextual factors. Furthermore, in a given context, these implementation challenges might arise in combination. We also look at solutions to these problems that are widely discussed in the scholarly literature and applied policy analysis.

5.3 Five Types of Implementation Problems

Implementation problems are hard to overlook. Regulators have failed to enforce emission standards for cars in countries like Germany for years (*The Economist* 2015); many developing countries and emerging economies have strict environmental or labour regulations on paper that are ignored in practice, and sanctions are not applied (cf. Brinks et al. 2020); examples of infrastructure projects running over budget and way beyond deadline abound (Berlin airport opening in 2020 eight years after was originally planned is just one of the most egregious). At the same time, many programmes work (maybe surprisingly) well, and deliver results under difficult conditions (Compton and 't Hart 2019). For example, conditional cash transfer programmes in Latin American countries are a success story (Paiva et al. 2019), as was New Zealand's response to the coronavirus pandemic in 2020 (Cousins 2020).

What are the obstacles or challenges that implementing agents have to overcome when they wish to deliver effective and politically viable policies? Across diverse fields, cases, and contexts, five recurring types of implementation problems can be identified, with the first two being related mainly to the implementation field and the other three linked to the target population and others affected by implementation (factors related to policy design are discussed in Chapter 4):

1. The problem of ensuring that the activities of implementing agencies and service delivery organizations are in line with the policy that has been adopted at a higher level. This is the problem of *vertical*

follow-through. It can manifest in inconsistent behaviour on the part of implementing agencies, delays in programme implementation, or diversion from policy objectives.

2. The problem of combining the activities of a number of agencies and authorities at the same administrative level that simultaneously affect the target group and influence the outcome of a policy. This is the problem of *horizontal coordination*, and it is seen in the uncoordinated activities of different agencies or departments dealing with overlapping target groups and pursuing different core tasks.

3. The problem of achieving compliance with norms and standards, possibly in the face of resistance among norm-takers. This is the problem of *enforcement*. Implementation deficits are manifested in a lack of compliance by (parts of) the target population.

4. The problem of motivating the target population to change behaviour patterns. This is the problem of *activation*. Behaviour patterns persist and lead to the continuation of the problem.

5. The problem of managing conflicting interests of different target groups or constituencies. This is the problem of *conflict management*. Escalation of conflicts between different groups would be a manifestation of implementation failures of this type.

Such problems and challenges mostly surface in the policy-making engine room, and one key for improving implementation is to involve superstructure actors in a way that takes into account the needs of the engine room. Box 5.1 summarizes how the city government in Berlin, Germany, has attempted to address four of these five implementation challenges in the context of persistent truancy. This case shows that implementation problems, while analytically distinct and hence requiring different strategies, often occur jointly. What may initially look like a relatively simple enforcement problem vis-à-vis a target population that is (partly) unwilling to comply turns out to be a rather complex problem involving elements of vertical follow-through (inconsistent application of rules across administrative districts) and horizontal coordination (between police forces, social workers, schools, school administration, and courts) as well as activation (raising interest in learning and education). We now discuss the five types of implementation problems in turn, referring when appropriate to the Berlin truancy case.

Box 5.1   School absenteeism in Berlin

School authorities and city governments in various countries have struggled to find ways to enforce compulsory schooling and to address high rates of school absenteeism. Since absenteeism is a marker for poor educational outcomes, authorities seek to reduce its rates, especially in neighbourhoods where the problem is widespread. In Berlin, Germany, the city government tightened its rules in response to persistently high rates of absenteeism. In the second term of the school year 2013/14 18.7 per cent of all high school students (grades 7–10) missed between one and ten days without a valid excuse such as a medical certificate, 2.4 per cent were absent between eleven and twenty days, and a small percentage (1.2 per cent) missed twenty-one to forty days (Abgeordnetenhaus von Berlin 2014a).

At the centre of the city government's measures was the tightening of reporting rules (Abgeordnetenhaus von Berlin 2013): the new rule, in force since November 2014, requires schools to inform the supervisory school authority about students who are absent for five (non-consecutive) days without excuse. (Previously, reporting was triggered by ten days of absence.) The school authority is required to inform the district administration's youth welfare department. Moreover, the school's psychological counselling service and the responsible teacher are obliged to invite the parents to discuss their child's attendance problem. Once notified, parents can be fined if their offspring is absent from school for more than five days. This coherent package of measures was adopted to address students and parents directly but also sought to reduce highly inconsistent implementation practices between city districts.

Other measures included an e-government project intended to create electronic student files accessible by all involved authorities, including police officers picking up youth outside school premises during school hours (Abgeordnetenhaus von Berlin 2014a). A cross-departmental working group was to be set up in each city district to include representatives from schools, school authorities, youth welfare offices, social workers, the police, and family court judges. Finally, schools were to be encouraged to establish mentoring networks among students, hoping to cultivate motivation for school attendance through peers (Abgeordnetenhaus von Berlin 2014b).

Contributing authors: Julia Melzer and Milan Thies.

5.3.1 Vertical follow-through

The problem of vertical follow-through can be subdivided into at least three major components, namely (1) the coordination of agencies in the implementation chain, (2) the relationship between implementing agencies and higher level authorities, and (3) the discretion of street-level bureaucrats and/or agencies.

The first component, vertical coordination, was originally identified in the classic study by Pressman and Wildavsky (1973) that established implementation research as a major area of policy analysis. They showed that even when support from the superstructure for a programme is strong and resources are available, the complexity of coordinating a large number of actors in the engine room can result in major implementation deficits. In their analysis of the subsidy programme of the Economic Development Agency in Oakland, California, which intended to create jobs for the long-term unemployed in the Black community, they showed how the need to coordinate the programme's details with a range of actors and institutions resulted in delays in implementation and deviations from the original plan. Even minor disagreement at any of these 'clearing points' could result in major interruptions and diversions.

Delays resulting from what Pressman and Wildavsky termed the 'complexity of joint action' have been observed in many more cases since then. A more recent example is Obamacare (the Patient Protection and Affordable Care Act) in the United States: even when carefully planned, the roll-out of a programme involving numerous federal and state agencies and non-state service providers is far more complex and difficult than one would expect—seen in various problems with the enrolment website and process after the programme's launch (May 2015). Coordination between the federal level and the US states was one of the major problems of the roll-out, including the unwillingness of some state actors to cooperate at all (Haeder and Weimer 2013).

A widespread recommendation for dealing with the complications that come with joint action is to reduce this complexity. Pressman and Wildavsky (1973) already recommended 'keeping it simple', starting at the level of programme design by targeting the problem in the most direct way possible. In their case, this meant directly supporting the hiring of the jobless rather than subsidizing investment and coupling it with requirements to hire unemployed Black people.

But the recommendation to keep things simple also extends to implementation structure, a piece of advice that is difficult to follow in the current age of multiple service providers and implementing agents that include for-profit companies and non-profit organizations. An example of successfully simplifying the implementation field is the widely acclaimed Bolsa Família conditional cash transfer programme of the Brazilian federal government. Key to effective implementation was the merger of four pre-existing conditional cash transfer programmes into one, the close cooperation of the federal government with municipalities, and the development of a central electronic registry. The conditions of the cash transfer programme were also kept simple, to allow for implementation by low-capacity municipalities (Paiva et al. 2019).

When simplification of the implementation field is not feasible, however, another widely voiced recommendation gains significance: the clarification of objectives, often combined with the setting of quantitative targets. In practice, vague formulation of objectives is one way to solicit sufficient support from actors with diverse interests or values for the adoption of a particular policy at the decision-making stage (cf. Zacka 2017, 45; Hacker et al. 2015). Another reason for the lack of clear targets in policies is that such targets come with the risk that executive politicians in the superstructure will be blamed for not achieving them; hence they will tend to avoid them (but see Boswell 2018 on why politicians might still rely on targets).

Despite these concerns, targets and performance management play an increasingly important role in policy implementation, in particular when it comes to managing the relationship between the delivery organization/implementing agency and higher level authorities, which constitutes a related but different component of the problem of vertical follow-through. Flaws in this relation can result in inconsistency in implementation practices among different lower level implementing agencies. In the Berlin case of school absenteeism, the widely varying practices of school district administrations in sanctioning the parents of truant students was one of the major implementation problems, and hence the clarification of rules for sanctioning was a main element of the reforms adopted in 2014 (see Box 5.2 on the reform's limited success). The specification of rules and clear incentives and sanctions for implementation agencies are therefore considered standard approaches to deal with inconsistent or lenient implementation practices. Setting performance targets is another way of doing this. However, such approaches will not be appropriate or feasible in all contexts, as discussed later in the chapter.

Moreover, tighter monitoring of implementing agencies and more intensive feedback between them and supervisory bodies might not always serve the institutional self-interest of the higher authority. Common wisdom would suggest that those higher level bodies have an inherent interest in knowing what is going on 'out there' in order to find out whether implementing agencies are doing their jobs properly, to intervene accordingly if they are not, and to adjust policy, rules, and regulations if feedback from implementing agencies reveals limitations or inconsistencies at that level. However, supervisors and supervisory bodies also have good reasons for not monitoring implementation practice too closely (Hucke and Bohne 1980). Feedback from the implementation field may actually reveal regulatory gaps and inconsistencies of policies that not only increase the workload at higher levels but also reopen political conflicts that were already dealt with (maybe through vague formulation of policies). Such revelations might also shift blame for implementation failures towards these higher levels. In short, higher-level authorities have incentives to detach themselves from implementation practice, especially if we assume that they are driven by political considerations of blame avoidance (Hood 2011).

The third component of the problem of vertical follow-through is the role of street-level bureaucracies (those organizations delivering public services and enforcing regulation on the ground), in particular concerning the degree of discretion that they have when implementing policies. Since the specification of all aspects of implementation in legislation or policy is neither possible nor always desirable (Zacka 2017), street-level bureaucrats have substantial discretion in applying general rules to specific cases and thereby 'make' policy as they implement it. That street-level bureaucrats have discretion does not always mean that they have a lot of slack and freedom. Instead, they often have to deal with limited resources, high workloads, and a set of often contradictory rules and prescriptions. In order to do their jobs, they have to simplify the tasks at hand and therefore use coping strategies, such as grouping clients by social status, age, gender, or ethnic background. Such coping strategies (Lipsky 2010) can lead to biases in the treatment of different client groups, such as biased grading of the schoolwork of disadvantaged pupils or racial profiling in police work. Recruitment and promotion policies that seek to increase the diversity of the public sector workforce, i.e. providing a stronger representation of different ethnic or religious groups and genders, are an effective means to address such biases, which are often unconscious (for studies showing the effects of gender and racial representation in police work, see Córdova and Kras 2020 and Nicholson-Crotty et al. 2017).

Performance management has been used to try to control street-level bureaucrats (Hupe and Hill 2014), with mixed results. While the introduction of performance targets and monitoring has indeed tightened control over street-level implementation by higher level authorities, it has also been noted that such measures can have demotivating effects and can lead to diverse forms of 'output distortions' and gaming (Hood 2012). Examples include schools teaching to the test in response to exam result-related performance targets, or police going for easy arrests in response to targets for arrests and cases cleared (see also Chapter 6). Higher levels of discretion normally result in street-level bureaucrats being more highly motivated to implement policies in meaningful ways (Tummers and Bekkers 2014; Thomann et al. 2018). Policies and regulations that deliberately grant street-level agencies leeway in figuring out the best way to achieve a result are sometimes called 'principle-based regulation' and distinguished from 'rule-based' approaches (nursing home inspection in Australia is one prominent example of such a 'principle-based' approach: Braithwaite 2002). With the advancement of AI-based systems of 'supporting' or automating decisions, the discretion of street-level bureaucrats might actually be reduced (but variation across different contexts is to be expected) (Bullock 2019; Busch and Henriksen 2018).

Yet the issue is not only about more or less discretion but also about the link or fit of a programme to the organizational context of implementation (cf. Elmore 1979). Successful policy implementation is in large part shaped by the fit of a policy to the institutional logics and needs of the front-line organization, as demonstrated by a study on prison management in the US (Lin 2000). That study showed that only when rehabilitation programmes help prisons to achieve their main objective—maintaining order and safety—will programme-related activities such as teaching be implemented in a meaningful way.

In summary, the problem of vertical follow-through is the Achilles' heel of policy implementation. The complexity of the implementation field leads to an abundance of coordination and monitoring problems. The call for clarification of policy objectives clashes with the realities of the politics of policy-making, and the simplification of implementation structures is difficult to achieve. Tools of performance management—another standard recommendation—are much more widely used today than even in the early 2000s. This trend is, however, in tension with the need for flexibility and discretion, which are also widely recognized as key factors for successful policy implementation that takes the context into account.

5.3.2 Horizontal coordination

The target groups of policies often face several different implementing agents and enforcement authorities. In the case of school absenteeism, the foremost implementing agent is the school, but school authorities (at the district level in Berlin, for example), social workers, youth courts, and the police play equally important roles, in particular for more problematic individuals in the target population. However, these organizations are difficult to coordinate (see Chapter 8 on coordination in policy-making more generally): because they work under different leadership, they have different tasks and hence priorities, and they follow different professional standards of good practice. For example, police officers picking up youth during school hours can often only suspect them of unexcused absenteeism, as they lack necessary information and have no way to communicate with other authorities. They also might not consider checking on youngster an important part of their jobs and hence might minimize effort, if they engage at all. Opportunities to catch truant students in the act are therefore missed. Lodge (2013, referring to former top British civil servant Sir Gus O'Donnell) has called this type of problem 'underlap': a particular issue, problem, or target group falls between the jurisdictional boundaries of different governmental organizations and becomes the responsibility of no one. Typical examples of underlap are instances of denial of responsibility for particular cases that do not fit into defined categories of jurisdiction (Wegrich and Štimac 2014: 45): for example, very young offenders who are under the age of criminal responsibility.

A widely discussed example of poor horizontal coordination is the failure of the various agencies of the US intelligence community to exchange information that might have prevented the terrorist attacks of 11 September 2001, often referred to simply as 9/11. As the report of the National Commission on Terrorist Attacks upon the United States

(2004) concluded, the failure to put scattered pieces of information to-gether was driven by poor information-sharing between these agencies. Some observers have suggested that 9/11 triggered a change in administrative doctrines, initiating a trend towards mergers of smaller agencies into larger ones such as the Department of Homeland Security, created in 2003 in response to the attacks, and a more general trend towards strengthening central coordination of policy implementation (Christensen and Lægreid 2007).

Of course, central solutions come with their own problems, and coordination problems still exist within larger, integrated agencies. The fiasco of the emergency response to Hurricane Katrina in and around New Orleans in 2005, in which more than 1,800 lives were lost, was attributed (among other factors) to coordination problems resulting from a combination of centralization and attention biased towards anti-terror activities. The previously independent agency for disaster response, the Federal Emergency Management Agency (FEMA), had been integrated into the new Department of Homeland Security and lost some of its capacity to directly coordinate with other agencies. In particular, coordination with state and local agencies became more difficult (Pollitt 2008, 3–4; Moynihan 2012).

Below the level of organizational redesign and the reshuffling of jurisdiction, attempts at improving horizontal coordination involve all kinds of cross-agency round tables, task forces, or interdepartmental committees. In the field of urban and land use planning, for example, cross-agency conferences to deal with applications from a variety of sector-specific perspectives have been used to avoid sending files back and forth between agencies. The standard approach to horizontal coordination is to set up cross-agency task forces that meet on a regular basis. The Berlin government intended to establish such cross-agency working groups at the district level to address the issue of school absenteeism. However, such attempts remained limited overall (see Box 5.2), as the urge of involved organizations to preserve their autonomy or 'turf' could not be overcome.

Difficulties are frequently reported in establishing strong cross-agency collaboration, with or without a task force. While 'collaborative governance' (Ansell and Gash 2008) is an increasingly popular approach and the involvement of the affected population and stakeholder groups is today considered a standard of good governance and policy-making, collaborative arrangements involving different governmental organizations are often ineffective. In other words, they may launch with enthusiasm and good intentions but too often fail to meet expectations. Failed attempts at cross-agency or cross-department collaboration reinforce images of bureaucratic silo mentality and limited interest in concerns that lie outside a department's jurisdiction. And indeed, attention to turf, i.e. defending one's jurisdiction, is a major concern for managers of bureaucratic agencies—not because of the prevalence of an outdated bureaucratic culture but because protecting jurisdiction or territory is critical for organizational maintenance and success and, at the end of the day, also performance (Wilson 1989).

Attention to turf is important because public agencies depend on public and political support for their missions. Such support is more likely to be won and kept when an agency's tasks are popular and not contested by other agencies intruding on its territory. At the same time, taking over tasks that are not part of an agency's core mission—for example, police officers checking on youth during school hours—will not be carried out with high motivation by the agency's workforce. Adding non-core tasks increases the need for internal monitoring and control, which will make the life of a manager more difficult and it is also likely lead to lower performance levels. Hence managers will seek to monopolize the task that fits their core mission—what Wilson (1989) calls the mission–jurisdiction match—and will avoid those tasks that fall outside it or potentially undermine its achievement. Therefore, agency managers should be careful about engaging in collaborative projects that not only distract from pursuing their core missions but might also lead to blame for failure or underachievement for which their agencies are not necessarily responsible.

Seeking to overcome the basic instinct of bureaucratic organizations towards turf protection, many governments have tried to change accountability arrangements via organizational reforms, including the introduction of matrix structures, joint targets, and joint budgets. But again, the instinct to defend the autonomy of a bureaucratic agency and the preference to control organizational resources has made the introduction of joined-up government via cross-cutting targets and shared budgets difficult and short-lived (Bogdanor 2005; cf. James 2004 on the UK experience; Christensen et al. 2014 on the case of welfare administration reform in Norway). Of course, it is not impossible to impose systems of collaboration and coordination in the public sector, as the proliferation of partnerships and public service networks suggests. However, the effectiveness of such networks to achieve coordination varies by case and is influenced by the difficulties of dealing with the autonomy, turf, and blame-avoidance instincts of bureaucratic agencies. A number of factors such as leadership, organizational capacity, and resource dependencies can shape cross-agency collaboration (Emerson et al. 2012; Bach and Wegrich 2019).

A particularly important mechanism that shapes the willingness of agencies to collaborate is the effect such joint ventures have on the reputation of the agencies, affecting the capability of agencies to deliver their core tasks effectively as evaluated by their audiences, such as the public and client groups. As Busuioc (2016) shows with respect to inter-agency cooperation between selected European Union agencies, turf-protection instincts can be overcome when cooperation helps to maintain or improve an agency's reputation for delivering a unique service. When managers believe that cooperation creates a reputational threat—for example, by putting at risk the key resources for the maintenance of reputation, such as intelligence and control over cases in police work—turf-protection instincts will have the upper hand. But when different agencies' resources and competences are complementary, cooperation is more likely (Heims 2019).

In sum, horizontal coordination is a challenge for effective policy implementation that stands in tension with the specialized structure of the public sector. And while cooperation might be necessary to achieve better policy outcomes, it puts the ability of individual agencies to perform at risk. Hence, attempts to improve cross-agency collaboration not only require leadership but also should take into account the effect such efforts will have on the capabilities of individual agencies. We extend the discussion on coordination of public policy beyond implementation issues in Chapter 8.

5.3.3 Enforcement

Implementation of regulatory policies is mainly about enforcement, i.e. securing the target population's compliance with behaviour prescribed by (regulatory) standards and rules. Environmental standards, for example, have to be enforced vis-à-vis industry; traffic rules vis-à-vis drivers, cyclists, pedestrians, and e-scooter riders; and food safety standards vis-à-vis restaurants, street vendors, and food processing companies. The challenge of enforcement is that regulated entities—individuals and organizations—will not necessarily behave according to the norm or standard without some threat of detection and sanctioning (see Chapter 4 on the programme theory behind regulatory instruments). This is because compliance comes at a cost: environmental or food safety standards, for example, impose compliance costs on the companies being regulated. In the case of compulsory schooling, the cost of complying with that norm is non-monetary, such as the forgone benefit of additional leisure time.

In order to avoid the cost of complying or to reap the benefits of unlawful behaviours such as selling kebabs with rotten meat or using industrial instead of comestible oil for food production, regulated entities may seek to actively avoid compliance, i.e. cover up violations of standards or find loopholes in existing regulations. Effective enforcement involves both the detection of violations of standards by monitoring regulated entities and sanctioning those who do not comply. Enforcement agencies face a number of difficulties. In many cases, enforcement authorities have to deal with large numbers of regulated entities. In food safety, for example, thousands of entities have to be controlled. Given the limited resources of enforcement agencies, constant monitoring of regulated companies is impossible. Besides human, financial, and technical resources, political support is also a scarce resource for enforcement authorities (cf. Short 2019; Brinks et al. 2020). Economically important or well-connected regulated entities might be able to mobilize political support so that they can avoid or deflect enforcement action. A major early study on implementation of environmental regulation in Germany (Mayntz et al. 1976) already identified scarcity of human resources and lack of political support, in particular at the local level, as the most important causes of enforcement deficits. In the twenty-first century, implementing agencies are troubled by the result of 'policy accumulation', i.e. the allocation of new tasks to implementing agencies without the provision of additional resources (Adam et al. 2019).

Studies on environmental policy implementation in developing countries and emerging economies (McAllister 2008; Milmanda and Garay 2020) show that similar though more salient deficits in resourcing of and political support for enforcement authorities are the causes of widely observed implementation gaps. Implementation research has demonstrated that enforcement authorities adapt their enforcement styles to these contextual factors, in particular by bargaining with regulated industries and trading flexibility in the application of standards for cooperative behaviour from the affected industry. In doing so, enforcement agencies not only compromise with powerful players; they also adapt the enforcement strategy to the context and balance the policy objectives of the regulation they have to enforce with wider objectives such as economic development.

Which strategies should enforcement agencies deploy to maximize compliance under these conditions? Two contrasting enforcement strategies have long shaped discussions about this question: deterrence and persuasion (cf. Lodge and Wegrich 2012; Gunningham 2010). While the first approach emphasizes clear and strict sanctions, the latter stresses support and advice. Both positions have been voiced in the Berlin case of school absenteeism, with some politicians arguing in favour of higher and more consistently applied sanctions for parents, while others claim that this would only increase pressure on those already disadvantaged in the current school system. Enforcement practices in Berlin districts are influenced by these different leitmotifs, and hence the use of sanctions varies substantially between districts.

The deterrence strategy assumes that compliance behaviour is the result of a calculation of the costs and benefits of (non-)compliant behaviour, i.e. regulatees are 'amoral calculators'. From this perspective, achieving compliance is mainly about changing the cost–benefit calculation of regulated actors: the result of the benefits of non-compliance—for example, the ticket price saved by fare dodgers—discounted against the costs of sanctions and the likelihood of getting caught (Becker 1968). This economic approach to compliance management argues that only when the threat of punishment is substantial and consistently enforced will regulated entities, including those who have not been caught in the act, be deterred from future non-compliance. When the likelihood of detection cannot be increased, for example, because of limited resources, the severity of sanctions should be amplified. In light of different distributions of costs and benefits of violating standards, overall compliance should improve among the targeted population of norm-takers.

However, research has shown that individuals and organizations do not respond in a uniform and rational way to a threat of punishment or the actual exercise of sanctions. A particularly tough approach to enforcement might undermine the willingness of 'regulatees' to cooperate with regulatory authorities (Baldwin and Cave 2020, 87–9). This holds in particular for regulated individuals or organizations who have not been (fully) aware of breaking the rules—such as a taxpayer making an 'honest mistake' in her tax declaration. The willingness to cooperate with tax authorities might decline in response to tough sanctioning practices of the tax authority (cf. Braithwaite 2007). In the future, that taxpayer might use tax advisers to help reduce the tax burden. In other words, an overly deterrence-oriented approach towards compliance can create a hostile and well-informed target population—and an overall lower rate of compliance. At the same time, making the risk of detection salient (for example, by sending reminder letters) has been shown to increase compliance rates (Fellner et al. 2013).

The opposing strategy stresses advice, persuasion, and information as its main tools, using sanctions only as a last resort. While this strategy is appropriate for dealing with involuntary non-compliance, it is open to exploitation from those who actually intend to evade compliance. Moreover, letting some regulated entities get away with breaking the rules can undermine the willingness of others to comply, starting a vicious cycle of non-compliance. There are of course situations in which a persuasion-based strategy is the only feasible option: when enforcement authorities lack the legal, monetary, human, or other resources to exercise sanctions, for example, variations of the persuasion strategy might be the only alternative. Gofen and Needham (2015) report how healthcare professionals engage in what they call 'deep personalization' to deal with parents that resist vaccination of toddlers. Deep personalization entails the typical elements of persuasion—personal conversations with parents about the benefits and risks of vaccination, and so forth—but also the tailoring of the vaccination itself, such as splitting vaccinations into separate doses to reduce what parents perceive as risks. The absence of sanctionable regulations can lead to a persuasion-based approach. But as already mentioned, enforcement agencies resort to persuasion and bargaining also when their de facto sanctioning power is limited.

Aiming to combine the strengths and offset the weaknesses of the persuasion and deterrence approaches, Ayres and Braithwaite (1992) introduced the 'enforcement pyramid'. Agencies following this strategy put strong emphasis on persuasion and advice but will move up the enforcement pyramid step by step (from warnings to fines and, ultimately, incapacitation, e.g. forced closure, revocation of licence, and the like) in response to the behaviour of a regulated entity. If the regulatee shows cooperation, the agency will reciprocate and de-escalate. This strategy is also known as 'responsive regulation', because the enforcement activity is adapting or responding to the behaviour of the regulated entity. The enforcement pyramid has been a leitmotif for many agencies across the globe in their efforts to reform their enforcement strategies by making compliance easier, improving information provision and advice, and thinking systematically about the application of sanctions.

Many challenges arise in applying the enforcement pyramid, ranging from concerns about the practicability of escalation and de-escalation to the question of how tolerant enforcement can and should be, for example, in high-risk areas such as nuclear power plants. But the main concern has been that the approach requires intense interaction between agency and regulated entity. As mentioned earlier, many agencies have to deal with so many regulatees that such intense interaction is not possible given limited agency resources and capacities. The enforcement strategy that takes this problem into account is called 'risk-based regulation' or 'risk-based enforcement' (Black and Baldwin 2010). The basic idea of this enforcement strategy is to classify regulated companies along two dimensions: the risk that they pose for achieving regulatory objectives and the likelihood that non-compliance will take place.

The first dimension is gauged by using risk assessment techniques that explore the generic nature of the activity, for example, concerning the health risks of water bottling versus meat processing in the area of food safety. The challenge here is to get the risk assessment right by focusing on the right type of risk and by taking into account the complexity of the policy issue. The example of the global financial crisis that began in 2007–8 shows how such risk analysis can go wrong. After the financial crisis, we learnt that risk-based enforcement systems in the financial sector completely overlooked the systemic risk stemming from the interdependence of financial institutions.

The other dimension of risk-based enforcement is the likelihood of non-compliance, which is assessed by tracking the compliance record of regulated entities. When one 'cannot control every steak', as one minister responsible for food safety succinctly stated (Lodge et al. 2010), resources must be allocated in a smart way, and those with poor compliance records and risky activities must be inspected more frequently and intensely. While risk-based regulation also raises issues of administrative fairness—not everyone is treated the same—the advancement of digital tools and data analytics will most likely result in more widespread usage of compliance-related assessments of regulated entities and more 'predictive' approaches to risk-based regulation (which might come with the risk of new biases, as different treatment of individuals or companies is shaped by previous events).

Compliance behaviour is influenced, however, not only by the enforcement activities of public agencies but also by the prevailing social and peer norms within the target population. For example, compliance with traffic rules varies according to social norms. Germany is known for high levels of pedestrian compliance with red signals, even when there is no traffic—and scolded jaywalkers are duly reminded of this norm, justified by the bad example a culprit could set for children. Other studies have identified the role of social and peer norms in fields ranging from compulsory military service (Levi 1997 on 'contingent consent') to tax collection (Rothstein 2005; Bergman 2009). Policy-makers try to make use of social norms for compliance and wider behavioural change policies, as we discussed in Chapter 4 in the context of designing nudges (of the social norm type). For the management of implementation, social and peer norms also play an important role in the context of activation, which we discuss next.

5.3.4 Activation

Many policies entail the active participation and cooperation of target populations for effectiveness ('co-production', discussed in greater depth in Chapter 7). This already applies to regulatory policies that require some degree of voluntary compliance, as discussed in the previous section. But cooperation is particularly important for achieving policy objectives when they target habitual behaviour patterns of individuals, such as unhealthy consumption behaviours.

The notion of activation has gained particular traction in the field of labour market policy, where it refers to various aspects of active labour market policies, i.e. efforts to get the jobless (back) into paid work. Such activation goes beyond simple job placement, in which qualification profiles of job-seekers are matched with job openings in companies. Especially since the rise of so-called welfare-to-work or workfare programmes since the mid-1990s, the concept of activation entails the further training and preparation of job-seekers, including personal development and behaviour (such as how to behave in a job interview) (Kenworthy 2010). These programmes have substantial—and controversial—political implications, in particular in the way the causes of unemployment or poverty are conceived (towards individual responsibility) (see Chapter 4, section 4.6.2 on the 'social construction of target population'). But they also come with particular challenges for implementing agents given the emphasis on personalized consultation and monitoring. Caseworkers not only decide on benefit payments, but in supporting their clients during job searches, they have to combine classic bureaucratic processing of eligibility and needs tests with counselling and monitoring of client behaviour. The challenge for implementation is not only that the different elements—control and support—are difficult to reconcile, but also that the segment of the target population requiring the most support is also usually the most difficult to deal with from the perspective of the street-level bureaucrat.

A related example of activation policy, in the sense of seeking changes in habitual behaviour patterns, is the so-called 'educational package' (*Bildungspaket*) of the federal German government introduced in 2015. Based on a diagnosis that children from socially disadvantaged families are also disadvantaged when it comes to extracurricular activities such as class outings, membership in sport associations, and private tutoring, the programme offers financial support for these activities via vouchers. However, uptake by socially deprived families was initially disappointing. At the same time, the programme's success varied substantially depending on location. Successful municipalities improved collaboration between different agencies, in particular between labour market offices (*Jobcenters*), the general administrative one-stop shops issuing the vouchers (*Bürgerämter*), and schools (see the earlier section on horizontal coordination). Above all, however, the programme's uptake and success were hindered by the time and effort required on the part of recipient parents, or enhanced in the case of municipalities which could reduce the time and effort required (cf. Bartelheimer et al. 2016).

In the policy analysis literature, this implementation problem is discussed in terms of removing an 'administrative burden' (Herd and Moynihan 2019) that presents obstacles to higher rates of uptake of such programmes. Note that such burdens that ultimately act as filters can also be established, or at least not removed, on purpose: it is well known but seldom researched that immigration offices, i.e. agencies dealing with work permits and visa issues, are in many countries neglected islands of Kafkaesque bureaucracies, possibly because foreigners are not (yet) voters. Herd and Moynihan (2019) show that some US states make access to abortion clinics particularly difficult; administrative burden becomes 'policy-making by other means' since abortions cannot be outright forbidden.

While these perspectives on administrative burden point to the problem of access to services from the perspective of clients and target groups, the key problem of activation in implementation concerns the implementing agencies' access to the target population. For example, in the case of school absenteeism, attempts to influence the behaviour of students directly might face several obstacles: parents, who can be sanctioned, might actually have limited influence on their children, and teachers and schools might not offer credible sanctions that induce behavioural change among the most hard-core truants. Behaviour patterns within student peer groups might be much more influential in shaping behaviour. One increasingly pop- ular approach among attempts to shape the behaviour of children and teenagers, not only in relation to school attendance, involves mentoring programmes that seek to establish positive peer role models (see the dis- cussion of peer norms in the context of programme theories of policy instruments in Chapter 4). From an implementation perspective, such ap- proaches come with the difficulty of finding and selecting appropriate role models that combine so-called street cred with the embodiment of the right social norms.

5.3.5 Conflict management

Some policies try to manage the conflicting interests of constituencies. Take the example of reintroducing wildlife in Western Europe. Since the beginning of the twenty-first century, wolves have successfully been reintroduced in various Western European countries. As an endangered species, wolves are protected from hunting by the European Union's Habi- tats Directive, under which the resettlement of wolves is official policy. However, as a number of incidents have shown, this does not come without problems and conflicts: wolves are predators and attack not only wild an- imals but also sheep and cattle. The resettlement of wolves is considered a direct threat by herders and farmers, and hunters are concerned about the impact wolves will have on wildlife. Wilson (1989) calls such a situation one of 'divided constituencies'. He argues that parks, fish, and wildlife de- partments in US state administrations, which are responsible for regulating hunting and protecting wildlife, avoid taking over the control of predators such as wolves and coyotes 'since the issue pits farmers who want predators killed to protect their livestock against ecologists who want them protected because they think these species are endangered' (Wilson 1989, 191).

Wilson suggests that bureaucratic agencies seek to avoid such divided constituencies; hence one strategy to deal with the problem is to allocate responsibility according to the client base of the agency, i.e. making an en- vironmental agency (rather than an agency with hunters or farmers as its client base) responsible for the protection of predators. But in many cases, an agency cannot shrug off responsibility and has to deal with divided constituencies and manage conflicts between affected groups with different preferences and interests.

One way to deal with this implementation problem is, again, to engage representatives of affected parties in some form of collaborative governance. In the case of managing conflicts associated with wildlife, wildlife conservation committees have been established in many countries (e.g. in Sweden; Duit and Löf 2018). While the institutional arrangements differ substantially, the general idea is to bring together various public agencies and the organized interests of affected parties, such as hunters, farmers, and nature conservation associations. The aim is to develop a common understanding among actors from diverse backgrounds by means of deliberation. However, such arrangements can also backfire when the different stakeholders use the forum to lobby for their position even more loudly.

Similar implementation problems occur in other policy areas. In immigration policy, for example, certain countries face a 'control dilemma' (Wright 2014) between, on the one hand, being responsive to populist calls to limit and restrict immigration and, on the other hand, serving the economy's demand for a greater supply of skilled workers through immigration.

In social and youth services, implementing agents have to manage the trade-off between keeping children safe, i.e. deciding about removing children from homes in which they might be neglected or abused, and the general principle of keeping children with their families (and in their culture, particularly when the culture is indigenous). Here, the trade-off in implementation does not result from divided constituencies but is inherent to the task, one that is amplified by the limited information that front-line workers have on the situation in the respective family.

5.4 Implementing Policies and Governing Implementation

Our discussion of the five recurring challenges of policy implementation shows that there is no one-size-fits-all recipe for success. Implementation problems come in many forms, and strategies for improving implementation need to be based on a sound analysis of the underlying (type of) implementation problem. Table 5.1 summarizes the five types of implementation problems and highlights their typical manifestations and main causes, as

Table 5.1 Types of implementation problems, their causes, and possible solutions

PROBLEM TYPE	MANIFESTATION	CAUSE	STRATEGIES
Vertical follow-through	Implementation activities at the front line deviate from policy design: delays, deviation, inconsistent application	o Diversity of involved actors, leading to coordination problems o Lack of monitoring o Street-level discretion	o Clear objectives o Simplification of implementation chain o Stronger control o Performance management o Automated decision-making based on artificial intelligence
Horizontal integration	Disparate, sometimes conflicting activities of different agencies, affecting the target group	o Different policy priorities and working styles o Blame avoidance and turf protection considerations	o Horizontal coordination via cross-cutting task forces and commissions o Joint targets and budgets
Enforcement	Lack of compliance with norms and standards by target groups	o Lack of enforcement capacities o Conflicting goals o Resistance of target population	o Responsive and risk-based regulation o Persuasion and personalization
Activation	Low response to policy measures	o Limited access to drivers of behaviour patterns o Barriers to changing behaviours that require intrinsic motivation	o Providing advice and consultation o Case managers o Drawing on peer groups
Conflict management	Escalation of conflict between different populations affected by policy	o Conflicting interests or values of populations affected by implementation activity	o Information and consultation o Collaborative governance

discussed in the policy process and implementation literature. The table also lists a selection of possible strategies for addressing these recurring implementation problems that are widely discussed in policy advice and consultancy circles. As our example of addressing school truancy shows, any case might be affected by more than one of these five implementation problems.

Whether these strategies can be effective in managing implementation challenges depends on the specific context and the details of their design and application. We do not offer 'best practices'; any claim that these exist is misleading because, as we argue throughout this chapter, the effectiveness of a strategy is a function of how well it aligns with the policy problem and with the institutional, political, and social context in which it is implemented. The concept of best practice ignores the varying nature of implementation tasks and the challenges they entail. However, what we can offer, drawing on insights from interactive policy analysis, are some clues as to potential difficulties that some of these strategies to solve implementation problems might run into or unintended effects that they might generate. In the hope that they might serve as a guide for policy-makers as they explore options, we summarize these clues and caveats according to proposed strategy:

- *Clear objectives*: The recommendation to formulate objectives precisely and operationalize them in the form of quantifiable targets is often unrealistic because it ignores political and administrative incentive structures and the (frequent) need to keep objectives vague in order to acquire and maintain support for a policy from diverse actors. There are other ways to bring as many actors as possible together. For example, those responsible for implementation can establish an understanding of what should constitute a programme's success and communicate this perspective upwards to the superstructure. In the superstructure, different, potentially conflicting criteria of success should be openly discussed (see also Chapter 6 on evaluation criteria).
- *Simplification*: The recommendation to keep the implementation structure simple often clashes with the reality of policy-making in the age of governance, in which power is dispersed both vertically (between levels of government) and horizontally (towards the private sector and other non-governmental actors and often among governmental agencies at the same level). And this dispersion of power also reflects the complexity of many policy problems, i.e. in some circumstances and policy fields, there

is no alternative to working with and managing multiple stakeholders (see Chapter 7).

- *Vertical control*: The recommendation to strengthen the monitoring of on-the-ground implementation needs to be considered in light of the institutional interest of politicians and administrators responsible for supervision. One should not assume that these actors invariably have a strong interest in knowing a lot about what is going on at the implementation level.
- *Performance management*: The prescription of performance management and target regimes might be one way to respond to lenient supervision and inconsistent street-level behaviour, but one should be aware that strong performance regimes will incentivize gaming and 'creative' compliance and could potentially undermine the professional motivation of street-level bureaucrats.
- *Automation/AI*: Policy-makers should be aware of both the value placed on discretion in implementation and the coping strategies of street-level bureaucracies. Limiting (racial, ethnic, class, or gender) biases by street-level bureaucrats is an important aim, and automated decision-making systems might have the potential to reduce discriminatory practices in implementation. However, the potential of automated decision-making to amplify pre-existing biases, introduce new ones, and reduce useful discretion of street-level bureaucrats (and also undermine their motivation) should be taken into account.
- *Coordination*: The recommendation to address horizontal coordination problems by creating cross-agency partnerships or by using shared accountability regimes (joint targets or budgets) should be considered in light of the organizational instincts of turf protection and monopolization of tasks and budgets. Powerful incentives must be in place to overcome these instincts.
- *Enforcement strategies*: Responsive and risk-based regulation can guide the consideration of appropriate enforcement strategies under conditions of limited resources and diverse target populations. But when applying these strategies, capacity limitations concerning the level of knowledge these systems require should be considered. These strategies should be used to inform the development of enforcement strategies that fit a particular context and not as a blueprint.

When exploring these different strategies, policy-makers should not only look at them individually but also consider the effects of combining them, in particular concerning potential trade-offs between strategies in light of different implementation problems that are present in a given context. There is, for example, a trade-off between the quest for vertical control, on the one hand, and the need for flexibility and discretion at the front line of implementation. This trade-off might be a matter of finding the right balance and design of control regimes. A second obvious trade-off is between the formulation of clear objectives and the simplification of implementation structure on the one hand, and the inclusion of a variety of agencies and stakeholders on the other. Different agencies and stakeholders will have their own ideas about policy objectives and good implementation, i.e. more horizontal coordination might make the definition of clear objectives and vertical control even more problematic. A third tension can be identified between the emphasis on horizontal coordination and the demands of street-level implementation for discretion and professional autonomy: commitments made in task forces, for example, might be in tension with the logics followed by those implementing a policy at street level.

In short, following popular or academic advice to address implementation problems cannot guarantee success, as the case of school absenteeism in Berlin shows us. Box 5.2 summarizes the state of the various measures five years after their introduction. With truancy rates slightly increasing, the policy cannot qualify as a major success (although, of course, these rates might be influenced by factors other than the policy). But the update shows that the policy does not meet its own procedural objectives, and many of the earlier ideas have not moved beyond the pilot stage.

Box 5.2 The persistence of implementation problems in addressing school absenteeism in Berlin

The approach the Berlin government adopted in 2014 to address persistently high rates of school absenteeism was in line with many of the recommendations voiced in scholarly literature and policy advice: to address the problem of vertical follow-through, standards were clarified, reporting lines streamlined, and sanctions unified; joint working groups and IT support were initiated to enhance horizontal coordination; and a combination of sanctioning and activation measures were introduced to change the behaviour of truant school kids and their parents. However, the track record of these measures in 2019, five years later, was mixed at best.

Enforcement styles still varied substantially across school districts, even between neighbouring inner-city districts, with some being more persuasion-oriented and others applying sanctions in a strict way (Abgeordnetenhaus von Berlin 2018). This is well illustrated by the different amounts of fines issued by the Berlin district governments as a response to school absenteeism. During the first half of the term 2018/2019, the district of Neukölln issued 415 fines. During the same time the district Charlottenburg-Wilmersdorf issued no fines at all (Abgeordnetenhaus von Berlin 2019).

Aside from the different sanctioning practices, working groups for horizontal coordination involving schools, school authorities, youth welfare offices, social workers, the police, and family court judges had been set up in some districts, but overall activities were patchy and limited (Abgeordnetenhaus von Berlin 2018). The IT project for the development of an electronic file to which different authorities have access was terminated after a pilot project, possibly because of high costs (€140,000 in a pilot school) and doubts about its effectiveness in addressing truancy. The launch of a new project for an 'integrated IT management in Berlin schools' early in 2020 might also have played a role (Senatsverwaltung für Bildung, Jugend und Familie 2015 and 2017).

What the Berlin example shows is how persistent implementation problems can be when there is a lack of political leadership in the superstructure to push implementation of the planned changes in a sustainable way and to overcome 'natural' resistance to change in the engine room (such as turf instincts that hampered horizontal coordination). This is not to say that the measures are generally not effective, but the structural challenges they address are hard to overcome. At the same time, school truancy as a policy problem continued.

Contributing authors: Milan Thies and Dustin Köhler.

5.5 Implementation, Politics, and Management

Successful policy hinges on successful implementation, and policy research over the decades has discovered not only how challenging implementation is, but also how much implementation continues to be shaped by political forces. Indeed, it can be seen as a continuation of politics at a different level (or stage). This by no means implies that the administrative factors and managerial approaches for improving the management of implementation that we discussed in this chapter are not relevant or are overshadowed by politics. But it does mean that implementation should not be considered an apolitical task of 'programming' an engine room to deliver public policies and putting it on autopilot; this would not even work if digital tools and artificial intelligence were employed for policy implementation and public service delivery.

In this chapter, we identified five key problems of implementation, or better said, challenges to successful implementation: vertical follow-through, horizontal coordination, enforcement, activation, and conflict management. We also discussed key approaches to dealing with these challenges, each of which comes with opportunities and limitations. It is important that the self-interests of both implementing agencies and those working in them are taken into account when using the approaches we summarized in Table 5.1.

And while each of these five implementation challenges is distinct, they often come in combination in a single case, as with the example of school truancy in Berlin. Hence, the potential trade-offs arising from the interaction of different solutions need to be recognized. One of the most frequently encountered trade-offs is between discretion and control. Implementing agencies and the street-level bureaucrats working in these organizations need to be able to take account of the context of implementation on the ground and the specifics of a particular case. Difficult implementation jobs can often only be managed by flexibly balancing different demands. At the same time, top-down control is necessary in order to make sure that policies are implemented as intended and that biases and deviations are limited.

In this chapter we have focused on how to implement a policy, i.e. turn input into outputs, outcomes, and eventually impact. Finding out to what extent an implemented policy actually generates the desired outcome is the quest of policy evaluation, the focus of the next chapter.

6

How to Evaluate Policies

Key concepts

- Evaluation criteria
- Impact evaluation
- Performance accountability
- Knowledge utilization

As we have seen throughout the previous chapters, public policy is about addressing societal problems by way of targeted interventions, i.e. policies. Having an impact on the perceived social problem—improving education, increasing road safety, reducing poverty, or cutting emissions—is the *raison d'être* of public policy, and the question 'did it work' is therefore key. Evaluation is both the stage of the policy process answering this question, and a subfield of policy analysis dealing with the scientific methods and approaches for evaluating public policies. This chapter discusses what good evaluation entails, and which challenges policy-makers face when designing policy evaluations in a context where the demand for evidence is growing but its role is often shaped by political logics.

6.1 The Different Faces of Policy Evaluation

In the ideal-typical policy cycle, evaluation is conceived of as the final stage. After a problem has been put on the agenda and properly defined so that a targeted policy can be developed, adopted, and implemented, the evaluation stage is when the jury assesses whether the policy delivered what it promised, i.e. whether it actually contributed to addressing the defined problem within the expected budget and time, failed to achieve any substantive results, required more resources, or yielded other (positive or negative) unintended effects. The outcome and impact of a policy, which is to say its effect on the actual state of the problem—poverty, homelessness, or environmental pollution—move into focus. Only on the basis of

How to Do Public Policy. Anke Hassel and Kai Wegrich, Oxford University Press.
© Anke Hassel and Kai Wegrich (2022). DOI: 10.1093/oso/9780198747000.003.0006

a proper evaluation can it be decided what kind of adjustments should be made to the policy design or to the implementing agents and rules guiding them. In the policy cycle model, the evaluation should lead to learning and requisite adjustment, or possibly to the policy's termination.

Considered that way, evaluation requires a policy to be in some way completed, or at least implemented for long enough that results can be meaningfully assessed and associated with the policy being examined. Accordingly, some policy-making organizations distinguish between evaluation, in the sense of an assessment of the results (or outcomes) of a policy intervention, and monitoring what is happening during the policy's implementation.

A proper evaluation is done according to the rules and standards of a professional and scientific study, with transparency in terms of criteria, methods, and data, as well as open discussion of any element of judgement and weighting between *evaluation criteria*. Such an approach to evaluation also requires the policy itself and the policy-makers involved to follow this logic of objective evaluation. Goals and criteria for policy success and failure need to be specified to allow for a precise assessment, and the goals should not be changed once the policy is on the implementation track; moving the goalposts during the game would render an evaluation exercise meaningless. This holds in particular for experimental evaluations, which have become a prominent approach to evaluating the effect of policy interventions since the late 1960s and early 1970s (Campbell 1969; Rivlin 1971). Since then, evaluation research has become an important component of problem-oriented policy analysis (combined with tools-oriented analysis). In the 2010s, experimental policy evaluations in particular were revived and reinvigorated in the context of 'behavioural approaches' to policy-making (see Chapter 4, especially Box 4.1) and in the international development community (Banerjee and Duflo 2019). Experimental evaluations are considered to be the superior method for separating the impact of the policy from all other external factors that could influence the outcome. For example, unemployment and poverty rates are often shaped more strongly by economic forces than by the quality of job placement services. Similarly, educational achievement is typically more heavily influenced by the social background of students than by the quality of teaching.

In the twenty-first century, policy-makers and implementing organizations, including non-governmental organizations (NGOs), face increasing pressure to justify programme choices and designs with 'hard' evidence based on 'rigorous' evaluations. These days, the bar is higher to show that policies actually do the job as intended. This also holds for political leaders in the superstructure, who have to justify policy interventions with reference to their effectiveness. At the same time, the conditions and criteria of good policy evaluation are difficult to adhere to in practice. While the criteria can be defined and the scope and methods can be established for any evaluation study, it is not likely that such choices will remain uncontested among diverse stakeholders.

The history of an early evaluation of a social action programme in the United States—Head Start, which offers early preschool educational services for disadvantaged children—is a case in point (see Fischer 1995). An evaluation conducted a few years after the programme's launch showed no strong impact on participants' educational achievement. While the evaluation was criticized for flawed research design (cf. Williams and Evans 1969), the 'leak' of findings from the evaluation study (known as the Westinghouse study) to the *New York Times* triggered a public debate about the programme, in the context of increasing political conflict over the wider 'War on Poverty' of President Johnson (1964–9). Having already attacked the War on Poverty during his election campaign, President Nixon (1969–74) used the early findings from the Westinghouse study to proclaim in his televised address to Congress that the Head Start programme was a 'proven failure' (cited in Fischer 1995, 54). His critique and the subsequent attempt to cut the programme spurred vigorous debate, in which educational experts, programme managers, and advocates for the poor questioned not only the Westinghouse study's methods but also the evaluation criteria deployed (Fischer 1995, 55): Some suggested that educational achievement as measured in standardized tests is too limited, and that the role of such programmes in socializing disadvantaged children into educational institutions is more important. Others argued that a programme such as Head Start should be evaluated as a 'normative contribution to the equal opportunity principle.... Compensatory programs such as Head Start were seen to be designed to nurture long-term harmony and stability in the social order and should be judged accordingly' (Fischer 1995, 55).

Despite criticism by top politicians in the superstructure and much controversy over the years (cf. Datta 1982), the Head Start programme survived these attacks, continuing to exist in the 2020s, and has been considered more successful over time. The story shows that the evaluation of a programme with a wide interest among various stakeholders will not necessarily close down contestation but will more likely trigger such debates. It also illustrates how evaluations are used as political ammunition in politics.

For the policy analyst or policy-maker, it is essential to understand the role of evaluation in the policy process in a broader sense than that underlying the mainstream tools-oriented branch. The field of evaluation research itself stresses that evaluation can—and should—happen throughout all the stages of the policy cycle (Vedung 2007). In the language of the evaluation community, this is called ex ante, ex post, and ongoing evaluation (Wollmann 2007). The term ex post evaluation—the assessment of a policy once it has had time to produce results—still reflects the most widely shared understanding of evaluation. But ongoing evaluation (or monitoring, as discussed in Chapter 5) and ex ante evaluation have gained currency. This is particularly the case for ex ante evaluations, also referred to as impact assessments, which should inform policy design while it is happening (see Chapter 4).

Moreover, evaluation in the sense of assessing the effects of a policy cannot be confined to those people carrying out or commissioning an evaluation study following the rules of scientific inquiry (Lindblom and Cohen 1979; Majone 1989). Actors with an interest in the policy will always in some way assess its merits and limitations, whether an evaluation study is carried out or not. Reports of government agencies and more or less independent audit bodies, media reporting, the work of think tanks and consultancies, court judgments, and the public debate in general, including via social media, can all qualify as forms of evaluation. And while such evaluation activities are obviously different from systematic evaluation studies following methodological standards, 'real' evaluation studies are not independent from such wider forms of appraisal: the way evaluation studies are commissioned and carried out, how findings are communicated, and the impact they have on policy-making are influenced by these broader forms of evaluation. All these actors will apply different criteria of success to the same policy, depending on their role and position. Some will focus on effectiveness in terms of goal attainment, others on efficiency and due process, and again others on issues of fairness and equity.[1] Evaluation in the sense of 'evaluation research' is merely one input in an ongoing process of assessing and debating the merits of policies (cf. Majone 1989, 168–9).

---

[1] What fairness and equity entail will often be disputed. For example, the meaning of fairness or equity in education will be contested when the starting conditions of children are shaped by social inequality. See Stone (2013, Chapter 2) on different dimensions of equity.

This chapter explores the challenges of evaluating public policies under these conditions, i.e. the tension between the demands of professional evaluations and the political context of policy-making, which influences how evaluations are carried out, interpreted, and used. The next section uses the Programme for International Student Assessment (better known as PISA) which assesses the performance of 15-year-old students across seventy-nine countries, as an example of a large-scale and very influential policy evaluation, in order to discuss the question of what constitutes a good policy evaluation. From there, we move to four key evaluation design challenges that policy-makers have to consider. We use these design challenges to explore the tensions between the different ways of engaging with evaluations, which—as we must disclose early on—cannot be resolved in the sense of any 'best practices', but call for weighing the options in light of trade-offs. In section 6.4 we explore the link between evaluation, control, and accountability. Accountability refers to the assessment of the conduct of officeholders, including politicians and leaders of implementing agencies from the public, non-profit, and private sectors. While accountability has always been a key dimension of governance, the late twentieth century saw an increasing emphasis on accountability with regard to 'outcomes' (i.e. that public sector organizations achieve specific targets, such as educational achievements of school students), shifting the focus from evaluating policies to evaluating those who carry them out. We discuss the merits and also the problems of this new type of performance or outcome accountability. Before concluding the chapter, we expand the perspective beyond issues of evaluation to discuss the issue of 'knowledge utilization' in the policy process more broadly—which plays an important role in all three core policy activities (design, implementation, and evaluation), but has been informed by debates around policy evaluation in particular. The chapter ends with recommendations on how to do good policy evaluations amid everyday politics.

6.2 What is (a) Good Evaluation?

From the standard perspective of (tools-oriented) policy analysis, a good evaluation clearly establishes how effectively a policy or programme addresses the policy problem at hand and how efficiently the intervention works. In other words, it relates the input (the policy instruments, resources, jurisdiction) to the output (activities of policy delivery organizations, such as courses a school has delivered) and outcome (the results produced by the policy intervention, i.e. education of children). Evaluation researchers distinguish between the immediate or medium-term outcomes (the changed behaviour of the target population, such as children at school) and the ultimate outcome, or impact (an increased level of education of children in a society) (see also Box 1.5 in Chapter 1 and the discussion in Chapter 5). In Chapter 4, we explored the role of 'programme theory', i.e. the underlying 'theory of change' that links a policy to the intended outcome or impact, and in Chapter 5, the process of implementation, by which inputs translate into action. Evaluation is about empirically establishing whether the theory was right, and indeed whether the outcome changed as a result of how the policy was implemented.

One example of a large-scale evaluation study is the international comparative assessment of the achievement of 15-year-old students by the OECD PISA (see Box 6.1). PISA is an unusual example of a policy evaluation because it does not measure the effect of one particular intervention; instead, it assesses the outcome produced by educational institutions by measuring how students perform. In other words, it focuses on the outcome dimension so that performance can be compared across a large number of countries—initially within the OECD, but more recently including a number of emerging market countries. PISA is known for its methodological rigour, although its approach to measuring educational achievement is not uncontested. At the same time, the study is highly influential in shaping the debate about education policy in a number of countries, and also in impacting the substance of policies and reforms. In fact, PISA has dominated education reforms in some countries by defining what good schooling is all about, and in particular how to measure good and bad schooling, namely via standardized tests.

Box 6.1 The OECD PISA study

Overseen by the OECD since its introduction in 2000, the Programme for International Student Assessment (PISA) is an international large-scale assessment which evaluates education systems by testing the knowledge and skills of 15-year-old students. Administered triennially, PISA's key objective is 'to share evidence of the best policies and practices, and to offer … timely and targeted support to help countries provide the best education possible' (Schleicher 2019, 2). The round conducted in 2018 included students from seventy-nine countries.

Especially since the mid-2000s, many countries have embedded PISA into normative policy instruments, for example by using PISA as a standard for goal-setting when constructing national indicators and performance targets (Breakspear 2012). An OECD-commissioned study found that twenty-four of the thirty-seven countries it covered had made changes to their national assessment strategies under the influence of PISA, including new, improved, or broadened assessments, as well as the linking of measurements and assessment frameworks to PISA (Breakspear 2012). Despite OECD claims that PISA does not take a curriculum approach to measurement, PISA reports often advance school-specific policy recommendations, and the growing practice of enfolding PISA competencies in national curriculum standards is evidence that policy-makers also interpret results as valid measures of school system performance.

Though causal relationships between PISA and policy change remain inconclusive, a growing body of research shows that governments also leverage PISA results to set agendas for policy dialogue, to evaluate the effectiveness of recent reforms, and as both an evidence base and broader 'policy rationale' to legitimate politicians' and policy-makers' reform choices (Fischman et al. 2018). In some cases, the media coverage and ensuing public debate surrounding newly published PISA results seems to be enough justification for reform, regardless of a country's actual performance (see Fischman et al., 2018). Certain policy lessons, often with reference to the early PISA success of Finland, have been transferred across education systems. And in even more countries, policy-makers have used PISA results to complement and/or validate existing national and regional assessments (as in Canada, Chile, Hong Kong, Mexico, Singapore, and Spain, among others), as well as to provide data for monitoring performance within certain groups or across subnational jurisdictions (such as in Germany, where PISA results were used to compare across federal states until a nationwide assessment strategy was fully implemented) (Breakspear, 2012). And while only a few countries and economies enacted large-scale reforms in response to the earliest PISA rounds, those that did were said to have experienced 'PISA shocks', with Germany amongst those caught most offguard by worse-than-expected results.

In the case of Germany, although experts had been long aware of the problems highlighted by PISA, the spike in public attention after the release of the first PISA results in 2001 exacerbated pressure on Germany's states, which have jurisdiction over education policy, while presenting an opportunity for the federal government to engage more directly. Over the next years, sweeping policy changes were adopted, legitimated in part by growing public demand and acceptance. Most notably, 'all-day schooling' of 6.5 hours, typical in most industrialized countries,

continued

Box 6.1 *continued*

---

was finally implemented; early childhood education was expanded; schools were awarded greater autonomy; the rigid secondary school tracking system was reformed; and the first national standards for student performance were created. The reforms appear to have paid off: today, Germany performs above OECD average in reading, science, and mathematics, though improvement in the latter two has stalled, and Germany's education system remains less equitable than the OECD average.

Not all countries, however, appear to buy into PISA to the same degree. When a new 'global competence' component was delivered in 2018, several countries, including Finland, Japan, and the US, declined to participate because of methodological differences. Questions about validity and cross-country reliability have also abounded since PISA launched. Researchers, especially experts in education policy, continue to debate the extent to which PISA's test topics and questions, target population, delivery mode (i.e. paper versus screen), and sampling and statistical methods create uncertainty and bias in scores (cf. Rutkowski and Rutkowski 2016). Language and translation effects, gender bias, and cultural differences (in general and, more specifically, in test-taking strategies) have also been identified as factors in PISA scores—despite efforts to account or adjust for these factors (Hopfenbeck et al. 2018). Nevertheless, the legitimation of PISA over time has certainly benefited its own creators: PISA's success has strengthened the position of the Directorate for Education within the OECD, which has itself become a global leader in education policy (Sellar and Lingard 2014).

Contributing authors: Jessica Leong Cohen and Milan Thies.

In short, PISA seems to have all that a good evaluation study needs: good data, clear policy implications, and high influence. At the same time, its design comes with trade-offs. While PISA is good at evaluating the overall performance of schools in a country or territory, other evaluation designs (e.g. experimental studies) are needed to evaluate the effect of a particular intervention, such as whether incentives for teachers in the form of performance-oriented pay make a difference in terms of learning outcomes. Policy analysts might observe that scores are higher in places where similar pay arrangements exist, but a simple correlation does not prove that such teacher incentives automatically and directly translate into better student performance. Experimental studies are seen as particularly suitable for exploring causal effects (e.g. Muralidharan and

Sundararaman 2011), although they come with their own limitations, in particular concerning the external validity of the experiment—that is, whether the causal relation found in the experimental trial setting would also be found in other settings. Another limitation regards the type of interventions that can realistically be tested via experiments, which is confined to specific, mostly small-scale policies. The evaluation approach followed by PISA, in contrast, allows for comparison—and ranking—of a number of different schools, and hence countries or regions, in terms of their performance.

However, neither the PISA approach—a large-scale measurement of outcomes—nor an experimental evaluation to test the impact of a particular intervention is likely to be helpful for policy-makers when they want to learn about how a policy should be or should have been implemented. For this purpose, more qualitative and process-oriented evaluations are the method of choice.

Even within PISA's logic and design choices, some concerns regarding the 'quality' of the evaluation can be raised. One question raised by critics is the extent to which standardized tests indeed measure educational achievement. This critique refers to both the method of testing as a way to evaluate the type of skills and knowledge that PISA wants to capture ('Does it actually measure what it intends to measure?') and whether it captures the 'right' skills and types of knowledge ('Does it measure the right things?').

It is, however, difficult to consider these questions and find meaningful answers to them without also taking into account the social and political context in which PISA is situated. Critics have raised the issue that PISA's conception allows for a better comparison across Western countries than across Asian and Arab countries (see Zhao 2020 for a synthesis of the critiques). Another issue was the lack of foreign languages as a subject in the PISA study (the OECD PISA project plans to run a foreign language test for the first time in 2025—but interestingly only focusing on English). An important consequence of the PISA method and its reputational significance is that it sets incentives for countries, i.e. the school authorities and responsible executives, to improve test scores from one round to the next round three years later. While educational reforms that have an impact on the quality of teaching, which in turn should have a downstream effect on the test performance of 15-year-olds, are difficult to achieve within three years, the administration of the test can be improved in a relatively short time, for example, by practising similar tests with students of the relevant age cohort. More generally, 'teaching to the test', i.e. focusing instruction on improving pupil performance on tests and exams rather than on the underlying competencies and skills, is a widely recognized unintended effect of performance-based approaches to educational reform (as well as in other policy fields) (Muller 2018, 91). The wider issue here is the effect of linking evaluation to accountability, which this chapter takes on in section 6.4.

Finally, a weakness of the PISA approach is the attribution problem. For example, Germany has somewhat improved its PISA scores since the first 'PISA shock' in 2001. One might attribute these modest improvements to various reforms of the educational system, such as the introduction of all-day schooling and the stronger emphasis on standardized testing and evaluation as measures to improve educational outcomes. Every round of PISA results triggers a public debate in which pundits discuss the effectiveness of these reforms. But beside improvement of the administration of the test, another factor might be the increasing amounts of money parents spend on private lessons.

These points are not meant to argue that PISA is not an example of a good evaluation. But they show that even, or in particular, a good evaluation is neither value-neutral nor unbiased. Choices of evaluation criteria and method reflect normative decisions about what a good policy is, and have an impact on the dimensions of a policy and its outcomes that are considered more important than others. It is this inevitable bias of any evaluation that makes it open to political contestation, no matter how 'good' in a technical sense the evaluation is (cf. Bovens et al. 2005). But as we discuss further in the next section, this caveat does not—or should not—lead to the conclusion that the quality of an evaluation study and the integrity of its design and execution are not of critical importance.

6.3 Four Challenges of Designing Evaluations

The observation that even good evaluation studies are not without trade-offs and biases translates into practical challenges and dilemmas for policy-makers seeking to find the best way to evaluate their work. We capture those challenges in four questions. What should be evaluated, how should that be evaluated, who should do the evaluation, and what should we do with the results?

6.3.1 What to evaluate

The first and foremost design question is what to evaluate. Remember that we argued earlier in this chapter that evaluation in a more general sense happens all the time and by any actor or organization with a stake in the policy game. The question for the policy-maker is for which policy issues or programmes a separate, formal evaluation promises added value. Once a particular policy has been selected for a formal evaluation, the follow-up question is which aspects of the policy will be subject to evaluation (for example, which skills of 15-year-olds will be tested in PISA and related studies).

In debates about improving policy-making capacity, the mainstream argument is that any policy needs to be evaluated after a certain period of existence. Advocates of evidence-based policy-making seek to strengthen the role of evaluation in the policy-making process as a standard operating procedure (e.g. OECD 2012; OECD 2020; cf. Parkhust 2017, Chapter 2). Such efforts suggest that so-called 'sunset clauses' (or expiry dates) and 'review clauses' should be incorporated into laws to require an evaluation some years after the law has been enacted (Bar-Simon-Tov 2018). The field of evaluation research received an important push from the review clauses that were included in various laws underpinning the War on Poverty initiative in the US in the 1960s to appease sceptics (Levine 1970; Aaron 1978). The contested nature of some policies and their underlying programmes make it necessary (and perhaps advisable) to build in evaluations. The inclusion of sunset or review clauses means a critical stock-taking of the law or programme's effects cannot be avoided by vested interests supporting the programme. However, the downside of sunset or review clauses applied too frequently is that a critical evaluation is unlikely to happen if a higher number of laws and programmes have to be constantly reviewed.

An alternative approach is to limit evaluations only to particularly important or contested policies or programmes. For example, the legislation setting out the so-called Hartz reforms of welfare provisions and labour market regulations adopted in Germany in the mid-2000s explicitly foresaw comprehensive evaluations of selected aspects, in particular the effects on unemployment and the labour market (Hassel and Schiller 2010). The significance of the reforms, as well as the political contestation about their risks and opportunities, triggered the mandate and budget for comprehensive evaluation.

A key question remains, however: who defines whether a policy or programme is important enough to require an evaluation? In the high-profile examples mentioned, parliaments were key drivers, but given that engine room policy-making is dominated by the executive bureaucracy, these remain exceptional cases. In reality, if the decision-making power for triggering an evaluation or determining what to evaluate is left entirely to the bureaucracy that is responsible for the law or programme in question, critical evaluations are rather unlikely. Some form of outside challenge—for example from an organization in the core executive of a government (finance ministry, prime minister's or president's office, or cabinet office), a legislative committee, or an NGO—could help to limit the power of engine room networks to call the shots on what to evaluate (and also how). Yet those outside challengers have to overcome the asymmetry in knowledge and expertise between the policy 'specialists' in the ministries and the 'generalists' outside (Jann and Wegrich 2019).

Once it is decided which policy or programme should be evaluated, there is the choice of what aspect to evaluate: inputs, outputs, outcomes, impacts, or even processes (Vedung 2007). While the ultimate aim of evaluation is to establish a link between the policy (including the input, i.e. the resources that went into the programme, and output) and its outcome, programme managers might find a process evaluation to be more useful for purposes of adapting the policy, in particular for newly established programmes that might take some time to generate impact. Such evaluations could establish whether the programme can be delivered in a meaningful way with the given resources, or whether the right target population is reached, for example. These aspects have been emphasized by so-called 'utilization focused' approaches to evaluation, which seek to engage users of evaluation studies in their design and implementation and consider the practical usage of an evaluation as the most important quality criterion (Patton 2008, 2012).

6.3.2 How to evaluate

The how question calls for decisions about the research methods that should be applied in evaluating public policy. As the chosen policy instrument needs to fit the programme theory (see Chapter 4), so the method needs to fit what is being evaluated and why. As mentioned earlier, the evaluation's purpose drives the choice of method. Providing useful information for programme managers and evaluating the performance of a policy-implementing organization are two purposes that lend themselves to methods of process evaluation and programme monitoring. While such 'implementation evaluation' (Patton 2008) is not linked to any particular method of data collection, the type of question lends itself more to descriptive assessments and detailed analyses of processes and structures (see Chapter 5 on implementation).

While process and implementation evaluation can be very valuable for policy-makers in terms of learning and adapting, the ambition of evaluation is often to find out 'what works' or 'if it works': to establish whether a policy has the intended impact on the policy problem, and to what extent. Such *impact evaluations* (not to be confused with the impact assessments we introduced in Chapter 4) seek to establish a causal link between the intervention—the policy, its inputs, processes, and outputs— and the outcome (cf. Gertler et al. 2016). As the now extensive literature on impact evaluation and field experiments (Gerber and Green 2012; Glennerster and Takavarasha 2013) argues, the leitmotif to follow is the experimental (or counterfactual) logic: the evaluation method that promises the best results—the most precise identification of a causal effect of an intervention—is an experimental study that compares a randomly selected 'treatment' group, i.e. those subject to the intervention, with a control group, which shares all statistical features of the treatment group but does not receive the intervention. For example, the reduction of class sizes as a means to improve educational outcomes could be experimentally tested by randomly choosing schools sharing certain socio-economic features in a selected region of a country. The measurement of the educational impact— through standardized tests that are administered in the treatment and the control group after a predefined time period—is achieved by comparing the performance of students on tests before and after the intervention between the two groups of schools.

Ever since the first major policy experiments were launched in the late 1960s and early 1970s (e.g. the Negative Income Tax experiments of the Nixon administration; see Box 6.2) (Widerquist 2005, 2019), policy experiments became a boom industry in the second decade of the twenty-first century—especially in developing countries, where they were pushed by donor organizations and the experimental arm of development economics. In the OECD world, policy experiments are linked to the 'nudge agenda' and the rise of behavioural economics as a meta-theory of policy interventions (see Chapter 4, Box 4.3). Examples of experiments today cover many important policy issues, such as universal basic income (see Box 6.2).

Box 6.2　Negative income tax and universal basic income experiments

---

Universal basic income (UBI), also called citizens' income or guaranteed minimum income, has been piloted and tested in a number of countries by both public and private actors. In April 2021, the Stanford Basic Income Lab identified fifty ongoing or past basic income experiments worldwide (Basic Income Lab n.d.), and seven proposals for future experiments, many of them carried out not by government institutions but by NGOs. Most of the experiments adhere to a randomized controlled trial (RCT) experimental design whereby a random sample of the population receives a guaranteed, unconditional income for the duration of the experiment, whereas a control group does not. There are variations in the dependent variables or consequences of interest, but frequently the motivation is to establish the effect of a UBI on employment, well-being, health, and education.

　　Early trailblazers of UBI experiments were the four negative income tax (NIT) experiments in the 1960s and 1970s in the US and the Manitoba Basic Income Experiment in Canada around the same time. Some thirty-five years later, the Finnish Basic Income Experiment in 2017–18 was seen as a prominent exhibit of the renewed interest in UBI experiments. These were government-run, large-scale, and politically significant experiments. Despite the different points in history at which these experiments took place, the experiments were framed and, consequently, evaluated in terms of labour market activation. In the Finnish case, the discussion revolved around reforming the social security system so as to reduce disincentive traps related to work, i.e. losing benefits once income rose to a certain level, which eroded the motivation to find adequate employment. The goal of the centre-right Finnish government was to reduce the country's unemployment rate, and the basic income trial was seen as a potential means to achieve this (Reynolds 2018). The Finnish Green Party, which had long advocated for UBI, notably said about basic income, 'We shall give everyone the opportunity to be active' (Perkiö 2020). Similarly, the four NIT experiments conducted in the US in the 1960s and 1970s had a narrow focus, aiming to determine whether any form of guaranteed income would reduce work incentives. This framing reflected the fact that one of the basic political obstacles to any policy initiatives such as guaranteed income is the widespread belief that they would kill work incentives (Levine et al. 2005).

This framing, in turn, played a role in the interpretation of the results and ultimate impact of the experiments. The Finnish government's decision not to extend the experiment, for instance, can be attributed to waning enthusiasm and even overt criticism from some parties, which had to do with limitations in the experimental design and implementation, as well as with results that showed basic income did not activate the long-term unemployed significantly. On the whole, evaluation studies of UBI (and negative income taxes) have persistently shown that it has a positive effect on health and well-being, while employment and hours worked tend to decrease (Forget 2011; Laín 2019).

Contributing author: Carlijn Straathof.

One set of concerns regarding policy experiments relates to ethics. For example, is it ethical to offer a (likely beneficial) treatment to one group but withhold it from another (MacKay 2020)? The response to this argument is that uncertainty and limited resources call for better evidence before scaling up interventions; only interventions that have been proven to be effective should be rolled out towards a larger population. Another critique on ethical grounds relates to the types of interventions tested (cf. Abramowicz and Szafarz 2020). For instance, the study 'randomising religion' (Bryan et al. 2020) tested the impact of religious values on economic outcomes (income) by providing 'theological education' of the Protestant branch of Christianity to the treatment group of 'ultra poor' Filipino households.

When RCTs are not practical or ruled out for ethical reasons, quasi-experimental designs that seek to emulate experimental designs using 'observational data' are next in the hierarchy of methods of the impact evaluation literature (Gertler et al. 2016). For example, when a government introduces a new curriculum across its school districts, the before-and-after comparison could potentially be used as a quasi-experimental design. In other cases, some external factor allows observation of the effect of a particular variable across an otherwise similar sample (regression discontinuity design, difference-in-difference)—for instance, when a tax is introduced in one locality but not in a neighbouring community that is otherwise similar.

Experimental and quasi-experimental methods are best applied to clearly confined, specific, and in this sense narrow interventions. One can hardly test complex combined policy interventions, such as new school management systems, teacher pay, and class sizes all at once. In other words, experimental evaluations are mostly limited to small-scale interventions, and the hope of the supporters of this approach is to facilitate improvements in policy-making through an ongoing cycle of incremental improvements (Halpern and Mason 2015).

Complex interventions are particularly difficult to evaluate when the different policy tools are interdependent. For example, it is possible that in a package of measures to reduce carbon emissions, which might include taxes, infrastructure investments, and regulatory standards, each measure has a separate effect and together they add up to a larger impact. Such policy packages can be evaluated by analysing the different policies separately. The situation is different when the impact of one policy is conditioned by the effect of another one: for example, investment in cycling infrastructure and public transport is linked to regulatory measures and disincentives for car use. The higher the level of complex interdependence in policy measures, the more difficult is the precise evaluation of its individual components. The so-called 'realist evaluation' approach to evaluation (Pawson and Tilley 1997) has been developed as response to the problem of evaluating complex interventions. It suggests that a general answer to the 'what works' question is impossible to achieve, as the effectiveness of a policy is the result of the interaction of the mechanism (of the policy intervention) with a given (local, historical, policy) context.

In sum, the debate about evaluation methods is very much driven by the goal to adhere to the high standards of policy evaluation. But it is also clear that precision in evaluation comes at the expense of comprehensiveness, or being able to capture complex interventions. The practice of policy evaluation is often only distantly related to these high standards. Methods to collect data on changes in output and outcome are possibly the mostly widely used forms of evaluation. However, subjective assessments of the policy by the target groups or other stakeholders (e.g. surveying students about the satisfaction with smaller class sizes) are also widely used. And indeed, the (narrow) focus on impact evaluation might not always be what policy-makers and public managers need to improve programmes.

6.3.3 Who should evaluate?

A third key design question is who should actually carry out the evaluation. 'Carrying out' the evaluation includes the actual work, i.e. evaluation design, data collection, and analysis, as well as the 'steering' of the evaluation, i.e. the definition of the parameters, the commissioning of research, and the handling of the findings.

From the perspective of evaluation research, the question 'who should evaluate' is a no-brainer: it should be those who are trained in the methods needed to design and carry out the evaluation in the most independent, objective way possible. As discussed earlier, the impartial execution of an evaluation is an important quality criterion, even if a bias in the form of the type of evaluation questions asked and criteria applied is unavoidable. Undue political influence—in the sense of both superstructure high politics and engine room bureaucratic politics—needs to be avoided. However, if policy learning is considered a goal of evaluations, close connection to (and even collaboration with) policy-makers is important as well. According to the 'utilization-focused' approach to evaluation we introduced earlier (Patton 2008, 2012), evaluations should be judged by their utility for practitioners and their actual use. The utility of an evaluation will, in all likelihood, increase when its design and execution are co-produced by policy-makers and possible implementing agents. In practice, many evaluation studies are carried out by think tanks and for-profit consulting groups.

A key skill for policy-makers in government is to be able to commission evaluation research in an informed way. Some governments have set up dedicated in-house units to support the commissioning of research and also to carry out some of it themselves. These range from independent watchdogs, such as audit institutions, to units within ministries directly supporting evaluation activities. For example, the UK National Audit Office has developed a strong track record of evaluating policies and service delivery, while the German federal ministry for economic cooperation and development has a directorate for 'policy issues, data and effectiveness' and one unit in this focuses on evaluation research.

An important question in this context is who within the government engine room should be in control of the evaluation. While aligning jurisdiction for the policy with responsibility for the evaluation might offer learning opportunities provided by direct feedback, there is a counterargument against leaving the design of evaluations to the policy-makers responsible for a policy or programme. Since they have 'skin in the game', they will probably not be very critical of 'their own' programmes. Many organizational and political incentives—ranging from the risk of budget cuts, to blame for failure, to relative power positions within the executive—make a self-critical assessment of a policy less likely. Carrying out evaluations also comes with opportunity costs. So why do they ever do it, as Aaron Wil-davsky (1972) asked in his classic account of evaluation in organizations? One answer is that the external pressure to justify policies with data and in-formation has increased, and policy-makers will use evaluations to make their case and defend their programmes (cf. Boswell 2018).

The 'who evaluates' question extends beyond the boundaries of the gov-ernment engine room towards the question of whether and how much other stakeholders, such as those affected by a policy, should be involved. In the evaluation literature, this is discussed as the tension between 'par-ticipatory' and 'expert' evaluations (Sager and Mavrot 2021). One of the key design questions in this context is who defines the evaluation crite-ria. The introduction to this chapter discussed the famous case of the Head Start preschool programme in the US. Much of the conflict and contesta-tion around this programme was about its impact, and whether to define impact purely in terms of educational achievements as measured by stan-dardized tests, or in terms of broader criteria such as socializing of children in educational institutions—or whether the programme should be consid-ered a right of children from disadvantaged backgrounds and not evaluated at all for impact. Impact evaluations pursue narrower evaluation questions, and are therefore often accused of taking on the lens of those in positions of power rather than the target groups and people subject to policy inter-ventions. Giving those at the receiving end of policies a say in designing (and even conducting) evaluations will likely lead to an emphasis on differ-ent aspects and on different evaluation criteria. Evaluating policies along a range of different criteria will often not result in a clear-cut answer to the 'what works' question, because there might be trade-offs between the criteria.

6.3.4 What to do with evaluations

In an ideal world, evaluations should inform policy learning. The data, in-formation, and evidence generated by evaluations should be used to adapt policies, reinforce elements that have worked, correct weaknesses, and, if called for, terminate programmes that are not effective. A widespread complaint in the world of policy analysis is that evaluations, and re-search and evidence more widely, are not properly used. As a result, it is frequently recommended that evaluations should be made mandatory and that transparency about the use of results (i.e. through reporting requirements, etc.) should be established. Making evaluations mandatory will not necessarily lead to either proper use of the results or formal compliance with such requirements without a change in the way evaluations and other sources of knowledge are used, as we discuss later in section 6.5.

However, as we have seen earlier, evaluations do not speak for themselves. Their initial framing is influenced by political interests and stakeholder preferences, as is the way they are used. Indeed, evaluation studies are only one input into the evaluation and development of policies, and making consequences automatic—for example, that a negative evaluation leads to the termination of a programme—would lead to the politicization of the whole evaluation process. In other words, evaluation results cannot be completely binding given the uncertainties, selectivity, and biases they inevitably come with. Full transparency regarding evaluation studies and results could also intensify, rather than rising above, the political debate surrounding the process itself. At the same time, accountability regarding the use of evaluations should be established to avoid gross misconduct. This includes establishing quality and transparency standards for evaluations, to prevent superstructure actors from cherry-picking results from a study without the risk that external scrutiny proves them wrong.

From the perspective of those seeking to influence policy using the results of evaluations, which could include both actors from the governmental policy-making engine room and NGOs such as advocacy groups, the communication of findings of an evaluation study is important. Relevant aspects include the building of credibility early on through transparency of evaluation criteria, design choices, and methods (Heider 2016). The development of a communication strategy targeting the right audience for the issue at hand is another important aspect, as is the communication (and visualization) of findings in an accessible way.

Evaluation studies are frequently used for agenda-setting purposes (see Chapter 3). If policy-makers are unhappy with policies or programmes, they might commission an evaluation in order to find legitimate arguments to terminate the policy. In other cases, evaluation studies are used to weed out badly performing parts of the public sector, or funding is tied to the results of evaluation studies. In the UK, the Research Excellence Framework (REF) is used to assess the research output of universities. As a result, university departments can be ranked by research quality, and the results are used for the allocation of research funding (REF n.d.).

Table 6.1 summarizes the challenges for designing evaluation studies and the related tensions and dilemmas.

Table 6.1 Evaluation design challenges

	QUESTION	TENSIONS / DILEMMAS
What to evaluate	Which policies, programmes, or aspects should be subject to a separate evaluation study?	Evaluation as standard obligation vs. selective evaluations of important policies
How to evaluate	Should more descriptive process and implementation evaluations or impact evaluations using experimental methods or regression analysis be used?	Precision vs. breadth and utilization of evaluations
Who should evaluate	Who is in charge of triggering, commissioning, and design of an evaluation?	Independent evaluators with high distance from interested parties (in government) vs. buy-in and feedback of policy-makers and stakeholders
What to do with evaluations	Should the utilization of evaluation results be mandatory?	Mandatory evaluations could lead to formal compliance but not deep engagement with evaluation results; politicization of evaluation process as a risk

6.4 Evaluation, Control, and Accountability

Evaluation is mostly discussed in relation to the policy under consideration. Its aim is to learn from experience to improve the design and implementation of a policy. But policies are designed and implemented by actors and organizations, and holding them accountable for the consequences of their work is a concern closely linked to the evaluation goal.

In essence, accountability is about who is responsible for results, whether good or bad. More specifically, the question of accountability refers to institutionalized processes to hold public agencies and officeholders responsible, i.e. to demand a report and explanation of conduct; this account giving is assessed in an accountability forum that delivers a verdict about conduct, including sanctions in case of misconduct (Bovens 2005). Accountability is not at all new, and it is traditionally focused on the conduct of government agencies and officeholders (e.g. whether public funds have been used properly). But *performance accountability* has gained relevance with the rise of the so-called New Public Management (cf. Hood 1991) since the 1980s, first in some Western countries (UK, US, New Zealand) and then globally.

An emphasis on performance management and target systems seeks to apply the logic of evidence-based, rational policy-making to the way the superstructure and the engine room are connected (see also Chapter 5 on 'vertical follow-through' in policy implementation). Here we focus on the accountability dimension of that relationship. According to the most basic model of performance accountability, the superstructure actors and institutions set the targets as the first step. Targets are aims and objectives transposed into numerical targets, which are often expressed as some form of indicator. For example, indicators for educational improvements are typically the results of some form of standardized test in key subject areas, such as reading and maths, as in the PISA example. In an ideal scenario, the targets are combined with the allocation of resources for service delivery organizations that are sufficient to achieve them. Targets are disaggregated to the level of individual implementing organizations, e.g. schools. The accountability element is established in 'performance contracts' which run from the superstructure down to the specific implementing organization. For example, school principals will be held accountable for the achievement of specified targets, as captured in standardized tests. Performance incentives range from bonus payments to the risk of contract termination (see Barber 2007 for a discussion of such a target system from a government insider's perspective).

The reach of the performance management approach varies substantially across countries and sectors, but a range of examples can be found in areas such as education, healthcare (hospital waiting times, diagnostic group-related payment models), policing (arrest and conviction rates), prisons (break-out rates), and so on. The rationale behind performance accountability is simple (cf. van Dooren et al. 2015 for a comprehensive introduction): when clear assignment of tasks is linked to the evaluation of their achievement, and hitting or missing the target has consequences for public managers, more effort will go into achieving the targets. But this logic also has a flip side: meeting the target might be achieved in ways other than improving individual or organizational performance (this is called 'gaming') or by focusing on only some aspect of performance, at the expense of those aspects of the work that are not captured in (quantitative) performance targets.

Performance accountability is not an invention of the twenty-first century, and unintended effects have been reported before. For example, 'payment by results' was already tried in English schools in the late nineteenth century, but was phased out by the turn of the new century after having triggered enhanced cheating and manipulation on the part of teachers and school managers and a narrowing of the curriculum to subjects upon which payments were based, among other unintended results (Jabbar 2013). Employment agencies are another early example. In a classic study of bureaucracy, Peter Blau (1955) discovered that numerical targets in an employment agency resulted in a drop in the quality of the counsellors' work. Since the performance assessment focused on the number of interviews carried out by the agency's employees, they maximized this number at the expense of engagement with the job-seekers.

Since the mid-1980s, the rise of New Public Management reforms in a number of countries (with varying zeal) has seen more examples of performance management gone wrong. Research since the 2000s has shown that gaming is widespread. Examples of such distortions of target systems can be found in Western democracies and authoritarian countries alike. Kostka (2016, 58) reports a range of difficulties in the use of a target-based approach to environmental policy implementation: 'target rigidity, cyclical behaviour, poor data quality, and the absence of an independent monitoring agency have generated adverse effects and contribute to a yawning gap between regulatory goals and outcomes'.

For the UK, Hood (2006) analyses different ways performance target systems are gamed. One example is the 'ratchet effect' (Hood 2006, 516), when efforts are minimized after a target is reached in order to avoid upward adjustment of the target next year. Hood (2006) reports that negotiations between 'spending departments' and the 'treasury' (finance ministry) in the UK are shaped by the departments' interest in avoiding more ambitious targets in the following year. Other forms of gaming include more direct manipulation of reporting, for example enhancing response times of accident and emergency vehicles (Hood 2012).

Another potentially negative effect of strict adherence to performance accountability has been called 'output distortion': here the behaviour is adapted to increase chances of hitting the performance target, but in ways that defy the purpose of the task. Examples range from police officers subject to evaluation on the basis of arrest rates focusing on 'easy targets' and petty offenses, to teachers 'teaching to the test' both in terms of subjects and students (ignoring the very good and poor students). Two more examples come from healthcare: hospitals evaluated on the basis of success rates in surgery (e.g. heart surgery) will try to select the 'input' and be reluctant to accept high-risk patients. Furthermore, hospitals in the UK that reached the target of reducing waiting times tended to have higher readmission rates of patients who had received treatment and been discharged; in other words, they met the specific performance target at the apparent expense of providing quality care (Elkomy and Cookson 2020). Despite the widespread reports of unintended effects of performance management linked to accountability, its use persists. Reviewing the evidence of the effects of target systems in healthcare and education in the UK, LeGrand (2007) suggests that they can deliver some improvement of performance within a relatively short period of time, but only from relatively low levels of performance. Boswell (2018) argues that the use of performance evaluation is driven by an attempt by executive politicians to signal trust and commitment to the electorate.

What is the implication for evaluating public sector organizations? As Majone (1989) and Wilson (1989) have argued, evaluation of performance in the public sector on the basis of outcomes is only meaningful when two sets of conditions are met. The first set requires that outcomes can be meaningfully captured in the form of quantitative indicators *and* these indicators capture the major aspects of the organizations' task. Otherwise, there is the risk that important tasks that cannot be easily quantified will be disregarded. The second set requires that the process of service provision can be both consistently observed *and* clearly linked to the outcome. Wilson (1989) calls entities that meet both sets of conditions 'production' organizations and mentions the post office and tax collection agencies as examples. For all other types of organizations, performance control is more problematic. For example, when knowledge about the outputs is limited and outcomes cannot be easily measured (or attributed to the service provision activity), monitoring should be limited to the input (e.g. the quality of professionals in education). As an example of a target for input-oriented monitoring, both Wilson and Majone mention teaching, the domain that has been subject to attempts at far-reaching performance control in various countries (not least fuelled by PISA). Wilson (1989) calls organizations in which the process can be observed but not the outcome 'procedural' organizations (since the procedures can be subject to controls). Armies in peacetime are an example of procedural organizations, but they become 'craft' organizations during wartime, when procedures become inaccessible to observers but outcomes become visible.

Advances in digital technology may increase knowledge about processes and the measurability of outcomes. But these experiences with performance evaluation and control are a warning against treating any organization as if it were a factory. Input and process controls might not be considered as 'state of the art' given the push for performance accountability, but relying on these modes of control and accountability can be more or less sensible depending on the nature of the task at hand. Finland, for example, has been hugely successful in the PISA rankings (at least in the early rounds of the PISA studies). Its success might have a lot to do with the level of economic development or social cohesion (Simola 2005). But it is notable that school policy in Finland does not rely on performance evaluation, standardized tests, or related tools, but puts strong emphasis on local autonomy and discretion of teachers (Kauko 2019).

6.5 Evaluation and Knowledge Utilization

The answer to the question posed by the fourth design challenge, 'What should be done with the results of evaluations?', seems straightforward: we should use them to learn about how good policies work, how effective they are, and how they can be improved. The underlying model of *knowledge utilization* has been called 'problem-solving' by Carol Weiss (1979). According to this model, the starting point is the identification and definition of a problem. As we explained in Chapter 3 when talking about agenda-setting, a problem is selected for increased attention in government (perhaps pushed by media, NGOs, or other actors), and in order to develop an appropriate policy response, policy-makers turn to research, either commissioning new studies or drawing on existing ones. This is the model that drives the main approaches to evidence-based policy-making. In this model, evaluation provides input regarding whether a particular approach is working or has worked and therefore whether to continue and adjust or adapt it.

Weiss (1979) also identified a second model of knowledge utilization that grants research a high degree of influence over policy; this is the 'knowledge-driven' model. Here, knowledge is produced independently of a policy problem, but policy-makers find ways to apply that knowledge (or technology or approach) to address their particular problem. Blockchain technology is an example: its potential for delivering public services has been promoted by advocates of the technology. For example, Allessie et al. (2019) present cases from different EU countries where this technology seems to hold promise, such as pension administration in the Netherlands or property registration and transfer in Sweden. The potential of artificial intelligence (AI) applied in public service delivery is another example (see Chapter 5 for a discussion of AI use in policy implementation).

Both models of knowledge utilization follow the script of research-driven policy-making, which raises high expectations while underestimating the role of different values (and evaluation criteria, as discussed above) and overestimating the potential of research to produce findings that need only to be 'used' rather than interpreted and adapted for policy purposes. Weiss observed several other models of knowledge utilization[2] that engage in different ways with the political dimension and the role of different stakeholders. One of these models, the 'interactive' model (which can also be traced back to the communicative model of Habermas), highlights that a range of stakeholders such as politicians, journalists, experts, and scientists engages in debates regarding the problem and solutions from their respective perspectives. All individual perspectives are limited, but they are limited in different ways, and collaborative engagement might bring about better solutions than relying on single perspectives.

However, there is no guarantee that stakeholders' interaction and their sense-making of information, knowledge, data, and research are driven by a joint problem-solving orientation. Examples of 'political' or 'tactical' use of information and knowledge (two more of Weiss's (1979) models) are hard to overlook, and they influence the full cycle of evaluation, from the decision to carry out an evaluation, its terms, and methods to the (non-)presentation of the findings (cf. Bovens et al. 2005). The terms of an evaluation study can be subject to political influence, that is, who carries the evaluation out, which evaluation question is adopted, and which methods are followed. The drafting of recommendations following from evaluation studies can selectively draw on data and information to present 'evidence' in support of a particular position (see Majone 1989, for this understanding of evidence). On the other hand, the presentation of findings—loud presentation or quiet shelving—is again a point in which political motivations and superstructure actors seek to influence the process.

---

[2] In addition to the knowledge-driven and problem-solving models, Weiss (1979) suggests the interactive, political, tactical, and enlightenment models.

Underlying these tactics are political motivations that range from avoiding blame for critical evaluations to boosting policy positions or delaying more substantive decisions on a policy that is controversial. For example, the regulation of small firearms in the US has been continuously prevented despite the high rates of arms-related deaths. This debate cannot be solved by evaluation studies or arguments. Sometimes such political stand-offs can be solved by pilot programmes. They can be used to gain political acceptance and facilitate political learning (understood as the updating of political preferences of stakeholders). For example, time-limited closures of inner-city roads for car traffic have been used to change the minds of shop owners who often resist that change out of fear of declining sales.

In short, the political tactics involved in using evaluation cannot be labelled as good or bad. While misuse of knowledge can be identified and should be named as such, the leitmotif for use of evaluations cannot be that political actors blindly follow evaluation results or just use knowledge as if this alone would lead to the best policy.

Moreover, the use of political tactics is not limited to the superstructure. Engine room actors also have material interests in programmes and will use evaluations and knowledge to defend 'their' programmes (cf. Baumgartner and Jones 2015, 1–2; Jann and Wegrich 2019). Here the competition between different government units for resources, attention, and jurisdiction are key motivations (see Chapter 2, section 2.3.4), but blame avoidance also plays an important role. As evaluation research was just beginning to take off, one of the key advocates of policy experiments Donald Campbell (1969) expressed the hope that the 'trapped administrator' who is afraid of negative evaluation can be replaced by the 'experimental evaluator' who embraces failure as part of a learning process. This sentiment resonates in the debates of the 2010s which call for a new failure-tolerant culture in the public sector: so-called public sector innovation labs have been set up as 'safe spaces' to allow for experimentation and risk-taking innovations (McGann et al. 2018). The extent to which these efforts will result in higher failure tolerance is, however, still an open question (cf. Timeus and Gascó 2018 for a case study of Barcelona).

What can we learn from this discussion of knowledge utilization models? The problem-solving and knowledge-driven models are part of the reality of policy evaluation and knowledge utilization, but their role is overestimated, and the complications involved in following either model are underestimated. The interactive model that involves a range of stakeholders sounds like a more promising leitmotif, and it is in line with the diagnosis this chapter started with, i.e. that no evaluation study alone can resolve disagreements between different stakeholders with different values and stakes in the game. As Majone (1989) emphasizes, deliberation between stakeholders about evaluation criteria can however help to clarify positions and identify common ground. Evaluations always come with a bias in terms of the criteria applied and methods used, their framing, and other aspects. However, they can be carried out in an unbiased and transparent way, and hence can and should provide an input to debates between stakeholders about evaluation.

This calls for multiple, even competing evaluations, or at least multiple criteria and perspectives in evaluations. While one cannot carry out multiple evaluations for every policy (or even a single evaluation for every policy), the underlying logic is key: competing perspectives must have a voice in evaluations of important and complex policies. How to avoid undue politicization of evaluations is another thorny issue. Formal provisions, such as transparency rules and publication requirements, can be gamed or circumvented. While not denying that such regulations can have positive effects, looking at the type of actors and stakeholders represented in the engine room that shapes policy evaluations in a given field seems to be as or more important.

The debate about knowledge utilization focuses mainly on how specific studies, data, or evidence are used (or not) in policy-making. But policy research can be very influential in an indirect way, as the enlightenment model in Weiss's typology shows. In the enlightenment model, concepts and theories diffuse from the field of research to the policy world. Instead of single studies, the generalizations and conceptualizations evolving from a number of studies lead to concepts that can influence policy in a very powerful way. Examples include regulatory enforcement (the enforcement pyramid; see Chapter 5) and policy design (nudges and behavioural insights; see Chapter 4). For policy-makers, engaging with such concepts is an important part of the framing of policy initiatives, discussed in Chapter 3 on how to set the agenda.

6.6 How to Evaluate

Policy evaluation seeks to contribute to the improvement of public policies through the production of knowledge and information about 'what works'. In doing so, most of the debate has focused on the production side of knowledge, i.e. how to produce precise impact evaluations when the policy intervention is usually only one of various factors shaping the outcome. On the utilization side, the tools-oriented branch of policy analysis has pushed for smartening up the engine room of policy-making for better use of evidence and evaluation. But since the invention of evaluation research as a branch of policy analysis, we have learnt time and again that evaluations of important policies are integral to the political process, and the political dimension is reflected in the diverging criteria that different stakeholders use to evaluate policies. The problem and challenge for policy analysis is that research results are indeed often inconclusive, open to alternative interpretations, and limited.

Evidence-based policy-making has overstated its case, but at the same time 'anything goes' and the denial of facts and findings further undermines problem-solving capacity. The second decade of the twenty-first century saw increasing contestation of knowledge and the rejection of science by some parts of society, a trend associated with the development of 'echo chambers' in social media and political polarization. The RAND Corporation introduced the term 'truth decay' to capture the trend of 'increasing disagreement about facts and analytical interpretations of facts and data' and 'a blurring of the line between opinion and fact' (Kavanagh and Rich 2018). But even before this trend was recognized, knowledge has been contested and the credibility of research findings undermined, as famously captured in the case of tobacco and environmental hazards in the book *Merchants of Doubt* (Oreskes and Conway 2010) and the 2014 documentary film inspired by it.

Finding the best way to create knowledge through evaluation and to use that knowledge well also requires finding a middle path between technocratic exaggeration about the role of evidence on the one hand and its undue politicization and manipulation on the other. Given the limitations of any kind of research, this is a difficult task.

So, what can we recommend?

- First, the ambiguities of programmes and disagreements about evaluation criteria cannot be resolved by improved measurement and methods, nor even by running experiments. However, as Majone (1989, 168) points out, these ambiguities 'can be represented and clarified by debate and mutual persuasion'.
- Second, that does not mean that objective analysis is not possible or useful. For the evaluation of a particular policy or programme or even

organization according to a particular set of criteria, studies can be carried out in an unbiased and transparent way and are in this (limited) sense 'objective'. But the findings from evaluations should be treated as one input to the debate, not as a substitute for this debate. Evaluations and data, information, and knowledge more generally need interpretation, sense-making, and argumentation. Data or findings do not speak for themselves.

- Third, the plurality of perspectives from different stakeholders should not be seen as a problem or limitation for evaluating policies in a useful way. Instead, diverse evaluation criteria should be seen as a way to tap into, engage with, and address underlying conflicts. As Majone (1989, 169) said, '[d]ebate among advocates of different criteria is often useful in reaching agreement and permits a more sophisticated understanding of public policy than is possible from a single perspective'. His point is in line with Weiss's interactive model of knowledge utilization. In some instances, multiple evaluations from different perspectives should be considered. A potential mismatch between evaluation focus and stakeholder perspectives should be on the radar of policymakers—a narrowly defined programme evaluation that focuses on goal achievement and administrative control while ignoring the programme's responsiveness to the values of different stakeholders with legitimate interests would not be helpful for problem-solving.

- Impact evaluation should not be considered the only valuable type of evaluation; the design of an evaluation should be adapted to the task at hand and the type of programme or organization evaluated. Process evaluations can be as valuable or more so than 'hard-nosed' impact evaluations. Policy teams should have available networks of experts able to carry out different types of evaluation studies.

PART III

CAPACITIES

Understanding Capacity

Capacity is the ability to carry out decisions (Skocpol and Finegold 1982, 260). It includes administrative capacity, but also the role of civil society, the organization of the business community, and the ability to coordinate with other actors, as well as the institutions that govern the political process itself. In order to make decisions and policies effective, many actors have to cooperate, coordinate, and share resources. Many potentially effective policy tools cannot be implemented because of a lack of state and administrative capacity (Lodge and Wegrich 2014a, 2014b). If administrative capacity is lacking, policy-makers have to mobilize other sources of support from the private business sector or civil society. Capacity can vary between policy problems, policy fields, and regions. Being aware of and compensating for limitations in capacity is essential for effective policy-making.

Consider, for instance, a commitment by the government to gender equality. Since the Women's Conference of the United Nations (UN) in Beijing in 1995, gender equality has officially been on the UN's agenda. Progress towards gender equality has however been painfully slow. In 2015, the Economic and Social Council of the UN adopted a political declaration on the occasion of the twentieth anniversary of the Fourth World Conference on Women, in which it expressed its concern that no country has fully

achieved equality and empowerment for women and girls and that significant levels of inequality between women and men and girls and boys persist
globally (UN Economic and Social Council 2015).

The slow progress towards gender equality highlights the problem of
capacity. Governments can only indirectly improve women's position in
labour markets by providing childcare, anti-discrimination legislation, and
support for women in the workplace. Very often, the division of labour
within families and traditional gender roles prevent women from participating fully in the labour market. Moreover, many employers believe that
women are less committed to their careers because of childcare responsibilities. Traditional values in society cannot be challenged by legislative
decrees alone.

For governments to address gender inequality effectively, they have to
employ resources such as public funding for childcare and high-quality
schools. The division of labour within families becomes part of the government agenda. This has many implications, with regard to social spending
on early childhood care, but also social protection schemes such as social
assistance and pensions.

Even if central governments are committed to the goal of achieving gender equality and have signed international conventions, it does not mean
that they are in a position to deliver. For instance, to the extent that gender equality depends on universal childcare for preschool children, this
is often the responsibility of subnational governments—either regions or
local authorities. How can the federal or national government nudge or
push lower-level governments to invest in childcare if they cannot command them to do so? They have to give incentives, and often bargain
over funds with local governments, in order to make the necessary investments in the public sector. Alternatively, national governments can
promote private sector childcare facilities and get employers on board to
install company-based childcare.

Moreover, changing employers' and men's attitudes towards women in
the workplace requires additional support by key actors in the business
community. Governments by themselves cannot single-handedly address
discrimination in the workplace, even if they put a strict regulatory framework in place. Employers and workers themselves have to buy into the
gender equality agenda. If governments can bring industry associations
and trade unions on board to pursue gender equality, the effectiveness of
government policies can be massively improved.

Finally, governments need to get approval and support for their policies from women themselves. Traditional roles of women in families and labour markets might be deeply engrained in cultural norms and belief systems. The capacity of governments therefore also includes the ability to engage in long-term institutional changes by reinterpreting existing norms in new and modern ways. With a modernization of gender norms among families, men and women, and the business community, a new institutional frame with regard to women in the workplace—and working mothers in particular—might emerge which can underpin new policies vis-à-vis childcare but also vis-à-vis the gender pay gap. Today, in many countries, we still find that professions that are dominated by women pay less than professions where the majority of employees are male. These disparities are rooted in outdated normative orientations of many (mainly male) policy actors, who judge that men have to provide for families while women provide the family's secondary income.

In this third part of the book, we engage with capacity in three chapters. Chapter 7 covers the role of stakeholders and actors in public policy. It analyses the different kinds of potential stakeholders and the capacity of the stakeholders themselves to become part of policy-making even beyond advocacy and agenda-setting. It shows that stakeholders play important roles in the policy process, both providing information on policy issues and taking on tasks themselves. The more organized stakeholders are, the more reliable they tend to be in the policy process and the more productive the relationship with policy-makers can be.

Chapter 8 deals with the necessity and ability of policy-makers to coordinate across different levels and national and other borders. Crossboundary coordination has become increasingly important, as many policy problems create externalities for other levels within a country or across countries. We identify different kinds of interdependencies and ways to address them. Effective solutions, in other words, need to be able to ensure that policies do not counteract but complement each other. We highlight that policy-makers can rarely rely on hierarchical decision-making power; increasingly, decisions must be reached in horizontal bargaining settings with many different actors.

Chapter 9 deals with the role of institutions. We discuss the importance of formal political institutions for decision-making processes. In addition, we address the role of incremental institutional change and the role of norm change and norm reinterpretation for policy-making. While institutions might change in moments of fundamental transformation, it is much more likely that gradual adjustment occurs over time. We talk about the effects of path dependence and how to overcome them. Finally, the chapter covers institution-building as an important part of policy-making, in particular (but not only) in developing countries. We propose ways of dealing with 'naïve institutionalism' (Roberts 2010) and offer some guidance on how to achieve meaningful progress towards institution-building.

Finally, in Chapter 10 we bring the different aspects of the preceding chapters together. Starting with our core aim to contribute to problem-solving, we show how to move from policy design to interactive policy analysis as a first step towards a better understanding of policy-making. We apply these insights to two areas. First, the role of evidence in evidence-based policy-making: here we discuss how the notion of evidence must be broadened to include more institutional and actor-related information. Second, we show that this also impacts the kind of skills students of public policy must acquire and employ. Skill sets can vary between the engine room and the superstructure, but in both cases must lead to a deep understanding of the task. At the very end, we look ahead to the challenges of policy-making in the future and the way practitioners can address them.

7

How to Engage with Stakeholders

Key concepts

- Stakeholder analysis
- Collective actors
- Stakeholder consultation
- Stakeholder collaboration
- Co-production
- Stakeholder delegation
- Policy capture

While the 'public' in public policies implies decisions taken by governments, there are many other non-governmental actors in both the superstructure and the engine room. Knowing and understanding these private political actors—stakeholders—and how they interact in the policy process is a key precondition for successful public policy-making. In this chapter we discuss the role of stakeholders in the policy process and analyse the potential for effective and productive involvement of private actors. We introduce stakeholder mapping as an essential tool in policy analysis. We focus on the types of stakeholders and their organizational properties as a way to better understand their role in the policy process. Finally, we show the limits of stakeholder involvement and which red lines should be drawn in order to prevent capture of the policy process by private interests.

7.1 Getting to Know Stakeholders

Politicians and government officials are not the only ones who work on public policies. The policy space is occupied by a vast number of actors who range from individuals to lobby groups, businesses, trade unions, civil society organizations, and think tanks. Knowing who these

How to Do Public Policy. Anke Hassel and Kai Wegrich, Oxford University Press.
© Anke Hassel and Kai Wegrich (2022). DOI: 10.1093/oso/9780198747000.003.0007

actors—also known as stakeholders—are and engaging in strategic relationships with them is a key condition for successful policy formulation and implementation.

Who are stakeholders? Stakeholders are individuals, groups, or organizations in a policy field who are affected by policy decisions and therefore have an interest or stake in that policy. Stakeholders can play very different roles in policy-making: they can influence the decision-making process, they can be part of the implementation and even evaluation of a policy, they might represent those who are the target of the policy, and they might react to policy changes. They also might undertake several of those roles in combination. The relationship between policy-makers and stakeholders is crucial for policy design (Chapter 4), policy implementation (Chapter 5), and increasingly evaluation (Chapter 6).

Liaising with stakeholders requires identifying, mapping, and managing productive relationships. The aim is primarily to optimize policy choices by taking into account stakeholders' concerns and the best available information about policy issues as well as to maximize societal support for policy change. In addition, stakeholders can perform public policy tasks themselves by participating in the design, implementation, or evaluation of policies.

Research on stakeholder management in public policy is not well developed. While stakeholder analysis is prominent in the business literature and has become a standard tool in business ethics, it has received only scant recognition in public policy with two exceptions. First, public management literature and project management toolboxes contain exercises in stakeholder analysis intended to build winning coalitions of stakeholders (Bryson 2003). Such exercises are based on the assumption that detailed knowledge of stakeholder preferences, power, and influence can improve decision-making in public (and private and non-profit) sector management (Nutt 2002). Second, international organizations such as the World Bank and the World Health Organization as well as development agencies advise their staff to engage in stakeholder analysis in contexts where agency staff come in as external actors and have to assess the situation in a policy field quickly (Schmeer 1999; World Bank 2004; USAID online). They aim to identify key actors who are powerful enough to promote or prevent policy decisions in order to address their concerns early on. Relationships with such actors often prove to be valuable resources.

In this chapter, we present the toolbox of stakeholder mapping and analysis. We introduce three key concepts: stakeholder analysis, a pyramid of stakeholder relations, and engagement with stakeholders. We advise policy-makers to establish strategic relationships with stakeholders and use their organizational capacities in order to formulate and implement policies more effectively. Stakeholder analysis involving collection of information about stakeholders' preferences and power is just one element among others. We also introduce a number of suggestions on how to engage with stakeholders interactively, such as consultation, collaboration, and delegation. But first we examine the role of stakeholders in the public policy superstructure and engine room.

7.2 The Role of Stakeholders in the Superstructure and Engine Room

In modern democracies, stakeholder engagement is part of the daily practice of policy-making both in the superstructure and in the engine room. In the superstructure, stakeholders aim to exert power over important policy decisions via lobbying, financing of election campaigns, or active agenda-setting (Baumgartner et al. 2009; Grossmann 2012; Bouwen 2004). Policy decisions on energy, transport, and health are never taken without the input of key stakeholders in the various business or non-profit communities affected. Many government ministries and agencies have outreach units for liaising with stakeholders as early warning systems for responses to policy changes. And, of course, legislators and their staff leave their doors open for their constituents and other stakeholders to have their say. Business groups invest large amounts of money in lobby organizations to ensure that policy decisions are in their interests. Other stakeholders, such as non-governmental organizations (NGOs) and labour and other interest groups, are also active in the superstructure. They focus on swaying public opinion and obtaining electoral promises to influence decision-makers regarding their constituencies and concerns. Different interest groups also form 'lobbying coalitions' with each other to enhance their success in influencing decisions (Klüver 2013).

Interest group influence on policy decisions in the superstructure is a common phenomenon and a key topic of political science. It is established in political science research that interest groups' influence is biased towards those with stronger financial and political resources (Schattschneider 1960; Schlozman et al. 2012). How and to what extent lobby and other advocacy groups affect decision-making depends on how they can impact the supply of information, mobilize citizen support, and represent the market power of lobbying coalitions (Halpin and Jordan 2012; Halpin 2014; Klüver 2013). Decision-makers are frequently put under pressure by such groups to take their interests into account when designing policies. The standard image of the work of lobby groups is behind-closed-doors meetings with parliamentarians and administrative staff to explain the lobbyists' policy goals and their potential power and influence to achieve these policy goals. However, the impact of lobby and other interest groups as stakeholders goes beyond the immediate effect on decision-making.

In the superstructure, stakeholder involvement usually results in either support for or opposition to key decisions by politicians. Their presence influences how policy fields are structured and the general approach towards their regulation. Stakeholder influence can be forced onto policy-makers by stakeholders who can pressure governments. Private sector companies, for example, can threaten to relocate or cut jobs if governments either prevent or actively pursue a policy. For instance, in September 2020 the social media and tech giant Facebook threatened to close down user accounts in EU member states if the EU pursued further regulation to ban sharing the data of European citizens with the US (Hern 2020). In February 2021, as a response to proposed legislation forcing platforms to pay publishers for linking to their content, Facebook also briefly banned Australian news organizations from posting on the platform and blocked users from sharing news from them (Paul 2021).

The role and influence of stakeholders can therefore severely limit policy-makers' room for manoeuvre. Even in areas where the government has a clear prerogative to make policy decisions, other stakeholders can heavily influence those decisions. In defence policy, for instance, governments are often dependent on contractors who produce military equipment and provide military services to such an extent that the defence ministry has limited control over key strategic decisions, such as prioritizing one military option (such as the air force) over others (such as the navy) (Adams 1981).

The interaction and long-standing relations with stakeholders also shape the general approach towards public service delivery. Take the case of childcare provision. On one hand, governments can keep childcare provision completely in the public domain by tasking local authorities with the running of daycare (Yerkes and Javornik 2019). This is the Scandinavian model. In many other continental European countries, on the other hand, childcare provision is very often facilitated and financed by the government but actually provided by private partners: welfare associations, churches, or non-profit and even for-profit organizations. Here the government provides the framework and financing, but private actors implement the provision. In many English-speaking countries, non-school childcare is completely in the private realm. Governments run some programmes, like Head Start in the United States (described in Chapter 6), but hardly get involved at all in comprehensive provision of childcare.

These models follow different philosophies of what the task of governments is and how public policies are best implemented. The relationships with stakeholders such as experts on education, private childcare providers, and family advice organizations vary considerably in these three settings. Where governments provide the service, stakeholders concentrate on lobbying the government over the quality and price of the service delivered (Gingrich 2011). Where governments contract out most services but still pay for them with taxpayers' money, stakeholders aim to influence the terms and conditions of the commissioning and put pressure on social spending for the service. In the case of private childcare services, stakeholders might seek tax allowances as an indirect subsidy, and families might push employers to facilitate childcare. In each of these cases, different types of stakeholder, be they family organizations, non-profit service providers, for-profit childcare providers, or consumer organizations, have different stakes in and influence over policy-making (Svallfors and Tyllström 2019).

The fundamental nature of these policies is thereby set in the superstructure and underpinned by theories and assumptions about the responsibility for childcare in the local community and by the national or local government. Once these basic structures have been set up, the engine room provides the policy space in which actors from the superstructure and engine room alike discuss the regulation of public and private childcare, the facilities, health and safety considerations, and so on (see Figure 7.1).

Stakeholder management in the engine room concerns mainly incremental adjustments to policy change, policy implementation, and service delivery. Many policies and public sector projects are carried out either by private actors directly or with the collaboration of private actors. Public sector agencies frequently commission private actors to conduct transport planning or the assessment of a biodiversity strategy. They also consult widely on policy concerns in order to pre-empt opposition to policy change or facilitate policy implementation. Here government officials are tasked with constant liaising with the most important stakeholders within a given

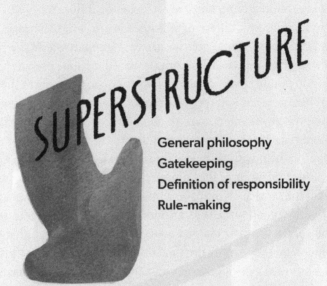

General philosophy
Gatekeeping
Definition of responsibility
Rule-making

Policy expertise
Delivery/subcontracting
Policy design

Fig. 7.1 Role of stakeholders in the superstructure and engine room

policy field. Knowledge about the power relationship between public and private actors and the expertise and capacity each brings is crucial for establishing a well-maintained stakeholder relationship. But stakeholders also play an important role in providing input to policy design in the form of information (e.g. concerning the feasibility of a policy) and also as demand and support for policy initiatives.

Stakeholder group composition and modes of collaboration vary by policy field and policy issue. Some policy fields are highly controlled by government with typically little room for other actors (e.g. secret service, policing, espionage), while others are more open and fluid with a multitude of different actors from the private sector and civil society (e.g. health, education, but also transport and energy). Superstructure decisions shape the room for stakeholders in policy fields, serving as gatekeepers for the policy field overall.

The scope of these stakeholders' involvement in public policies primarily varies with the general philosophy regarding the size and mandate of government per se. It is subject to trends and changes over time. During the twentieth century, both what is expected of governments and their size have continuously increased. Growing government responsibility has resulted in more regulation and more intense cooperation between the public and private sectors. Government approaches vis-à-vis the private sector and private sector involvement have shifted generally, from a strong emphasis on government prerogatives in the immediate post-war period until the 1970s, to a more private sector orientation from the 1980s onwards. Naturally, this has implications for who is considered a proper stakeholder and who has influence at the superstructure or engine room level at any given time point.

7.3 Stakeholder Analysis

Stakeholder analysis is an important task in the formulation of public policy. It has the primary goal of identifying the relevant actors of a policy field with regard to their interest in the issue at stake and their capacity to influence the decision or each other. Stakeholder analysis aims to assess with whom policy-makers can work, who can provide input or join in design or implementation, and who might work against a proposed policy. This information is extremely useful not only in a policy's inception phase but also throughout the entire policy process.

Stakeholders can range from individuals such as investors, business owners, workers, or neighbours, to organizations such as business associations or NGOs, to large movements without clear structures such as anti-corruption demonstrations or the Black Lives Matter movement. They might include the nominally powerless (often but not always the target population) as well as politically dominant actors.

7.3.1 Identify potential stakeholders

To illustrate how a stakeholder analysis might work, let's take a policy field like workplace health and safety and fire standards regulation. Though a rather narrow, well-established policy field in most wealthy countries, it is not so in others. In Bangladesh, for example, tragedy has prompted the Bangladeshi government to consider improving and enforcing health and safety regulations in the textile industry (see Box 7.1). At the outset of efforts to do so, a stakeholder analysis would start with a list of those actually or potentially affected by such a policy (see Table 7.1).

Box 7.1 The Bangladesh Accord

On 24 April 2013 a factory building in Dhaka, Bangladesh, collapsed, killing more than 1,100 people. The factory produced garments for the global textile market, primarily for low-cost fashion retailers. The reaction to the disaster was a global outcry. The fire and building safety standards in factories in Bangladesh had been under scrutiny for many years, and private regulation and inspection had long been seen as unsatisfactory.

Given the high level of interest by the wider public, the German Ministry for International Development sponsored a meeting of retailers and non-governmental organizations (NGOs) in early May 2013 in order to develop a joint agreement. Major retailers and apparel producers covering more than 1,000 Bangladeshi garment factories signed up to the agreement, which was forged by the IndustriALL Global Union and the UNI Global Union in alliance with leading NGOs, such as the Clean Clothes Campaign and the Worker Rights Consortium (Greenhouse 2013). The Accord requires regular building inspections and better enforcement of fire and safety standards as well as payment of compensation by the retailers to ensure adequate building safety, estimated to amount to up to USD 500,000 per factory. The International Labour Organization (ILO) and the government of Bangladesh were to participate in monitoring.

The 2013 Accord was a milestone for identification and remediation of hazard and safety issues in Bangladesh (Bangladesh Accord 2013). In the aftermath engineers inspected more than 2,000 ready-made garment factories and found more than 150,000 safety hazards. Moreover, companies committed to a Safety Training Program initiative to train workers in textile companies in workplace safety.

A follow-up agreement was signed in June 2017. This so-called Transition Key Accord consolidated the progress that was achieved thus far and provides for the disclosure of inspection reports and corrective action plans (Bangladesh Accord 2017). Moreover, it gives workers the right to refuse unsafe work. In June 2020, the Ready-Made Garments Sustainability Council (RSC) was set up as a permanent safety monitoring and compliance body in the garment sector in Bangladesh. Additional sources: Ashwin et al 2020; USAID 2016; Greenhouse 2013; Bangladesh Accord 2018.

Table 7.1 Stakeholder analysis in the Bangladesh Accord

SUPERSTRUCTURE	ENGINE ROOM
○ Big textile companies in Bangladesh	○ Government bureaucrats in ministries and parliament
○ Textile trade union leaders	○ Textile companies Local and regional administrations
○ Key labour representatives	○ Technical experts on planning permission and compensation claims
○ Insurance and re-insurance companies handling fire insurance	○ Law firms
○ Local communities and regions where textile firms exist	○ Architects
○ Investors	○ Community of scientists dealing with health and safety and building regulations
○ Major international retail companies	○ Local employees and labour unions of textile companies (and their families and dependants)
○ Minister of Labour and Social Affairs	
○ Minister for Construction and Housing	

Not everyone who works in the policy field or deals with the policy is included in the stakeholder analysis. The media, for instance, frequently express a position on the policy field, especially when a tragedy occurs, but generally would not be seen as a stakeholder with their own interest. However, in some countries media organizations have taken active positions on certain policy issues and run their own campaigns. For instance, in the UK, some media outlets of Rupert Murdoch's News Corporation engaged directly in the ultimately successful campaign to leave the European Union by openly supporting Vote Leave (Gavin 2018). They would be included as a powerful actor in a stakeholder analysis on that topic. Similarly, the legal system likely has to deal with the policy, and judges might have clear views on the suitability of a policy. As part of the independent judiciary, however, courts and judges are not necessarily part of a stakeholder analysis. At the same time, policy analysts would pay attention to the way in which the media portrays the issue as well as the legal discourse around the policy. They would in particular monitor the access of stakeholders to the media and the legal system as instruments that enhance their power position.

Other groups who are not included in stakeholder analysis are consumers, taxpayers, and the general electorate. These groups are too large and undefined, until they are organized in consumer protection groups, taxpayer alliances, or special issue pressure groups.

7.3.2 Assess stakeholder power and interest

In a second step, the stakeholders will be sorted according to various policy dimensions and their preferences regarding the proposed policy. In the case of the garment industry in Bangladesh, and more specifically the field of health and safety and building regulations and those relating to places where export goods are produced, we could think of the following dimensions:

- Export-based development strategy
- World market prices for textiles and competition with other producers
- Public health and occupational hazards
- Environmental considerations
- Employment
- Investment
- Tax revenue
- Regional and local development

Table 7.2 Stakeholder power and interest

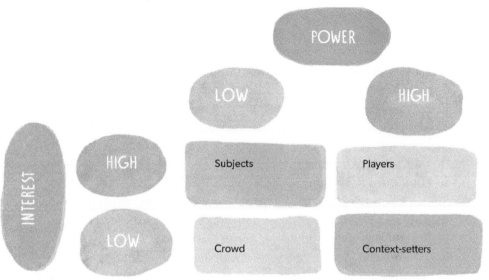

Source: Based on Eden and Ackermann (1998, 122). Reprinted with permission. © SAGE Publications Ltd Books.

- Infrastructure
- Architectural and landscape considerations.

At this point, the importance of the policy dimension for each of the stakeholders is identified and categorized. Labour groups are obviously most concerned with health and safety issues as well as employment impact, while governments are likely to seek to preserve the export-led growth model. This looks relatively straightforward, but gets more complicated as it might vary in different regions and local communities.

Stakeholders might also be split among themselves on some of these dimensions. While some textile factory employees and their labour unions are for obvious reasons worried about their own health and safety, others might prioritize their concern about the risk of losing their jobs over their own health. To estimate which concern outweighs the other is not an easy exercise. In order to assess stakeholder preferences, analysts can use interviews, surveys, or stakeholder meetings.

Using the power-versus-interest grid advanced by Eden and Ackermann (1998, 122) and refined by Bryson (2003), a policy analyst would then proceed to categorize stakeholders according to the extent of their interest and power (see Figure 7.2). Thus, stakeholders can be grouped as key 'players' who have both high power and strong interest in the policy field (e.g. big garment factories in Bangladesh), as 'subjects' who have high interest but little power (e.g. scientists working on health and safety in global supply chains, local labour unions, local administration, local employees), and as 'context-setters' who have significant power but little interest (e.g. other investors, government bureaucrats).

Using this scheme, one can assess to what extent various stakeholders might be able to influence or control each other. For instance, local communities are under the influence of higher political administrations and the federal or national government and can be swayed in one direction or another by other means. Local communities can be directed or paid off by higher level government to support their policies, even if they are not supportive at the outset. Also, advocacy organizations can influence the debate by using other actors who are not initially stakeholders. For example, they can pressure international donors in Bangladesh to support their cause in other arenas or use the courts and judges in order to pre-empt certain policies.

As noted earlier, assessing the importance of the issues for individual stakeholders is an important but difficult exercise. In the superstructure, a change in policy usually engenders a political struggle. When engaging in the struggle, stakeholders have to overstate their concern and the importance of the policy in order to attract attention and support for their position (see Chapter 3). How strongly the populace of a local community feels about the regulation of health and safety in textile factories is very hard to assess. Local policy-makers have to juggle such regulations' impact on employment, public finances, and the local infrastructure. At the same time, a town with a strong manufacturing base tends to have more opportunities than other towns. For the analyst, it is therefore very hard to surmise what local politicians' position on this is likely to be. Local communities can even be split on the issue, as only some groups will benefit from additional employment, while others might worry about rising costs of real estate and might lose their small businesses.

Ultimately, stakeholder analysis will identify how various actors are likely to respond to a change in policy. It can therefore be used to strategically develop consensus between different actors in decision-making processes and anticipate opposition to change. Far-sighted policy analysts will base their judgement of the political power necessary to launch change processes on a sound understanding of the preferences and roles of key stakeholders in the policy field.

7.3.3 Focus first on collective actors

When assessing the stakeholder scene, the policy analyst will likely first focus on *collective actors* rather than individual ones (though the latter can sometimes also have a significant impact). For collective actors in particular, their organizational properties, including their purposes and the resources available to them, are as important as their power and interest. As worthy as all stakeholders might be, some collective actors are better suited than others to strategic interaction.

Fritz Scharpf (1997) introduced a helpful classification of different types of collective actors who could be considered stakeholders or partners, according to their collective or particular purposes and resources (see Table 7.3).

Table 7.3 Types of collective actors

Source: Based on Scharpf 1997, 55. Copyright © 1997 Reproduced by permission of Taylor & Francis Group, LLC, a division of Informa plc.

Stakeholders who strive for a collective purpose tend to be politically motivated. These include protest movements, NGOs, business and labour associations, and political pressure groups. Their motives are generally oriented to political and societal goals and not to immediate personal gain. The motivation is important insofar as they generally act on behalf of others, be it society at large, workers, communities, or future generations. They therefore need to appeal to a wider constituency to increase their advantage, in particular for their members.

Such collective actors can be divided into two groups according to their organizational structure: movements and associations. Movements and protest groups are able to organize activities such as demonstrations and public actions, but cannot enter into binding negotiations or formal contracts with policy-makers, as they have no mechanisms for delegating power apart from charismatic leaders. As these leaders only have spontaneous support, policy-makers would not likely engage with them on a long-term basis. Movements can therefore exert temporary pressure, but no lasting relations can be developed. It is for instance difficult to liaise with groups such as the *gilets jaunes*, Fridays for Future, or Extinction Rebellion activists, as their structure is fluid. In contrast, associations have a formal structure, including mechanisms for electing or appointing leaders who can speak and act on behalf of their constituencies. They are able to engage in long-term relations with other policy-makers, and are generally partners in policy fields, as long as they do not get so incorporated into the structure that they lose their independence. As they usually rely on memberships and/or donations, they also have collective resources and are more professional, whereas movements can generally only count on mainly irregular or temporary resources.

Stakeholders who pursue individual and private concerns as collective actors can take the form of either clubs or coalitions. Clubs are organizational forms where resources are shared among members and the benefits return mainly to the individual members. Some lobby groups set up shared facilities, such as offices and legal representation and are clubs in the sense that the outcome of their activities is for the benefit of each individual member of the organization and not a public good per se. In Scharpf's (1997) framework, coalitions are stakeholders seeking separate gains who do not share resources with each other. Most big companies have government relations offices in capitals, to make their voices heard in the policy process. They might join coalitions to coordinate actions with others on a temporary basis, until the shared goal is met.

The dynamics of the relationship between policy-makers and stakeholders depend largely on the type of stakeholders involved, i.e. whether they are associations, clubs, movements, or coalitions. Resource-sharing presupposes a decision-making mechanism within the organization (association or club), which is again based on firm structures, organizational boundaries, and procedures. Usually, decision-making is based on voting. Associations and clubs have organizational structures where members tend to participate in goal formation through annual general meetings to decide key themes. While such structures and procedures might make associations and clubs slower to act, they also ensure that the organization as a whole is on board, thus leading to a more robust stakeholder relationship. Coalitions and movements, on the other hand, need to seek consensus on an ad hoc basis in order to act jointly. These forms of decision-making tend to be temporary and loose. In general, policy fields with a high density of highly organized stakeholders are more stable, predictable, and dependable compared to those which are characterized by few and very fluid stakeholders.

7.4 A Pyramid of Stakeholder Relations

Stakeholder analysis is only the first preparatory step toward strategic interaction between policy-makers and stakeholders. Understanding the nature of the policy field and the composition of stakeholders is the precondition for strategic interaction, but that interaction typically goes much further. In this section we introduce four types of stakeholder interaction which take place in the policy world. They range from consultation to collaboration, co-production, and delegation. The different types of interaction range from easy and ad hoc, such as consultation, to more resource-intensive and long-term (delegation). One could imagine a pyramid illustrating the progression of interactions (Figure 7.2): the higher on the pyramid, the more long-term the relationship is.

7.4.1 Consultation

Consultation is the most common kind of stakeholder relations. It is the first step after a stakeholder analysis, or is sometimes even part of it. As noted earlier, the stakeholder analysis aims to identify both those who might be

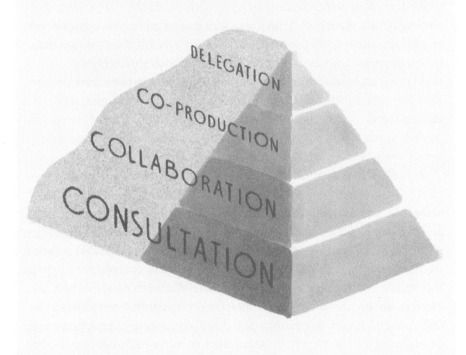

Fig. 7.2 Types of stakeholder engagement in the policy process

most supportive of change and those who might most strongly oppose it, and maps them with their potential influence on the process.

The management of policy change involves strategic communication with stakeholders, which is tailored to their position and influence. Key players with substantial power over the process should be targeted and involved in decision-making processes, while less powerful actors with low interests, the 'crowd' in Table 7.2, should at least be informed via general information campaigns. Those who are powerful but in opposition to change could be brought on board through active involvement.

The most straightforward instances of consultation with stakeholders are public infrastructure projects (Römmele and Schober 2013). As examples, one can think of a major restructuring of a local neighbourhood by way of a bypass, the building of an airport or railway station, or the closure of public libraries. Here, policy-makers may use communication and negotiations with local stakeholders to pre-empt public criticism of relocation decisions. Stakeholder participation can take the form of town hall meetings, surveys, or more elaborately organized consultation processes. Such deliberate involvement can pre-empt lawsuits against policy decisions, help smooth implementation, and build public support.

Consultation with stakeholders is also relevant for the preparation of proactive policy change. Let's take the example of digital technology at work. The diffusion of digital technology has wide-ranging implications for employment and skills. Small companies might struggle with the implementation of digital tools, and employees lack the necessary skills to use them productively. Proactive policy analysts would host consultation fora with businesses, local communities, and labour unions on the opportunities and consequences of digital technologies in order to assess support that might be needed by businesses and the education sector. These fora could be in the form of workshops, conferences, or surveys. Through consultation and participation, policy analysts could pick up the major concerns of businesses and employees, but might also come across innovative policy solutions that are already being employed.

For instance, some companies experiment with new policies providing home offices for staff, in order to cut down on commuting costs and facilitate work–life balance (in particular for working parents). Even before the COVID-19 pandemic led to unprecedented lockdowns and stay-at-home orders starting in early 2020, working from home had become a standard feature in many industries and had been particularly popular among younger workers. Mobile working has also spread, as many employees are on the road visiting clients or suppliers and spend many working hours either driving or in trains or airplanes. Mobile working and home offices have implications for employers and for public policy more broadly. Some companies have developed innovative formats for home workplaces, working time monitoring, and collaboration. Public policy issues concern the potential regulation of insurance-related issues (e.g. covering work-related accidents at home), working time monitoring, and health and safety issues (e.g. assessment of work equipment).

In order to get a handle on the policy field, policy analysts would first craft a policy agenda regarding mobile working, identifying the potential policy issues and the implications for regulation and supervision (see Chapter 3 on agenda-setting). In order to develop new policy solutions and tools, the policy analyst would organize workshops with businesses and other actors that are known for innovative solutions, in order to anticipate potential calls for reregulation of workplaces and occupational health and safety. These workshops would identify practices which can serve as examples for other firms. Policy analysts would then disseminate the results of these workshops through publications, events, or social media (video websites, web-based publications and films, interviews with experts, and the like). Moreover, they would assess the results with regard to the need for changes and adjustments in public policy. A subsequent policy paper would again be used for consultation with businesses, labour unions, and other stakeholders, in order to gather additional responses and commentaries. Finally, the government would launch a government white paper on 'Technology at Work' or 'Mobile Working'.[1]

As such consultation does not typically lead to formal agreements or contracts between policy-makers and stakeholders, it can be—as in the case of stakeholder analysis—employed with almost anyone. Street protesters can be consulted in the same way as labour unions, businesses, or experts. Consultation can be more open, and select participants only to keep out potential troublemakers and for cost purposes. This is different when it comes to collaboration, co-production, and delegation: when planning to engage in more formal cooperative relationships, policy-makers need to be aware of the organizational capacities of their partners and their internal organizational set-up. Nevertheless, such informal consultation processes

---

[1] An example for exactly this process is the Work 4.0 exercise by the German Federal Ministry for Labour and Social Affairs (Bundesministerium für Arbeit und Soziales 2017).

can lead to more intense forms of involvement, such as collaboration or co-production of policies.

In many countries, consultations are a mandatory and highly regulated aspect of policy formulation. This follows the early model of the US, where the Administrative Procedures Act of 1946 prescribes that federal agencies need to publish drafts of their proposed regulations; these draft rules need to be open for public comment during a 'notice and comment' period; and agencies need to respond to these comments in their final rule-making (Yackee 2019; Potter 2019). The EU has an elaborate system of consultation, which applies to the legislative procedure and other policy initiatives which starts with a draft from the EU Commission (see Box 7.2). Among the key challenges of such public reviews is the aggregation and weighting of different inputs from diverse stakeholders in online consultation procedures (Balla, Beck, Meehan, and Prasad 2020).

Box 7.2 Consultation processes in the EU

The European Union (EU) introduced a formalized online consultation process for civil society organizations in the early 2000s, in addition to existing consultation procedures. The European Commission (EC) defines 'consultation' as the process by which the Commission wishes to involve the external parties concerned in policy-making, prior to a decision by the College of Commissioners (European Commission 2002: 10). Consultation serves a dual purpose. First, it contributes to the improvement of the quality of policy and the involvement of stakeholders and the general public. Second, transparent and coherent consultation procedures on the part of the Commission do not only allow greater involvement of the general public, but also improve the possibilities for the legislature to scrutinize the Commission's activities (e.g. by providing summary documents of the results of the consultation) (European Commission 2002: 4). The EC promotes consultations as a tool to foster the participation of non-business groups such as environmental NGOs, consumer groups, and labour interests (Quittkat 2011; Klüver 2013; Bunea 2017), but in reality consultation responses are dominated by business groups (Beyers and Arras 2020).

The EC is in control of the consultative fora and monitors their proceedings closely. The system has closed/targeted as well as open/public consultations. Public consultations are online and similar to the 'notice and comment'

continued

Box 7.2 *continued*

---

practice of the US federal administration (Bunea 2017). Based on further consultations in 2012 and 2014, the European Commission redesigned these consultation practices and incorporated them into the Better Regulation package (May 2015) and the 'Inter-Institutional Agreement on Better Law Making' (April 2016).

Through these measures, a new approach is pursued in which stakeholders are consulted more comprehensively throughout the policy cycle and on a broader set of activities, including roadmaps, impact assessments, legislative proposals and implementing acts (Bunea 2017). In its 2021 Communication on Better Regulation, the EU Commission announced the streamlining of consultation procedures, seeking to avoid separate consultation procedures for each policy (European Commission 2021). In June 2020, the Commission revamped its 'Have Your Say' portal, encouraging 'stakeholders and citizens—including those without an in-depth knowledge of EU policy-making—to contribute to the Commission's initiatives as they take shape before and after their adoption by the Commission' (European Commission 2020b).

Contributing author: Julia Seefeld.

7.4.2 Collaboration

Collaboration with stakeholders requires a clear purpose, and organizational capacities that allow stakeholders to enter into formal relationships with policy-makers. Through such collaboration, policy-makers and stakeholders jointly address policy issues with a clear view to developing shared solutions. Policy-makers thereby invite stakeholders to actively contribute not only their opinions but also their efforts.

Think of the issues of anti-discrimination and affirmative action. Many governments are concerned about discrimination at the workplace, but also discrimination against consumers and have developed policies that not only punish discriminatory behaviour but also actively aim to prevent and reduce discrimination. Some governments have introduced legal penalties for discrimination by employers and retailers. Where these exist, those who do business have to treat all employees and customers the same, and cannot treat anyone differently on the basis of religion, race, gender, or sexual orientation, although this is sometimes in conflict with freedom of expression. High-profile court cases, for instance in the US, have signalled that the government is serious about prosecuting discriminatory behaviour (*The Economist* 2020).

In addition to enshrining anti-discrimination in the legal codes, policy-makers have actively sought to set up alliances with civil society organizations (CSOs) and businesses, in order to facilitate the implementation of anti-discrimination strategies and behaviour. Sponsors and organizers of large sports events have committed themselves to finance advertisements that carry the message of open societies against racism and discrimination. Multicultural workplaces are featured in ads by businesses, and codes of conduct of businesses and CSOs are encouraged and disseminated across societies. Businesses often engage in anti-discrimination alliances because it helps companies to recruit employees and manage diversity, but also in order to pre-empt further regulation. Governments, businesses, and CSOs thereby cooperate in the dissemination of anti-discrimination practices and participate in joint activities. In the US, for example, the Business Coalition for the Equality Act, under the umbrella of the Human Rights Campaign, is a group of leading US employers that support the Equality Act, a federal bill that would provide the same basic protections that are already afforded to workers across the country to lesbian, gay, bisexual, and transgender Americans (Human Rights Campaign, n.d.).

Similarly, youth unemployment and the transition from school to work are a topic for many governments, especially where youth unemployment is higher than adult unemployment. Therefore, governments and business communities work on better collaboration to improve this transition. Many business associations have set up networks of public schools and businesses which organize internships for career orientation of school children, host events with local companies, and work on innovation in education (Schulewirtschaft Deutschland n.d.; Business in the Community n.d.). Local businesspeople host and attend school events, facilitate technological progress in schools, and participate in job fairs for school-leavers.

These business groups are 'clubs', as they pursue self-interested goals (better recruitment opportunities). Nevertheless, they also support policies by governments to enhance recruitment and skill formation. The interests of governments (place students in jobs and keep youth unemployment down) overlap with the interest of business (recruit new workers and improve the quality of education of future workers). The networks can make the government policies of anti-discrimination and youth transition to work more effective by disseminating ideas and practical advice for implementation. Because business networks often function as monitoring devices (businesses observing each other), implementation of best practices is more likely to be enhanced.

Policy-makers can therefore nurture initiatives and networks like these by attending their events, giving out prizes, or supporting them locally or at a regional or federal level. A policy collaboration with stakeholders can create win–win situations where private resources are used to pursue a common public good.

7.4.3 Co-production of policies

Co-production, like delegation, which is discussed separately in the next section, is a form of stakeholder engagement that is long-term and depends on a number of preconditions, which are rooted in the policy field but also in the participating stakeholders. Ostrom (1996) defined co-production as a process through which inputs from individuals who are not in the same organization are transformed into goods and services. In terms of the policy process, it gives private actors a larger role than they would have through collaboration. Co-production takes place when stakeholders actively participate in the design and implementation of policies that will affect them. It has developed over decades of experience of public–private co-management of policies.[2]

An important policy field that is characterized by policy co-production in industrialized countries is the labour market. While the government sets the regulatory framework (dismissal protection, working time limits, health and safety protections, and the like), many aspects of working conditions are regulated by trade unions and employers' associations. Often called 'social partners', these two groups of stakeholders do not only set wages for a vast number of employees, but also negotiate about a whole range of other issues such as access to training, pension funds and contributions (see Chapter 2, Box 2.3), and healthcare, among others. For those covered by these agreements, they are often as binding as the labour and health and safety laws that are set by the national government. In some countries, collective agreements supersede legislation, and in other countries the government refrains from legislating in this field as it encourages

---

[2] In public management there is a similar concept of co-creation, which refers to the co-production of innovations in the public sector, such as a redesign of a public service by public officials, citizens, and other private sector actors. See Torfing et al. (2019).

the social partners to find solutions—policies—themselves. In Germany, for example, labour laws include a clause that permits companies to deviate from the law if they do so in accordance with a collective agreement. And in Scandinavia, governments have not set a statutory minimum wage, as the collective agreements are so comprehensive that everyone is covered by collective bargaining. Here we also find that unemployment insurance is not provided by the government but administered by trade unions, a policy which we will discuss in the next section on delegation.

Another example of co-production is the vocational training system in countries such as Austria, Germany, Denmark, Switzerland, and Luxembourg. School-leavers can take up apprenticeships with companies. As apprentices, young workers are paid less than a regular adult worker and follow a strict schedule of training and schooling. The apprenticeship ends with an exam that is set by the local chamber of commerce. The content of the training is regulated by federal decrees, but the formulation of those decrees is the responsibility of relevant businesses, trade unions, and chambers.[3] Public authorities and private associations—employers' and trade unions—cooperate in the planning, organization, and implementation of vocational training. The precondition for such a system to work is a tight network of employers' associations and high participation rates of companies who train apprentices; this reduces opportunities for free-riding of the system. As training involves investment of time and other resources, cost-sharing between businesses, employees, and the public authorities who monitor and supervise the training is crucial. The whole system relies on the constant and trusting cooperation of all actors involved. Everyone, in particular employers' associations and trade unions as well as vocational schools and chambers, must have the organizational capacities to enter binding agreements on content and participation. The system has been proven highly successful in facilitating the school to work transition for school-leavers, but almost impossible to introduce in other institutional settings where employers' and business associations operate under very different conditions.

In the case of the Bangladesh Accord, companies from the Global North participated in the regulation and enforcement of health and safety standards in garment factories in Bangladesh that were part of their supply

---

[3] Chambers of commerce can be private industry organizations. In continental European countries such as Germany and Austria, chambers of commerce and artisanal chambers are legally mandated organizations of local businesses which are charged with particular tasks, mainly with regard to vocational training certification.

chain. Without active co-production on the part of these retailers, the inadequacy of health and safety standards in garment factories would not have been addressed. However, the Bangladesh Accord took inspections out of the hands of government, which led to ongoing contention.

7.4.4 Delegation

The *delegation* of policy-making to private stakeholders is often rooted in the historic evolution of the policy field. In many cases, as with the regulation of internet platform companies and financial markets today, the policy starts as a private issue, often in the market or business sphere, and only becomes a public policy concern later on. Common forms of delegation can be found in the operation of unemployment insurance (see Box 7.3), in standard-setting, and in the regulation of professions, such as law, medicine, and others, but also in codes of conduct such as the German corporate governance codex (cf. Lodge and Wegrich 2012, 102–4).

Box 7.3 The Ghent system

Some European countries (the Nordic countries and Belgium) have delegated the administration of their unemployment insurance systems to trade unions (the Ghent system). For instance, in Sweden, the Ghent system is based on voluntary membership in unemployment insurance regimes, which are subsidized by state funds. Trade unions administer these funds on a sectoral basis. They are responsible for collecting membership fees and handling benefit payments. They also are heavily involved in developing policies regarding these funds. In Sweden, the Ghent system was reformed in 2007, resulting in increased membership fees and reduced benefit levels. Along with other factors, this contributed to the decline in trade union membership in Sweden (Kjellberg 2009).

In the international arena, we find private standard-setting through organizations such as the Internet Corporation for Assigned Names and Numbers (ICANN) for the regulation of the internet, or the International Organization for Standardization (ISO) for the formulation of global standards of various sorts. ICANN is a non-profit organization responsible for coordinating the maintenance and procedures of several databases related to the namespaces and numerical spaces of the internet, ensuring the network's stable and secure operation (ICANN 2019). It is part of a global multi-stakeholder community, which engages in the technical maintenance work of the central internet address pools and the Domain Name System (DNS) root zone registries as part of the Internet Assigned Numbers Authority (IANA) function contract. The global DNS is key for the operation of root name servers and therefore of the internet. ICANN manages the Internet Protocol (IP) and maintains registries of Internet Protocol identifiers (cf. Flonk et al. 2020).

The principles of operation of ICANN are to preserve the operational stability of the internet; to promote competition; to achieve broad representation of the global internet community; and to develop policies appropriate to its mission through bottom-up, consensus-based processes. The organization's role and function were initially based on a Memorandum of Understanding between the US Department of Commerce and ICANN, which handed over the management of the DNS to the non-profit organization ICANN (ICANN 1999). Given the crucial role of the internet these days, not only for everyday life but also for almost all economic activities, the delegation of the management of IPs and domains to a private entity is no small feat. Until 2016, the US had the power to withdraw this delegation of responsibility at any time and appoint a new organization instead through a contractual arrangement. In 2016, the US government gave up this contractual control (Becker 2019).

A similar sort of delegation has occurred with the founding and operation of the ISO. The ISO is a private association which was founded in 1947 in Geneva, by national standard-setting organizations which are often also non-governmental organizations and essentially national-level examples of policy delegation.[4] ISO develops industry norms for products and services, but also organizational standards. ISO norms do not have the status of decrees or legislation. Companies comply with the norms voluntarily, since they can trade and build supply chains more easily if their production processes are based on ISO norms. However, governments can declare ISO norms as legally binding by referring to them in laws and administrative decrees. In the EU, the European Committee for Standardization (CEN), the umbrella body for thirty-four standard-setting institutions in Europe, usually adopts ISO norms and disseminates them (see Box 7.4).

---

[4] Examples of standard-setting organizations are the Instituto Argentino de Normalización y Certificación (IRAM), Standards Australia, the American National Standards Institute (ANSI), and the British Standards Institution. These organizations usually have a a Memorandum of Understanding with the respective government to be recognized as the main or leading national standards body.

Box 7.4 Delegated standard-setting in Europe

CEN is one of three standardization organizations in Europe. The other two are CENELEC (European Committee for Electrotechnical Standardization) and ETSI (European Telecommunications Standards Institute). ETSI, established in 1988 by the European Conference of Postal and Telecommunications Administrations (CEPT) after the European Commission floated the idea, produces standards for ICT-enabled systems. All three are officially recognized by the European Union and by the European Free Trade Association (EFTA) as responsible for developing and defining voluntary standards at European level. The rules regarding cooperation between European standardization organizations, national standard-setting bodies, member states, and the Commission were later adopted in EU Regulation (1025/2012), which sets out the legal framework for standardization.

These are two examples of the delegation of public policy concerns to private actors. In both cases, they take place under the auspices of public authorities. The norms are reinforced by public policy whenever governments refer to the standards set by ICANN or ISO. The underlying stakeholder structures include both private and non-profit organizations and public authorities. In many cases, non-profit organizations have been contracted or recognized by governments to act as their official representatives in these structures. In the end, the lines between public and private regulation can be blurred, with private actors performing public authority functions.

Delegation also takes place in other forms of economic governance such as stock exchanges, which are still private corporations but serving an important public function, and professional associations such as the Royal Colleges of Doctors (in Canada and Australia), who regulate access to professions and training. The delegation of public policies to private actors can be a powerful and convenient tool for policy-makers, as private actors sometimes have more knowledge of the policy issue and also a keen interest in these policies. They will therefore monitor the implementation and enforcement of the policy and try to influence the process. At the same time, policy-makers risk losing influence over the policy field and becoming dependent on private actors who might develop too much control over the policy.

7.5 How to Manage Stakeholders

Overall, an organized polity with many participation points for stakeholders is better than one with no or little stakeholder engagement. Public policy depends on other, non-public actors to help make and implement policies. Government policy has to be designed, implemented, and evaluated. If policy-making were reduced to decision-making by governments and implementation by public agencies, policies would be less effective and slower to take hold. Only through cooperation with others can sensitive information be effectively shared. In other words, stakeholders are a precious resource for public policy.

On the other hand, not all stakeholders have public goods or public benefit in mind, and many are in the business of public policy with the goal of private gain. There are different competing claims about what public goals should be. Many stakeholders are rent-seekers, and therefore seek access to policy-makers in order to profit from policy that benefits their business or purpose. This can be in the field of government commissions (e.g. defence contractors) or market regulation (e.g. access to product markets), but also control over public resources for specific groups in societies (e.g. the privileges for religious organizations in many societies). For policy-makers, the task is to strike a balance that allows them to create strategic and productive relationships with stakeholders without becoming dependent on particular stakeholders, devoting too large a share of public resources to them, or being captured by an entire industry or pressure group.

In this section, we offer some examples of productive and destructive relationships with stakeholders in order to derive some lessons on how to find the right balance.

7.5.1 Disastrous stakeholder relations: capture

One of the greatest threats stakeholders pose to public policy is the capture of a policy field or policy issue in order to make financial or other private gains at the expense of others or the taxpayer.[5] The danger of *policy capture* by stakeholders is highest where the policy issue requires a high

---

[5] In extreme cases, the polity itself is captured by private interests and turns to clientelism and patronage. This is not what we discuss here. Here we assume that the polity is generally healthy (non-corrupt, non-clientelist) but that stakeholders in some policy fields have become too dominant.

level of technical expertise which might not be present within the public administration, and where the salience of the issue is high, or private power is concentrated and public interest is dispersed (Wilson 1980). Capture by stakeholders can be found in the fields of energy, infrastructure, defence, and finance, among others (OECD 2017).

A prominent example is the role of the financial services industry in the run-up to the global financial crisis that began in 2007, and its influence over the regulation of financial markets. A key feature of the regulation of financial markets after the Wall Street crash in 1929 was the separation of investment and retail banking, in order to protect high-street banking activity from the higher risk investment banking entails. In the US the 1993 Glass-Steagall legislation restricted affiliations between banks and securities trading firms.

Over the course of the 1990s, with the rise of financial services as a key sector, several legislative changes weakened the regulation, until the Gramm-Leach-Bliley Act of 1999 repealed most of it altogether. The liberalization and globalization of the financial system led to a fundamental restructuring of the industry, including the evolution of companies that became 'too big to fail': in other words, the costs associated with their bankruptcy or closure would be greater than the cost of rescuing them. Once the financial crisis hit in 2007, the US government had to bail most of them out rather than letting them fail. One response to the financial crisis was the Dodd-Frank Act of 2010, which aims to restrict securities trading by retail banks.

The repeal of Glass-Steagall was primarily pushed by the financial services industry, which has pursued close relations with successive US administrations over several decades. Personal ties became closer, and a network of experts arose which comprised academics, parts of the administration, and big banks (Dash and Story 2009).

The collusion between investment banks and the US administration is a prime example of capture. Regulatory changes, such as the repeal of the Glass-Steagall legislation, the authorization of more complex financial products, and the lack of technical expertise in regulatory agencies, as well as less oversight of the industry, contributed to increasing securitization of mortgages and thereby to the financial crisis. Disastrous stakeholder relations can only be reined in by strong oppositional forces in the superstructure, which can force policy-makers to distance themselves from predatory business interests.

7.5.2 Productive relationships: cooperation

In contrast, productive relationships include the types described earlier in this chapter in which stakeholders and public policy-makers cooperate in order to achieve common goals. Established cooperation, as in the fields of vocational training and collective bargaining, is a precious resource for policy-makers, even though it has proven harder to pursue in countries with more liberal labour market regulations such as the US.

An example of such cooperative relationships can be seen in the attempts to hold companies accountable for their operations overseas. Since the 1990s, multinational companies have been called upon by public institutions and NGOs to more closely oversee and introduce standards in their supply chains, in particular in countries where the rule of law is weak. The United Nations Global Compact (launched in 2000) and the subsequent Guiding Principles of Business and Human Rights (adopted in 2011 after some six years of development) have aimed to introduce public policies on the effective enforcement of human rights in the international arena. While UN and ILO conventions make demands on governments to adopt and implement human rights in their countries, the Global Compact and the Guiding Principles address both governments and multinational firms. They encourage firms to develop and adopt standards on labour rights, anti-corruption, and the environment, and to provide tools in order to facilitate application of these standards in the supply chain. Companies outsourcing manufacturing to developing countries are thereby charged to ensure that their business partners should take account of the human rights impact of their business relationships. This is an example of strategic co-production of policies by the UN and multinational firms. Participation in the network of the Global Compact is entirely voluntary. Large firms do however engage in the initiative in order to boost their brands' reputations and reduce the risk of being attacked for poor labour practices. As the Global Compact has often been accused of blue-washing (masking the bad deeds of companies through participation in UN activities), a range of subsequent developments have aimed to make these policies stick. For example, within the framework of the Guiding Principles, a due diligence toolbox was developed which companies should adopt when investing abroad.

Another instrument for enforcing responsible business practices is the OECD Guidelines for Multinational Enterprises (OECD 2011).

These Guidelines are part of the OECD Declaration on International Investment and Multinational Companies signed in 1976, and apply to all thirty-four OECD countries and twelve adhering states. The most recent revision of the OECD Guidelines, in 2011, took up some of the demands by trade unions and CSOs to include due diligence for supply chains, a stronger focus on human rights—a result of the UN's Guiding Principles—and the inclusion of fair pay in transnational companies, to name but a few.

The OECD Guidelines have a complaints procedure for violations of the guidelines, which works through national contact points (NCPs). These procedures, which are still seen as weak by many observers and lack support from some national governments, can help to profile cases of business irresponsibility, facilitate discussions, and increase scrutiny of corporate behaviour (OECD 2015; ECCHR 2011; Müller-Hoff 2018). Cases of companies' irresponsible behaviour that are brought to the attention of the NCPs can result in bringing parties together and facilitating mediated outcomes that lead to concrete improvements and, in some cases, compensation. Some NCPs undertake fact-finding missions and issue final statements that determine whether the guidelines have been breached (OECD Watch n.d.).

According to the UN Guiding Principles and OECD Guidelines, companies should conduct due diligence processes in order to identify, prevent or mitigate, and account for actual and potential adverse impacts on human rights. Therefore, in 2018, the OECD Council adopted a guidance document to promote a common understanding of due diligence requirements (Bonnitcha and McCorquodale 2017). In addition, the OECD published sector-specific guidance, for example, for the garment and footwear and the extractive and mineral sectors (OECD 2011). Both the UN Guiding Principles and the OECD Guidelines strengthen the Bangladesh Accord by giving the stakeholder initiative a policy framework and thereby a stronger sense of legitimacy and stability.

7.5.3 Finding the right balance

A number of mechanisms can help policy-makers to strike a healthy balance in relation to key stakeholders. Knowing stakeholders, their interests, and their power is obviously the first task of stakeholder management. Preventing capture is crucially important but not sufficient for developing healthy stakeholder relations. Indeed, there are many more steps, some of which are highlighted here and listed in Box 7.5.

- **Draw red lines for privileged business groups**. Each country has a couple of industries or sectors that are of dominant importance for the economic well-being of that country; the same is usually true for regions, cities, and towns. In the US and UK financial services are dominant; in Germany the car and engineering industries matter a lot. Governments will do almost anything to protect the competitive advantage of these industries (Hassel and Palier 2021). This bears the risk of capture. The US administration was captured by the financial services industries. Similarly, the German government is heavily influenced by the car industry, which led to a lack of supervision and was conducive to the 'dieselgate' scandal. Government–industry relations in these key sectors are often unhealthy, and key figures move between government and industry through the so-called revolving door. Whistle-blowing frequently fails. Policy-makers should be aware of the risk of capture by key industries and develop 'red lines'. Codes of conduct of government officials should limit the financial and otherwise attractiveness for politicians and policy-makers of engaging in relations that are or could be deemed too close. For instance, the EU Commission of Jean-Claude Juncker adopted a stronger Code of Conduct for Commissioners in 2018 in order to identify potential conflicts of interest and keep Commissioners from moving to lucrative private sector positions too quickly (European Commission 2018).
- **Embrace transparency**. In this context, lobby registers and transparency rules help watchdogs and other groups hold the government and its officials to account. The European Union, for example, has sought to become more transparent by introducing a lobby register and making meetings of Commissioners with stakeholders public, though the system does not apply evenly across EU institutions. Too much transparency can sometimes hinder the development of otherwise healthy relationships. For instance, full disclosure of the content of conversations between government officials and human rights groups might alert oppressive regimes and enable them to anticipate (and possibly avoid) sanctions. Nevertheless, transparency helps to prevent capture by stakeholders (OECD 2018).
- **Encourage interaction and consultation**. Most governments have become more open towards a wider range of stakeholders in recent years,

and engage more actively in stakeholder management. Frequent consultations, town hall meetings, and dialogue with an array of stakeholders are useful exercises which gather information not only about policy fields but also about valid concerns and potential resistance. Policymakers should routinely engage in these practices.

- **Provide and defend an active stakeholder infrastructure by facilitating access to resources**. Stakeholders need a beneficial environment and supportive context in which to operate. In many countries, human rights groups are banned, or their financing from abroad is regulated in order to undermine their activities (Carothers and Brechenmacher 2014). Authoritarian governments fear public criticism by stakeholders and try to silence them by eroding their resource base. An active stakeholder policy should aim to do the opposite. A healthy policy context provides infrastructure for stakeholders by way of charitable status, tax deductions, and other forms of indirect support. Policy-makers should generally want active stakeholders and should seek to nurture them.

- **Privileged access makes for stable relationships**. Where policy-makers seek more than consultation, they should afford privileged access to selected stakeholders. While this seems contradictory to wide consultation processes and fairness, this is in fact not the case. When policy-makers have identified a project or policy that can best be pushed forward through collaboration or co-production, they should identify partners and give them a privileged status in order to stabilize the relationship. Privileged partners should be kept closer to the policy field and the decision-making process. They should have access to information and be part of consultation procedures. Privileged partners tend to be more ready to support policy proposals.

- **Structure the field of stakeholders**. Finally, policy-makers should aim to structure the policy field by engaging with some stakeholders more than others. They should make strategic choices about how crowded and regulated they want the policy field to be. They can also engage in mediating conflicts between stakeholders, and establish privileged relationships with very valuable stakeholders (see previous). The constellation of stakeholders in a given field is not completely under the control of the policy-maker, but it is also not completely externally determined. Over a longer period, policy-makers can reduce or eliminate the involvement of stakeholders that are too destructive in their approach, or incorporate others into the government's decision-making process.

Box 7.5   Mechanisms for a healthy relationship with stakeholders

---

- Set revolving door rules and codes of conduct
- Ensure transparency
- Encourage stakeholders through broad consultation
- Provide and defend infrastructure by enabling resources
- Afford privileged access to maintain stable relationships
- Structure the field of stakeholders

Finally, what about the democratic quality of stakeholder relations? As explained earlier, stakeholders can become problematic once they capture a policy field and constrain governments from independent decision-making. This often leads to clientelistic political structures, which undermine a polity's democratic quality. As long as capture is prevented or at least contained, an active group of diverse stakeholders in a policy field is generally an asset, not just for the policy process but also for democratic processes. Stakeholders transmit public discussions about policies; they engage and involve larger groups of societies between elections. As long as the field of stakeholders is open for newcomers and activities are encouraged rather than banned or blocked, policy-makers should welcome other actors as part of the policy process.

8

How to Coordinate Public Policy

Key concepts

- Policy interdependence
- Externalities
- Arbitrage
- Public goods and free-riding
- Horizontal coordination
- Positive and negative coordination
- Mutual adjustment
- Coordination capacity

As the world becomes more open, problems, as well as the policies designed to address them, have become more complex. Policy problems are caused and shaped by developments in other domains and by actors who are not part of the problem's policy space. The mismatch between the allocation of policy capacities (legal authority and resources) and the actual manifestation of policy problems creates interdependence. This chapter introduces various types of problems arising from policy interdependence and proposes potential ways to coordinate policies. The main types of policy interdependence problems are externalities, policy arbitrage, and free-riding. Coordination of policies is essential for responding to policy interdependence, but it is inherently difficult to achieve in light of power dispersion and fragmented authority. Hierarchical coordination is often unfeasible for addressing transboundary problems, but mechanisms of horizontal coordination, such as bargaining and mutual adjustment, come with their own limitations. Against this background, this chapter discusses options for increasing coordination capacity and their advantages and disadvantages.

How to Do Public Policy. Anke Hassel and Kai Wegrich, Oxford University Press.
© Anke Hassel and Kai Wegrich (2022). DOI: 10.1093/oso/9780198747000.003.0008

8.1 Policy-Making in a Complex World

On 16 October 2009, the government of the Maldives, an island nation in the Indian Ocean, held a cabinet meeting under water using scuba gear and hand signals. President Mohammed Nasheed and thirteen other government officials took their seats at a table on the sea floor—about 6 metres below the surface of a lagoon off Girifushi, an island usually used for military training (Associated Press 2009). The meeting aimed to draw international attention to the islanders' fears that global warming and melting polar ice caps threaten the survival of the island, which is, on average, 2.1 metres above sea level.

In a complex world, many problems manifest themselves in places where they were not caused and/or cannot be solved. The Maldives by themselves will not be able to stop global warming. Other policy problems, such as migration, international security, and the spread of infectious diseases, are 'transboundary' by nature. Within the boundaries of nation states, we have different levels of government that are responsible for policies, the implications of which are felt by others, for example in public transport and infrastructure provision. Even within the same level of government, horizontal interdependencies exist, for example between cities and surrounding municipalities and between different policy domains, such as agriculture and environment.

To address such problems, the right policy design is only one aspect of policy-making. Just as important as design is coordination or collaboration between different parts of governments, across levels of government, and across sectors—both in terms of setting (common) standards and in terms of aligning administrative and political action. Because of its strong focus on seeking policy solutions to substantive problems—how to create jobs, eliminate pollution, reduce crime, increase educational achievement, and the like—the field of policy analysis has rarely engaged with the transboundary nature of policy issues. Most contributions to policy analysis rest on an institutional model of democratic politics that can be characterized as majoritarian, hierarchical, and unitary (Scharpf 1993). Policies are decided by parliamentary majorities and the executive resting on such majorities (or their direct election); these decision-makers are responsible for a particular territorial unit, such as a municipality or a federal or central state. The policies are executed on the basis of the state's jurisdiction, including its powers to implement policies using force. Under such assumptions, the search for good policies can rightly focus on defining the problem, exploring alternatives, selecting the best possible so-lution, implementing this solution, and evaluating its effects as a basis for adjustment and change, i.e. the standard policy process.

However, as the world has become increasingly connected, open, and integrated, power has been dispersed in various directions: upwards to in-ternational and transnational institutions, downwards to subnational and local government levels, and sideways to non-state actors. In the policy world of the early twenty-first century, coordination across organizational, territorial, and sectoral boundaries is as important for successful policies as the work on policy substance, if not more so; it is also often an integral part of that work. The analytical tools to understand coordination processes and how to shape them, that are provided by research areas ranging from pub-lic administration (Peters 2015, 2018) to the analysis of multi-level systems (Scharpf 1999; Jachtenfuchs and Kasack 2017), need to be connected with and integrated into policy analysis.

This chapter addresses different types of cross-boundary policy prob-lems and possible solutions that involve different types of coordination. Coordination refers to the alignment of the activities of interdependent actors or organizations (or units within an organization) towards some common aim (cf. Koop and Lodge 2014, 1313; Peters 1998, 2015). Co-ordination hence refers to the process of adjusting decisions and actions as required by interdependence. In the following discussion, we take a broad view, including any way that actors take the effects of their action on other organizations or actors into account when pursuing these activities. Policy actors engage in coordination to take into account existing inter-dependencies in the pursuit of more coherent policies. The results can be evaluated in terms of the benefits for actors involved and for overall welfare (Scharpf 1994). As Metcalfe (1994, 278) succinctly formulated it, often co-ordination is about not 'imped[ing], frustrat[ing] or negat[ing] each other's activities'.

While coordination can be achieved by various means, including hier-archical direction from higher levels, cooperation and collaboration entail stronger elements of working together. Chapter 7 on stakeholder relations already explored forms of cooperation between government policy-makers and other stakeholders, in particular businesses and NGOs. In this chapter, we focus mainly on coordination among governmental actors and delve into mechanisms of coordination. Note that, in the practice of governing, coordination is ubiquitous, but so is refusal to coordinate; being unwill-ing to take the other's concern into account and refusing to take part in addressing a problem are important parts of this reality (Bach and Wegrich 2019).

Before exploring the mechanisms of coordination in more detail, the next section introduces three problem constellations that call for co-ordination, ranging from relatively simple externalities to the arbitrage of regulatory settings and free-riding of public and collective goods in transboundary contexts. This is followed by an analysis of coordination mechanisms for dealing with such problems. In the final sections, we discuss how to increase the coordination capacity of policy-making systems and highlight the importance of institutions to underpin it.

8.2 Interdependence as a Key Challenge in Policy-Making

In much of policy analysis, policy problems are discussed as if they were isolated affairs when in fact many are so complex and multifaceted that all purported solutions will have some repercussion on other policy problems and/or be affected by them. In other words, many policies are interdependent. Some policies might have indirect effects on other jurisdictions; for example, variance in corporate tax regulations affects where mobile transnational companies shift their profits, which then has an impact on tax regulations and revenues in other countries. The high-profile case of the negotiated tax bill of Apple in Ireland is a case in point as it deprives other governments of potential tax revenues from sales of Apple products and services in the European Union (EU).[1] Many multinational companies engage in profit-shifting and thereby enjoy minimal tax bills compared to other firms. Other policies have more immediate and direct effects on neighbouring countries, as the case of the Grand Ethiopian Renaissance Dam (GERD) shows (Box 8.1). The Ethiopian government's energy policy, of which GERD is a manifestation, will likely have significant impact on its neighbours. Such interdependencies can be a source of conflict, big and small.

Policy interdependence takes place not only between nation states but also—not surprisingly—within a country, between different territorial and

---

[1] The EU Commission investigated the case and fined Ireland but ultimately lost the case in the European General Court. In September 2020, it was decided to appeal before the European Court of Justice (ECJ). Ireland is one of the major tax havens for multinational firms doing business in the EU (European Commission 2020c).

governmental levels (local versus regional or national), and between organizational units, such as ministries. The transport systems of cities affect local residents as well as commuters who live outside cities but work in them. Decisions on petrol and car taxes taken at the national level affect local traffic and transport policies at the subnational level. Housing policy in the commuter belt can affect housing prices in the city. If more housing is provided in the city, the public health and quality of life of residents might be harmed because parks and public spaces might be built on. Any policy-making entity therefore must be aware of the fact that its policies are impacted by the policies of other jurisdictions without necessarily being able to control their policies or shape them.

Interdependence is a general feature of all policy-making, and only few— if any—decisions are free of any impact from or on others. Even within specialized departments, coordination is necessary. Within the ministry of agriculture, decisions on animal protection will affect not only dairy farmers but also, indirectly, those who produce animal feed or grains. In the ministry for transport, subunits for different modes of transport (road, train, air, water, cycling, and walking) need to coordinate to account for their varying impacts on quality of life and the environment.

From a policy-making perspective, it is critical to know the ways policies can be interdependent in order to understand and shape the coordination mechanisms or activities needed to deal with the challenges related to each. Here, we identify three key types of problems stemming from policy interdependence: externalities, arbitrage, and free-riding from the provision of public goods. These types of interdependence-related problems are rooted in governance structures and capacities but also in the policy problems themselves: some policy problems are more prone to generate issues of interdependence than others. All three types of policy interdependence problems affect the distribution of benefits and costs of policies, which are not necessarily within the domain of the policy-maker's concern, and therefore coordination is required to address these issues.

8.2.1 Policy externalities

Policy *externalities* are illustrated most clearly by the GERD case (Box 8.1). Ethiopia will control the energy produced by the dam, but the water flow downstream in Sudan and Egypt will be affected by it. Both downstream countries will likely be impacted by Ethiopia's policies even if Ethiopia does not deliberately want to harm them. Externalities occur when the jurisdiction of the decision-making actor creates costs for third parties without them reaping the benefits.[2] We can frequently observe policy externalities between neighbouring countries, both regarding observable phenomena, such as pollution, and regarding risks, such as nuclear accidents. Nuclear power plants are often built near international borders, increasing anxieties in neighbouring countries. One example is the Belgian nuclear power plant, Tihange, which has been deemed unsafe and has been the subject of many complaints and lawsuits by neighbouring countries: Germany and the Netherlands (Strauss and Biesemans 2020).

There are also policy externalities between territories or different levels of government. National or federal governments often introduce policies that are beneficial to their own budgets but costly to lower level governments. For instance, where social assistance or unemployment benefits are paid for at the local level, national policy changes that impact employment, either across the board or in certain regions, can affect local authorities' finances substantially (Trampusch 2020).

Box 8.1 The Grand Ethiopian Renaissance Dam (GERD)

In 2020, the Grand Ethiopian Renaissance Dam (GERD) was under construction on the Blue Nile River about 40 km east of Sudan. It is owned by the state-owned Ethiopian Electric Power Corporation and is intended to serve primarily Ethiopia, but also Sudan and Egypt. All three countries depend on the Nile River for water, although Ethiopia's highlands supply most (more than 85 per cent) of the water flowing into it.

Construction started in 2011 and has led to conflict, especially between Egypt and Ethiopia. Ethiopia argues that it has the right to utilize its natural resources to alleviate poverty. Ethiopia also states that the dam will not significantly impact the water flow into the Nile. Egypt sees the dam as a major threat to its water security and argues that existing agreements (the water rights granted to Egypt by the 1929 Anglo-Egyptian Treaty and the 1959 agreement between Egypt and Sudan) give it a veto right over infrastructure projects on the Nile. Such a veto could prohibit Ethiopia from using the dam.

---

[2] There are also positive externalities, i.e. creating benefits for the third party without the burden of extra costs.

In 2020, about 70 per cent of the dam had been completed, at a cost of US$4.6bn. It was projected to provide 6,450 megawatts of electricity and thereby double Ethiopia's power output. Ethiopia was also hoping to export electricity to neighbouring states, starting in 2022.

There have been long-standing conflicts between Egypt and Sudan, on the one hand, and Ethiopia, on the other, over the allocation of the waters of the Nile. When Ethiopia announced in July 2020 that it had started filling the GERD's reservoir, Egypt complained to the international community, as it had asked for a legally binding agreement before the dam could be used. The international community, including the US, threatened to cut aid to Ethiopia if the conflict were not resolved.

As Ethiopia started filling the dam's reservoir, Egypt sought to secure a political agreement on the timetable and on how the GERD would be managed, particularly during droughts. Sudan initially opposed the dam's construction but later warmed to it because of a perceived beneficial impact on domestic development. There was, however, fear that the GERD could threaten Sudan's own dams.

Talks held under the auspices of the African Union led to a possible compromise on the reservoir, but not on the role of the dam during droughts. While the three countries agreed on a definition of a drought (when the flow of Nile water to the dam falls below 35–40 b.c.m. per year), how Ethiopia would deal with droughts remains unsettled (Mukum Mbaku 2020).

There is already a regional framework for the management of the Nile in place— the Nile Basin Initiative (NBI). It is a partnership between the Nile riparian states that was launched in 1999 and has already helped to outline rights and responsibilities for cooperative management of the resources of the Nile. In 2010, a Cooperative Framework Agreement (CFA) was concluded in the context of the NBI but not signed by Egypt and Sudan (Ifimes 2020). The three countries also signed a Declaration of Principles in 2015 as a first step towards a detailed technical agreement, which so far has not been agreed upon (Tawfik 2015; El Tawil 2020).

Contributing author: Julia Seefeld.
Additional source: Gorvett (2021); The Economist (2021).

Between policy fields, we can also observe externalities. Agricultural policies might benefit farmers but can affect the health of the population and impact health campaigns carried out by health ministries. For instance, the use of antibiotics in meat production increases the productivity of cattle farming, but can have severe implications for consumers. As bacteria become more resistant to antibiotics, the efficacy of antibiotics will decline, and the general population (not only consumers of meat) will become more vulnerable.

8.2.2 Policy arbitrage

Policy *arbitrage* refers to the competition between different regulatory regimes enabled by the mobility of citizens or companies that allows them to choose the most favourable. In many areas related to global financial markets but also trade and investment decisions, wealthy individuals and companies have considerable leeway as to where they invest their capital or incorporate their companies. In its original usage, 'arbitrage' refers to the exploitation of price differences, but we use it to refer to the exploitation of policy differences, especially in relation to taxes and regulatory standards, for example labour and environmental standards, across jurisdictions.

The clearest example of such exploitation stems from the competition policy-makers face from other jurisdictions when setting tax rates, company law, and tax enforcement (Genschel and Schwarz 2011; Genschel and Seelkopf 2016; Rodrik 2011). Governments try to lure investment and companies, and therefore jobs, to their jurisdictions by offering favourable conditions. Since all governments are facing the same situation, there is the risk of a race to the bottom by undercutting taxes and regulation. In the EU, countries such as Ireland and the Netherlands have become highly attractive locations for investments and the incorporation of firms because of their tax and other regulatory policies (Shaheen 2017). In the US context, such a race to the bottom is known as the Delaware effect, after the state that is renowned for its reduced regulatory barriers, which draw firms to incorporate there (Vogel 1997). Regulatory competition might include lowering labour or environmental standards, or even requirements for receiving residence visas or passports (see the 'golden visa' example, described in Chapter 3, especially Box 3.1), in comparison with competing jurisdictions.

At the same time, high-quality public services and living conditions can also be an asset in international competition, and a race to the bottom is not always the outcome. Moreover, companies might be interested in adapting to higher regulatory standards early when the expectation is that standards will be tightened eventually across jurisdictions. Higher regulatory standards might also limit competition from smaller companies lacking capacities to comply. The resulting effect, a 'race to the top', has also been called the California effect in the US context, which describes the upward adjustment of regulatory regimes towards stricter regulations to apply uniform rules across corporations (Vogel 1997).

8.2.3 Free-riding

With the provision of *public goods* come problems of *free-riding*. Public goods are those that are non-excludable, i.e. it would be extremely costly to prevent someone from benefiting from them, and non-rivalrous, i.e. one person's use does not reduce what is available to someone else. At the global level, political order rests to a large extent on public goods, such as non-violence in daily life, the rule of law, trust in institutions and media, infrastructure, a healthy or at least non-toxic environment, general levels of education, and scientific research, as well as general product and food safety. These public goods lay the foundation for prosperous societies and must be nurtured. In general, the beneficiaries of public goods are not necessarily the same as their producers, and costs and benefits are unequally distributed. Therefore, there is a temptation for participants to try to take a 'free ride' in the process; in other words, some might contribute less or even nothing at all, but still enjoy the benefits

As we know from the example of the tragedy of the commons (Ostrom 1990; Hardin 1968), introduced briefly in Chapter 3, the overuse of a open-access resources leads to its depletion and lower welfare overall. Collective action is required to protect the commons and therefore also the public good. If all users of a common-pool resource, such as fishing grounds, follow only their individual self-interest, the resource will be over-used and eventually exhausted. Note that this problem is not one of simple narrow-mindedness; if one user restricts her use of the resource, another user will likely compensate for her self-constraint and extract more resources.

If left unattended, policy problems stemming from interdependence can lead to not only conflict but also inferior policy outcomes. If Ethiopia ignores the concerns of its neighbouring countries along the Nile, regarding the negative externalities its dam could produce, it might face aggression and even military responses. From an overall perspective, the costs for the neighbouring countries might outweigh the benefits that Ethiopia can yield from building the dam. Policy arbitrage could also be harmful if not addressed. If countries compete against each other for investments and capital by lowering regulatory standards and taxes, all countries (or jurisdictions) will ultimately suffer as the downward spiral will continue. But in the absence of a global (or even European) tax policy regime, individual countries gain from this tax competition and hence have an incentive to continue the practice. Finally, the production of public goods might be stalled if too many policy actors engage in free-riding and do not contribute to the production of the public good.

8.3 Coordination Mechanisms

Coordination is the answer to the problems arising from interdependence. Interdependence is created by the mismatch between the allocation of policy capacities (legal authority and resources) and the actual manifestation of policy problems. Coordination can address these mismatches and should improve the quality of policy outcomes. However, positive outcomes that enhance the overall welfare of all involved actors are far from guaranteed. Different mechanisms of coordination come with their own preconditions, strengths, and weaknesses.

Governments have developed mechanisms for dealing with interdependence and resulting problems: negotiating conventions in international organizations and agencies; co-signing procedures between different departments and information channels on activities in different parts as routine procedures for daily business; and intra- and inter-ministerial coordination committees for cross-cutting issues with political priority (cf. Scharpf 1994; Peters 2018; Benz and Sonnicksen 2017). In the transnational context, coordination is less structured and more difficult to realize.

The way coordination mechanisms are defined has been influenced by concepts in economics and by the question of how best to organize 'transactions'. The perspective of transaction cost economics (developed by R. Coase in 1937) has compared two basic coordination mechanisms available to companies: they can either purchase services or products on the market or they can produce these goods or services in-house. Market mechanisms and surrogate forms of competition are also widespread within government; think of competitive tendering processes in the procurement of goods and services, league tables in education, or rankings between organizations or jurisdictions. The interdependence problem, described earlier as policy arbitrage, is driven by forces of competition. However, market mechanisms (or surrogates) are of limited value for addressing the policy interdependencies discussed earlier, since they usually require some form of collaboration.

The first and most visible alternative to market-based coordination mechanisms is hierarchy, in particular within the hierarchical structures of the superstructure (the equivalent to in-house production in the transaction cost perspective).[3] But as mentioned previously, even within the executive organization, hierarchy is not the only, and maybe not even the dominant, mechanism of coordination (Table 8.1). In addition, there are other non-market coordination mechanisms used to overcome issues relating to interdependence. Such mechanisms include formal bargaining structures, networks, stable relationships between different legal and political authorities, self-organization in co-operatives, patterns of information sharing, and mutual adjustments. Mixed forms of horizontal self-coordination and hierarchy also exist. None of these coordination mechanisms emerges by itself; all of them must be nurtured and encouraged. In the following, we discuss the main coordination mechanisms (and their subtypes) in turn, before moving to hybrid types.

8.3.1 Hierarchical coordination

Hierarchical coordination—exercised either by a single actor, such as an executive politician, or by a majority vote in parliament—can in theory achieve welfare-maximizing decisions, since the distribution of costs and benefits to the individual players affected by the hierarchical decision can be weighed against collective welfare gains. For instance, one actor's losses might be accepted if they come with a higher level of well-being for everyone (Scharpf 1997). Solutions are possible that maximize overall welfare in a way that the situation cannot be improved without making someone worse off (Pareto optimal). Hence, one of the proposed solutions for collective action problems, such as the tragedy of the commons, has been *hierarchy* (just like the proposed utopia for solving global problems is often a 'global government'). Hierarchy is synonymous with follow-through: if a national government regulates subnational decision-making, lower level units have to comply with national regulations. Similarly, in hierarchical organizations, executives can overrule staff at lower levels. Hierarchy is therefore the potentially most direct and effective form of coordination.

However, as Scharpf has shown, hierarchy has its limitations as a coordination device (Scharpf 1994, 1997; see also Wegrich and Štimac 2014;

---

[3] This point is taken from Fritz Scharpf's path-breaking work on hierarchy—and its limits—in policy-making (Scharpf 1997).

Adam et al. 2019). First, hierarchical decision-making does not automatically serve the general welfare if the motivation behind the hierarchical rules is not to pursue it. If heads of government can hierarchically arbitrate between different government agencies or ministries, they are likely to follow the interests of their office when taking the decision (such as claiming credit and avoiding blame) and not necessarily societal welfare. For instance, when balancing farmers' protests and biodiversity commitments, a central government might be tempted to avoid conflict with its core voters instead of trying to work out a longer term solution by mediating between the agriculture and environment departments. Thus, the motives (Scharpf 1994, 32–3) behind hierarchical decision-making are a key factor in explaining outcomes. In functioning democracies, mechanisms of accountability through voting and judicial review and established norms of democracy and fairness keep the motivation problem in check. While these checks and balances are essential for controlling and limiting executive power, they also limit the potential of hierarchical coordination.

Second, hierarchical decision-making suffers from limited information-processing capacity at the top of governments or organizations, the 'information problem' according to Scharpf (1994, 33–4). Hierarchical decisions are taken in the superstructure and are only loosely based on detailed policy knowledge available in the engine room (see Chapter 2). In the process of bringing evidence up the hierarchy from lower levels, some form of selection and filtering needs to take place to avoid overloading the processing capacity of the peak. Decision-making concentrated at the top of the hierarchy is therefore prone to either 'information impoverishment' because input has been tailored to support the interests at the top or 'information overload' because it has not been filtered at all. To avoid these risks, according to Scharpf's analysis (1994), hierarchical intervention should only be used sparingly. But, as Scharpf argues, the efficacy of such selective intervention rests on the assumption that most interdependencies between organizational units can be subsumed within the hierarchical structures. In other words: the more cross-cutting interdependencies exist, the more limited is the value of hierarchical coordination. For example, if the issue of 'digitalization' consists of so many aspects and angles that basically all existing ministries of a government have some interest in the issue, creating a new ministry with responsibility for digitalization will not be very helpful: this ministry would still have to rely on the capacity of many other ministries to develop and implement policy in this cross-cutting field.

Beyond these limitations of hierarchical decision-making, there is another perhaps more fundamental one: its reliance on the model of the unitary and majoritarian state. Hierarchy in response to transboundary problems can only be used on the basis of voluntary delegation of decision-making powers to a third party. For example, an international agreement to ban the hunting of whales can be enforced by the International Whaling Commission (IWC), trade rules are monitored by the World Trade Organization, and so on. But even if the enforcement of negotiated standards is delegated to transnational bodies, the acceptance of those delegated powers during enforcement might be more easily challenged. Looking again at the case of whaling, 'research' exemptions from the IWC's hunting ban have been gamed by several countries, with some abandoning the agreement entirely and some remaining without sanction (*The Economist* 2019; BBC News 2019).

8.3.2 Horizontal coordination

The second basic coordination mechanism is *horizontal coordination*. As an ideal type, horizontal coordination is characterized by the absence of hierarchy: the involved parties voluntarily engage in coordination because the results might bring higher benefits than uncoordinated or unilateral action. Hence horizontal coordination is done via negotiation and bargaining and is characterized by the search for compromises, the binding of 'package deals', and other forms of coming to an agreement (Sebenius 1983). The key challenge of horizontal coordination stems from the condition that each participant generally has veto power, making such negotiations prone to compromises on the lowest common denominator. While, in theory, negotiations can lead to results that maximize overall welfare, such agreements are not easy to reach.

As Scharpf (1993) has argued, achieving welfare-maximizing solutions requires package deals, side payments, and issue linkages, which need time and effort to design; in other words, negotiations that seek welfare-maximizing solutions come with high transaction costs. Moreover, negotiations work best when the actors engage in high-trust, open exchange and follow a joint problem-solving orientation. But such behaviour can be exploited by actors who aggressively pursue individual or organizational self-interest. As a result, horizontal coordination can result in stalemate and limited policy change.

Table 8.1 Coordination mechanisms and types of problems stemming from policy interdependence

	EXTERNALITIES	ARBITRAGE	PUBLIC GOOD
HIERARCHY	National or central government decision on sharing costs and benefits of policy: **Cabinet decision on coal power plants**	Setting minimum standards by lead actor: **Federal government sets minimum tax rates for local authorities**	National or central government decision that lower-level government has to contribute to financing of public good: **Disaster fund; social investment**
HORIZONTAL COORDINATION (POSITIVE)	Negotiations over costs and benefits of different options: **GERD**	Negotiations on common (minimum) standards: **EU corporation tax**	Alliances in international organizations: **Paris Agreement**
HORIZONTAL COORDINATION (NEGATIVE)	Veto mechanisms on international climate projects: **UN Green Climate Fund changed rules on voting**	Veto right of governments in taxation: **Power of smaller EU member states to veto tax harmonization**	Veto right in international organizations: **UN Security Council**
MUTUAL ADJUSTMENT	Iterative standard-setting process: **Convergence of humanitarian aid for refugees**	Trading up regulatory standards: **Open method of coordination (OMC)**	Shared orientation point: **Shared research facilities; learning networks; Global Compact**

In order to explore ways to increase the capacity of horizontal coordination to address problems of policy interdependence, it is useful to consider some of the many variations. Observing interdepartmental policy coordination across government ministries, Scharpf (1997, 1994) identified two such variations (cf. Hustedt and Seyfried 2016 on climate policy coordination in the EU Commission): positive and negative. These two subtypes of horizontal coordination are distinguished by their level of ambition and procedure. *Positive coordination* actively seeks to develop a joint, integrated solution to a policy problem using input from various specialized units. The aim is to find a combination of measures incorporating elements from the range of perspectives. The most fitting procedure is often a taskforce type of structure, where information and proposals for solutions are pooled and a blend of interventions is jointly developed (Hustedt and Danken 2017). Positive coordination requires the open exchange of ideas and a cooperative orientation on the part of all involved actors. While positive coordination is appropriate for addressing complex, cross-cutting policy issues, the procedure itself can also become complex and stretch the capacities of the actors involved in it.

The ambition of *negative coordination* is lower: it seeks mainly to avoid negative externalities of policy decisions by one unit in the area of responsibility of another unit. The most fitting procedure here is sequential consultation: while one of the actors is in the lead (for instance, when designing new environmental policies), other policy-makers are consulted on the proposed measure and the extent to which it affects them or might be undermined by other policies. The purposes of negative coordination are to vet proposals that are on the agenda and to avoid negative effects of the proposed activity that are not on the lead unit's radar (Scharpf 1972, 1994; Mayntz and Scharpf 1975). Negative coordination helps to reduce the complexity of policy-making, as it allows the processing of many different policy issues at the same time. If applied to transboundary coordination, the countries downstream from Ethiopia would be consulted in planning the GERD (and in all likelihood they would veto the plan if no concessions were made). When complex policy issues cannot be addressed in a 'positive' way, negative coordination avoids harm in situations of interdependence. For instance, the government of Ethiopia might not engage in active negotiations about the GERD with neighbouring countries but might inform them ahead of time so that they can prepare for the fall-out of the dam.

A third variation of horizontal coordination exists, namely *mutual adjustment* (cf. Lindblom 1965). This mode of coordination does not require any direct interaction between the interdependent actors, but the actors consciously adjust their behaviours to those of others. Under mutual adjustment, the actors involved neither pursue a joint policy, as they would with positive coordination, nor aim to address inconsistencies, as they would through negative coordination. Rather, mutual adjustment takes place in polycentric networks, in which actors inform each other about their activities with the expectation that others will follow or adjust to the new situation. Mutual adjustment does not aim to actively pursue coordination, but it is nevertheless a coordination device that can be pursued proactively to avoid negative consequences.

Coordination via mutual adjustment can be observed in some socio-economic institutions of highly advanced countries. For instance, private, firm-sponsored training regimes have developed into highly coordinated vocational education systems in German-speaking countries (as an example of co-production, see Chapter 7). Here, firms overcome their fear of poaching skilled labour (Becker 1964) via decentralized coordination, in which each firm commits to invest in training (Hall and Soskice 2001). Firms monitor each other's behaviour and are pressured by local policy-makers to stick to the vocational training system.

For policy-makers, mutual adjustment is the least accessible form of coordination as it relies on decentralized decision-making. However, information sharing, transparency, and regular updates regarding the developments of joint interest can lead to policy networks that facilitate other forms of coordination further down the line. If nothing else is available, mutual adjustment is certainly better than no coordination at all. Facilitating information exchange and the understanding of the rationale of counterparts in other organizations, sectors, or governments is also key to supporting horizontal coordination from the bottom up (see section 8.4). Furthermore, mutual adjustment can lead to more active forms of horizontal coordination, which can be very effective in solving problems on the ground without unnecessary formalism and wading through complex hierarchical structures.

As noted at the outset of this section on horizontal coordination, participation is ostensibly voluntary. Still, many policy actors might feel compelled to participate in such processes because they might face disadvantages if they pull out: the remaining actors decide on solutions at the expense of those who are not present in the negotiations, or other actors have ways to punish those who are absent. There is therefore a strong incentive to participate in horizontal coordination processes in order to gain access to information about other actors' behaviour as well as to pre-empt measures that might cause harm. Self-interest therefore tends to reinforce participation. In addition, there might be direct punishment for those who decline participation, for example, exclusion from other forms of cooperation in the future or in other fields (issue linkage). Often horizontal coordination leads to the linking of policies in terms of exchange of favours (or penalties). For instance, in September 2020 the US suspended a portion of its development aid to Ethiopia in an attempt to push it towards an agreement with Egypt and Sudan on GERD, but the new Biden administration decided to de-link issues and restored most of the aid in early 2021 (*The Economist* 2021; Solomon 2021).

At the same time, the organizational self-interest in having a voice in horizontal coordination might be offset by an interest in avoiding blame for failure or ineffective solutions. Issues and problems that are not among an organization's priorities might be better ignored and left alone. We discuss this problem in the context of policy implementation (in Chapter 5) as the challenge of 'horizontal coordination', illustrating the problem with the case of failing collaboration between schools, police forces, social workers, and judges in dealing with school absenteeism in Berlin. We can expect horizontal coordination to emerge when interests and preferences are congruent, which is often the case in tight-knit policy communities (e.g. in the field of agriculture). But, when policy problems are seen as blame magnets or deviate from an organization's core mission, horizontal coordination might not emerge without hierarchy pushing it. Cross-cutting policy issues such as racial, religious, and gender equality or digitalization can thus fall between the cracks of organizational (or territorial) attention.

8.3.3 Hybrid forms of coordination

In the practice of governing, hierarchical and horizontal forms are often combined. In the coordination of cross-cutting policy issues within a political executive, horizontal self-government is usually embedded in a 'shadow of hierarchy' (Scharpf 1993). Actors from different departments have substantial autonomy in coordinating with other departments and seek to solve interdependence problems with limited involvement from the top executives. That holds both for coordination within single departments, where the minister only gets involved in the few contentious issues that need her attention, and for coordination across departments. However, the hierarchy serves as a 'shadow', a potential intervention from the top that disciplines the negotiation partners. Those working in the engine room have some incentive to solve problems through horizontal coordination, including preserving their autonomy and not overloading the political leadership. At the same time, if stalemate occurs, they can delegate issues that cannot be resolved in the engine room to the top.

A second, more 'designed' form of hybrid coordination is called 'experimentalist governance' (Sabel and Zeitlin 2012). The basic idea is to combine centralized goal-setting with decentralized implementation *and* a process of learning from different implementation practices and peer review from other actors. The role of the central unit is to set goals—usually in agreement with the dispersed units—and to monitor goal attainment over time. Moreover, the central unit is responsible for organizing a peer review process based on the reporting of the implementation practices of the various units. The idea of experimentalist governance grew out of observing the EU's open method of coordination (OMC) (see Box 8.2). Note that critics have pointed out several of the approach's disadvantages, including the strong reliance on written reporting that can deflect from real developments on the ground and the incentives to hide problems and critical development (Chalmers and Lodge 2003).

Box 8.2   Open method of coordination (OMC)

Within the EU, some policy fields are the responsibility of the European Commission based on the Treaty on the Functioning of the European Union (TFEU). Other issues are of increasing importance for the functioning of the European single market but are not part of the EU polity. In order achieve progress along the lines of jointly developed goals in a variety of social policy fields, such as employment, education, and poverty, the European Commission has started a process described as the open method of coordination (OMC). The term dates back to the Lisbon European Council in March 2000, although the method has been around for much longer. A precursor of OMC was the European Employment Strategy (EES), introduced by the 1997 Amsterdam Treaty (European Parliament 2014).

  The OMC is a method of soft law and does not result in EU legislation. It focuses rather on disseminating best practice and achieving convergence with regard to EU goals in policy areas, which are within the partial or full competence of the member states. The aim of the OMC is to encourage policy laggards (those who do not meet the jointly defined goals) to learn from policy leaders in orchestrated policy learning exercises. Further mechanisms to achieve convergence between the member states involve the establishment of guidelines, quantitative and qualitative indicators, benchmarks, periodic evaluations, and peer reviews of national and regional targets. There are no sanctions for those who do not meet the targets. However, the terms 'peer pressure' and 'naming and shaming' are often used in connection with this process of learning and improvement. This may hint at processes of greater weight than the apparently 'soft' nature of the governance tool implies. According to the European Commission, it works together with EU countries using the OMC in the areas of social inclusion, healthcare, long-term care, and pensions (social OMC).[4] Quite distinct areas, such as education, research, immigration, and enterprise policy, have been subject to partial OMC processes that have been restricted to more or less institutionalized benchmarking procedures. Since there is a wide variety in terms of strength, duration, and compliance mechanisms, some argue that it seems more relevant to use the term OMC in the plural (De la Rosa 2006, 620).

In the OMC process, policy objectives are first proposed by the European Commission. Thereafter, the member states decide, first in Council formations and then at the yearly meetings of the Spring European Council, which objectives the member states will pursue. Next, the member states report their efforts to meet the objectives agreed upon for the given OMC process, which are reviewed by peer member states and at the EU level (Commission-Council) via performance assessments. Though the OMC has had some positive effects in policy areas, such as labour market activation and the reduction of child poverty, in terms of mutual learning at the EU level and horizontal networking among non-state and subnational actors, there are doubts about the effectiveness of this hybrid coordination mechanism due to a low political impact on the national level and a lack of monitoring mechanisms (Prpic 2014; Zeitlin 2011).

Additional sources: Hatzopoulos (2007); Vanhercke (2019).

---

[4] 'The social OMC is a voluntary process for political cooperation based on agreeing common objectives and measuring progress towards these goals using common indicators. The process also involves close co-operation with stakeholders, including Social Partners and civil society.' (European Commission n.d.-e).

8.4 Coordination Capacity

Efforts to enhance the capacity of governing systems—within a nation state or in an international context—to coordinate boundary-spanning issues have to grapple with the fact that there is no perfect coordination mechanism. All mechanisms described in this chapter come with disadvantages, blind spots, and limitations and depend on the willingness of the involved actors to play along in the coordination game. But some lessons can be derived from the research on cross-cutting policy coordination and the attempts to reform policy-making systems to better address problems arising from interdependence.

An important element in building *coordination capacity* is the skill set of public servants and the staff of non-governmental actors. Addressing interdependence requires what Hood and Lodge (2006) called 'boundary spanning skills', i.e. the competence to understand the logic of counterparts in other organizations and to communicate across boundaries.

Another set of recommendations refers to proposals to align formal capacities—competences and jurisdiction—with the nature of cross-cutting issues. Such proposals, ranging from territorial reforms, such as the merger of smaller municipalities into a single, larger one, allowing for better regional coordination, to the creation of transnational institutions, such as the United Nations Environment Programme, which among other tasks seeks coherence in the UN's environmental activities, are very familiar in debates about dealing with interdependence. Mergers of agencies have also been promoted as a way to improve horizontal coordination (Christensen et al. 2014; see also the US Department of Homeland Security example in Chapter 5). On a general level, institutional reform might be a very important tool in adapting to interdependencies. However, the difficulty of institutional reform (see Chapter 9) is only one reason that this approach should not be overemphasized. Another concern is that institutional reforms might not solve those problems of interdependence.

Let us illustrate this with the idea of creating a new ministry at the central government level that would assume responsibility for emergent, cross-cutting topics, such as digitalization. Such 'super-ministries', which merge several ministries or government agencies, are set up when cross-policy solutions are sought for particular problems. For example, super-ministries for digitalization are expected to come up with faster ways to introduce new technologies and innovation. The rationale behind such a proposal is that the role of hierarchical coordination will be enhanced and that of horizontal coordination, which has apparently failed, would be reduced. One minister would be politically accountable to push that agenda, and she could draw on the expertise, budget, and jurisdiction concentrated in the ministry.

The critical question for assessing the potential success of the approach is how many of the policy interdependencies can really be concentrated within a single ministry in order to shift from inter-departmental horizontal to intra-departmental vertical (hierarchical) coordination. In the case of digitalization, the answer might be: not many! As mentioned, this is an issue area that affects every policy domain and requires specialized expertise in numerous fields—science, education, transport, health, security, and financial markets, to name just a few. Concentrating all these competencies in one ministry would leave the other ministries devoid of relevant expertise in the field. Much more likely is a new ministry for digitalization that can only rely on hierarchy to a very limited extent and needs to coordinate horizontally with other ministries to achieve substantial results. Hence, in pushing digitalization, many countries added jurisdiction for this issue to an existing ministerial portfolio, such as economic policy or infrastructure, rather than creating a new stand-alone ministry.

The hypothetical super-ministry example points to the risks and limitations of pursuing institutional reforms as a panacea for addressing policy interdependence (see also Chapter 9). Of course, the potential for institutional reform needs to be assessed anew for each context, and there are several alternatives to the leitmotif of concentrating interdependencies in one organization to enhance hierarchical coordination. One option is to enhance the role of hierarchy by establishing temporary structures, such as taskforces, that are to address cross-cutting issues. At the executive level, a taskforce could be coordinated by a commissioner who has the direct support of the top executive politician in the superstructure (prime minister, president, or the like). This kind of approach can be used to enhance horizontal coordination between ministries and, as noted earlier, to call selectively on hierarchical intervention from the top to overcome stalemate in negotiations. The limitation of such an approach is that it can only be used for a small number of high-level issues because its success depends on the credible 'shadow of hierarchy' of the political executive. The institutional capacities of the executive can be enhanced by establishing or strengthening staff and resources for such coordination functions.

There are clearly circumstances in which hierarchical or vertical cooperation is opportune. However, the key to enhancing coordination capacity lies primarily in questions about enhancing horizontal coordination. We discuss two main directions, namely the improvement of cross-boundary negotiations and the improvement of conditions for spontaneous interaction and coordination from the bottom up.

As noted above, the main bottleneck of negotiations that should lead to horizontal coordination is that the participants can veto decisions that might enhance overall welfare but not benefit this one actor. Let us consider the case of the European Green Deal (Box 8.3). The EU as a whole benefits from an ambitious climate change policy, but some countries might bear substantial economic costs because their economy or energy system relies on fossil fuels. In such cases, side payments and package deals likely need to be arranged in order to get the parties to come to an agreement. For example, countries such as Poland will likely need to be compensated for the negative effect of climate change policies on its coal industry. The capacity of negotiation systems to develop such solutions can be enhanced by establishing issue-spanning negotiations (Sebenius 1983; Scharpf 1993). This usually requires top executives in the superstructure to get involved in order to shift negotiations from individual issue areas towards a higher level. As the distribution of costs and benefits is likely to be different between sectors (in some issues, Poland would benefit from climate change policies), issue-spanning negotiations increase the chances of finding package deals that distribute costs and benefits in a way that all participants can agree upon.

Box 8.3   The European Green Deal

The European Green Deal is an action plan to respond to climate change and environmental degradation by making the EU's economy sustainable. It was presented by the European Commission on 11 December 2019 (European Commission 2019b).

As part of the deal, the EU aims to be climate neutral by 2050 and therefore proposed a European Climate Law to turn this political commitment into a legal obligation. The law includes a binding target of net zero greenhouse gas emissions by 2050. The EU institutions and the member states are obligated to take the necessary measures at an EU and national level to meet the target, taking into account the importance of promoting fairness and solidarity among member states. Reaching this target will require action on the part of all sectors of the EU economy. Such actions include investing in environmentally friendly technologies, supporting industry innovation, rolling out cleaner, cheaper, and healthier forms of private and public transport, decarbonizing the energy sector, ensuring buildings are more energy efficient, and working with international partners to improve global environmental standards.

The European Green Deal also envisions financial support and technical assistance to help those that are most affected by the move towards the green economy. Called the Just Transition Mechanism, it is to help mobilize at least €100 billion over the period 2021–7 in the most affected regions (European Commission n.d.-f).

Among the EU member states that will be most affected is Poland as it relies on coal for more than 75 per cent of its electricity needs (Simon 2020). When the Green Deal was announced, Poland was the only EU member state to refuse to pledge climate neutrality by 2050, with the ruling Law and Justice party saying that it needed more time and money to shift its economy from coal to cleaner energy sources. Though it seemed to indicate a change of heart in September 2020, Poland had still not officially committed to the common goal as of January 2021. The EU Commission has pledged a subsidy of €2bn from the EU's Just Transition Fund to phase out coal, but, according to an EU budget deal struck in July 2020, Poland would be eligible for only half of the EU funds if it did not sign up to the bloc's climate neutrality objective.

Contributing author: Julia Seefeld.

Another negotiation-related strategy is to separate debates about distributive issues from discussions about problem-solving. Research on international regimes, be they issue- or sector-specific, has shown that the institutionalization of attention to a particular issue can support the development of an epistemic community around this issue and split areas of consensus on what needs to be done from more contentious issues of distributional effects, which need to be dealt with through position-oriented bargaining (Haas 2016; Gehring 1994; Haas 1992; Zürn 2018). For example, in the context of climate change, the international regime supported early on the establishment of an international network of professionals with significant knowledge, reputation, and skill in the field that eventually became an influential advisory body, i.e. the Intergovernmental Panel on Climate Change (IPCC). Boundary-spanning institutions have also proven effective in enhancing coordination in fields such as metropolitan governance. Increasing social, economic, and political interdependence between neighbouring countries or regions has been used as a deliberate strategy to nurture a joint problem-solving orientation (Benz et al. 1992).

A second set of measures to improve horizontal coordination targets the engine room, not the superstructure. The underlying idea is that many problems related to policy interdependence are best addressed by spontaneous and undirected interaction in the engine room. An empirical study on coordination in the multi-organizational public transport system in the San Francisco Bay area has highlighted the many benefits of 'coordination without hierarchy' (Chisholm 1989). Chisholm argues that spontaneous coordination evolves in response to problems of interdependence when the people dealing with this problem are not hindered from doing so. An important and often overlooked task for improving cross-boundary coordination is to consider such barriers and find ways to reduce or overcome them. In turn, increasing exposure to the realities of other organizations (or countries, sectors, roles, and the like) increases understanding of these realities and facilitates informal coordination. Developing a web of informal relations across organizational boundaries is a very effective, although possibly not very direct way of improving coordination (Scharpf 1993; Chisholm 1989; Héritier 1999).

8.5　How to Coordinate

For the policy-maker in the twenty-first century, coordination of policies across sectoral and territorial boundaries is as important as the design and implementation of substantive policies. Interdependencies have increased and have undermined the implicit governance model of policy analysis, namely the model of an integrated and independent state that can autonomously make policies for its own constituencies. Interdependencies already abound within the normal context of one central government, but with economic and social globalization, and later digitalization, those interdependencies present a key challenge for policy-making in the twenty-first century. Governing them successfully will be crucial for effective policy-making.

However, finding solutions to problems arising from interdependence is not an easy task. Solutions might look obvious from an outsider's perspective, but the actors involved at different ends of interdependent policies are accountable to their constituencies—be that a particular country, region, or local community or the sector an organization is working in. 'Local' rationalities and interests cannot be ignored when exploring solutions that take interdependence into account. But the first lesson from research on interdependence is that these interests can and should be anticipated and acknowledged: representatives of Ethiopia should be aware of the downstream effect that building a dam has on bordering countries dependent on the Nile River. Becoming aware of such interdependence is the first step towards reconsidering short-term or sectorally confined benefits in light of the long-term costs of the project resulting from the relationship with downstream countries and the implications of a deteriorating relationship.

Building structures and institutions that address interdependencies is critical but the challenges of reforming and building institutions should be kept in mind. Often ideas for institution-building aim for an ideal hierarchical coordination, for example, when 'super-ministries' are summoned up to address cross-sectoral interdependencies or when transnational institutions should 'govern' global problems. For many problems stemming from interdependence, hierarchical coordination is neither feasible nor appropriate, given the manifold disadvantages and limitations of this type of coordination. Institution-building and development should not only be considered from the perspective of concentrating power but also conceived to improve horizontal coordination and voluntary cooperation. Institutions play an important role in allowing horizontal coordination to balance out asymmetric interests between stakeholders, for example, by combining different issues in negotiations (to allow for package deals) as well as by institutionalizing a process to search for common interests and specific solutions to foster these.

Institutions for coordination should also not be limited to formal rules and structures, but also include informal patterns of interaction. These include consultation procedures such as the EU's 'Have Your Say' portal (Chapter 7). Direct interaction across organizational and territorial boundaries is an often invisible but critically important means to improve coordination. Such patterns can evolve in response to emerging problems and needs but require an enabling context and can be facilitated by 'staging' direct exchange. We take up the role of institutions for policy-making in Chapter 9.

9

How to Work with Institutions

Key concepts

- Institutional elements
- Electoral rules
- Veto positions
- Path dependence
- Incremental change
- Institutional change
- Institution-building

Policy-making takes place in the context of institutions. Institutions consist of rules, norms, and mental maps; they guide the behaviour of individuals and organizations. In the superstructure, political institutions shape the allocation of power and the ability of political actors to veto decisions. In the engine room, policy fields are structured by sectoral institutions. They not only inform the general orientation of experts and the populace but also decisions regarding how a policy field is governed. This chapter focuses on three aspects of institutions in the policy process. We examine how to work with institutions in the superstructure, how to facilitate incremental change in the engine room, and how to build strong institutions.

9.1 Institutions Matter for Policy-Making

If you want to solve a policy problem that requires a change in behaviour, it might not be enough to simply pick the right policy instrument. When addressing wicked problems, such as poverty, corruption, or economic development (Chapter 3), policies need the support of the broader institutional context to be effective. As we explain in Chapter 4, a measure by the government will only show an impact if it reaches the target population and if it results in the desired behavioural change. Policy instruments do not generate an impact on their own; they require effective institutions.

How to Do Public Policy. Anke Hassel and Kai Wegrich, Oxford University Press.
© Anke Hassel and Kai Wegrich (2022). DOI: 10.1093/oso/9780198747000.003.0009

In this chapter, we address the role of institutions for policy-making in both the superstructure and the engine room. At the superstructure level, political institutions structure politics. There are several key political institutions, such as the rule of law, and checks and balances, but also electoral rules, the role of organized interests, and federalism, which affect decision-making processes and have a lasting effect on policy decisions. Electoral rules shape party systems by having either winner-takes-all systems or more proportional representation in parliament. These in turn lead to one- or multi-party governments and different kinds of negotiations and opportunities to exert veto power in decision-making.

At the engine room level, institutions that are specific to policy fields (which we call sectoral institutions) are crucial for policy design, implementation, and ultimately success. Sectoral institutions shape the interactions between stakeholders and affect the normative orientation of experts in the field. These institutions also protect the power balance in the engine room and very often need to be adjusted in order to effect actual policy change.

Finally, in places with weak institutions, policy-making is often about institution-building or at least strengthening institutions. Since the 1990s, international development policy has often focused on institution-building. Governments were advised to set up independent agencies for fighting corruption or improving tax collection or monetary policies, among other purposes. As experience has shown, these agencies only function in the desired way if they are backed up by broader institutional change.

This chapter addresses all three ways to work with institutions: understanding political institutions in the superstructure as a precondition for effective policy-making, reforming institutions to support policy change, and building institutions in the context of institutional weakness. But first, we briefly summarize relevant lessons from the rich literature on institutions.

9.2 The Effects of Institutions

The great advances of institutional analysis in economics, political science, and sociology since the 1990s allow us to make some general observations about the nature of institutions as they relate to making public policy (Hall 1993; Mahoney and Thelen 2015; Ostrom 1990; Polski and Ostrom 1999;

Streeck and Thelen 2005). We start with the finding that institutions are highly abstract and frequently invisible elements of the policy environment (Polski and Ostrom 1999, 2). North (1991, 97) neatly defines institutions as the 'humanly devised constraints that structure political, economic and social interaction. They consist of both informal constraints (sanctions, taboos, customs, traditions, and codes of conduct), and formal rules (constitutions, laws, property rights)'. Similarly, Crawford and Ostrom (1995) define institutions as widely understood rules, norms, or strategies, such as laws, policies, procedures, practices, and habits, that create incentives for behaviour in repetitive situations.

It is therefore widely accepted that institutions reach far beyond formal rules (such as constitutions and laws) and embrace informal practices and habits as well. The strength of institutions is therefore not solely embodied in a strong set of official rules. Only if these rules create a shared concept that influences the minds and routines of those who participate in policy-making can we see the effect of institutions. Formal institutions generate compliance because they are reinforced by strong social norms (Brinks et al. 2020, 12; Levi 1988).

The inherent nature of institutions is to provide stability. Institutions are the basic rules of the game of any political or other human and societal interaction. In the policy world, an institutional order is the foundation on which all political governance structures rest. Institutions provide a material, substantial set of formal rules. In the political realm, these are constitutions, electoral rules, and a body of law, as well as government decrees, bureaucracies, and policies. These rules are formalized in rule books with enforcement mechanisms (agencies, courts, penalties, and the like) behind them. Political actors and the polity's citizens are generally aware of the basic rules of a governance system.

To understand better the effects and functions of institutions, we can use the distinction made by organizational theorists between three *institutional elements*. Scott (2014), for example, argues that institutional arrangements usually combine regulative, normative, and cognitive elements. Regulative elements are legal norms (and policies), which make up the formal framework of institutions. Actors follow the rules for fear of punishment and because they 'have to'. Normative elements are based on moral or ethical systems, which work through habits and are based on a sense of duty and obligation. Norms create a feeling of 'ought to', i.e. shaping perceptions of what constitutes 'appropriate behaviour' (cf. March and Olsen 2006). Obligation is a very powerful motivation for behaviour and stronger than being forced to act in a particular way. Finally, cognitive elements are based on cultural norms, internalized values, and perceptions about how the world works. They correspond to social identity and desire. These norms are followed because actors 'want to' (Palthe 2014). Cognitive maps are the most powerful factors guiding behaviour because actors do not even see alternatives for their actions and consider it completely natural to behave in a particular way. However, cognitive maps are very difficult to change through policy-making.

When we apply this distinction between institutional elements to the analysis of policy-making and institutional change, the challenges and opportunities for impactful change become clear. Policy-making often addresses the regulative element of institutions because it is the easiest to change and the limitations of such a strategy of institutional change are not easily detected. For example, debates about the need to create 'independent institutions'—e.g. central banks, regulatory agencies, tax collection authorities, or even a 'carbon central bank' (to regulate emissions trading)—are often limited to the formal dimensions of independence (such as statutory rules). They underestimate, however, the powerful influence of informal norms that can undermine or support real independence from undue political interference.

By contrast, cognitive elements of institutions can be effective without the need for constant enforcement. For example, if central bank independence is taken for granted across political parties, economists, and interest groups as the key for successful monetary policy, the support for independence is strong. However, changing cognitive maps is very difficult and limited to the cultural context of a given locality and policy field.

Considering the normative dimensions of institutions is therefore critical for making policies stick and institutional change effective. It is important that policy actors develop a moral duty or obligation to follow a particular policy. In addition to regulatory change (banning smoking or corporate bribes), actors need to be convinced that this is the right thing to do (and that other actors also consider the unwanted behaviour to be inappropriate). In order to address the normative institutional dimension in change processes, policy-makers need to provide information, educate, and advocate for change. A convincing narrative becomes an important element of successful institutional change.

Political institutions frequently provide a normative frame for action. In the superstructure, policy-makers trust in the rule of law not just in the formal sense that its implementation can be enforced by courts. In ideal cases, abuse of power can be redressed, and politicians can be held accountable, at least at the level of formal use of power and money. Formal regulatory systems do not need to provide perfect control if political leaders follow the rules of appropriate behaviour (and provide little protection against abuses of power when leaders do not respect those rules—unless they face a robust response from civil society—as we can see in cases of democratic backsliding, Levitsky and Ziblatt 2018). Furthermore, policy-makers and citizens are accustomed to the rules and develop a normative understanding of right and wrong. Democracy, for example, is an institution of governance that has highly normative foundations. The rule of law, the peaceful transition of power from one elected government to another, and the recognition of human rights are not just neutral legal norms; rather, they motivate people to stand up in their defence and are taught in schools as normative orientations.

The normative frame of institutions might even exist where the institution itself is absent. In authoritarian countries, governments go to great lengths to pretend that they comply with basic democratic procedures like elections. Even though they find ways to secure their positions of power outside the rule of law, it is important for them to adopt the language of democracy, even if only at a superficial level.

Of course, not all policy changes need to address institutions or pursue institutional change. Many complex (wicked) problems require attention at the normative level in addition to the regulatory level. If a policy is only situated at the regulatory level, it is less effective than if it is embodied in broader institutional settings. Achieving normative or behavioural effects via institutions requires the provision of information, explanation, and enforcement of regulatory standards. If policies change but are not enforced, they might be counterproductive. At the same time, many (formal) regulatory changes are adopted in the hope that they will subsequently generate changes in norms and values. One example of such 'aspirational laws' is the policies to reduce violence against women in Mexico (Htun and Jensenius 2020).

In sum, we know that institutions matter for policy-making. They make policy decisions stick by shaping the practice and behaviour of policy-makers and those affected by the policy. In particular, the normative element of institutions, i.e. the element signalling duty or obligation, is important to reinforce regulatory change. Moreover, the strength of institutions is critical to their ultimate effectiveness. Often policy change is about strengthening or building institutions, both in the superstructure and in the engine room.

9.3 Understanding Political Institutions in the Superstructure

Political institutions fundamentally shape the policy-making process through (at least) three different ways. The first way involves the allocation of power and the aggregation of interest, primarily via electoral rules. The second extends beyond electoral rules to a wider perspective regarding political institutions, especially power-sharing mechanisms, which is prevalent in heterogeneous societies. Here, we refer to consociationalism or consensus versus majoritarian democracies. The third way involves the process of decision-making in parliamentary democracies and the number and capacities of other actors to veto decisions. For all three channels, there is a broad and well-established literature, primarily in the field of comparative political science. It is worth considering the evidence and arguments of this literature in more detail to make it fruitful for policy analysis.

9.3.1 Power allocation

The most powerful channelling effect of political institutions runs through the *electoral rules* of parliamentary and presidential democracies. It is well established that electoral rules divide parliamentary democracies into two groups: those with majoritarian systems and those with systems based on proportional representation. Majoritarian systems are those where elections are held in single-member districts and winners are determined by simple majorities. In such a first-past-the-post system, the candidate with the most votes wins the seat with no regard for the votes opposing the candidate. In contrast, in systems with proportional representation, all votes (beyond a certain threshold) influence the composition of parliament as seats are allocated in proportion to the votes won by each party receiving votes.

In practice, majoritarian systems tend to lead to two-party systems. Voters consider the chances of each candidate and tend to opt for those who have a chance of winning the seat. If the choice is for a multitude of different parties divided along one dominating cleavage, voters will abandon radical parties and opt for moderate parties to prevent the opposing party family from winning the seat. Over time, smaller parties will merge with bigger ones or just be abandoned, as they have no chance of winning seats. By contrast, in systems with proportional representation, multi-party systems flourish and, over time, tend to lead to more parties. This general effect of electoral rules on party systems is called Duverger's Law (Duverger 1972).

The effect electoral rules have on policy-making is thus substantial. The number of political parties in parliament generally determines not only whether governments are unitary actors (single-party governments) or coalitions (multi-party governments) but also what kind of parties end up in government. Multi-party governments tend to pursue different kinds of policies than single-party governments. Moreover, research by Iversen and Soskice (2006) has shown that majoritarian systems tend to favour right-wing parties, while proportional representation systems tend to advantage parties on the left. In proportional electoral systems, the number of years with left-wing parties in government was almost three times higher than that of right-wing parties, but the opposite was true in majoritarian systems, i.e. the number of years right-wing governments were in office was almost triple that of left-wing parties.

9.3.2 Power sharing

The British Westminster system of electoral rules is a majoritarian parliamentary system. These electoral rules are the most characteristic feature of the system but not the only one and are embedded in a whole set of other institutions and norms which make the system distinct. The Westminster system embodies an approach to democracy in which the parliamentary group that has a majority of seats in parliament has far-reaching powers. It is highly competitive but also adversarial. The system's other distinctions include a high level of centralization, a lack of a written constitution, and a rather weak upper legislative house. Majority rule works particularly well in relatively homogeneous societies, in which the system serves even minority groups sufficiently well.

In contrast to the Westminster political system, most continental European political systems are based on consensus, with majority rule as a minimum condition. However, the key feature of consensus democracies is that power is shared, dispersed, and limited (Lijphart 2012). Such consensus institutions have emerged in less homogeneous societies, in particular societies that are divided along religious, linguistic, racial, or ethnic lines, i.e. beyond mere socio-economic or class cleavages. In divided societies, minorities would be excluded if no consensus-seeking mechanism existed. Countries with consensus models, such as Switzerland, Belgium, and the Netherlands, have developed their political institutions in a context of multi-ethnic or multi-religious societies (Lehmbruch 1975; Fakhoury 2019, on consociationalism in Lebanon). Because these countries were heterogeneous in terms of language, religion, and regional autonomy at the time of democratization, mechanisms were established to ensure that one societal group would not dominate the other but had to negotiate power relationships.

In consensus systems, proportional representation is important as it provides minority groups greater opportunity to participate via multi-party parliaments and coalition governments. In addition, the power-sharing mechanisms developed in consensus systems typically result in strong interest groups (often organized centrally as corporatist groups), a high degree of decentralization to lower levels of government, effective bicameralism, robust constitutions, and a powerful judiciary. These institutions protect minority rights and strive to balance the needs and demands of different groups in society. Consensus-based political institutions find it easy to accept sharing power with other actors and are based on the negotiation of compromise, which is alien to the Westminster system (see Box 9.1).

Box 9.1 Leaving the European Union: the Westminster system and EU politics from an institutional perspective

The United Kingdom was a latecomer to the European Union. Only after the prominence of the British Empire fundamentally declined after the Second World War and hopes for economic recovery were attached to joining the European Community (EC) did the British government decide to apply for membership to the EC, eventually joining in 1973.

The relationship between the UK and the EC (and later EU) was always uneasy. The UK was reluctant to join the deeper mechanisms of European integration, such as the Schengen Agreement on free movement or the European Monetary System. The UK saw the EU more as a free trade zone than as a nascent political union, which it never shared as the final goal. This scepticism also applied to the role of the European Court of Justice. The British approach towards judicial review is more limited as the UK does not have a codified constitution and the judicial review of legislation is rare. Parliament is the strongest institution in the Westminster system, and the idea of power sharing between the judicial and parliamentary systems is not well received (Odermatt 2017). Finally, EU decision-making rests on either unanimity or qualified majority voting. The European Parliament and the EU Council usually require a supermajority to adopt legislation. This involves long negotiations and compromises on many different levels.

Power sharing and compromise are alien to the British political system. EU Council compromise decisions were therefore frequently seen in the UK as political failures rather than as standard procedures of decision-making. The strong impression of the EU as unfair and unduly constraining to British political endeavours reflects the possible lack of compatibility of a strong Westminster system, that relies on very few constraints for Parliament and prime minister, and the European political system, in which power sharing and negotiation have been institutionalized.

When the potential benefits of EU membership for the UK economy and society appeared to decline and responsibilities grew, important sections of the British Conservative Party, one of the main pillars in the party system, started to rebel. At the heart of the push to leave the EU remained the ill fit between the Westminster system and the mechanism of European negotiated politics, along with the judicial review process of the European Court of Justice (ECJ).

The process of leaving the EU proved to be politically difficult, as the British Parliament found it hard to agree on the terms and conditions of leaving. In the final Withdrawal Agreement with the EU, a key topic was again the role of the ECJ in policing the governance of the agreement (Morris 2020). The European Union Act 2020 was passed by the British Parliament on 22 January 2020—nine days before the UK withdrew from the European Union.

9.3.3 Making decisions in the superstructure

The dynamics of decision-making in the superstructure depend on the number of actors who can potentially veto a proposition and thus hold a *veto position*. Political institutions in the superstructure give different actors influence over the decision-making process. In countries with frequent referenda over policy decisions, such as Switzerland, political actors can organize referenda to push governments to adopt certain policies. If the electoral rules produce large majorities, as they do in the UK and Sweden, the parliamentary group has high levels of control over the decision-making process. Finally, if majorities are small and parliamentary groups divided, the government might have some influence over decision-making but might also have to compromise with conflicting groups and even other stakeholders, such as professional associations, consumer groups, and the like. Immergut (1992) has shown how differences in the institutional superstructure shaped the prospects of healthcare reform policies in France, Sweden, and Switzerland. In Switzerland, the influence of doctors' associations was strongest, while it was weakest in Sweden, where large parliamentary majorities are the norm. A later study on healthcare reform across Europe (Immergut et al. 2021) reinforced the importance of considering such veto positions.

Veto positions are not necessarily inherent to particular political institutions. Actors hold a veto position if they can stop the government from adopting or proceeding with a policy (Tsebelis 2002). It is key to identify those actors who, either because of their institutional decision-making power or because of their voting rights, can make a difference in the policy process: if the government's majority in parliament is slim, and a subgroup of parliamentarians is not willing to support the government on a particular policy, that subgroup can veto the process, even if it is very small. On the other hand, even a powerful president or a second chamber cannot be said to hold a veto position, and will not make a difference in the policy process, if it supports the position of the government on a policy proposal (Tsebelis 2002).

If many veto positions exist in the superstructure's decision-making process, policy stability is more likely than change, as it is hard to overcome the veto of so many actors. Policy stability (or stalemate) can, however, lead to political instability: if the political system lacks the capacity to resolve problems, the mounting problem load can lead to unstable political regimes and eventually a change of government (or even regime). Also, if it is impossible to change the legislative status quo, other actors, such as bureaucrats and judges, will tend to be more active and independent from the political system. Thus, decision-makers in the superstructure need to understand these veto opportunities and constellations as they embrace policy proposals.

Unlike in centralized political systems with majority rules, in systems with numerous veto positions, decision-making requires negotiation. This is why in complex political institutions, such as the EU, with very high numbers of veto players, it can take a very long time and many side arrangements to find a compromise on which every necessary actor can agree.

At the same time, Lindvall (2017) argues that the need to forge larger coalitions in power-sharing systems (with many veto positions) forces the government to compensate the losers in reforms and allows for reforms that are likely to be more sustainable in the long term. More actors have to agree to the policy, making more demands in exchange. The same actors will also support the policy afterwards and work towards its implementation.

9.3.4 Working with political institutions

As should be evident at this point, policy-making in systems with consensus-based institutions differs substantially from policy-making in majoritarian systems. Power-sharing mechanisms, checks and balances, and coalition governments lead to dynamics in the policy process that are quite different from those experienced by single-party governments in a highly centralized political setting. This also has implications for policy-making at subnational levels. Institutional context is key: both policy analysts and policy-makers need to understand the formal electoral and political rules of the game. Therefore, it is paramount to make sure that the formal electoral and political rules of the game are well understood, while keeping in mind that the difference between institutional types is not as clear cut as the literature suggests. Indeed, there are several mixed systems (such as the French), and even in majoritarian systems, veto players constrain the national government (Congress in the United States; devolved governments in the case of the UK).

Since the turn of the twenty-first century, political authority has fragmented in all political systems, and new actors, in particular new parties, have proliferated. Even though electoral rules in majoritarian systems still favour a two-party system, there have been a number of instances in which other parties have come to power. Examples include the coalition government in the UK between 2010 and 2015, in which the Liberal Democrats joined the Conservatives, and the minority government in the UK in 2017, which featured a deal between the Conservatives and the Democratic Unionist Party of Northern Ireland.

Furthermore, in the framework of international organizations, almost all negotiations are based on unanimity and consensus. Thus, the ability to compromise and formulate a broad win-set for all policy-makers is relevant for actors not only in systems with proportional representation but also in many other settings.

In the following, we offer some general recommendations to the policy analyst as how to understand and work with political institutions in the superstructure.

- **Identify core policy content.** In most political processes, policy proposals are subject to negotiation and influence by other actors, particularly veto players. To ensure that policies are not stripped bare or watered down to the extent that they are meaningless, policy proposals must have a core policy content that is non-negotiable. Policy analysts must be able to differentiate between nice-to-have policy features and those that cannot be abandoned in the negotiation process. These core policy features must be communicated to those involved in negotiations and those stakeholders who are needed to support the decision-making.
- **Identify room for manoeuvre.** Along the same lines, anticipating the policy preferences of other actors in the policy process can help to identify possible compromises in order to increase the potential win-sets for all actors involved: Make sure that aspects of the policy are potentially attractive for other actors or veto players in the process. Include compensation mechanisms for those who stand to lose because of the policy, and use such compensation to make the overall policy attractive for a broader audience. Build policy coalitions in the political system; underlying policy arguments addressing the constituencies of different coalition partners must be formulated clearly.
- **Secure credible commitments.** Ensure that key decision-makers in the superstructure can make credible commitments on the core and secondary aspects of the policy. Political actors need to be able to count on parliamentary backing for the policy proposal they present in negotiations with other actors. If policy-makers' commitment to the core of the policy is not credible, supporters might abandon the cause and not accept a necessary compromise (see Box 9.2).

9.4 Changing Institutions: How to Embed Policies

In the engine room of the policy world, institutions provide formal rules and normative frames. These frames not only influence the decisions made by individuals with regard to their own lives and those of their families but also shape the scope for policy change. For instance, an education system is usually based on a clear mandate of obligatory schooling for a minimum number of years, a structure of different types of schools, the type of teaching in each type of school, and the permeability between different schools. Some countries, such as the UK, France, and the US, have elitist education systems, where certificates from particular higher education institutions (Oxbridge, ENA, Ivy League) in combination with particular schools (private versus state schools) largely determine life chances. Other countries have a less stratified education system. Most families develop normative orientations towards the education system in order to give their children the best possible opportunities. They will engage with the system as it is and try to make it work for them. They might employ private tutors to get into elitist schools or acquire other skills through vocational training or internships. The underlying institutions, in particular the set of special rules for elite schools, tax breaks, and privileges for private education, protect the elitist versus meritocratic education system. In order to make elitist education systems more inclusive, change would need to be made not only to the regulation of schools but also to the wider context in which these schools operate.

The example of the education system shows how policy fields are institutionalized in particular ways that structure certain outcomes. Everyone affected by the policy field will adjust their expectations accordingly. Those who are privileged by an institution have a strong interest in maintaining that institution. As they are the beneficiaries, they are also motivated to exert influence on the policy field. The institutional context of education systems is usually informed by the role of private versus public schools, the importance and selectiveness of schools and higher education, as well as the kind of education ideals a society holds. Key actors are school administration bodies at the local and regional level, but also private schools—where relevant—and teachers' and/or parents' associations. These actors frame the general normative orientation of the field: in the education sector, the normative orientation might prioritize excellence over inclusion based on the privileged position of private schools. In that case, policy-makers will aim to educate a small number of the elite at high-quality schools, while not devoting much energy to general access to education.

Sectoral institutions, therefore, are comprised of the basic structure of a policy field, as well as the policy history of the field, the actor constellation, and the general approach (cognitive map) towards the policy field. When combined over time, these components form a cohesive understanding about the core values of the policy field, what kind of expert is likely to be active in the field, and whose interests dominate. For instance, in many countries, teachers' unions are very influential and might seek to protect themselves from overly high expectations on the part of parents. School administrators might try to keep schools and parents under control, while government bureaucrats aim to limit the costs of schools. In this context, improving school performance is no mean feat.

How can a policy be made effective in the context of such sectoral institutions? How can the attention of school administrators be shifted from protecting teachers (if that is the problem) to engaging in a discourse on teaching quality and inclusion? Changing institutions requires a good understanding of how policies feed into institutions and vice versa (see Figure. 9.1).

9.4.1 Path dependence

How do institutions evolve? In public policy (as in organizations and technology), initial design decisions can substantially shape later development. Decisions in the superstructure on basic institutional design or heavy investment in a particular kind of public infrastructure will often determine policies for decades to come. In most countries of the Organization for Economic Co-operation and Development (OECD), pension and education systems were conceived in the late nineteenth century, and their basic structure, rules, and norms have remained roughly the same almost everywhere. This is the effect of *path dependence* (see Box 9.2).

As with technological innovations, initial designs favour certain stakeholders and discriminate against others. They can shape the trajectory of a policy and limit other options. In policy design, the decision by many big cities, at the turn of the twentieth century, to organize mobility via public transport rather than individual cars has had important repercussions not only for individuals but also for business. The introduction of a free-of-charge healthcare system (the National Health Service) in the UK after the Second World War has had enormous implications for the delivery of health services, mobilization of resources, and planning capacity of medical care in the UK. These initial decisions also draw on specific resources from public administrations.

In short, initial policy decisions lead to a basic policy design, which cannot be changed easily at a later stage and therefore, over time, itself turns into an institutional context. Once policy-makers start down a particular path, reversal is difficult. Policy change, therefore, must take into account the existing policy design and its legacy. As existing policy designs privilege some groups and policy actors at the expense of others, this can lead to the accumulation of advantages over time (increasing returns). These increasing returns stabilize the basic policy design over long periods of time, despite changes of government and even, perhaps, public opinion. The stability of policy design is, therefore, the result of initial decisions and the logic of path dependence. Both constrain the policy choices available to future policy-makers.

The concept of path dependence makes two major contributions to the understanding of policies. First, it underlines the importance of the historical evolution of policy fields and the role of timing. As Paul Pierson (2000) points out, the timing of policy decisions is crucial, particularly since politicians' time horizons are shorter than those for people in the business community and in public administration (Pierson 2000; Howlett and Goetz 2014). Policy-makers are rewarded for their policies within the electoral term; thus, reforms that will only show benefits over a longer time perspective are unlikely to be prioritized (cf. Jacobs 2011, who argues that a low risk of losing office for imposing short-term costs is one precondition for politicians to take future-oriented decisions). Path-breaking decisions, on the other hand, require decision-making power and a long time horizon. That does not mean that policy-makers shy away from policy decisions that have a long-lasting impact. The UK government's decision to hold the Brexit referendum had enormous consequences for the country. However, among many political actors, the motives for pursuing Brexit were short-term electoral gains. The short-term time horizon of policy-makers in the superstructure combined with the effects of path dependence works against the pursuit of long-term strategies and investments and will shape the incremental adjustment that is usually pursued instead.

Box 9.2   Policies as institutions: the concept of path dependence

---

Path dependence is a concept that has its roots in technology, science and economics but has found its way into political science and policy research. Path dependence describes the phenomenon where decisions and developments are overwhelmingly shaped by earlier choices made relating to the design of technologies and of policies. Initial decisions on technology and policy leave room for adjustment and reforms in some directions, but preclude other choices due to the high costs of substantially changing direction. The claim of path dependence is that the initial design establishes a path, which not only aligns the expectations of stakeholders but also distributes rewards for those who are on the path while discriminating against those who challenge the path. The further we travel down the path and the more we invest in an initial policy design, the higher are reversal costs and the more likely it is that we will pursue this path further and only change direction slightly.

An initial (policy) decision may serve as an orientation point for all actors in the (policy) field. This is clearly the case for many technical standards, from the worldwide proliferation of the QWERTY keyboard layout to the continued dominance of the Windows operating system for personal computers. As more and more office workers are trained on the QWERTY keyboard and in Windows-based applications, switching to a new base design becomes more costly. Future technological developments will have to take the current standards as their starting point. For the foreseeable future, new keyboard models will copy the QWERTY keyboard, and computer hardware will be designed to accommodate the standards of Microsoft.

In policy fields, path dependence evolves when policy-makers, particularly in the engine room, are trained in a particular policy approach, for instance when a database is developed for a specific administrative task but also when the population has invested heavily in particular systems, such as pension funds or private education.

The second contribution the notion of path dependence makes for understanding policies is that it helps to explain the dynamics of change. Although institutions can be normative straitjackets, they are also frequently contested. Opposition to institutional frameworks comes from losers of the established systems, from young generations, who strive for modernization, and from technological and political change. Not everyone supports a free healthcare system like the NHS. Private health providers might lobby for more private healthcare. Younger generations might push for better healthcare and campaign against waiting lists for surgery. Technological advances in medical science might revolutionize healthcare through companies that cannot be integrated into a free healthcare system. Pushbacks against established policies, therefore, also have an effect on the institutional context. While new policies have to be adapted to the existing institutional context if they are to be effective, institutions must eventually take these new policies into account. In short, policy change and institutional change have to go hand in hand in order to make any difference (Figure. 9.1).

Taking path dependence seriously, the policy-maker will need to carve out a policy approach that builds on the existing policy path and aims to shift the path in a new direction. There is rarely the opportunity for radical change, which is only possible in moments of revolutionary 'punctuations', i.e. critical junctures in history. In moments of critical juncture, institutions and policy fields can be set on a different path. Critical junctures are times of major upheaval (systemic change as after the fall of the Berlin Wall in Germany, wars, or revolutions). The shift between institutional stability and radical change has been termed 'punctuated equilibrium' (see Box 9.3 and Chapter 2).

More frequent than radical change is *incremental change*. Even though institutions are relatively unfluctuating sets of rules of the game and 'reified conventions', they are not immune to gradual change, which can be deliberately pursued and orchestrated. Such institutional change opens a new world of agency for policy-makers to pursue strategies of change. Rather than aiming or waiting for an unpredictable exogenous shock, pursuing incremental endogenous institutional change builds a policy repertoire they can employ to adjust or reform institutional settings.

Box 9.3   Punctuated equilibrium

Punctuated equilibrium is borrowed from research in biology, where it was used to challenge the Darwinian notion of gradual change through mutation. It was put forward by natural historians, Eldredge and Gould (1972), who proposed that lineages exist in essentially static form (equilibrium) over most of their histories, and

continued

Box 9.3 *continued*

new species arise abruptly through sudden, revolutionary 'punctuations' of rapid change, at which point—as in the Darwinian model—environmental selection determines the fate of new variations. In political science, punctuated equilibrium was introduced in studies on agenda-setting by Jones and Baumgartner (2005).

9.4.2 Incremental institutional change

Gradual *institutional change* can occur in different ways. Mahoney and Thelen (2009, 16) have identified three mechanisms of change (layering, drift, and conversion) in addition to basic rule change. If new rules are introduced in addition to old ones, we find a process of layering. Layering can be found in situations in which governments seek to respond to a changing context but do not have the capacity or willingness to pursue more comprehensive change, and hence introduce new rules 'on top' of existing ones. The new rules gradually change the institutions without requiring a major repeal of laws by introducing tensions towards pre-existing rules that build up over time. For example, rules on political asylum have been tightened without dismantling the general idea of granting asylum to those who are politically persecuted. The institution of political asylum has thereby acquired a new meaning. Similarly, the interpretation of human rights has changed over time through the issuance of new conventions on social and economic rights, which were not part of the classic understanding of human rights.

If old rules persist and no new rules are introduced, institutions might nevertheless change. For instance, the rules already in place might be neglected (drift), or their impact might be redirected to serve different purposes beyond their original intention (conversion). In some cases, old rules are simply no longer applied or enforced, and therefore drift occurs. A prominent example is drug policy. The recreational use of marijuana has become habitual among younger generations and generally more accepted. The enforcement of sanctions on the use of soft drugs in cities in Western Europe and the US has gradually diminished or disappeared. Instead, a new drug policy has slowly developed which is more permissive and has led to the legalization of marijuana use in some places (some US states, Canada, Uruguay, among others). The policy first drifted and then led to new legislation.

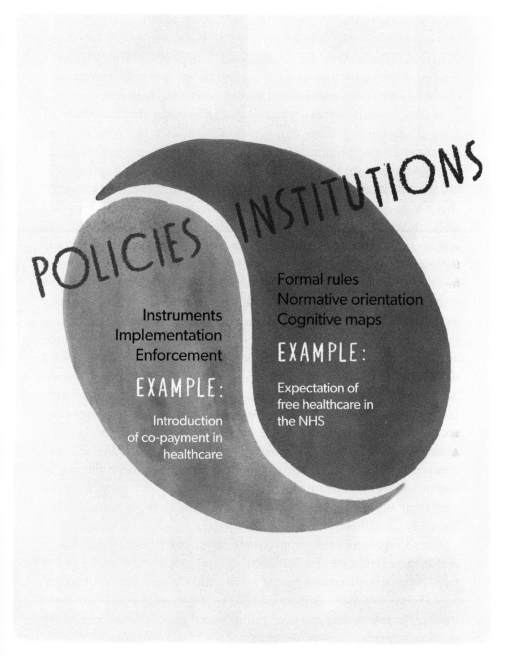

Fig. 9.1 The complementarities of policies and institutions

Understanding the process of incremental institutional change allows policy-makers to consider possibilities for transforming institutions without (fundamentally) changing their formal set-up. Rather than waiting for a big bang and politically tumultuous circumstances, in which major changes must be decided on and implemented, gradual change might transform into fundamental change once a tipping or turning point is reached. Gradual change does not depend on exceptional circumstances but can emerge from day-to-day adjustments to new challenges.

Neglect, erosion, and newly introduced rules might shift a policy from one path to the next without a big bang. As society and business continue to evolve in certain directions, the meanings of institutions might transform even if the regulations are pretty much the same. Or specific regulations will be altered and adjusted to such an extent that the old regime changes its character or just collapses. For instance, the liberalization of labour markets that started in Western countries in the early 1980s was accompanied by a decline in labour inspections in many countries. While the regulatory standards of health and safety often increased on paper, enforcement produced high costs for state budgets and businesses and few results. Lack of coherence and guidance often undermined the capacity to enforce regulatory measures (Blanc 2012). A good example is working time regulations, which often include very clear norms of maximum hours and minimum breaks.[1] In reality, adherence to the working time rules for white-collar workers in many industries is neither monitored nor enforced, and so the rule has lost its grip. In start-up firms and in parts of the financial services industries, firms leave working time to the discretion of their employees.

The three mechanisms of gradual institutional change, layering, drift and conversion, can also reinforce each other, as Graf shows with the case of German skill formation, in which firms and universities have acquired an important role in offering hybrid forms of post-secondary education (Graf 2018, 187).

A key insight from the perspective of incremental institutional change is that there might also be declining returns from a well-trodden policy path as policies are constantly contested and lose their relevance (cf. Jacobs and Weaver 2015). Opposition to a particular policy path might make it less attractive to continue in that direction if it is less and less likely to produce pay-offs. Thus, while recognition of path dependence is essential for the policy analyst to understand the policy field, it is not sufficient

---

[1] For instance, German working time legislation demands that there must be an eleven-hour break between two working days. Employees who respond to work e-mails in the evening must, by law, wait eleven hours before they can start working again. This is not enforced in practice.

for understanding the full expanse of the room available for policy reforms.

9.4.3 How to achieve gradual but transformative change

The possibility of embarking on gradual but transformative change assigns policy-makers and analysts much greater agency than would the assumption that big external events are the precondition for major policy change. In a rapidly changing world that presents many challenges for policy-makers and exerts high pressure to deal with these challenges, policy-makers have a range of options for preparing for and engaging in gradual institutional change. Here we list a range of measures that activists and policy-makers in the superstructure and engine room could pursue.

- **Analyse and reinforce existing countertrends**. Even though path dependence implies that policy fields follow a particular trajectory, broader societal, economic, and political trends might disrupt the policy path. Take the example of same-sex marriage. In many countries, heterosexual marriage is privileged, regarding taxation, pension, inheritance, and adoption rights, and, in some, gay marriage is banned outright. As heterosexual families are the vast majority, there is little reason to assume that they would like to share their rights and that minority rights would be on the agenda or part of the institutional trajectory. Nevertheless, in many countries over the last decade, the rights of same-sex couples were strengthened to almost the same level as heterosexual marriages in all but name. Even as conservative governments in some countries did not dare to remove the protection of heterosexual marriage, some gave in to stronger demands from the lesbian and gay communities to give them access to similar privileges. Behind this layered incremental change are primarily more liberal values in some societies and general trends towards diversity, which have been used successfully by many minority groups to advocate for change.
- **Enforce norms more rigorously or work towards forbearance.** This is not a call for policy-makers to break the law of the land or to encourage people to break laws. But compliance with norms could take place on many different levels, from full support to nominal acceptance. For instance, in the example of the dominance of individual car transportation vis-à-vis public transportation, there are many ways to give a clear sign

that the car industry and car owners must contribute more to reversing climate change. Parking restrictions could be enforced more strictly, while public transportation could be made more accessible. Car park spaces could be repurposed as bicycle parking spaces. A differentiated approach towards rule compliance and enforcement aims to send signals about the earnestness of policy change. Civil society campaign groups could run projects to showcase change. For instance, in public welfare systems, benefit cuts and sanctions are commonly used to punish those benefit recipients who do not comply with the rules on activation, such as seeking a job. Citizen campaign groups have set up funds to pay sanctions on behalf of specific individuals to highlight the injustice and ineffectiveness of the existing system. On the other hand, a more lenient practice of enforcement could be the starting point of policy change, as we discussed earlier in relation to the example of cannabis consumption. 'Forbearance' (Holland 2017) is used by politicians in the absence of other policy means to support constituents (i.e. as 'informal welfare'), but could also be used to initiate change.

- **Exploit ambiguity.** In many policy regimes, norms and regulations are ambiguous. Laws and judicial rulings might include general norms about fairness and justice that could be exploited by policy-makers and policy activists to expand the room for interpretation of the policy field. Climate activists, for example, have been pushing to grant asylum rights to 'climate refugees'. The ambiguous nature of asylum laws allows them to convincingly make these claims.

- **Introduce friction.** Most policy trajectories operate in relative peace as long as they deliver the expected results. Those who aim to change the institutional set-up of the system could start by pointing to the system's weaknesses and actively emphasize the loss in social justice or the high public costs the system produces. For instance, access to private schools and issues of diversity have long been the Achilles heel of private school systems. Policy-makers could actively evaluate the composition of students in private education systems in order to force them to adopt more inclusive admission policies. Alternatively, strategic litigation (strategic use of the judicial system to highlight the flaws of existing policies) could help to put pressure on a system's insiders to change their behaviour.

- **Mobilize the losers**. Where some actors benefit from policy regimes, others might lose. Often the losers do not know that they are disadvantaged by the policy. Policy-makers could make losers aware of their losses through research reports and evaluation studies and create awareness of the distributional effects of policies. In most countries, spending on bicycle and pedestrian infrastructure is only a fraction of public spending on roads, even though, relatively speaking, many more people use bikes and walk daily. In a situation of rapidly rising rents and only little leeway to change the regulation on rent control, policy-makers could actively support tenants' associations in their assessment of the situation. These associations could be included more intensively in the policy discourse, perhaps at the expense of investors and landlords. Tenants could be made aware of their rights, and landlords who extract high rents could be publicly shamed. When the city of Berlin introduced rent control in early 2020, it launched an information campaign and forced landlords to inform tenants of their new rights.[2]

These measures aim at creating a new narrative (see also Chapter 3) about the workings of a policy regime to introduce gradual but transformative change. They require the knowledge and mobilization of other actors, especially stakeholders, and analysis of the distributive effects of particular policy fields. As the beneficiaries of existing policies will observe these activities and likely oppose them, policy-makers who engage in gradual but transformative change need to anticipate such responses and strategically engage with losers as well as change-makers. They also need to be aware of the time horizon and the general and secular trends in public opinion regarding particular topics. Diversity and citizens' rights, which are very high on the agenda in the politics of the 2020s, could be mobilized for strategic discussions in a variety of policy themes including foreign affairs, financial regulation, and social policies. As policy-makers are not in control of major exogenous events, gradual transformative change is usually the only option available for transforming the institutions shaping a policy field.

9.5 Building Institutions

In the field of development economics and assistance, the lack of robust institutions has long been identified as a major obstacle to economic development (Acemoglu and Robinson 2012). From the 1980s onwards,

---

[2] The Berlin's (state) law for rent control has been overturned by the Federal Constitutional Court in March 2021.

international organizations have therefore recommended institutional reforms as a path to success. The World Bank called for the improvement of 'institutional capabilities' for reaching development goals (World Bank 1997; Roberts 2010, 15). Earlier, Samuel Huntington (1968, 1) emphasized that 'the most important political distinction among countries concerns not their form of government but their degree of government', in other words, the quality of their institutions.

Institution-building is an enormously difficult task as fundamental change of behaviour is required to make a new institution work. Many governments have tried to address wicked problems by setting up new institutions. New institutions were supposed to insulate policy-making and policy delivery from political influence. For instance, from the 1970s onwards, independent monetary institutions (central banks) were seen as superior to central banks under the control of the government. Many governments therefore started to give central banks an independent mandate. Economic analysis supported the claim that central bank independence works: countries with more independent central banks had lower inflation rates (the studies controlled for all kinds of other factors, cf. Roberts 2010, 23–46).

Arm's-length administrative bodies, removed from direct political influence (for example, from the minister responsible for the agency's policy portfolio) that have been charged with regulating economic sectors, ranging from financial services to telecommunications, electricity, railways, and pharmaceuticals, have diffused globally as a model promising unbiased and expert-based regulation of these sectors (see Jordana et al. 2018 for a global data set on regulatory agencies). Insulation of agencies from political influence has been seen as critical because investors require stable and predictable regulatory frameworks for making long-term investments. If private enterprises were to make investments in infrastructure, for example, the risk of political interference (to, say, reduce consumer prices for electricity) would need to be minimized. The limited possibility for competition in sectors tending towards natural monopolies (electricity, water, telecommunications) also requires unbiased regulatory intervention, for example regarding pricing or access to infrastructure by competitors.

Thus, establishing independent administrative bodies was seen as an institutional solution for many policy problems, and developing countries in particular have been at the receiving end of such recommendations from international organizations, such as the World Bank and the International

Monetary Fund (IMF). But, as Roberts (2010) found, such recommendations were based on a naive understanding of how institutions work and how they can be changed. The case of the so-called 'autonomous revenue authority' (Roberts 2010, 65–74) is particularly instructive. Diminishing tax collection, due to political unrest, economic crises, and a public sector in decline, was a widespread problem in the 1970s and 1980s in developing countries. In the 1980s, Ghana found a way out of this problem: after defaulting on a loan, it negotiated a solution with the IMF that included the separation of its two tax collection bureaucracies from the finance ministry. The new National Revenue Secretariat was granted wide autonomy; oversight was exercised by a new board rather than the finance ministry. Revenues collected beyond targets could then be used for performance bonuses and investment in facilities. Indeed, the new autonomous agency was effective, and the tax-to-GDP ratio (the size of the tax revenue of a country in relation to its economy) increased from 5 to 17 per cent at the end of the 1980s.

Uganda was the first country to copy Ghana's success and then Peru followed. The reform yielded successes in both countries, as indicated by increasing tax rates. By the mid-1990s, the reforms in the three countries were turned into a template, the semi-autonomous revenue authority (ARA). Broadly modelled after the template of independent central banks, ARAs were to remove the incentives for politicians to interfere in tax collection for short-term political gains, a practice which had the effect of undermining the agency's enforcement capacities and the population's tax morale. Promoted as a successful model by the IMF, the World Bank, and leading national development cooperation institutions (such as the UK's Department for International Development, DFID), twenty-three developing countries had adopted some variation of the model by 2005 (Roberts 2010, 70). However, most of the adopting countries could not achieve similar gains in tax collection rates, and even the three leading countries could not sustain their success.

Roberts's analysis of the weaknesses of the ARA reforms points to two mechanisms inherent to institutions discussed at the outset of this chapter. First, formal institutional change does not equal real institutional change. The 'autonomy' of the revenue agencies was put into laws and statutes, rules and regulations, but this did not automatically change the existing power relations. 'The ARA model created a situation in which a new organization became the rival of the most powerful player in the bureaucracy' (Roberts 2010, 71). The finance ministries also fought back in the post-reform years, taking back control over tax enforcement. Second, the formal or regulative dimension is not sufficient to change norms of 'appropriate behaviour' (the normative element of institutions Scott (2014) discusses). Norms of corruption and nepotism prevailed and influenced the enforcement practices in these new tax collection authorities.

The hard lesson to be drawn from the case of the ARAs is that institution-building cannot be achieved through formal institutional change that is limited to the regulative component of institutions. Many capacity-building efforts in development assistance suffer from the underlying theory of change that Roberts (2010) calls 'naïve institutionalism'. While corruption remains one of these wicked problems that is very difficult to address (Mungiu-Pippidi 2015), international cooperation also has examples of institutional change that take into account both the regulative and normative elements of institutions. In 1997, the OECD adopted the Anti-Bribery Convention and changed the discourse on bribes. After a concerted campaign, OECD member countries committed to making it a criminal offence for companies to offer bribes to foreign public officials because it undermined the rule of law in countries with weak institutions. It took some time for the corporate regulatory regime to support the shift away from corporate bribes and towards cleaner corporate governance for overseas investment. Only after companies were prosecuted for bribing foreign governments and public opinion in the home countries turned against those firms did the regulation stick (see Box 9.4).

Box 9.4 Fighting bribery

Until the adoption of the OECD Anti-Bribery Convention, officially the Convention on Combating Bribery of Foreign Public Officials in International Business Transactions, in 1997, it was common among multinational companies to bribe local officials in countries in which they invested in order to obtain planning permission, tax privileges, or other favours. In some countries, the practice was legal, and such payments were even tax deductible in the companies' home countries. After the US introduced criminal sanctions for bribes in the Foreign Corrupt Practices Act in 1977, a more systematic discussion started in the OECD. The OECD set up a working group on anti-bribery in 1989, and the member states chose the soft instrument of a recommendation on bribery in international business transactions in 1994. The ad hoc working group was turned into a formalized Working Group on

Bribery and drafted the Convention. In 2009, the OECD added two recommendations to its anti-bribery framework: one introduced a monitoring process based
on accelerated phases of evaluations, on-site visits, and public reports and the
second called for changing tax law to disallow the tax-deductibility of bribes.

In December 2019, data for 2018 was published by the OECD (OECD 2019b) that
shows the number of individuals and entities who have received sanctions for
foreign bribery since the Convention entered into force as well as the number of
investigations and ongoing criminal proceedings.

The risks of noncompliance increased for firms subject to the Anti-Bribery
Convention with the onset of Phase 3 in 2010. Frequent evaluations as well as academic research have shown that multinational companies that are subject to the
Convention have reduced their actual bribery behaviour relative to competitors
who are not covered by the Convention (Jensen and Malesky 2018). However, a
report by Transparency International (2020b) claims that active enforcement of
the Convention declined considerably between 2018 and 2020.

While corruption remains a wicked problem in many countries, bribery, as part
of multinational companies' business practices, has been banned, even though
few countries have actually gone so far as to sanction companies. Scandals
involving large bribes attract media attention and lead to legal action in a number of fields including international sports events, such as international football
tournaments (US Department of Justice 2015; Meier and García 2015).

The anti-bribery case shows the close relationship between institutions
and policies. Institutions are the context of policy-making, and policies
are the measures taken by governments as a response to policy problems.
Context and action are interdependent: policies have an effect on the institutions, while institutions have an effect on the policies. The Anti-Bribery
Convention was conceived in a broader institutional context, in which corruption had low priority. By adopting a regulation banning bribes and
monitoring prosecution, governments and companies have been pressured
to take the costs of bribery more seriously. Repeated prosecution or at least
the threat of sanctions could potentially convince firms that bribery is not a
sustainable business practice. In theory and increasingly in practice, anti-
bribery has become a stable norm even if the norm's strength still varies
cross-nationally.

Effective institution-building rests on four components of policy-
making: First, it depends on establishing a new norm of behaviour. Norms
tell individuals, businesses, policy-makers, and officeholders what is right

and wrong. It could be said that anti-bribery has been established within the multinational business community around the world as a guiding norm, even though many companies still violate it. Second, norm violation must be sanctioned through consistent enforcement. Only if bribery at a certain level and frequency leads to painful punishment will actors stick to the norm. Third, institutional norms require establishment via repeated behaviour. A norm does not arise out of singular events but out of everyday action. Only if repeated actions follow the same norm will the norm be effectively complied with. Finally, effective institution-building rests on complementarity. Institutional complementarity refers to institutional settings, in which the presence of one institution is necessary for the effectiveness of another (Hall and Soskice 2001). Many institutional systems are based on complementary institutions. Most obviously, the rule of law is based on the separation of power within political institutions. In the context of bribery: anti-bribery norms are effectively complementary to decent public sector wages and a professional ethos of the public sector.

9.6 How to Harness Institutions

Institutions are the most powerful drivers of policy success and failure. If strong institutions support a policy, implementation is comparatively straightforward, and enforcement takes place without extraordinary effort. In contrast, if policies are not in line with the institutional environment, they are very likely to fail. Knowing the force of institutions and being able to use them to one's own advantage is therefore a key skill for policy-makers to have. Successful policy change goes in tandem with institutional change.

In this chapter, we have introduced three different arenas of institutional effects: the arena of working with political institutions, the arena of gradual institutional change, and the arena of institution-building. For each we introduced a number of guidelines for the policy analyst or policy-maker to apply (see overview in Table 9.1).

In the first arena, when working with institutions, the toolkit refers mainly to the preparation for negotiations in systems of power sharing. As we show, political institutions are devices for power sharing but with different effects. In all political institutions, policy actors in the superstructure must negotiate with others to push their agenda through. Having a potential win-set in one's pocket for negotiations with other actors is therefore a key precondition for successful decision-making.

Table 9.1 The institutional toolkit

WORKING WITH POLITICAL INSTITUTIONS	PURSUING INCREMENTAL CHANGE	BUILDING INSTITUTIONS
○ Identify core policy content	○ Analyse and reinforce existing countertrends	○ Establish new norms
○ Identify room for manoeuvre	○ Enforce norms or work towards forbearance	○ Ensure compliance
○ Secure credible commitment	○ Exploit ambiguity	○ Ensure repeated behaviour
	○ Introduce friction	○ Reinforce institutional complementarities
	○ Mobilise the losers	

When pursuing incremental change in the second arena, the toolkit shows how norms can be tweaked by adjusting enforcement practices and introducing friction, among other tactics. As norms are often ambiguous to some extent, the different interpretations of norms could be exploited. The losers of particular institutional settings could also be mobilized to push towards a reinterpretation of norms.

Finally, when it comes to the third arena of institution-building, policy-makers and analysts need to work towards the establishment of a new norm for guiding behaviour (paying taxes, not paying bribes, or reducing pollution). The norms must be rooted in the population's awareness, but behaviour must also be monitored and repeatedly practised. Only through practice, penalties, and normative orientations will institutions stick. This works better in an environment of institutional complementarities where norms reinforce each other.

10

Conclusions

Key concepts

- Policy learning
- Actor-centred policy-making
- Specialists and Generalists
- Public Policy Schools

Public policy is much more than adopting a specific measure. It is a complex process of creating new norms or reinforcing existing ones, liaising with other stakeholders, and securing support and legitimacy for a particular path of action. It aims to steer the behaviour of individuals, businesses, stakeholders, but also of policy-makers themselves. Effective policy-making is based on complementary norms, instruments, and actors that all reinforce each other. Policy-makers aim to align policy instruments with the institutional context and the stakeholders at hand. Because the context and actors vary across policy fields and countries, solutions to wicked problems need to be tailor-made; one-size-fits-all solutions seldom exist.

In this final chapter, we first summarize the key messages of the book. We consolidate our general approach to the policy process and combine the key components: process, policies, and capacity. Returning to the Paris Agreement and climate change policies we began with in Chapter 1, we illustrate how our understanding of public policy can be applied to a specific yet wicked policy issue. We discuss how the concept impacts the notion of evidence-based policy-making and propose a broader understanding of the policy process. Finally, we illustrate what kind of skills a policy analyst needs in today's policy world.

10.1 Problem-Solving

Climate change is a wicked problem. It affects, and is affected by, many policy decisions in a wide range of different domains, such as transport,

How to Do Public Policy. Anke Hassel and Kai Wegrich, Oxford University Press.
© Anke Hassel and Kai Wegrich (2022). DOI: 10.1093/oso/9780198747000.003.0010

housing, and energy, to name but a few. Each of these domains presents policy trade-offs. Experts in the various policy fields make recommendations regarding how to reduce emissions. Some experts put the greatest emphasis on technological change, for instance, carbon-neutral jet fuels, zero-emission steel plants, or new types of building insulation. But, beyond technological innovation, climate policies are expected to involve major behavioural changes on the part of individuals and businesses (Sachs et al. 2019).

In large part, because the affluence of Western lifestyles and the growth models of emerging economies are fundamentally based on fossil fuel consumption, there is, at times, strong opposition to climate change policy that ranges from denying that climate change is happening or that humans have had any role in it to questioning specific measures. Affected individuals worry about possible income loss and a lower quality of life; companies about higher costs and reduced profit margins; countries and subnational governments about weakened industries and slower economies. Potential winners of climate change policies, such as renewable energy producers, face a battle against strongly mobilized losers. Potential beneficiaries, such as the people of the Maldives, who are at risk from rising sea levels (see Chapter 8), find it hard to make their voices heard. As the example of the *gilets jaunes* in Chapter 1 shows, trying to address climate change is less about the lack of policies than the lack of political support.

How can interactive policy analysis help in the response to climate change? In this final chapter, we draw general conclusions from the preceding chapters to show how a broader interactive understanding of public policy can inform actors and thus help them develop more effective strategies. Understanding the political nature of public policy and identifying key levers for change will help policy analysts and actors to actually make the desired change.

Integrating the political dimension of policy-making into the analytical repertoire of policy analysis improves problem-solving. Policy analysts need to be able to read the behaviour of stakeholders and anticipate the responses of actors from other units, departments, sectors, or countries to policy initiatives in order to be prepared to influence these processes. But politics is more than a constraint that needs to be worked around. Problem-solving needs politics; it needs the investment of political capital—the legitimacy to act and the resources to mobilize the machinery of government, to connect stakeholders, and to enact policy—in order to make or change policy.

The critical role of politics, actors, and institutions in policy-making calls for bringing together the three branches of policy analysis and research (see Chapter 1). Substantive and tools-oriented policy analysis are essential for finding good solutions to policy problems. Nevertheless, the interactive branch of policy analysis that focuses on understanding the policy process must also be brought back into the conversation and needs to be developed as an integral part of the problem-solving toolkit. The coronavirus pandemic that started in 2020 has shown the importance of scientific knowledge and research in dealing with crisis. But it has also shown how the uncertainty about 'what works' requires political choices, deliberation between stakeholders, and political leadership. The pandemic has also shown that 'evidence' is not just 'out there' but is endogenous to the policy process, i.e. evidence is created by various actors.

More generally, for policies to be successful in the longer term, they also need to be politically successful. Policies that are somewhat effective on the programme level, i.e. yield some positive results in relation to the problem level, are undermined in the longer term when they do not enjoy support and legitimacy (Compton and 't Hart 2019). To avoid such a negative feedback loop is as much a task of policy-makers as it is to design and implement policies that promise to generate positive results on the immediate, programmatic level (Meckling et al. 2017).

The discussion on climate change (see Box 10.1) illustrates that there are already many policy tools available to tackle the problem. We also know that many policy instruments that have been suggested by the scientific community are implemented too slowly or not at all. The reasons for the mismatch between scientific policy advice and political will are to be found in the policy process, which is dominated by political imperatives. Decision-makers worry about the political fallout from climate change policies. Rising energy prices, less mobility via cars and airplanes, and ailing industries will have negative effects on citizens and businesses, who might punish governments for their policies. The evidence, knowledge, and expertise of the scientific community are not powerful enough by themselves to facilitate necessary decisions.

Box 10.1   Interactive policy analysis and climate policies

Many climate policies affect the underlying economic model of rich Western societies. CO_2 emissions per capita in the OECD are more than twice the level of the world's average (OECD 2020). China is catching up fast in absolute terms, but its per capita emissions are still far below the OECD average (Our World in Data n.d.). At the global level, the primary sources of greenhouse gas emissions in 2013 were electricity and heat (31 per cent), transportation (15 per cent), manufacturing (12 per cent), agriculture (11 per cent), and forestry (6 per cent). Energy production of all types accounted for 72 per cent of all emissions (Center for Climate and Energy Solutions n.d.). To reduce the carbon footprint of rich countries requires, at a minimum, the transformation of energy production, agriculture, construction, and mobility.

Each of these sources of greenhouse gas emissions is the basis for employment and wealth. Fossil fuel energy production (coal, oil, and gas) is a sector with high-paid employment. Similarly, fossil fuel-based transportation creates millions of well-paid jobs in the car industry and its suppliers. Millions are also employed in agriculture-related jobs, including small farmers without many alternatives. The transition to a reduced- or zero-emissions economy will therefore be painful for many people, as their employment prospects and livelihoods will be affected. Governments and policy-makers in the superstructure must consider the negative political fallout when closing coalmines, regulating agriculture, or introducing a carbon tax.

The transformation creates rather immediate potential losers (e.g. those who work in affected industries) and potential winners (e.g. those who will find employment in new energy sectors). Climate change policies therefore involve not only the obvious 'regulating the commons' policy problem, but also equity policy problems (see Chapter 3; Rao et al. 2017). Moreover, the losers can be mobilized politically by parties that promise to protect their jobs against climate change policies that are too far-reaching. A stakeholder mapping (Chapter 7) would identify the fossil fuel-mining industries and others, whose business model is entrenched in carbon use, as highly influential lobby groups in the policy process. These stakeholder groups would include not only mining companies and coal power plant operators, but also internal combustion engine manufacturers (and their value chain), chemical industries, and the like.

Interactive policy analysis addresses climate policy primarily as an equity policy problem in a stakeholder setting that is characterized by powerful private stakeholders (Meckling et al. 2015; Pahle et al. 2018). The level of conflict in the distributive politics of climate change is further amplified by the politicization of knowledge and evidence itself, linking to broader developments of polarization and declining trust in government (in countries such as the US). These perspectives drawn from an interactive approach to policy analysis are increasingly influential in the climate-related policy network and help us to better understand why there is a wide gap between the politics in the superstructure and the analysis in the engine room, as illustrated by the failure of governments to meet the targets of the Paris Agreement. The 'super-wickedness' of the climate policy field demands a degree of change in the power constellation of the superstructure that has not fully materialized in many countries (Levin et al. 2012).

The discourse in the climate change academic community has realized the importance of the political economy of climate change since the turn of the century. Stakeholder involvement and consultation has become a standard practice in many settings. Institutional barriers have also been addressed (see Pahle et al. 2018; Meckling et al. 2015). Climate change policy analysis is, in many ways, exemplary for interactive policy analysis.

The policy analyst will also pay attention to the historical trajectory of energy policies. The more recent history of coal mining, for instance, shows that closing mines can be highly conflictual (see pit closures in the UK during the 1980s; Winterton and Winterton 1989) or very expensive (see mine closures in Germany in the 1990s and 2000s; Kommission 'Wachstum, Strukturwandel und Beschäftigung' 2019; also Groll 2019). Furthermore, the analyst will assess the importance of the industry in the context of the national economy. The government of Norway, an oil-exporting country that nevertheless prides itself on its environmentally friendly e-mobility strategy, decided as late as 2020 to explore oil drilling in the Arctic (Pryser Libell and Bryson Taylor 2020). Although Australia is highly vulnerable to global warming, it is the world's largest coal exporter, and the Australian government is partially captured by the mining industry (Transparency International 2017).

Among the key insights derived from interactive policy analysis of climate change is that the losers of climate policies are too powerful to be ignored and that new coalitions have to be formed (Meckling et al. 2017). Therefore, strategies for compensating actual and potential losers must be part of the policy process and the policy package for it to be politically successful (Dorsch et al. 2020).

The distinction between what goes on in the political superstructure—the visible political actors and institutions 'on deck'—and the policy-making in the engine room—the sphere of specialized experts and officials who work on policy—is our basic framework to grasp the role of politics in policy-making. Understanding the logic of both spheres and how they interact is the key to reading (and influencing) the policy process. The first part of the book therefore explored these two spheres and how their different logics shape the prospects for problem-solving. Policy analysts need to understand why and how considerations of power (and survival) shape the behaviour of superstructure actors and their receptiveness to policy ideas and initiatives coming from the engine room. Looking at agenda-setting through this lens helps to identify a set of strategies that can support launching policy initiatives. As we have discussed in Chapter 3, analysis is a critical part of these tactics—not as separate from the politics but as a tool to influence the process (as with the reframing strategy of Transparency International in the case of the 'golden visa').

The chapters of Part II of the book zoomed into the three core tasks of policy-making—policy design, implementation, and evaluation. The central role of the engine room is evident across these three tasks, but so is the recurring role of the political superstructure. The chapters in this part also show how the interactive branch of policy analysis can enhance the way these three tasks are perceived. Policy design, as we argue in Chapter 4, is more than the assessment of alternative policy options in terms of their costs, benefits, and unintended effects. Smart policy-making expands this perspective to include the fit of a new policy to the institutional context and pre-existing policies. However, smart policy-makers also need to consider how a new policy influences the standing of their organization in the policy subsystem: is the policy providing new opportunities for more effectively pursuing core tasks, or possibly creating new dependencies undermining the autonomy and reputation of one's own organization?

Policy implementation is also shaped by the logics of both superstructure and engine room: for example, when policies remain vague or even contradictory at the policy formulation stage in such a way that conflicts are to be resolved as the policy is being implemented. Strategies for improving policy implementation require a good understanding of how politics—at the micro level of the street-level engine room and the macro level of the superstructure—influences the behaviour of the different players, including front-line bureaucrats. Similarly, policy evaluations cannot be separated from political influence. While quality standards are important for avoiding political misuse, the idea that such an evaluation can objectively identify good and poor policies underestimates the extent to which different stakeholders will evaluate the same policy from different perspectives. Good and poor policy choices are in the eye of the beholder.

In short, even core policy work—designing, implementing, and evaluating—is intertwined with politics, both the high politics of the superstructure and the micro-politics of the engine room. The toolbox of policy analysts needs to be enhanced with models of thought and heuristics that help to deal with, and make use of, these political mechanisms and forces.

A key message of this book is that good policy cannot be achieved by only focusing on optimizing the design, implementation, and evaluation of single policies. Instead, the capacity of policy-making systems to produce policies, to implement or enforce them, and to evaluate them need to be nurtured and maintained as well, as the chapters of Part II make plain. Analytical, coordination, delivery, and regulatory capacities (cf. Lodge and Wegrich 2014b) are clearly essential for policy work at the design, implementation, and evaluation stages (Wegrich 2021).

Nevertheless, there are also critical capacities that cut across the different stages of policy work; Part III focuses on these. As is evident from Chapter 7, stakeholder mapping and management are central to being able to mobilize non-governmental actors in the policy process. Our key analytical heuristic in this chapter is the pyramid of stakeholder engagement that extends from consultation to the full delegation of policy-making. Assessing the best form of stakeholder engagement in a given context depends on the organizational properties of stakeholders and their relationship with the decision-makers. Our discussion of capture versus collaboration provides a yardstick for policy-makers to assess stakeholder relations. The ability to build and draw upon productive relationships with all kinds of stakeholders constitutes an important capacity for good policy-making.

The increasing complexity of policy issues implies that coordinating policy-making across territorial and sectoral boundaries is an ever more important task of policy work. However, the nature of cross-boundary policy issues limits the ability to deploy coordination tools that work within a single government or organization. A key competency of policy-makers is, therefore, to be familiar with, and know when to use, the different mechanisms and tools of horizontal coordination (and even hierarchical coordination). Distinguishing different types of policy interdependencies makes it easier to understand the potential responses of other organizations, countries, or levels of government to policy initiatives that have an impact on them.

Finally, the ability to work strategically with institutions is the third key capacity. Political research on institutions leaves us with two core takeaways. First, institutions shape the preferences and worldviews of actors in the superstructure and the engine room. How actors behave in the politics of policy-making is driven by their institutional context. Second, strong institutions are important preconditions for effective policy-making, as weak institutions lack the capacity to give orientation to individual and collective stakeholders. Changing institutions, and in particular building weak institutions into strong ones, is inherently difficult as institutions are intertwined with wider societal and economic conditions. But we know from many studies, both in developing countries and the OECD world, that institutional change cannot be achieved by changing only the formal or regulatory element of institutions.

Political science research has made strong contributions to our understanding of these three cross-cutting capacities, but this knowledge needs to be included in the analytical toolbox of policy-makers. For example, we know that some policies enhance capacities, while others undermine them (Wegrich 2021), but the capacities that policy-making and policies demand and their implications are often lost in debates focusing mainly on the immediate effects, costs, and benefits of policies (Adam et al. 2019). How to make investments in capacities politically attractive when these investments might only yield results in the medium and long term, i.e. beyond the time horizon of many superstructure actors, is one of the important puzzles of policy-making in the twenty-first century.

In this concluding chapter, we apply the key concepts we have just reviewed to illustrate the potential of a more comprehensive approach. We start by moving from interactive policy analysis (IPA) to actor-centred policy-making using the example of climate change, as introduced here and in Chapter 1. In the third section, we spell out the implications of IPA for evidence-based policy-making, which is often seen as the most promising approach in a complex and data-driven policy world. We also demonstrate how the agenda of evidence-based policy-making could be enriched by integrating IPA. Finally, we turn to challenges and opportunities for research and for the education of policy analysts and policy-makers into the future.

10.2 From Analysis to Policy-Making

The making of public policy goes beyond adopting policy instruments as a response to problems that find their way onto the government's agenda. As we laid out in the preceding chapters, public policy strives to introduce new norms or change existing norms. Successful policy-making builds on liaising with other stakeholders and makes sure that policies gain support and legitimacy. Effective public policies help to steer and guide the behaviour of individuals, businesses, stakeholders, and policy-makers themselves. When policy-making can build on existing norms and enlist other stakeholders in policy design and implementation, it can leverage its potential far beyond the resources of the government. Therefore, for policy-making to be effective, decision-makers need to look at how to make norms, instruments, and actors complementary and how to introduce a process with positive feedback loops. These processes are often time- and place-specific as institutional contexts and stakeholders vary across countries as well as policy fields. There are no one-size-fits-all solutions or universal best practices to solve wicked problems; there are only approaches and models that worked in a particular place and at a particular time. *Policy learning* is about the mutual exchange of such experiences. But even if there is no single solution or model that works everywhere all the time, it is possible to develop guidelines for making policies for tackling wicked problems more effective by addressing more concretely the role of actors, instruments, and institutions. We discuss these guidelines now in turn and then apply them to the case of climate change policies.

10.3 Actor-Centred Policy-Making

Public policies need to reach the hearts and minds of individuals, businesses, civil society organizations, and policy-makers if they are to have behavioural effects.[1] Economists often base policy on incentives for actors to do the right thing. Emissions trading systems, for instance, introduce a limited supply of certificates that can be traded with others as a price signal for emissions (see Box 10.2). The higher the price of emissions, the more actors will try to reduce emissions—so the theory goes. But actors might

---

[1] The term 'actor-centre policy-making' is borrowed from the work by Fritz Scharpf and Renate Mayntz on actor-centred institutionalism as a concept in the social sciences (Mayntz and Scharpf 1995; Scharpf 1997).

also respond to the incentives in alternative ways. They might try to change the rules of the game by negotiating the price signals downwards to make them less painful, by requesting compensation, by moving high-emissions production abroad, or by passing the price on to their customers. In these cases, the emissions trading system does not necessarily have a positive effect on reducing emissions. Incentives might therefore work in other ways than intended by the policy instrument.

Box 10.2   Emissions trading as a pathway towards decarbonization

Emissions trading has been the key policy instrument to reduce CO_2 emissions in the EU since 2005 and covers about 40 per cent of all greenhouse gas (GHG) emissions there. Total emissions allowances are capped and reduced annually (European Commission n.d.-g). These allowance certificates can be traded between firms and give a signal to participating companies that they can reduce costs if they reduce GHG emissions. The EU Emissions Trading System (ETS) is not without faults, as it allows businesses to transfer production to other countries with laxer emission constraints (carbon leakage). Also, in the past, the volume of certificates was too high, meaning the price was too low to give strong price signals to firms (Bundesministerium für Wirtschaft und Energie 2021). A 2019 reform of the EU ETS, that introduced the stability of prices through the Market Stability Reserve, was successful in establishing a more significant price signal (Flachsland et al. 2020).

The ETS is a market-based regulatory system that relies on price signals. Price signals are well understood and accepted in the business community. However, it is widely acknowledged that emissions trading does not work in isolation to reduce GHG emissions and mitigate climate change. Complementary policies would, for instance, ensure grid access for renewable energies or provide additional subsidies to facilitate innovation in renewable energy production. In 2018, the EU therefore adopted the Clean Energy for All Europeans package. This package included a recast Renewable Energy Directive with provisions favouring renewable energy and the Regulation on the governance of the energy union with requirements for the drafting of climate and energy plans (European Commission n.d.-h). Thus, the EU ETS interacts with multiple other instruments to shape incentives for governments, businesses, and consumers in taking energy investment and consumption decisions.

In addition, governments of EU member states need to develop more active strategies to pursue the transformation towards a carbon-free economy. This includes a focus on energy use (power, heating, construction) and clearer guidelines for emissions reductions at the local and sectoral level to avoid free-riding and ensure a buy-in from all sectors and regions. The transformation of industries goes far beyond simple incentives to increase renewable energy production and higher costs for fossil fuel energy. It requires an industrial policy, major public investments (Sachs et al. 2019), and the reorganization of major industries. These policies can build on a long-term trajectory of high-quality investment in infrastructure during the post-war period, which can help to mobilize support for further action.

Additional sources: Searchinger et al. (2018); Bayer and Aklin (2020).

Actor-centred policy-making seeks to include stakeholders as much as possible when formulating, implementing, and evaluating policies. Climate change research has emphasized the role of stakeholder buy-in as crucial for policy success (Waisman et al. 2019). Researchers in the engine room of climate policy have realized that, in order to find a common language, streamline policy goals, and facilitate communication, it is essential to involve collective actors with a stake in the policy, each of whom has different properties in terms of members, networks, and resources. As we argue in Chapter 7, such stakeholders can be a strong channel for communicating policies to the target population. Rather than being a nuisance or barrier to change, groups, organizations, and businesses can also be crucial facilitators for policy change. Winning stakeholders over to support a policy is a major endeavour for policy-making. If key stakeholders, such as energy companies and labour unions in fossil fuel industries and regions which largely depend on these industries, can be brought in, climate change policies might be adopted more quickly and more effectively.

Inviting key leaders from among the winners and the losers for consultations on targets and transformations is therefore a prime approach in climate change policies. Even if some industries try to deflect from more ambitious targets, consultation and involvement is a more direct way to promote transformation strategies than drafting such strategies without their input. Among key stakeholders, a few change leaders can be identified and rewarded for their cooperation by keeping them close to decision-making processes. Others can be carefully excluded from consultation to minimize their sphere of influence. The normative goal of ensuring broad participation in developing policies that affect people's lives notwithstanding, stakeholder engagement must follow strategic aims.

10.4 Agile Processes and Policy-Making to Create Support

Policy instruments address policy problems in different ways (Chapters 4 and 5). To ensure long-lasting effects, policy instruments should be responsive to reactions from the target population and adjustable. When deciding on which instruments to employ, governments often choose a mixture of regulatory, information-based, and financial instruments and direct provision. Different policy instruments have different political effects. In other words, it matters whether regulations ban certain behaviours or financial instruments reward particular behaviours or investments. Regulatory instruments, such as banning fossil fuel cars, create clear losers of the policy. In contrast, funding instruments, such as subsidies for renewable energies, create winners who have a vested interest in the policy and dispersed losers paying (indirectly) for them with little incentive to mobilize.

Both winners and losers have preferences and will support policies that advance those preferences. Policy-makers should think about the political effects of policy instruments in terms of the generation of followers and supporters of the policy. This includes identifying the co-beneficiaries and externalities of particular policies. For instance, replacing combustible engine cars and trucks with electric ones has further beneficial effects for residents, such as reducing noise and pollution on the streets. Families with children and people with pre-existing health conditions might especially appreciate better air quality and less noise, as would residents who live on busy roads. They are likely to actively support the move towards quieter, non-polluting electric cars.

When puzzling over policy instruments, policy-makers in the superstructure should pay attention to the composition of experts in the engine room. As policies are largely path dependent (Chapter 9), the engine room is likely to be dominated by beneficiaries of current policies. Transport policy engine rooms are likely to be populated by specialists in car or truck transport. In order to promote transportation based on renewable energy sources, space needs to be created in the engine room for experts on renewables, for instance on government advisory boards and through funding for policy research. Policy-makers can thereby steer the debate in the engine room by generating and introducing new evidence.

Changing the composition of actors in the engine room is a strong tool for making the policy process more effective. This new mix extends beyond government and includes the proliferation of new non-governmental organizations (NGOs) and think tanks (McGann and Whelan 2020). By strategically including and excluding NGOs and think tanks in the engine room, policy-makers can change the discourse on policy developments.

Finally, when introducing policies, it is essential to strengthen the link between planning and execution. As we know from design thinking processes (Chapter 4), innovation in product development can be sped up by introducing experimentation and feedback loops. Governments have set up policy labs (Gofen and Golan 2020), regulatory sandboxes (Goo and Heo 2020),[2] and other spaces for experimentation, such as 'living labs'. When policy change can be tried out in practice without tedious and strongly contested policy-making procedures, policy-makers can identify effects and evaluate them strategically. Agile policy-making in designated areas can lead to fruitful policy innovation and bring in new experiences. It might also change the existing power structure in a given policy field—the distribution of supporters of, and opponents to, a policy—by demonstrating the positive effect of change on a small scale before planning more comprehensive change. This lesson from agile urban development, known as 'tactical urbanism' (Lydon and Garcia 2015), is gaining traction in other policy fields. For example, in relation to climate change, the smart sequencing of policies to 'ratchet up' measures has become an important element in policy strategies (Pahle et al. 2018).

10.5 Institutional Context as Leverage

The institutional context gives policies a normative and cognitive underpinning. As argued in Chapter 9, not only are institutions ubiquitous; they also guide actions and orientations. They go beyond formal norms and regulations to provide informal normative guidance. Policies that build on existing institutions are much easier to adopt and to implement in comparison to those that aim to challenge or change the institutional context. If possible, policy-makers should connect their policy options to existing institutional norms. For instance, the protection of earth and nature is consistent with basic norms in all societies. The negative effects of the

---

[2] Primarily in the field of fintech (the application of digital technologies in the delivery of financial services).

intense use of fossil fuels on the earth's climate and atmosphere are not congruent with most people's understanding of environmental protection. Climate change policies could therefore be based on the normative understanding of the importance of environmental protection in a broader setting, such as religious beliefs (protection of creation) and appreciation of natural habitats for quality of life.

Climate policies also connect to norms relating to externalities (see Chapter 8) and the 'polluter pays' principle. For a long time, the externalities of fossil fuel production and consumption were overlooked or suppressed in policy-making. As their effect on climate change (and life on earth) became ever more evident, climate policies have sought to adapt standard regulations that had been applied for years to polluters, such as making them pay for and mitigate the damage, to target greenhouse gas emitters. Policy-makers should tighten these connections with established norms and principles when advocating and developing policies.

To strengthen the institutional context of climate policies, policy-makers can use various techniques to better explain the effects of pollution and the need for decarbonization. The Paris Agreement requires each signatory government to submit a nationally determined contribution (NDC) which represents the government's efforts to reduce emissions and mitigate climate change. These NDCs need to be translated into decarbonization strategies or pathways that show clear steps towards decarbonization at the national and sectoral level. The use of indicators and dashboards to set goals and measure progress toward them can help illustrate how big the policy gap still is. Monitoring and evaluating policies and their outcomes are tools not only for communication but also for connecting with the wider institutional context. Evaluation reports can, for instance, strengthen the 'polluter pays' principle, by assessing policy instruments on their capacity to make heavily emitting firms pay for the damage they cause. They can reinforce the underlying normative orientation of policy-makers and regulators by emphasizing that those who pollute or emit greenhouse gases should contribute to cleaning up or reducing them.

10.6 Implications for Evidence-Based Policy-Making

Evidence-based (or evidence-informed) policy-making has become the gold standard of public policy (see Chapter 1). Policy-making should be based on the best available knowledge to address policy problems. Substantive and tools-oriented policy analyses underline the importance of using the best available evidence for making policy decisions and situate the use of evidence in the complexity of the political context for decision-making. What does interactive policy analysis mean for evidence-based policy-making?

Evidence is a term most often used to broadly refer to all knowledge and data that are produced by scientific methods as well as official statistics. However, evidence is always an interpretation of such data and knowledge. Majone (1989) distinguishes data and information from evidence. In his view, information is data that have been analysed, using statistical methods in particular. In contrast, evidence is 'information selected from the available stock and introduced at a specific point in an argument' (1989, 48). Given the growing volume of raw data available because of pervasive digitalization and the increasingly sophisticated processing of data using statistical methods and data science, the use of evidence as information selected for the purpose of persuasion will become ever more important.

What this means in practice is that evidence is not neutral, not an objective property that can be taken off the shelf. Evidence can be strategically produced and used (Chapter 1). Businesses in industries with high negative externalities have often commissioned research projects to counteract accusations of damage to health or the environment. Prominent examples are the tobacco industry in the 1970s (WHO 2012) and the soft drink and sugar industries (Litman et al. 2018). Social media and tech companies also frequently fund or conduct research with clear expectations as to the research topics and to some extent the interpretation of results (Dave and Dastin 2020). Research organized or funded by interest groups who have a stake in the policy field are likely to be biased towards certain outcomes. Similarly, think tanks and non-governmental advocacy groups shape and frame the results of their research to have a certain effect on a problem or audience.

Despite the potential bias of external research, it is crucial for policy-makers in both the superstructure and the engine room to keep the engine room open to new (sources of) evidence. Policy fields tend to create policy images and monopolies (see Chapter 3), which dominate the interpretation of a given policy field. For instance, for decades fossil fuel was seen as an unproblematic source of energy. It took much effort on the part of the climate research community to draw attention to the negative externalities of fossil fuels and the impact of greenhouse gases on climate change. To address the problem comprehensively in the interest of problem-solving, the engine room should be amenable to incorporating new research methods, approaches, and evidence.

As the existing data on climate change increase rapidly and more evidence of the effectiveness of climate policies is produced, evidence-based policy-making should be built on the foundations of experience. This must include existing evaluations of policies and the history of the policy field. For policies to be evaluated effectively (Chapter 6), policy-makers need to have a clear image of what kind of evidence has already been produced and by whom. Evidence, in other words, goes far beyond specific evaluations of individual policies—for instance through randomized control trials (RCTs)—and should cover the broader policy environment. When policy-makers in the engine room commission research in the policy field they work in, they should expand their research to include questions regarding the institutional context and the policy environment.

Evaluations, in particular those based on economic models, very often focus on the attainment of specific goals, such as the maximization of growth, welfare, and taxes or the reduction of greenhouse gases. They frequently neglect the effects of policies on the relative gains and losses of those affected. For instance, research on globalization and the specialization of production through trade has often concluded that the overall welfare effect of trade is positive without taking into account that there are those who lose because of trade and financial openness (Rodrik 2020). This includes workers, who might lose their jobs and income, as well as governments that might lose their capacity to tax. Evidence produced to address policy problems should cover the effects on income distribution as well as the main drivers of political competition. Regarding climate policies, this is the main lesson from the *gilets jaunes* movement, which gained momentum because French President Macron's administration did not seem to pay attention to distributional effects when introducing higher fuel taxes (see Chapter 1 and Box 10.1).

Moreover, the policy process should also be fed with evidence on likely implementation challenges. Often the input to evidence-based policy-making relies too much on abstract assumptions regarding the effects of particular policies. It is thus important to pay attention to the (expected and actual) implementation practices of street-level bureaucracies and the prevailing social norms of the target population in policy evaluations that might be contrary to the standard assumptions. Similarly, stakeholder responses can counteract policy measures and delay or even stop policy implementation. Hence, attention to implementation challenges and stakeholder responses should be strengthened in ex ante policy evaluations, such as impact assessments (see Chapter 4). In climate change policy, the European Climate Change Programme has embraced this well by identifying potential impacts on other policy areas and co-benefits early on, for instance in terms of energy security and air quality (European Commission n.d.-i).

Finally, while evidence is produced at a rapid rate in many policy fields, it is not always accessible or comprehensible in a policy context. The *communication* of the results of academic studies to the policy community should be organized in a transparent and effective way in order to speed the dissemination and uptake of research results. Encouragingly, information producers are increasingly presenting their output in the form of dashboards and general indicators (Waisman 2019; OECD 2019c), often accompanied by visualization tools or by full or partial data sets that allow users to tinker with the data. Such dashboards are particularly helpful for making comparisons. More generally, there is a basic need for publication and presentation of reports containing policy evidence produced by independent, non-governmental research centres. Nevertheless, academics tend to write primarily for the community of scholars and too rarely for the policy community, at least partly because, for career advancement, publication in scholarly journals is judged more favourably than a presentation of policy reports. 'Policy implications' are often presented as doing more of what is missing (more coordination, better implementation, more engagement, etc.) without contributing to the key question of how to achieve this. The transfer of research results often relies heavily on the policy of individual research institutions. Governments should invest in ways that improve practical policy formulation based on existing independent research by ensuring access to journals and other scholarly outlets, supporting open access, and allowing policy experts time to actually read it.

Working towards better communication and channels of mutual understanding is increasingly important (Box 10.3). In recent years, the evidence-based policy-making community has increased the quality of policy research and advice within governments and intergovernmental bodies. The European Commission set up the Joint Research Centre (JRC), which, in 2020, had over 3,000 employees to provide in-house research for better informed policy. Also, many OECD countries that already have strong institutions and scientific expertise have established advisory committees to increase the quality of policy advice.

These efforts can be further improved by adding different perspectives that are not directly related to the core programme theory of the policy.

For instance, beyond the discussion of the basic mechanics of a CO_2 emissions tax as a climate change policy instrument, policy-makers could seek an analysis of the effects of such a tax on various societal groups as well as proposals considering compensation schemes for those most adversely affected.[3] Moreover, based on our insights of the policy process, we know that policy-making should be based on mixed teams from a variety of disciplines and fields, including climate experts, economists, and other social scientists. Throughout the entire policy process, effort must be devoted to identifying crucial issues in other fields that might be relevant to the policy problem in focus. What is the effect of a CO_2 emissions tax on mobility, on rural areas, on social mobility, and on the labour market? How could the concerns and perspectives of the *gilets jaunes* have been integrated into decision-making processes?

Box 10.3 Evidence-based policy-making on climate change

As a policy field, climate change has fully embraced evidence-based policy-making. The field has been built on four decades of scientific analysis of global warming and the effects of man-made greenhouse gases and other contributors. The body of evidence is based on several 100,000 research papers (Minx 2018). Beginning with the 1972 publication of the Club of Rome's *The Limits to Growth*, several generations of scientists have researched and analysed the toll of Western growth models on the earth's capacity to digest pollution and other outputs of fossil fuel consumption.

The scientific community was essential for setting up many climate change policies, including the (now many) emissions trading systems and the Paris Agreement. Nevertheless, the growth models of industrialized and emerging economies are still highly dependent on fossil fuels. The transformation of economic models towards decarbonization and more climate-friendly approaches has moved onto the agenda only since the turn of the century. There is still evidence missing and research to be done on how such a transformation can take place and which policy instruments are most effective.

Above all, the research will need to ask more profound institutional questions about path dependence (Pahle et al. 2018), and transformative change might require more complex paths towards decarbonization (Waisman 2019). It will take

---

[3] A good example is Edenhofer et al. (2019), who contributed an expert report for the German Council of Economic Advisers proposing different models of price reforms of the emissions trading system.

major interdisciplinary efforts of policy analysis, economics, other social sciences, and natural sciences to develop strategies that address the political costs and benefits of deep decarbonization. Social scientists can contribute to understanding the distributional and other social impacts of such policies and their effects in the context of rising populism.

10.7 Skills for Making Public Policy

University-based public policy programmes have spread around the globe since the 1960s, with the aim of improving policy-making by educating policy analysts, public policy experts in the private sector, and decision-makers. Since the early 2000s, public policy programmes have strengthened quantitative skills (statistics), economics, and, more recently, big data and data science in their coursework, often at the expense of specific policy fields, which students are more or less expected to acquire on the job. New approaches towards policy-making coming from behavioural and development economics, social psychology, and organizational studies have moved our attention towards examining specific policy interventions through experiments.

Graduates of public policy programmes are expected to apply their knowledge of primarily academic research when starting to work for government bureaucracies, consultancies, NGOs, or government affairs sections of the corporate sector. In their various roles, they are no longer part of the academic setting and are, in most cases, not expected to conduct scholarly research. However, in some selected policy fields, in-house research plays a significant role, particularly in international organizations. For instance, in the World Bank, the OECD, and the World Health Organization, a sizeable number of programmes have their own departments conducting high-quality, professional research. In this case, senior policy analysts and researchers often obtain Ph.D. degrees in order to have the methods training to work in a more research-based environment.

In most other positions, policy analysts are not primarily researchers but practitioners. They work with academic knowledge and evidence to find the best solution for the task at hand. They have to be savvy consumers of empirical evidence and must know how to judge the merits of a particular output or result, as well as its source. Typically, they work in the superstructure or engine rooms of the policy process and are responsible for specific tasks, divisions, or projects. Their professional roles range from advocacy campaign manager in an NGO to civil servant monitoring security in nuclear power plants. These many roles share some job characteristics that demand particular skills.

A key question graduate students ask when enrolling in a public policy programme is the degree of required *specialization* on a particular topic. Capstone projects and master theses enable students to show craftsmanship in relation to policies, topics, or research methods. This might include the application of highly sophisticated economic models to large data sets, critical evaluation studies of existing policies, or case studies on new policy issues. These bigger pieces of applied research are steps towards specialization in a particular field, method, or approach. They give students the opportunity to be on top of that field, method, or approach and in command of existing knowledge and evidence in it.

In established policy fields, the engine room is filled with specialists on particular aspects of it. With regard to climate change policies, there is a large community of researchers and policy experts who have a deep knowledge on specific policies (e.g. emissions trading) or technologies (e.g. wind or solar energy). Because their expertise allows them to play down or minimize challenges from the perhaps less knowledgeable generalists in the superstructure, these specialists are often in powerful positions (Jann and Wegrich 2019). A higher level of specialization is therefore desirable if policy analysts are seeking to play an influential role in the engine room, particularly if they can build a bridge between the academic research community and the policy-makers in the superstructure. Government bureaucracies are full of specialist gatekeepers of a certain policy, who make sure that evidence is in line with government policy.

In the superstructure, professional roles usually require different skills. Here we find many policy analysts as staffers for members of parliament, aides of decision-makers, and managers of political parties or interest groups. Their primary role is to strengthen the organization they work for by using organizational skills and relationships and creating followers for their superiors. These tasks are based on more generalist skill sets (project management, campaign management, organizational skills). In the superstructure, relationships are the key to maintaining power (either electorally or within the political establishment), and loyalty and rewards for support are the currency (Chapter 2). Policy analysts who work in the superstructure must spend more time than their engine room counterparts on relationship maintenance. This includes knowing who's who (within the organization, legislature, or executive) and being up to date on the key topics of the moment. It is often noted that an address book with private mobile numbers is the most important tool of successful superstructure actors. As a policy analyst in the superstructure, a similar understanding of the relationships between key actors is a condition for success. Maintaining and grooming relationships is a skill that is transferable to the boardrooms of the corporate sector, which often works with similar approaches at the top level.

Whether policy analysts land in the superstructure or in the engine room, they must develop an approach towards the other sphere based on understanding and not on disdain. Policy experts often have a cynical view of the politics that plays out mainly in the superstructure. For their part, political analysts often think of policy specialists in the engine room as naive. Neither approach is helpful. In order to deal with wicked problems and even more mundane ones, both sides need to develop a better understanding of each other.

As we have emphasized throughout the book, stakeholders are important actors. Mapping stakeholders is a natural first step towards healthy stakeholder relations. Still, policy analysts in both spheres need to be able to work with stakeholders in an effective and professional way. This requires not only interpersonal skills but also an understanding of both the stakeholders' organizational properties and their power base. On whose behalf can the young Swedish environmental activist Greta Thunberg speak other than her own? Whom do the activists of Extinction Rebellion, an action-oriented environmental group, represent? For whom or for which interests does today's visitor engage in lobbying? Can policy experts in the engine room have stable relationships with actors who are neither elected nor appointed but just speak for themselves? These questions need to be clearly stated and answered when consulting with external experts or organizing a consultation exercise regarding, for example, a permit to destroy a forest to make way for a new power plant, car factory, or highway.

In both spheres of policy-making, policy analysts must have a deep understanding of policy problems beyond specific tools. For instance, experts in tool-based policy approaches, such as nudging, tend to apply the same set of behavioural tools to a number of policy questions. In most cases, the tool (nudging) is well understood, but conflicts arise around issues not related to the tool itself. Policies might incentivize residents to use public transport more than cars by restricting car parks or facilitating bike riding through health insurance rebates. Small steps towards biking and away from car transport through pop-up bike lanes might accumulate to bigger steps, such as car-free inner cities, as pursued in Paris and Barcelona, for example. Incremental policy change at various levels towards a defined goal can be a successful policy approach. Developing such strategies requires detailed knowledge of the problem (traffic) and the context (mobility policy).

To make these incremental policy changes sustainable, they need to be embedded and understood in the deeper policy context of mobility issues. For instance, commuting to work varies significantly between countries and regions in terms of distance, time required, and modes of transportation, among other factors (Eurostat 2016). It is important to understand the scope and implications of long-distance commuting for mobility within and between cities and have an understanding of how they impact traffic evolution. Therefore, the policy analyst charged with encouraging biking in inner cities needs to gain a fuller understanding of the context surrounding mobility.

Being able to bring evidence into policy-making and use it advantageously is an integral part of the policy analyst's skill set. Deep knowledge is based on many different sources, ranging from informally acquired information regarding actors' preferences and worries to formal research studies on behavioural impact. As the data revolution is gaining momentum, it is important to keep up with new advances in academic research. In the early 2020s, one of the most important assets of policy analysts is their insight into how the data revolution will play out for policy-making and how to take advantage of it.

Acquired knowledge must be continuously updated in specialized training courses, which should become part of the lifelong learning experience of policy-makers. The inability of individuals to keep up with the wealth of new knowledge underlines the need for specialization and the importance of finding a policy niche in which the policy analyst is the undisputed expert in the engine room or superstructure (as noted earlier). At the same time, it is essential to remain open to other disciplines and discourses. As the policy constellation can radically shift, particularly in the dynamic field of climate change, students and practitioners of public policy need to keep an eye open for new developments to avoid being surprised by fast-moving events. They should look for, among other sources, scoping studies that summarize the most important trends in research on a particular issue. They should also incorporate street-level experiences and knowledge in their analyses. How effective are public services in dealing with policy implementation? What are the constraints front-line bureaucracies (including NGOs or private firms delivering policy) have to deal with on a daily basis? How satisfied is the populace with the authorities responsible for environmental protection?

Finally, as our key messages throughout this book indicate, policy analysts must be trained to think in terms of processes and organizational logics, not only in terms of the analytical tools of policy analysis. Public policy-making is a process not an action. Processes take time to evolve, and actors need time to adjust to new practices. Often the reorientation of actors towards new norms and policy goals precedes the adoption of a particular measure. In many countries, when same-sex marriage was formalized and became part of civil law, this was not a breakthrough but a decision that was long overdue. Similarly, many arguments coming from the climate change engine room to push for faster decarbonization have taken a long time to reach the superstructure. Once these arguments are accepted, coalmines might be closed and renewable energy made available more quickly. Procrastination for political reasons might still take place but might be called out more forcefully than before. In short, once the fossil fuel industry's institutional line of defence falls, a whole range of measures might become possible which were unthinkable a few years ago. For example, as the COVID-19 pandemic made obvious, many business trips are less essential than corporate managers or employees thought. Similarly, high-energy-consuming industries, such as the steel and construction industries, are now having to transform their production processes towards lower energy consumption. When policy analysts start thinking in terms of processes, milestones, and ratcheting up achievements, their room for manoeuvre expands into new fields. They become the plumber of a broken system rather than the designer of a new one. We should consider this as a positive move, even though the system might need a complete overhaul, either now or at some point in the future.

10.8 The Way Ahead

Since the 1960s, policy analysis has evolved as an academic field of study and as a profession (Radin 2018). Now in the early 2020s, our knowledge about the policy process, the actors involved, and the instruments available is more sophisticated and fine-tuned than ever before. But policy problems have become more complex. As the world has opened up, the interdependence of policies and their effects has grown. Indeed, the

COVID-19 pandemic showed the world the new level of connectedness of people and problems. With the first cases officially reported in December 2019 in Wuhan, China, the virus spread within a couple of months across the planet. The pandemic has also underlined that governments today have far more responsibilities than their predecessors. Many policy fields that are central for policy-makers today, such as the environment, economic development, and healthcare, did not exist, or were only in their infancies, in the second half of the twentieth century.

We are now at another threshold of addressing global problems. Climate change poses many problems for nations and communities and contributes to political conflict over resources. The number of refugees at the global level is unprecedented, at a time when many traditional countries for receiving immigration have adopted strong measures to control and restrict inflows.[4] The digital economy challenges established growth models and appears to be shifting economic and political power to a few towering tech companies. The list of wicked problems and related challenges goes on.

Clearly, better policy analysis is needed to support decision-makers as they seek answers to these and other pressing questions, and thus the practice of policy analysis will have to evolve further. Evidence-based policy-making will need to expand the kind of evidence that feeds into decision-making. It must embrace actor-centred and institutional analysis to open and develop new approaches in the pursuit of policy change.

Evidence-based policy-making also should reorganize the communication between the engine room of the policy community and the academic community. Research questions and results have to be presented in formats that are accessible, understandable, and open to all for discussion. The policy community and the scientific community will have to invest more resources in intermediary organizations or mechanisms that can facilitate the matching of knowledge with policy needs.

Policy learning is an essential part of policy analysis. Good practice scoring is one way to try to find out how and why some governments or agencies solve policy problems better than others. But the contextual and institutional factors for good practice comparisons will have to become part of the analysis. Policy learning will increasingly span the global scale. Many developing countries continue to follow policy advice from the richer North as policy practice in standard policy fields (administration, taxation) still

---

[4] At the end of 2019, the number of refugees stood at 79.5 million, an all-time high (Auswärtiges Amt 2020).

informs economic development in the South. They are, however, also increasingly a source for policy learning in rich countries, which also need to develop policy solutions in an environment of weak institutional contexts.

A key question for the years ahead is how to reconcile goal attainment (the main focus of policy analysis) with system maintenance (maintaining the stability of political institutions despite increasing challenges to democracy).[5] The mature political institutions of the West are in danger of backsliding in light of polarization and populism and can no longer be taken for granted. In other words, there are more and more problems to solve, while the capacity to solve them seems to have declined. Smart governments should recognize the challenge and leverage the resources at their disposal, which are embedded in high-quality research organizations, well organized civil societies, and the business community. The introduction of policy labs and higher spending for problem-oriented research indicates that some governments have started to embrace this course.

The most promising way to go is to increase the learning potential of practitioners. A *reflective practitioner* (Schon 1983) mixes established routines with experimentation and has an open mind, welcoming new research results and new research methods and weighing them against the tried and true. Data science can help to address wicked policy problems, if it is employed in a way that takes context and institutions seriously. There will not be one solution for climate change or any other policy problem that can be applied across the world. But there can be policy platforms, based on evidence and research, that provide the toolbox for supranational, national, and local policy-makers to act in the interest of the populace for a better world.

---

[5] We owe this point to Fritz Scharpf. The distinction between goal attainment and system maintenance goes back to Talcott Parsons's systems theory.

How to write for public policy

1. Writing for Public Policy

Writing is a craft that can be learned through guidance and practice (Chrisinger 2017). Good writing for public policy makes a difference; it has a higher impact on actors in the superstructure and the engine room than poor writing. Policy actors in all fields have busy schedules, little time, and often many different topics to juggle. They appreciate policy writing that is accessible, succinct, and clear.

Writing for public policy is different from writing for academia, on the one hand, but also from writing for the media, on the other hand. Academic writing targets the academic community and is situated in a particular research context. Journalistic writing addresses a broad and often diffuse audience and needs to combine news reporting with deeper insights. The audience of policy writing is primarily policy-makers and stakeholders in the superstructure and the engine room with regard to a particular policy problem. Policy writing is solution-oriented, based on research results, and often prescriptive. Policy papers are written to give decision-makers a basis to take decisions and make choices.

For readers of policy papers, it is important to keep in mind that policy reports are not politically neutral but mission-driven. Therefore, it is key for good policy-making that every policy report must state who financed, commissioned, and wrote the report. There are many policy reports that are allegedly neutral but have been quietly or openly financed by parties who have vested interest in the outcome (Bero 2003).

There are many different forms of policy papers. They range from policy reports, policy memos, and policy briefs to more official papers such as green and white papers. Green and white papers are policy reports produced by governments and intergovernmental bodies, such as the European Commission and some United Nations agencies. While green papers aim to engage in discussions and float proposals at a formative stage, white papers tend to be statements by governments on concrete policy or action, sometimes proposing legislative changes. Policy reports, memos, and briefs differ by length and purpose, with policy briefs being basically short versions of policy reports. Before going into each of these in greater detail, we first highlight some general guidelines for policy writing.

2. General Guidelines for Policy Writing

Policy papers must be written in a clear language. They should avoid exaggeration and value judgement, as well as strong adjectives and scandalizing language. A policy paper is written in an analytical (not normative) fashion. It should not come across as an (un)informed opinion or as overtly biased—even if, as noted earlier, it is mission-driven. Every statement in a policy paper must be supported by evidence.

2.1 Language and style

While the bulk of a policy report should be written out in full sentences, the information should be presented in a way that facilitates the location of important points, using titles, bold type, visualization, and bullet points. Other important formatting and style tips include:

- A policy report should have a straightforward numbering of sections and clearly defined paragraphs.
- Numbered or bulleted lists are useful where necessary, but the entire report should not be one long enumeration, i.e. a laundry list of things to consider.
- Lengthy descriptions of data or case studies should not interrupt the flow of the text. They should be placed in an appendix, numbering and labelling figures and tables.
- Sources should be cited in a fashion that least disrupts the flow of text, such as footnotes or endnotes.
- Policy papers have to be written in plain language rather than in academic or field-specific jargon.
- Crafting an argument and presenting evidence in a clear way can be learned and practised.[1]
- Spelling and grammatical errors should be avoided, as should sloppy formatting. These can distract from the message and make the authors seem less competent.

---

[1] See Chrisinger (2017) for ways to develop and structure clear arguments.

2.2 Evidence

The data and information that are used in policy papers can be based on publicly available documents or also private documents, which are owned by organizations or individuals and not in the public domain. In addition, evidence can be drawn from data, other reports, news reporting, interviews, film footage, or photos, as well as mainstream academic research. In principle there is no limit on what kind of information can be used in a policy paper.

However, all information must be verified (especially if not first-hand), and sources must be clear. Written sources such as academic research, documents, public data, reports, and websites are easy to cite and reference. Policy papers must have a bibliography. Each bit of information cited in the document, particularly quantities, needs to have a source including a page number, if quoted from other sources. Each direct quote needs to be marked by quotation marks, and again a source with page number or other precise identifying information needs to be given. The point of such detailed citation is that the sceptical or curious reader should be able to locate the information and its original source with relative ease.

Informal information, oral interviews, witness reports, and documents classified as secret might be harder to verify. Authors of policy papers must make sure that the sources of data and information are reliable and real. The background of interview partners and informants must be checked and, if necessary, verified by triangulation. Triangulation in the social sciences describes the way to verify information using two or more different methods or sources (Rothbauer 2008).[2] If interview partners or witnesses to crimes or political oppression cannot be named for safety reasons, this must be explained in the text of the report. Sources must also be protected if evidence can lead to negative repercussions. If data have been obtained unofficially, check with legal counsel whether and which part of the data can be used.

The more controversial the evidence is likely to be, the more effort needs to be undertaken to verify the information. The effect of homelessness on health is not disputed; health statistics and survey evidence are likely to be robust enough as the substance of a policy paper. On the other hand, evidence of torture in civil wars that might be cited in tribunals has to be backed up by several sources, and needs to be checked for its validity, both legally and factually.

---

[2] For verification methods see also Human Rights Watch (n.d.).

Sometimes a policy paper is also supposed to address a topic for which the evidence is still developing, as in the case of the COVID-19 pandemic. In such cases, authors need to be particularly meticulous in letting the reader know about the character of the information used (e.g. preliminary, contested, peer-reviewed, and the like).

2.3 Graphs and visualization

Graphs, tables, and other visualizations are useful for succinctly presenting evidence, as well as for promoting the policy paper on social and other media. Some policy writings contain simple but key bits of information such as 'homelessness increased by 15 per cent last year' or 'more than 200 women were killed by their partners in the first six months of 2020'. These data can have a stronger effect if they are visualized and used as key information in promoting the policy paper. More complex information such as comparative data is best presented by graphs. For instance, a policy brief on minimum wages contains cross-national comparative data on minimum wage levels. The author could write that Luxembourg's minimum wage is €12.38/hour and Bulgaria's €1.87/hour, but with a bar chart, the reader sees quite clearly the massive difference (Müller and Schulten 2020). Visualization of data is used to 'tell a story', emphasize a point, and highlight particular messages (Bennett 2017).

Visualization can include data graphs (bars, pie charts, line graphs, radar graphs, and the like) or process graphs (flow charts). Think of compressing complex material into graphs or tables to attract attention. All graphs, tables, and charts must be referred to and explained in the text. The source of all data in graphs must be identified so that the curious reader can locate it if desired. Finally, all graphs, tables, and charts must have a title which ideally encapsulates the essence of the information.

3. How to Write a Policy Report

A policy report is an analysis of a particular policy problem and of potential solutions to the problem. Policy reports are written from a specific perspective. They are neither academic research reports nor journalistic coverage about a particular topic. They have a purpose in mind, which links back to the actor or stakeholder who writes or commissions the policy report. Actors in the superstructure (ministries, companies, non-governmental organizations, associations, politicians) commission or write policy reports to further their goals: either to shape a policy field (reduce homelessness or greenhouse gases) or to become politically more attractive (by being seen to address policy problem). Actors in the engine room work with and write policy reports continuously as part of working on a policy field. They summarize new research or new developments in the policy field, frame the issue in a different light, or use policy reports for evaluations.

The purpose of a policy report is a deeper investigation into an issue that can lead to action in the form of a green or white paper or a bill or legislative proposal. It might also lead to broader policy discussion or reforms such as the establishment of new agencies or institutions. Longer and comprehensive policy reports can have a lasting impact on the policy discourse. For instance, the report by the Club of Rome, *Limits to Growth*, has become the classic reference point about the impact of exponential population and economic growth on the earth's resources (Meadows 1972).

3.1 Target audience

The policy report primarily informs other members of the engine room and decision-makers in the superstructure about the problem, its importance, and potential measures to address the problem. It might be picked up by quality media and might change the public discourse about a problem. A well-researched policy report might be included in academic research, even though it is not written for an academic audience.

3.2 Purpose

The purpose of a policy report is to raise awareness (agenda-setting; see Chapter 3) and/or present ways to address the problem by assessing evidence on different policy instruments. Policy reports are essential tools in policy-making as they provide available knowledge in an accessible way to those working in a particular policy field.

3.3 Content

The range of topics covered by policy reports is as wide as the range of policy problems. Policy reports can cover impact assessments of policies or cost-benefit analyses of policy proposals. A policy report can also be about some part of the policy process itself: for instance, a stakeholder analysis, the analysis of political institutions, or a study on the party system. The content of a policy report addresses topics that are problematic in some way. There are few policy reports purely about the beauty of the rainforest, but many about the dangers to biodiversity posed by logging and deforestation. However, policy reports also highlight the (positive) effects of policy: for example, in protecting biodiversity (EASME 2020).

The scope of a policy report should be clearly defined from the outset, and depends on how much we already know about a policy problem. There are already thousands of reports on climate change. An additional policy report dealing with climate change must address a specific angle or new phenomenon and should not cover climate change per se. It can also address the results of a recent international summit or new evidence. In contrast, relatively new policy problems such as online hate speech, the coronavirus pandemic that began in 2020, or the platform economy allow for a broader treatment of issues. In any case, the policy report must be clear about the definition of the problem, the extent and seriousness of the problem, indicators to measure the problem, and developments over time (see Chapter 3 on problem definition).

When deciding about the topic and angle of a policy report, policy analysts have to keep their potential audience in mind. Who is meant to read the report and why? As noted above, a policy report's main audience is typically other members of the engine room and decision-makers in the superstructure. It can be written for public consumption as part of an advocacy campaign (see Annex 2) or be kept confidential within the organization. The report's status as public or confidential will impact the content and the presentation. Confidential reports can be more candid, whereas public reports have to keep in mind the response by other stakeholders, not to mention privacy concerns.

Is it addressed to government agencies responsible for covering the policy problem, or to a wider audience, highlighting failures of the government? Is there a policy community which will reinforce the findings of the report, or is it breaking new ground? Is the problem an open secret in society or in fact unknown to a wider public? Will it stir a reaction beyond the policy community? Will it contain fierce criticism of government action or a benevolent suggestion to improve some policy measures? The content of the report and recommendations must be in sync: when policy papers uncover government failures that are well known among the general public and for which there is broad agreement that change must occur, the recommendations can be far-reaching. But when policy reports are likely to receive a mixed response because some parts of the public might not see the topic as critical, report writers have to consider which recommendations might be acceptable for which groups.

For instance, policy reports about child labour in diamond mines in Africa might get a strong pushback by leading jewellery companies who source their diamonds with these mines (Human Rights Watch 2020). It is therefore important that the tone of the report must be factual, but also directly address the jewellers' responsibility along the supply chain of diamonds, and therefore also for the working conditions of children.

3.3.1 Executive summary

A longer policy report (all reports with more than five pages) must have an executive summary or a bulleted list of key points. It gives the reader a first-glance overview of the main points covered in the report, including at a minimum the problem definition, the key results of any analysis, and the recommendation(s). The executive summary is (most often) the last part of the policy report to be written, and should contain all the information that is needed to understand what the report is about. It is not a narrative of the different sections of the report but a succinct overview. As a rule of thumb, the executive summary should not exceed 5 per cent of the word count of the report itself, but can be several pages if the report is of substantial length.

3.3.2 Background

A policy report needs a background section that situates the report in a broader context. The background section summarizes key events and facts that describe and introduce the policy problem. It also gives the policy problem a time perspective (whether it is a recent development or a long-standing problem) and, if so desired, offers a rationale for the report's timing, e.g. an upcoming election, an investigation, or the negotiation of an international treaty or agreement. In essence, the background section sets the scene for the policy report.

The background section can also contain the policy history. In the case of a long-standing policy problem, the report should give an overview as to why past policies have failed to address the issue. If these failures are the focus of the report, however, they should rather be discussed in the main section.

3.3.3 Policy analysis

The policy analysis is the core of the policy report. A problem is examined via data analysis and/or testimonies of those concerned or experts. The aim of the policy analysis is to give a deeper understanding of the problem at hand and to present a new interpretation or evidence that leads to a clear conclusion. The policy analysis can be based on complex statistical analyses, but equations and complex tables should be placed in the annex and not in the main text. This core text should be accessible to an informed reader without higher-level statistical training.

3.3.4 Stakeholder analysis and institutional context

Analyses of stakeholders (Chapter 7) and the institutional context (Chapter 9) are essential information for policy-making. A policy report can even focus solely on a stakeholder analysis: for instance, in preparation for the negotiation of a new emissions trading system, to give decision-makers an overview of key actors, or in preparation for a consultation procedure in the search for a suitable place to dump nuclear waste.

However, when stakeholders are not the main topic of the policy report, it might be useful to consider them in a separate section to strengthen the overall policy analysis. A more detailed stakeholder analysis can also be part of the appendix to the policy report.

The same holds for the analysis of the institutional context. It rarely appears as a separate or explicit part of policy reports. Often the institutional context is taken as a given in a particular polity but not explicitly addressed. However, there are other circumstances in which it might be helpful for the policy analysis to address the institutional context directly. This can be done either in a separate section or appendix, or even in a separate report. For instance, the EU is formally not responsible for minimum wages or minimum incomes in the member states, but the EU Commission wants to initiate discussion about a policy on minimum wages. A policy report covering the evolution of minimum wages across the EU needs to address this discussion regarding EU competencies to set minimum wages in EU member states (Müller and Schulten 2020). Moreover, if member states have radically different approaches to wage-setting, including some member states that have categorically ruled out statutory minimum wages in order to protect their national collective bargaining institutions, this should be discussed in a policy report, perhaps in a separate textbox.

3.3.5 Recommendations

A policy report must contain recommendations for addressing the policy issue. This should not just be a statement of the conclusions or implications from the analysis, but rather a section explicitly dedicated to recommendations addressing those who can adopt measures to solve the problem. It should be clear who the addressees of these recommendations are. While some recommendations might target governments or public sector agencies, others might be addressed to private businesses or multi-stakeholder organizations.

Recommendations should be formulated in such a way that those addressed have the formal responsibility and the capacity to implement the recommendations. As the case of the golden visa programmes (Chapter 3) has shown, the EU has only limited responsibility for member states' residency permits and visas. This should be made clear in the recommendation section. The main responsibility for visas stays with the governments of member states and should be addressed as such. Local governments cannot be held responsible for national policies and vice versa. Proper targeting requires a prior analysis of who is responsible for a particular policy issue.

3.4 Format and structure

Policy reports can be based on academic knowledge (based on specific research projects, data analysis or case studies) but do not have to be. In any case, they have to be factually accurate and balanced in the presentation of information. When based on scientific knowledge, policy reports should refrain from using academic jargon, statistical or economic models, equations, and other terms that are not accessible to the broader policy community. More complex technical details should be moved to the appendix, with the expectation that the report can be read without understanding the information given in the appendix. All data and all quotes by sources must be referenced in footnotes or in a reference list.

The length of a policy report can vary, ranging from short overview reports of around five pages to detailed reports of several hundred pages. The length reflects the purpose of the report, the depth of the analysis, the amount of data, and the comprehensiveness of the treatment. A ten-page policy report either covers a relatively small problem (schedules to clean a local playground) or one angle of the problem, or gives only a rough overview of a topic. These are usually called policy briefs (see section 5).

3.5 Launching a report

The publication of a report should be timed to coincide with a particular situation or event. Policy reports on climate change are often launched before international conferences addressing climate change. Policy reports on human rights abuses are published around certain investigations, but also ahead of the UN Human Rights Day on 10 December every year, as media outlets aim to cover these events and look for material. The chance of the report being picked up by media is therefore higher.

Only major reports merit being launched by press conferences, as media outlets will only attend these for bigger news items. Smaller reports can also be launched through press releases, events such as conferences or talks, or social media campaigns. Often a combination of an event, media campaign, and press release is organized to attract attention to the report. Most importantly, those groups addressed in the recommendations must receive the report in a prominent way and should be directly targeted by communication strategies. In addition, other actors in the engine room of the policy field must be made aware of the report.

4. How to Write a Policy Memo

A memo is a brief analysis of a policy issue prepared by an aide for a decision-taker in the superstructure or engine room, in order to prepare for an event, speech, strategy, or decision. It is written from the perspective of the decision-taker and takes their priorities into account.

4.1 Target audience

A policy memo is written exclusively for an addressee within an organization. In a larger organization and depending on the position of the author of the memo, the memo will likely be reviewed by one or several superiors before reaching the person who will use the material. This is an iterative process in which the author can be asked to alter all or parts of the text.

4.2 Purpose

The primary purpose of a memo is to brief or advise the addressee on a policy matter, assuming that they are aware of the context in which the issue arises but are not aware of the details or all of the issue's implications.

The specific purpose of a memo may vary depending on the context in which it is written and the organizational culture and routine in which you work. Regardless, it is important to first of all clarify what the purpose of the particular memo is in order to tailor it to that purpose. Common categories include:

- *Information*: Information memos may have the purpose of briefing a superior (e.g. the Secretary) on matters that she/he might be asked about. Such policy memos may typically be called 'policy notes'.
- *Recommendation*: Very often, a policy note is written in response to a request from a superior or another agency asking for guidance. In addition to the policy notes, such a memo will need to include a recommendation. Such memos may be called 'briefings'.
- *Action*: 'Action' memos require that the addressee make a decision (approve, not approve, or discuss) or take further action.
- *Speaking points*: This is a memo that was called for by someone who will need to speak about a certain topic. Likely, the memo will first need to provide relevant information before suggesting speaking points. In some instances, you may be called upon to write out an actual *speech*.
- *Press briefing*: Such a memo is very similar to a 'speaking points' memo but designed to respond in a press conference setting. It can take on the form of a fully spelled out speech and/or press release.

4.3. Content

A memo addresses the issue in a direct and straightforward manner. The key questions and considerations need to be put up front. Decision-makers want to know the bottom line of the memo quickly: are there conclusions or implications they should be aware of? If it is a recommendation or action memo, is there reasoned advice on where they should position themselves on this issue? It is important that the memo reflects the task and/or mission of the organization.

A memo constitutes a concise policy analysis. The memo is written about a specific topic. Therefore, the memo is written in an analytical (not normative) fashion. If opinions are voiced in a memo, they should be situated as part of the assessment of the facts, but it should not come across as uninformed opinion or bias.

4.4 Format and structure

A memo comes in one piece, with an executive summary at the outset, a brief introduction (usually labelled 'background'), an analytical section (e.g. options to be considered), and a recommendation or concluding section (depending on the aim of the paper).

It should be as succinct as possible and usually two to five pages in length. The memo should be written in full sentences. To summarize information more succinctly, it can use occasional bullet points, subtitles, bold type, and forms of visualization such as tables and graphs. The bulk of the text should not exceed two pages, not counting appendices or other supplementary material. The format of the policy memo should allow the recipient space to comment and amend by leaving ample margins.

A memo has a clear header structure (To, From, Date, Re:), which is often supplied by the agency (be sure to check!). The subject (Re:) should be treated like a 'headline' and contain sufficient information for future reference.

Considering that some of the points may need follow-up on your part or someone else's, it is key that sources of information are cited. This should be done in the least disruptive fashion, such as footnotes or endnotes; but used sparingly and only for sources.

5. How to Write a Policy Brief

A policy brief can take various forms. It can be an abbreviated version of a policy report or even be based on a policy report. A lengthy and comprehensive policy report might lead to several policy briefs that outline key results and conclusions. A policy brief can also be a short intervention by a policy expert on a current topic or an assessment of a recent policy announcement or legislative proposal. For instance, when the EU Commission announced its 'New Pact on Asylum and Migration' on 23 September 2020, the policy think tank Jacques Delors Centre at the Hertie School in Berlin published a policy brief titled 'EU Border Procedures: Clear, Fair and Fast? The New Pact in Review', in which the authors Lucas Rasche and Marie Walter-Franke analysed the strength and weaknesses of the proposal (Rasche and Franke 2020).

5.1 Target audience

The target group of policy briefs is policy-makers in both the superstructure and the engine room as well as journalists and a broader public audience. Policy-makers and journalists seek out policy briefs in order to save time when trying to digest complex information and look for arguments when negotiating or reporting about policy problems.

5.2 Purpose

The purpose of a policy brief is to give policy-makers a quick overview of a specific policy issue, a policy question, or a recent event. It informs policy-makers but also tries to shape perceptions about that policy issue. It therefore has a clear point of view and a clear message. By providing an interpretation or a short intervention, the policy brief author tries to influence the discourse on a current issue.

5.3 Content

The content of policy briefs is usually a response to a current event, a short overview of a policy problem or policy instrument, with a clear point of view. Policy briefs can also be used as the basis for op-eds in newspapers and magazines, both print and online. The policy analysis in a policy brief is more elaborate than in a policy memo but shorter than in a policy report. It does not contain complex statistical analysis.

A policy brief typically also contains recommendations which are more short-term oriented and realistic. The target audience should be able to influence or even implement the recommendations. They provide practical solutions for the problem at hand.

5.4 Format and structure

A policy brief runs between five and ten pages and can be a summary of a longer policy report. It contains an executive summary but otherwise does not follow a specific structure. The language of a policy brief needs to be more accessible than a policy report or a policy memo as the target group is more diffuse.

Because a policy brief competes with media products and is more in the domain of heated political discussions, it has to present itself as attractive to readers. It has to be timely in a particular discussion and relevant to policy-makers. It is important for policy briefs to have a catchy title and an attractive design. The language should engage the target audience and include direct points of action.

How to Design a Policy Advocacy Campaign

Casey Kelso

Advertising campaigns sell things. Election campaigns win a public office for politicians. And corporate advocacy changes draft legislation in their favour. Often there is a common perception that advocacy and campaigning are unethical or only manipulate public perceptions. Not true! (See Box A2.1.)

Box A2.1 Freedom of opinion and expression

The essence of a democratic society lies in the legitimate endeavour of people who want to change the policies and practices of governments, businesses, and public attitudes that make important decisions affecting people's lives. That advocacy in the public interest is underpinned by fundamental human rights to free expression and the right to participate in public affairs.

(Universal Declaration of Human Rights, articles 19 and 21)

In practice, campaigning means engaging the public in influencing efforts, while advocacy has a wider scope and includes all sorts of strategically planned influencing, including lobbying directly with a decision-maker and public engagement campaigns. However, advocacy and campaigning can mean the same thing, according to Ian Chandler, an advocacy expert trainer. He defines both as 'an organised process of influencing selected people or institutions in order to achieve desired policy, practice, social, behavioural or political changes that will benefit particular groups or causes' (The Pressure Group Consultancy n.d.). Like Chandler, this guide uses the term 'advocacy campaigning' to embrace all these various elements.

A good advocacy campaign strategy should identify your target audiences and narrow influencing objectives for each; create messages for these audiences conveyed through their channels (such as social media, trusted commentators, direct lobbying); and plan for key moments and levers of influence on a decision-maker to achieve your advocacy goals.

Common problems include unclear or vague objectives relating to too many issues; poor monitoring that allows over-optimistic wishful thinking; or inappropriate tactics dictated by personal preferences or past precedent. Other difficulties include a lack of research into the actors involved, so you end up talking to the wrong audiences, and wasting resources by creating key advocacy messages that sound great to an internal audience but disappear unnoticed by those who matter most in a policy decision. This guide describes four ways to avoid these problems when planning an advocacy campaign, whether it is an international multi-year advocacy campaign or a research report.

1. Make Objectives, Strategy, and Tactics Smart

The planning of advocacy campaigning should not be seen as value-neutral. Rather, values and sparking an emotional reaction are just as important as a cool recitation of facts. Advocacy plans should be modified by feedback. Advocacy planning is iterative.

Research and analysis are at the heart of good planning for evidence-based advocacy. If you are going to conduct advocacy, especially at the international level, you will need solid evidence showing that this is an important problem and that existing policies are not working. You will also need strong evidence to reinforce your proposed solution. It is much more difficult to advocate to solve a vaguely defined problem, or a problem whose nuances you do not completely understand, than one that is clearly defined, researched, and analysed. The way a problem is worded and understood has a huge impact on the number, quality, and type of proposed solutions that you can think up and advocate for.

A traditional tool for understanding problems is the Problem/Solution Tree analysis. It is best carried out with a group of people using flip chart paper or an online whiteboard. Planning is easiest with knowledgeable staff members but ideally needs to be done with the inclusion of the people for and with whom the change is being advocated. Participatory and collective processes are essential for buy-in by actors involved in the issue.

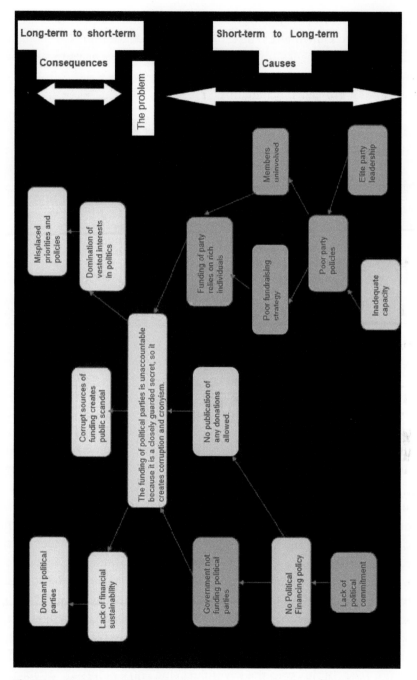

Fig. A2.1 Creating a problem tree

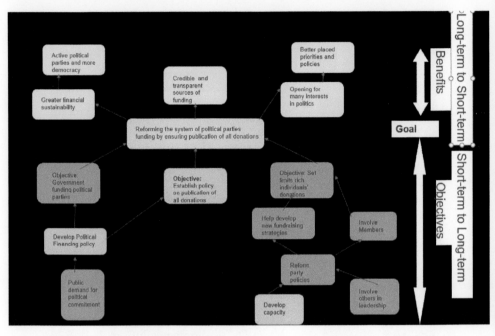

Fig. A2.2   Creating a solution tree

In the example provided in Figures A2.1 and A2.2, this specific analysis exercise surrounding the broad problem of political party funding could be conducted with the involvement of political party leaders, members of the governmental electoral commission, and academics studying political finance reform, among others.

The first step is to discuss and agree on the broad problem or issue to be analysed. That problem, in the case depicted in Figure A2.1 'The funding of political parties is unaccountable …', is written in the centre of the flip chart and becomes the 'trunk' of the tree. The second step is to identify the causes, which become the roots—arranged in a cause-and-effect logic—with major contributors located closer to the problem and background fundamental issues further below. The third step is then to identify the consequences, which become the branches above the problem 'trunk'. In the last step, causes and consequences are rephrased into positive solutions or objectives and desirable outcomes or benefits, respectively, as depicted in Figure A2.2. In this way, the key influencing entry points are established in a 'Solution Tree' (VeneKlasen and Miller, 2007, 147–62; Hovland, 2005, 12–13). Once the tree has taken shape, ask the group: which are the most serious consequences, and which easier or more difficult to address? And who can best solve them: government, international agencies, business, or communities?

Having five to seven objectives is too much, scattering your energies and spreading scarce resources too thinly. Narrowing down your advocacy to two or maximum three lines of attack is necessary. One way to do this is called 'cutting the issue', which some activist organizations find reduces a complex problem into one or more 'bite-sized' issues. You can 'cut' or reduce the scope of a problem in creative brainstorming discussions in a group to find narrow approaches on the most immediate, specific, and realizable (winnable) aspects of the problem (Whelan and La Rocca n.d.).

A tool called 'Picking a winning issue' can also help. Whether in a horse race or in a government's industrial strategy to encourage certain economic sectors or companies (Wade 2015), 'picking a winner' depends on the questions you ask. Using a checklist to rank potential solutions allows you to prioritize issues in order of impact and importance and regroup them along common lines (Figari and Kelso 2013). Questions include the following. Will this result in a real improvement in people's lives? Is this widely felt? Is there a clear political and policy solution? Is this issue winnable?

Sometimes, in multi-stakeholder contexts with various actors all involved, planning and problem analysis can become an advocacy tool in itself. The Open Contracting Partnership (Sklar 2020) developed 'The Challenge Wheel' in which stakeholders were brought together in a meaningful and productive conversation despite widely different areas of expertise. Each actor contributed unique perspectives on how to address the problem, gaining grudging agreement about the nature of the problem itself. After such a workshop, some advocacy was already accomplished!

No planning guide can omit SMART elements. Narrowing the focus SMART-ly creates crisp planning (Figari and Kelso 2013, 20):

- Specific: clear, indicating exactly what is expected, why it is important, and who is involved;
- Measurable: include specific criteria for measuring progress;
- Achievable: realistically achievable within a given timeframe and with the available resources;
- Relevant: address the scope of the problem and feature appropriate steps that can be implemented, and whether activities are 'hooked' to an interesting event or anniversary;
- Time-bound: include a specific timeframe for achieving the objective.

2. Monitor to Adapt your Strategy Flexibly

Measuring the amount and type of changes you have created through your advocacy demonstrates your effectiveness in the 'upward' accountability demanded by donors and other funders. Responding to constituents and partners in 'sideways' accountability is also important for participatory knowledge and maintaining relationships, while good management means 'inward' accountability from and to staff by monitoring performance and drawing lessons. Organization legitimacy ultimately depends upon that accountability 'outward' to the public and to your mission to show you are 'doing right things' as well as 'doing things right' (Fox and Brown 1998).

A good 'theory of change' gives a roadmap to sequencing advocacy activities. Also called an outcome map, they usually illustrate in a diagram how, and why, you think change will happen and how you will know if you are making progress in advocacy. By breaking down the plan into a 'pathway' of events, advocacy goals become manageable—defining the many changes that must occur along the way, such as laws, policies, and practice in government, attitudes and behaviour of people and institutions, or conditions for children, adults, families, or communities. These changes can be defined as impact.

In developing a theory of change, veteran campaign trainer Jonathan Ellis suggests thinking about a 'so that' chain—doing something *so that* something else happens *so that* something else then happens, and so forth. No activity should exist by itself but contributes to another (Ellis 2020; see also Organizational Research Services 2004, 12–17). Ellis also emphasizes the importance of a monthly review meeting on the theory of change and progress following the 'so that' chain: If you have got stuck, why? What have you learnt about getting stuck? And what changes are you going to make to your theory of change?

There are many types of monitoring, evaluation, and learning (MEL) systems. To keep it workable, use only a few indicators to track progress. If you are depending upon partners or colleagues, keep it simple but precise; otherwise, a lot of time is spent cajoling them into reporting. Types of indicators range from the adoption of law (which may take years) to website visitors and retweets on social media (with weekly averages) or commitments by authorities, numbers of partners in a coalition, or institutional development, such as fundraising targets and a multi-stakeholder process agreed upon.

In measuring advocacy, ask yourself:

- Have we **framed debates** on the political agenda? This is about attitudinal change.
- Have we encouraged **clearly stated commitments**? This is about influencing others' language and rhetoric.
- Have we **changed procedures** at the domestic or international level? This is about how a policy decision was made, i.e. transparency and inclusion.
- Have we affected **policy content**? Changes in law can be lasting.
- Have we influenced **behaviour change?** Changes are made in how society sees the issue.

A great tool for planning advocacy and anticipating risks is the 'premortem', the opposite of a post-mortem. It helps you identify risks at the outset and break the bias of unwarranted optimism. As described by decision scientist Gary Klein (2007) a premortem

> comes at the beginning of a project rather than the end, so that the project can be improved rather than autopsied. Unlike a typical critiquing session, in which project team members are asked what *might* go wrong, the premortem operates on the assumption that the 'patient' has died, and so asks what *did* go wrong. The team members' task is to generate plausible reasons for the project's failure.

In this challenging exercise, you make a (hypothetical!) presentation to your board, boss, or funders about why your advocacy failed, explaining lessons learned, and how you would have done things differently. It is a 'realism' test.

3. Know your Context and the Actors in it

Perhaps the most difficult and thought-provoking step in planning advocacy campaigning is to analyse the context in which you are advocating. This involves mapping a long list of stakeholders and then visually portraying them according to (1) their agreement or opposition to your advocacy goal; (2) their influence upon the specific decision-maker key to the change you seek; and (3) the interest they have in the issue itself.

The key to making the map useful is to discuss and decide upon the key decision-maker you must persuade—it could be a government official, a majority in parliament, or a segment of the public. The map helps identify your target audiences. Defining your target audiences will allow you to agree on advocacy tactics, what communications channels to use, the tools, and measurement. The more precise you can be about your target audiences, even naming them, the greater the chances of a successful strategy. Use your objectives to define the target audiences to reach (Chandler 2015, The Pressure Group Consultancy n.d.).

Researching the likes, beliefs, and interests of these key audiences is critical in gaining valuable information on the knowledge and behaviour of your target audiences. Sometimes it comes down to a micro-aspect of the target audience, such as 'Minister X is heavily influenced by lobby Y', or 'The government makes its final budget decisions by March 31'. Others can include: 'Our best champion in the new government is member Z', or 'Journalist A has more influence with the government than journalist B', and 'NGO C successfully lobbied the government on environmental issues last year'.

After you set the goal and objectives, you need to decide on tactics and strategies. The stakeholder map can contribute to the design of approaches, activities, and materials to influence the targeted decision-maker(s). Among the possible advocacy approaches, important activities are:

- **Persuading the 'moveable middle'** to help you influence the decision-maker(s) by persuading them of your position and motivating them to take action.
- **Creating interest** among an apathetic 'middle' to convince them of the issue's importance is a traditional aim of public awareness-raising, particularly if there is an election coming up.
- **Building alliances or coalitions** means activities such as joint letters, pooled resources for a video, partners in campaigning, and the like. Even without a coalition, use a champion to speak out.
- Taking an approach of **giving less influential allies a boost in visibility** can mean featuring them in a video highlighting their views, or meeting officials together in a joint delegation.
- **Monitoring an opponent's public statements** is always smart, so one can anticipate objections and answer criticisms.

4. Shape your Messages so your Audience Listens

A key message is a short phrase (no more than twenty-five words) that specifies the core message that you want to communicate to audiences and want them to remember. They vary in complexity and can be adapted to suit the level of knowledge of each audience: government ministers and local companies will not be receptive to or understand the same kind of message as allies and local communities. The golden rule of communications is to start where the audience is at, not where you want them to be. This is called framing, defined as 'the boundaries that highlight specific parts of an issue, place others in the background, and leave out some entirely. The frame influences how an audience thinks about an issue, including who is responsible for the cause and its possible solution' (VeneKlasen and Miller, 2007, 235). More tips for effective communication are found in, among others, the European Union Agency for Fundamental Rights (2018): *Ten Keys to Effectively Communicating Human Rights.*

Seriously consider whether you have honestly addressed your opponents' arguments in your advocacy campaign messages. Jonathan Ellis (2017, 51) reflects: 'As campaigners, we very often choose the messages that motivate ourselves. Campaigning is not about motivating ourselves … It is about choosing the most effective method and message to tackle the arguments of your opponents.'

In 2020, former United States president Barack Obama continued this debate when he criticized activists' use of the slogan 'Defund the Police' (Evelyn 2020). He argued that the slogan lost a big audience, making advocacy for police reform a lot less likely. 'So the key is deciding, do you want to actually get something done, or do you want to feel good among the people you already agree with?' Obama said. 'And if you want to get something done in a democracy, in a country as big and diverse as ours, then you've got to be able to meet people where they are' (Evelyn 2020).[1] In reply, progressive Congressperson Alexandria Ocasio-Cortez (2020) tweeted: 'The thing that critics of activists don't get is that they tried playing the "polite language" policy game and all it did was make them easier to ignore. It wasn't until they made folks uncomfortable that there was traction to do ANYTHING even if it wasn't their full demands.' Answering her, Obama (2020) stuck to his point: 'The issue to me is not making them comfortable. It is, can we be precise with our language enough that people who might be persuaded around that particular issue to make a particular change that gets a particular result that we want, what's the best way for us to describe that?' The conclusion? Both sides are right. The point is that you must consciously choose your style, either confrontational or solutions-oriented but make the choice based on analysis.

---

[1] The quote by former president Obama is part of a video interview on the Guardian website (Evelyn 2020).

5. Putting it All Together

So, you have analysed the issue, framed SMART objectives, picked 'winning issues', developed a theory of change 'so that' your advocacy follows a logic, identified risks and indicators, and analysed your stakeholders to frame advocacy messages to persuade key audiences. Now the final step in advocacy is implementation. A good strategy sets out milestones in a timeline of key opportunities and events to influence the decision-maker. Bear in mind that your tactics (or activities) should not just be a succession of self-organized meetings and reports, but should be linked to real-world anniversaries, negotiations, and elections.

Congratulations! Whether you win or lose, by doing advocacy you are changing the way decision-making happens in your society to be more inclusive and open to all.

References

Aaron, H. 1978. *Politics and the Professors: The Great Society in Perspective*. Washington, DC: Brookings Institution.

Abgeordnetenhaus Berlin. 2014. 'Schriftliche Anfrage des Abgeordneten Joschka Langenbrinck'. Drucksache 17/14183.

Abgeordnetenhaus Berlin. 2013. 'Alle Berliner Kinder müssen die Schule besuchen—die Prävention gegen Schulschwänzen stärken, die Schulpflicht konsequent durchsetzen!' Drucksache 17/1004.

Abgeordnetenhaus Berlin. 2014a. 'Entwicklung der Schulschwänzer/innen in den Bezirken im 2. Schulhalbjahr 2013/2014'. Drucksache 17/15184.

Abgeordnetenhaus Berlin. 2014b. 'Alle schulpflichtigen Kinder in Berlin müssen die Schule besuchen—Prävention gegen Schulschwänzen stärken, die Schulpflicht konsequent durchsetzen'. Drucksache 17/1612.

Abgeordnetenhaus Berlin. 2018. 'Schuldistanz—Maßnahmen zur Prävention und Intervention in den Bezirken: Auswertung und Schlussfolgerungen'. Drucksache 18/0777.

Abgeordnetenhaus Berlin. 2019. 'Schriftliche Anfrage des Abgeordneten Joschka Langenbrinck (SPD) vom 15. August 2019 zum Thema: Entwicklung der Schulschwänzer/innen in den Bezirken im 1. Schulhalbjahr 2018/2019 und Antwort vom 10. September 2019'. Drucksache 18/20601.

Abramowicz, M., and Szafarz, A. 2020. 'Ethics of RCTs: Should Economists Care about Equipoise?' In B. Florent, I. Guérin, and F. Roubaud (eds), *Randomized Control Trials in Development: A Critical Perspective*. Oxford: Oxford University Press, 280–292.

Acemoglu, D., and Robinson, J. A. 2012. *Why Nations Fail*. New York: Crown.

Adam, C., Hurka, S., Knill, C., and Steinebach, Y. 2019a. 'Introducing Vertical Policy Coordination to Comparative Policy Analysis: The Missing Link between Policy Production and Implementation', *Journal of Comparative Policy Analysis: Research and Practice* 21(5): 499–517. https://doi.org/10.1080/13876988.2019.1599161.

Adam, C., Hurka, S., Knill, C., and Steinebach, Y. 2019b. *Policy Accumulation and the Democratic Responsiveness Trap*. Cambridge: Cambridge University Press.

Adams, G. 1981. *The Politics of Defense Contracting: The Iron Triangle*. New York: Routledge.

Adams, R. 2021. 'UK Universities Facing "Unaffordable" Hike in Pension Contributions', *The Guardian*, 3 March. Retrieved 3 March 2021 from <https://www.theguardian.com/education/2021/mar/03/uk-universities-facing-unaffordable-hike-in-pension-contributions>.

Alcohol Awareness. 2019. 'Are you Pushing the Sausage?' Retrieved 2 October 2019, from <https://alcoholcampaign.org/2019/10/02/are-you-pushing-the-sausage/>.

Alesina, A., and Paradisi, M. 2014. *Political Budget Cycles: Evidence from Italian Cities*. Cambridge, MA: National Bureau of Economic Research.

Allcott, H., Lockwood, B. B., and Taubinsky, D. 2019. 'Should we Tax Sugar-Sweetened Beverages? An Overview of Theory and Evidence', *Journal of Economic Perspectives* 33(3): 202–27. <https://doi.org/10.1257/jep.33.3.202>.

Allessie, D., Sobolewski, M., and Vaccari, L. 2019. *Blockchain for Digital Government: An Assessment of Pioneering Implementations in Public Services*. Science for Policy Report (JRC). Luxembourg: Publications Office of the European Union.

Altmann, S., and Traxler, C. 2014. 'Nudges at the Dentist', *European Economic Review* 72: 19–38. <https://doi.org/10.1016/j.euroecorev.2014.07.007>.

Anheier, H. K. 2019. 'On the Future of the Public Policy School', *Global Policy* 10(1): 75–83. <https://doi.org/10.1111/1758-5899.12599>.

Anheier, H. K., Haber, M., and Kayser, M. A. (eds). 2018. *Governance Indicators: Approaches, Progress, Promise*. Oxford: Oxford University Press.

Ansell, C., and Gash, A. 2008. 'Collaborative Governance in Theory and Practice', *Journal of Public Administration Research and Theory* 18(4): 543–71. <https://doi.org/10.1093/jopart/mum032>.

Ashwin, S., Kabeer, N., and Schüßler, E. 2020. 'Contested Understandings in the Global Garment Industry after Rana Plaza', *Development and Change* 51(5): 1296–1305. <https://doi.org/10.1111/dech.12573>.

Associated Press. 2009. 'Cabinet Makes Splash with Underwater Meeting', *NBC News*, 17 October. Retrieved 8 May 2021 from <https://www.nbcnews.com/id/wbna33354627#.XwjMDuexU2w.2013/2995(RSP)>.

Auerbach, A. M. 2020. *Demanding Development: The Politics of Public Goods Provision in India's Urban Slums*. Cambridge: Cambridge University Press.

Auswärtiges Amt (Federal Foreign Office). 2020. 'UNHCR Announces Figures on Refugees and Displaced Persons—All-Time High'. 18 June. Retrieved 20 April 2021 from <https://www.auswaertiges-amt.de/en/aussenpolitikthemen/migration/unhcr-figures-refugees-displaced-persons/2354468>.

Ayres, I., and Braithwaite, J. 1992. *Responsive Regulation: Transcending the Deregulation Debate*. Oxford: Oxford University Press.

Bach, T., and Wegrich, K. 2019. 'Blind Spots, Biased Attention, and the Politics of Non-coordination', in T. Bach and K. Wegrich (eds), *The Blind Spots of Public Bureaucracy and the Politics of Non-Coordination*. Cham: Palgrave Macmillan, 3–28.

Bach, T., and Wegrich, K. 2020. 'Politicians and Bureaucrats in Executive Government', in R. B. Andeweg, R. Elgie, L. Helms, J. Kaarbo, and F. Müller-Rommel (eds), *The Oxford Handbook of Political Executives*. Oxford: Oxford University Press, 525–46.

Baldwin, R., and Cave, M. 2020. *Taming the Corporation: How to Regulate for Success*, Oxford: Oxford University Press.

Balla, S. J., Beck, Alexander R., Meehan, E., and Prasad, A. 2020. 'Lost in the Flood? Agency Responsiveness to Mass Comment Campaigns in Administrative Rulemaking', *Regulation and Governance*. <https://doi.org/10.1111/rego.12318>.

Banerjee, A. V., and Duflo, E. 2019. *Good Economics for Hard Times: Better Answers to our Biggest Problems*. London: Penguin UK.

Bangladesh Accord. 2013. 'Accord on Fire and Building Safety in Bangladesh'. 13 May. Retrieved 28 February 2021 from <https://bangladesh.wpengine.com/wp-content/uploads/2018/08/2013-Accord.pdf>.

Bangladesh Accord. 2017. 'Transition to The RMG Sustainability Council (RSC)'. 21 June. Retrieved 28 February 2021 from <https://bangladesh.wpengine.com/wp-content/uploads/2020/11/2018-Accord.pdf>.

Bangladesh Accord. 2018. 'Safe Workplaces'. Retrieved 1 March 2021 from <www.bangladeshaccord.org>.

Barber, M. 2007. *Instruction to Deliver: Tony Blair, Public Services and the Challenge of Achieving Targets*. London: Politico's Publishing.

Bardach, E. 1977. *The Implementation Game: What Happens After a Bill Becomes a Law*. Cambridge, MA: MIT Press.

Bardach, E., and Patashnik, E. M. 2019. *Practical Guide for Policy Analysis: The Eightfold Path to More Effective Problem Solving*. Los Angeles: CQ Press, Sage.

Bar-Siman-Tov, I. 2018. 'Temporary Legislation, Better Regulation, and Experimentalist Governance: An Empirical Study', *Regulation and Governance* 12(2): 192–219. <https://doi.org/10.1111/rego.12148>.

Bartelheimer, P., Henke, J., Kaps, P., Kotlenga, S., Marquardsen, K. Nägele, B., Wagner, A., Söhn, N., Achatz, J., and Wenzig, C. 2016. 'Evaluation der bundesweiten Inanspruchnahme und Umsetzung der Leistungen für Bildung und Teilhabe'. Schlussbericht. Göttingen Nürnberg.

Basic Income Lab. n.d. 'Map of Universal Basic Income Experiments and Related Programs'. Retrieved 14 April 2021 from <https://basicincome.stanford.edu/experiments-map/>.

Bason, C. 2017. *Leading Public Design: Discovering Human-Centred Governance*. Bristol: Policy Press.

Bason, C. 2018. *Leading Public Sector Innovation: Co-creating for a Better Society*. 2nd ed. Bristol: Policy Press.

Baumgartner, F. R., Berry, J. M., Hojnacki, M., Kimball, D. C., and Leech, B. L. 2009. *Lobbying and Policy Change: Who Wins, Who Loses, and Why*. Chicago: University of Chicago Press.

Baumgartner, F. R., and Jones, B. D. 2009. *Agendas and Instability in American Politics*. 2nd ed. Chicago: University of Chicago Press.

Baumgartner, F. R., and Jones, B. D. 2015. *The Politics of Information: Problem Definition and the Course of Public Policy in America*. Chicago: University of Chicago Press.

Bayer, P., and Aklin, M. 2020. 'The European Union Emissions Trading Scheme Reduced Emissions Despite Low Prices', *PNAS* 117(16): 8804–12. <https://doi.org/10.1073/pnas.1918128117>.

BBC News. 2006. 'Asbos Viewed as "Badge of Honour"'. 2 May. Retrieved 8 May 2021 from <http://news.bbc.co.uk/2/hi/6107028.stm>.

BBC News. 2018. 'France Protests: PM Philippe Suspends Fuel Tax Rises'. 4 December. Retrieved 8 May 2021 from https://www.bbc.com/news/world-europe-46437904.

BBC News. 2019. 'Japan Whaling: Why Commercial Hunts have Resumed Despite Outcry'. 2 July. Retrieved 8 May 2021 from <https://www.bbc.com/news/world-asia-48592682>.

Beck, U., and Beck-Gernsheim, E. 2001. *Individualization: Institutionalized Individualism and its Social and Political Consequences*. London: SAGE Publications.

Becker, G. S. 1964. *Human Capital: A Theoretical and Empirical Analysis, with Special Reference to Education*. New York: National Bureau of Economic Research, distributed by Columbia University Press.

Becker, G. S. 1968. 'Crime and Punishment: An Economic Approach', in N. Fielding, A. Clarke, and R. Witt (eds), *The Economic Dimensions of Crime*. London: Palgrave Macmillan, 13–68.

Becker, M. 2019. 'When Public Principals Give up Control over Private Agents: The New Independence of ICANN in Internet Governance', *Regulation and Governance* 13(4): 561–76. https://doi.org/10.1111/rego.12250.

Bekkers, V., Fenger, M., and Scholten, P. 2017. *Public Policy in Action: Perspectives on the Policy Process*. Cheltenham and Northampton, MA: Edward Elgar.

Bemelmans-Videc, M.-L., Rist, R. C., and Vedung, E. 1998. *Carrots, Sticks and Sermons. Policy Instruments and their Evaluation*. New Brunswick, NJ, and London: Transaction Publishers.

Benjamin, R. 2019. *Race After Technology: Abolitionist Tools for the New Jim Code*. London: John Wiley & Sons.

Bennett, J. 2017. 'Make Figures, Tables, Graphs Work for You', in D. Chrisinger (ed.), *Public Policy Writing that Matters*. Baltimore: Johns Hopkins University Press, 95–108.

Benz, A., and Sonnicksen, J. 2017. 'Patterns of Federal Democracy: Tensions, Friction, or Balance between Two Government Dimensions', *European Political Science Review* 9(1): 3–25. <https://doi.org/10.1017/S1755773915000259>.

Benz, A., Scharpf, F. W., and Zintl, R. 1992. *Horizontale Politikverflechtung: Zur Theorie von Verhandlungssystemen*. Frankfurt a. M.: Campus Verlag.

Bergman, M. 2009. *Tax Evasion and the Rule of Law in Latin America: The Political Culture of Cheating and Compliance in Argentina and Chile*. University Park, PA: Pennsylvania State University Press.

Bero, L. 2003. 'Implications of the Tobacco Industry Documents for Public Health and Policy', *Annual Review of Public Health* 24(1): 267–88. <https://doi.org/10.1146/annurev.publhealth.24.100901.140813>.

Beyers, J., and Arras, S. 2020. 'Who Feeds Information to Regulators? Stakeholder Diversity in European Union Regulatory Agency Consultations', *Journal of Public Policy* 40(4): 573–98. <https://doi.org/10.1017/S0143814X19000126>.

Bezes, P. 2007. 'The Hidden Politics of Administrative Reform: Cutting French Civil Service Wages with a Low-Profile Instrument', *Governance* 20(1): 23–56.

Bhatti, Y., and Erikson, R. S. 2011. 'How Poorly are the Poor Represented in the US Senate?', in P. K. Enns and C. Wlezien (eds), *Who Gets Represented?* New York: Russell Sage Foundation, 223–46.

Black, J., and Baldwin, R. 2010. 'Really Responsive Risk-Based Regulation', *Law and Policy* 32(2): 181–213. <http://dx.doi.org/10.1111/j.1467-9930.2010.00318.x>.

Blanc, F. 2012. *Inspection Reforms: Why, How, and with What Results*. Paris: OECD.

Blau, P. M. 1955. *The Dynamics of Bureaucracy*. Chicago: University of Chicago Press.

Boden, R., and Epstein, D. 2006. 'Managing the Research Imagination? Globalisation and Research in Higher Education', *Globalisation, Societies and Education* 4(2): 223–36. <https://doi.org/10.1080/14767720600752619>.

Bogdanor, V. (ed.). 2005. *Joined-up Government*. Oxford: Oxford University Press.

Boin, A., 't Hart, P., Stern, E., and Sundelius, B. 2017. *The Politics of Crisis Management: Public Leadership under Pressure*. Cambridge: Cambridge University Press.

Bonilla-Chaín, M. E., Iglesias, R., Suaya, A., Trezza, C., and Macías, C. 2016. *Learning from the Mexican Experience with Taxes on Sugar-Sweetened Beverages and Energy-Dense Foods of Low Nutritional Value*. Washington, DC: World Bank.

Bonnitcha, J., and McCorquodale, R. 2017. 'The Concept of "Due Diligence" in the UN Guiding Principles on Business and Human Rights', *European Journal of International Law* 28(3): 899–919. <https://doi.org/10.1093/ejil/chx042>.

Bonoli, G., and Liechti, F. 2018. 'Good Intentions and Matthew Effects: Access Biases in Participation in Active Labour Market Policies', *Journal of European Public Policy* 25(6): 894–911. <https://doi.org/10.1080/13501763.2017.1401105>.

Börzel, T. A. 1998. 'Organizing Babylon: On the Different Conceptions of Policy Networks', *Public Administration* 76(2): 253–73.

Boswell, C. 2018. *Manufacturing Political Trust*. Cambridge: Cambridge University Press.

Bouwen, P. 2004. 'Exchanging Access Goods for Access: A Comparative Study of Business Lobbying in the European Union Institutions', *European Journal of Political Research* 43(3): 337–69. https://doi.org/10.1111/j.1475-6765.2004.00157.x.

Bovens, M. 2005. 'Public Accountability', in E. Ferlie, L. E. Lynn and C. Pollitt (eds), *The Oxford Handbook of Public Management*. Oxford: Oxford University Press, 182–208.

Bovens, M., 't Hart, P., and Kuipers, S. 2005. 'The Politics of Policy Evaluation', in M. Moran, M. Rein, and R. E. Goodin (eds), *The Oxford Handbook of Public Policy*. Oxford: Oxford University Press, 317–33.

Braithwaite, J. 2002. 'Rules and Principles: A Theory of Legal Certainty', *Australian Journal of Legal Philosophy* 27: 47–82.

Braithwaite, J. 2007. *Regulatory Capitalism: How it Works, Ideas for Making it Work Better*. Cheltenham and Northampton, MA: Edward Elgar.

Breakspear, S. 2012. *The Policy Impact of PISA: An Exploration of the Normative Effects of International Benchmarking in School System Performance*. OECD Education Working Papers, 71. Paris: OECD Publishing.

Brinks, D. M., Levitsky, S., and Murillo, M. V. (eds). 2020. *The Politics of Institutional Weakness in Latin America*. Cambridge: Cambridge University Press.

Bryan, G., Choi, J. J., and Karlan, D. 2020. 'Randomizing Religion: The Impact of Protestant Evangelism on Economic Outcomes', *Quarterly Journal of Economics* 136(1): 293–380. <https://doi.org/10.1093/qje/qjaa023>.

Bryson, J. M. 2003. 'What to Do When Stakeholders Matter: A Guide to Stakeholder Identification and Analysis Techniques', paper presented at the London School of Economics and Political Science, 10 February.

Bullock, J. B. 2019. 'Artificial Intelligence, Discretion, and Bureaucracy', *American Review of Public Administration* 49(7): 751–61. <https://doi.org/10.1177%2F0275074019856123>.

Bundesministerium für Arbeit und Soziales (Federal Ministry of Labour and Social Affairs). 2017. *White Paper. Work 4.0*. Berlin: BMAS. Retrieved 8 May 2021 from <https://www.bmas.de/EN/Services/Publications/a883-white-paper.html;jsessionid=%203CD9A4A06A2A73168CBE59EB7EC25178>.

Bundesministerium für Wirtschaft und Energie (Federal Ministry for Economic Affairs and Energy). 2021. 'The EU Emissions Trading System—Essential for the Energy Transition'. Retrieved 8 March 2021 from <https://www.bmwi.deRedaktion/EN/Artikel/Energy/emissions-trading.html>.

Bunea, A. 2017. 'Designing Stakeholder Consultations: Reinforcing or Alleviating Bias in the European Union System of Governance?', *European Journal of Political Research* 56(1): 46–69. <https://doi.org/10.1111/1475-6765.12165>.

Busch, P. A., and Henriksen, H. Z. 2018. 'Digital Discretion: A Systematic Literature Review of ICT and Street-Level Discretion', *Information Polity* 23(1): 3–28. <https://doi.org/10.3233/IP-170050>.

Busemeyer, M. R., and Trampusch, C. (eds). 2012. *The Political Economy of Collective Skill Formation*. Oxford and New York: Oxford University Press.

Business in the Community. n.d. 'Education. Every Child Able to Achieve in Education'. Retrieved 19 April 2021 from <https://www.bitc.org.uk/education/>.

Busuioc, E. M. 2016. 'Friend or Foe? Inter-Agency Cooperation, Organizational Reputation, and Turf', *Public Administration* 94(1): 40–56.

Cabinet Office. 1999. *Modernising Government*. London: Cabinet Office. Retrieved 8 May 2021 from <https://ntouk.files.wordpress.com/2015/06/modgov.pdf>.

Cairney, P. 2016. *The Politics of Evidence-Based Policy Making*. Basingstoke: Palgrave Macmillan.

Cairney, P. 2019. 'The Transformation of UK Tobacco Control', in M. Compton and P. T. 't Hart (eds), *Great Policy Successes: How Governments Get it Right in a Big Way at Least Some of the Time*. Oxford: Oxford University Press, 84–103.

Cairney, P. 2021. *The Politics of Policy Analysis*. London: Palgrave Macmillan.

Calvert, R., McCubbins, M., and Weingast, B. 1989. 'A Theory of Political Control and Agency Discretion', *American Journal of Political Science* 33(3): 588–611.

Campbell, D. T. 1969. 'Reforms as Experiments', *American Psychologist* 24(4): 409–29.

Carothers, T., and Brechenmacher, S. 2014. *Closing Space: Democracy and Human Rights Support Under Fire*. Washington, DC: Carnegie Endowment for International Peace.

Center for Climate and Energy Solutions. n.d. 'Global Emissions'. Retrieved 21 March 2021 from <https://www.c2es.org/content/international-emissions/>

Chalmers, D., and Lodge, M. 2003. *The Open Method of Co-ordination and the European Welfare State*. CARR Discussion paper, 11. London: ESRC Centre for Analysis of Risk and Regulation. <http://wwww.lse.ac.uk/accounting/assets/CARR/documents/D-P/Disspaper11.pdf>.

Chandler, I. 2015. 'Advocacy and Campaign Planning Mini-Guide #1 Advocacy and Campaigning: An Overview'. The Pressure Group. Retrieved 8 May 2021 from <http://thepressuregroup.org/index.php/download/mini-guide-1-advocacy-campaign-in-an-overview/>.

Chisholm, D. W. 1989. *Coordination without Hierarchy: Informal Structures in Multiorganizational Systems*. Berkeley, CA: University of California Press.

Chrisinger, D. 2017. *Public Policy Writing that Matters*. Baltimore, MD: Johns Hopkins University Press.

Christensen, T., and Lægreid, P. 2007. 'The Whole-of-Government Approach to Public Sector Reform', *Public Administration Review* 67(6): 1059–66.

Christensen, T., Fimreite, A. L., and Lægreid, P. 2014. 'Joined-up Government for Welfare Administration Reform in Norway', *Public Organization Review* 14(4): 439–56. <https://doi.org/10.1007/s11115-013-0237-8>.

Citizenship by Investment. 2018. 'CBI/RBI Industry has Grown into $13 Billion Dollar Industry'. Retrieved 25 March 2021 from <https://citizenshipbyinvestment.ch/index.php/2018/0728/cbi-rbi-industry-has-grown-to-13-billion-dollar-industry/>.

Clarke, A., and Craft, J. 2019. 'The Twin Faces of Public Sector Design', *Governance* 32(1): 5–21. <https://doi.org/10.1111/gove.12342>.

Coase, R. H. 1937. 'The Nature of the Firm', *Economica* 4(16): 386–405.

Cobb, R. W., and Elder, C. D. 1971. 'The Politics of Agenda-Building: An Alternative Perspective for Modern Democratic Theory', *Journal of Politics* 33(4): 892–915.

Cohen, M. D., March, J. G., and Olsen, J. P. 1972. 'A Garbage Can Model of Organizational Choice', *Administrative Science Quarterly* 17(1): 1–25.

Colchero, M. A., Rivera-Dommarco J., Popkin B. M., and Ng, S. W. 2017. 'In Mexico, Evidence of Sustained Consumer Response Two Years After Implementing a Sugar-Sweetened Beverage Tax', *Health Affairs* 36(3): 564–71. <https://doi.org/10.1377/hlthaff.2016.1231>.

Compton, M. E., and 't Hart, P. T. 2019. 'Looping to Success (and Failure): Second-Order Mechanisms and Policy Outcomes', in G. Capano, M. Howlett, M. Ramesh, and A. Virani (eds), *Making Policies Work*. Cheltenham: Edward Elgar Publishing, 191–210.

Córdova, A., and Kras, H. 2020. 'Addressing Violence Against Women: The Effect of Women's Police Stations on Police Legitimacy', *Comparative Political Studies* 53(5): 775–808. <https://doi.org/10.1177/0010414019879959>.

Cousins, S. 2020. 'New Zealand Eliminates Covid-19', *The Lancet Regional Health—Europe* 395(10235): 1474. <https://doi.org/10.1016/S0140-6736(20)31097-7>.

Craft, J., and Halligan, J. 2020. *Advising Governments in the Westminster Tradition: Policy Advisory Systems in Australia, Britain, Canada and New Zealand*. Cambridge: Cambridge University Press.

Crawford, K., Dobbe, R., Dryer, T., Fried, G., Green, B., Kaziunas, E., Kak, A., Mathur, V., McElroy, E., Nill Sánchez, A., Raji, D., Rankin, J. L., Richardson, R., Schultz, J., West, S. M., and Whittaker, M. 2019. *AI Now 2019 Report*. New York: AI Now Institute, New York University. Retrieved 8 May 2021 from <https://ainowinstitute.org/AI_Now_2019_Report.pdf>.

Crawford, S. E., and Ostrom, E. 1995. 'A Grammar of Institutions', *American Political Science Review* 89(3): 582–600.

Crenson, M. A. 1971. *The Un-Politics of Air Pollution: A Study of Non-Decisionmaking in the Cities*. Baltimore, MD, and London: Johns Hopkins Press.

Crouch, C., Finegold, D., and Sako, M. 1999. *Are Skills the Answer? The Political Economy of Skill Creation in Advanced Industrial Countries*. Oxford and New York: Oxford University Press.

Culpepper, P. D. 2010. *Quiet Politics and Business Power: Corporate Control in Europe and Japan*. Cambridge: Cambridge University Press.

Danielsson, J. 2018. 'The McNamara fallacy in financial policymaking', Voxeu (Column), 1 June, https://voxeu.org/content/mcnamara-fallacy-financial-policymaking

Dash, E., and Story, L. 2009. 'Rubin Leaving Citigroup; Smith Barney for Sale', *New York Times*, 9 January. Retrieved 8 May 2021 from <https://www.nytimes.com/2009/01/10/business/10rubin.html?_r=1&hp>.

Datta, L. 1982. 'A Tale of Two Studies: The Westinghouse-Ohio Evaluation of Project Head Start and the Consortium for Longitudinal Studies Report', *Studies in Educational Evaluation* 8(3): 271–80.

Dave, P., and Dastin, J. 2020. 'Google Told its Scientists to "Strike a Positive Tone" in AI Research—Documents'. Reuters, 23 December. Retrieved on 8 May 2021 from <https://www.reuters.com/article/us-alphabet-google-research-focus-idUSK BN28X1CB>.

de la Rosa, S. 2006. 'The Open Method of Coordination in the New Member States: The Perspectives for its Use as a Tool of Soft Law', *European Law Journal* 11(5): 618–40. <https://doi.org/10.1111/j.1468-0386.2005.00279.x>.

De Souza Leão, L., and Eyal, G. 2019. 'The Rise of Randomized Controlled Trials (RCTs) in International Development in Historical Perspective', *Theory and Society* 48(3): 383–418.

Dewey, M., and Di Carlo, D. 2021. 'Governing through Non-Enforcement: Regulatory Forbearance as Industrial Policy in Advanced Economies', *Regulation and Governance*. <https://doi.org/10.1111/rego.12382>.

Dorsch, M. J., Flachsland, C., and Kornek, U. 2020. 'Building and Enhancing Climate Policy Ambition with Transfers: Allowance Allocation and Revenue Spending in the EU ETS', *Environmental Politics* 29(5): 781–803. <https://doi.org/10.1080/09644016.2019.1659576>.

Duit, A., and Löf, A. 2018. 'Dealing with a Wicked Problem? A Dark Tale of Carnivore Management in Sweden 2007–2011', *Administration and Society* 50(8): 1072–96. <https://doi.org/10.1177%2F0095399715595668>.

Dunlop, C. A., and Radaelli, C. M. 2019. 'Policy Instruments, Policy Learning and Politics: Impact Assessment in the European Union', in G. Capano, M. Howlett, M. Ramesh, and A. Virani (eds), *Making Policies Work*. Cheltenham and Northampton, MA: Edward Elgar Publishing, 115–36.

Duverger, M. 1972. *Party Politics and Pressure Groups: A Comparative Introduction.* New York: Crowell.

Dye, T. R. 1976. *Policy Analysis: What Governments Do, Why they Do it, and What Difference it Makes.* Tuscaloosa, AL: University of Alabama Press.

EASME. 2020. *Bringing Nature back through LIFE.* Brussels: Executive Agency for Small and Medium-Sized Enterprises.

ECCHR. 2011. 'A Comparison of National Contact Points: Best Practices in OECD Complaints Procedures'. Policy Paper 011. <https://www.ecchr.eu/fileadmin/Publikationen/OECD_A_comparison_of_NCPs_Policy_Paper_2011-11.pdf>.

Eden, C., and Ackermann, F. 1998. *Making Strategy: The Journey of Strategic Management.* London: Sage.

Eldredge, N., and Gould, S. J. 1972. 'Punctuated Equilibria: An Alternative to Phyletic Gradualism', in T. Schopf (ed.), *Models in Paleobiology.* San Francisco: Freeman Cooper & Co., 82–115.

Elkomy, S., and Cookson, G. 2020. 'Performance Management Strategy: Waiting Time in the English National Health Services', *Public Organization Review* 20(1): 95–112. <https://link.springer.com/article/10.1007/s11115-018-0425-7>.

Ellis, J. 2017. *Campaigning for Change: An Essential Guide to Campaigning around the World.* Independently published.

Ellis, J. 2020. *Making your Campaign Happen: How to Use a Theory of Change or a Future Story for Your Campaigning.* Retrieved 21 May 2021 <http://jonathanelliscampaigns.com/wp-content/uploads/2020/01/Making-your-campaign-happen.pdf>.

Elmore, R. F. 1979. 'Backward Mapping: Implementation Research and Policy Decisions', *Political Science Quarterly* 94(4): 601–16.

El Tawil, N. 2020. 'Declaration of Principles on Renaissance Dam is "Exclusive Agreement" Binding Egypt, Ethiopia, Sudan Together: Intl. Law Expert', *Egypt Today*, 23 June. Retrieved 21 May 2021 from <https://www.egypttoday.com/Article/1/88909/Declaration-of-Principles-on-Renaissance-Dam-is-exclusive-agreement-binding>.

Emerson, K., Nabatchi, T., and Balogh, S. 2012. 'An Integrative Framework for Collaborative Governance', *Journal of Public Administration Research and Theory* 22(1): 1–29. <https://doi.org/10.1093/jopart/mur011>.

Enns, P. 2016. *Incarceration Nation: How the United States Became the Most Punitive Democracy in the World.* Cambridge: Cambridge University Press.

Epstein, D., and O'Halloran, S. 1999. *Delegating Powers: A Transaction Cost Politics Approach to Policy Making under Separate Powers.* Cambridge: Cambridge University Press.

Eubanks, V. 2018. *Automating Inequality: How High-Tech Tools Profile, Police, and Punish the Poor.* New York: St Martin's Press.

European Commission. 2002. 'Consultation Document: Towards a Reinforced Culture of Consultation and Dialogue. Proposal for General Principles and Minimum Standards for Consultation of Interested Parties by the Commission', COM(2002) 277 final. Retrieved 22 April 2021 from <https://www.europarl.europa.eu/meetdocs/committees/juri/20040218/020277EN.pdf>.

European Commission. 2017. 'Better regulation guidelines – Impact assessment. Retrieved 23 September 2021 from https://ec.europa.eu/info/law/law-making-process/planning-and-proposing-law/better-regulation-why-and-how/better-regulation-guidelines-and-toolbox_en.

European Commission. 2018. 'Commission Decision of 31.1.2018 on a Code of Conduct for the Members of the European Commission', 2018 700 final. 31 January. Retrieved

22 April 2021 from <https://ec.europa.eu/info/sites/default/files/code-of-conduct-for-commissioners-2018_en_0.pdf>.

European Commission. 2019a. 'Report from the Commission to the European Parliament, the Council, the European Economic and Social Committee and the Committee of the Regions on Investor Citizenship and Residence Schemes in the European Union'. 23 January. Retrieved 2 March 2021 from <https://ec.europa.eu/info/files/report-commission-european-parliament-council-european-economic-and-social-committee-and-committee-regions-investor-citizenship-and-residence-schemes-european-union_en>.

European Commission. 2019b. 'Communication from the Commission to the European Parliament, the European Council, the Council, the European Economic and Social Committee and the Committee of the Regions. The European Green Deal', COM(2019) 640 final. 11 December. Retrieved 22 April 2021 from <https://eur-lex.europa.eu/resource.html?uri=cellar:b828d165-1c22-11ea-8c1f-01aa75ed71a1.0002.02/DOC_1&format=PDF>.

European Commission. 2020a. 'Investor Citizenship Schemes: European Commission Opens Infringements Against Cyprus and Malta for "Selling" EU Citizenship'. 20 October. Retrieved 22 April 2021 from <https://ec.europa.eu/cyprus/news_2020 1020_2_en>.

European Commission. 2020b. 'European Commission Revamps its "Have your Say" Portal'. 3 July. Retrieved 2 March 2021 from <https://ec.europa.eu/commission/presscorner/detail/en/IP_20_1240>.

European Commission. 2020c. 'Statement by Executive Vice-President Margrethe Vestager on the Commission's Decision to Appeal the General Court's Judgment on the Apple Tax State Aid Case in Ireland'. 26 September. Retrieved 2 March 2021 from <https://ec.europa.eu/commission/presscorner/detail/en/STATEMENT_20_1746>.

European Commission. 2021. 'Better Regulation. Joining Forces for Better Laws' Communication from the Commission to the European Parliament, the Council, the European and Social Committee and the Committee of the Regions, 29 April 2021, Retrieved 26 September 2021 from https://ec.europa.eu/info/sites/default/files/better_regulation_joining_forces_to_make_better_laws_en_0.pdf.

European Commission. n.d.-a. 'Mission Statement of the Secretariat-General'. Retrieved 2 March 2021 from <https://ec.europa.eu/info/departments/secretariat-general/mission-statement-secretariat-general_en>.

European Commission. n.d.-b. 'Better Regulation: Guidelines and Toolbox'. Retrieved 22 April 2021 from <https://ec.europa.eu/info/law/law-making-process/planning-and-proposing-law/better-regulation-why-and-how/better-regulation-guidelines-and-toolbox_en>.

European Commission. n.d.-c. 'Have your Say'. Retrieved 22 April 2021 from <https://ec.europa.eu/info/law/better-regulation/have-your-say>.

European Commission. n.d.-d. 'Activities of the Group of Member State Experts on Investor Citizenship and Residence Schemes'. Retrieved 22 April 2021 from <https://ec.europa.eu/info/policies/justice-and-fundamental-rights/eu-citizenship/eu-citizenshipactivities-group-member-state-experts-investor-citizenship-and-residence-schemes_en>.

European Commission. n.d.-e. 'Employment, Social Affairs and Inclusion'. Retrieved 2 March 2021 from <https://ec.europa.eu/social/main.jsp?langId=en&catId=750>.

European Commission. n.d.-f 'The Just Transition Mechanism: Making Sure No One is Left Behind'. Retrieved 2 March 2021 from <https://ec.europa.eu/info/strategy/priorities-

2019-2024european-green-deal/actions-being-taken-eu/just-transition-mechanism_ en>.

European Commission. n.d.-g. 'EU Emissions Trading System (EU ETS)'. Retrieved 22 April 2021 from <https://ec.europa.eu/clima/policies/ets_en>.

European Commission. n.d.-h. 'Energy Union'. Retrieved 20 March 2021 from <https://ec.europa.eu/energy/topics/energy-strategy/energy-union_en#regulation-on-the-governance-of-the-energy-union-and-climate-action>.

European Commission. n.d.-i. 'European Climate Change Programme'. Retrieved 22 April 2021 from <https://ec.europa.eu/clima/policies/eccp_en>.

European Economic and Social Committee. 2019. 'EESC Demands an End to All Investor Citizenship and Residence Schemes in the EU'. 18 November. Retrieved 14 April 2021 from <https://www.eesc.europa.eu/en/news-media/news/eesc-demands-end-all-investor-citizenship-and-residence-schemes-eu>.

European Parliament. 2014. 'The Open Method of Coordination. At a Glance. The Open Method of Coordination'. Retrieved 14 April 2021 from <https://www.europarl.europa.eu/EPRS/EPRS-AaG-542142-Open-Method-of-Coordination-FINAL.pdf>.

European Parliament and Council of the European Union. 2018. 'Directive (EU) 2018/2001 of the European Parliament and of the Council of 11 December 2018 on the Promotion of the Use of Energy from Renewable Sources (Recast)'. Retrieved 14 April 2021 fom <https://eur-lex.europa.eu/legal-content/EN/TXT/PDF/?uri=CELEX:32018L2001&from=DE>.

European Union Agency for Fundamental Rights. 2018. *Ten Keys to Effectively Communicating Human Rights*. Luxembourg: Publications Office of the European Union.

Eurostat. 2016. 'Statistics on Commuting Patterns at Regional Level. Statistics Explained. Data Extracted in April 2016'. Retrieved 22 March 2021 from <http://ec.europa.eu/eurostatstatisticsexplained/>.

Evelyn, K. 2020. 'Barack Obama Criticizes "Defund the Police" Slogan But Faces Backlash', *The Guardian*, 2 December. Retrieved 8 May 2021 from <https://www.theguardian.com/us-news/2020/dec/02/barack-obama-criticizes-defund-the-police-slogan-backlash>.

Fakhoury, T. 2019. 'Power-Sharing After the Arab Spring? Insights from Lebanon's Political Transition', *Nationalism and Ethnic Politics* 25(1): 9–26. <https://doi.org/10.1080/13537113.2019.1565173>.

Farolfi, S., Pegg, D., and Orphanides, S. 2017. 'Cyprus "Selling" EU Citizenship to Super Rich of Russia and Ukraine', *The Guardian*, 8 March 2021. Retrieved 8 May 2021 from <https://www.theguardian.com/world/2017/sep/17/cyprus-selling-eu-citizenship-to-super-rich-of-russia-and-ukraine>.

Fellner, G., Sausgruber, R., and Traxler, C. 2013. 'Testing Enforcement Strategies in the Field: Threat, Moral Appeal and Social Information', *Journal of the European Economic Association* 11(3): 634–60. <https://doi.org/10.1111/jeea.12013>.

Figari, A., and Kelso, C. 2013. *Developing an Anti-Corruption Advocacy Plan: A Step-by-Step Guide*. Berlin: Transparency International. <https://oc-hub.org/community/wp-content/uploads/2020/10/2019-05-08developing-an-advocacy-plan-a-step-by-step-guide-transparency-international-1.pdf>. Last accessed 22 March 2021.

Fischer, F. 1995. *Evaluating Public Policy*. Chicago: Nelson-Hall Inc.

Fischer, F., Miller, G. J., and Sidney, M. S. (eds). 2007. *Handbook of Public Policy Analysis Theory, Politics, and Methods*. Boca Raton, FL: CRC Press.

Fischman, G. E., Topper, A. M., Silova, I., Goebel, J., Holloway, J. L. 2018. 'Examining the Influence of International Large-Scale Assessments on National Education Policies', *Journal of Education Policy* 34(4): 470–99. <https://doi.org/10.1080/02680939.2018.1460493>.

Flachsland, C., Pahle, M. Burtraw, D., Edenhofer, O., Elkerbout, M., Fischer, C., Tietjen, O., and Zetterberg, L. 2020. 'How to Avoid History Repeating Itself: The Case for an EU Emissions Trading System (EU ETS) Price Floor Revisited', *Climate Policy* 20(1): 133–42. <https://doi.org/10.1080/14693062.2019.1682494>.

Fletcher, J. M., Frisvold, D. E., and Tefft, N. 2010. 'The Effects of Soft Drink Taxes on Child and Adolescent Consumption and Weight Outcomes', *Journal of Public Economics* 94(11–12): 967–74. <http://dx.doi.org/10.1016/j.jpubeco.2010.09.005>.

Flonk, D. Jachtenfuchs, M., and Obendiek, A. S. 2020. 'Authority Conflicts in Internet Governance: Liberals vs. Sovereigntists?', *Global Constitutionalism* 9(2): 364–86. <http://dx.doi.org/10.1017/S2045381720000167>.

Forget, E. L. 2011. 'The Town with No Poverty: The Health Effects of a Canadian Guaranteed Annual Income Field Experiment', *Canadian Public Policy* 37(3): 283–305. <https://doi.org/10.3138/cpp.37.3.283>.

Fox, J. A., and Brown, L. D. 1998. 'Assessing the Impact of NGO Advocacy Campaigns on World Bank Projects and Policies', in J. A. Fox and L. D. Brown (eds), *The Struggle for Accountability: The World Bank, NGOs, and Grassroots Movements*. Cambridge, MA, and London: MIT Press, 485–552.

Frank, M. 2020. 'No Drama Smalltalk mit Wolfgang Schmidt'. Youtube. 18 June. Retrieved 8 May 2021 from <https://www.youtube.com/watch?v=iZFnFTj-flc>.

Fraser, A., Tan, S., Lagarde, M., and Mays, N. 2018. 'Narratives of Promise, Narratives of Caution: A Review of the Literature on Social Impact Bonds', *Social Policy and Administration* 52(1): 4–28. <https://doi.org/10.1111/spol.12260>.

Funnell, S. C., and Rogers, P. J. 2011. *Purposeful Program Theory: Effective Use of Theories of Change and Logic Models*. San Francisco: Jossey-Bass Wiley.

Gautier, M. 2020. 'Number of Deaths during the Yellow Vest Protests in France 2018–2019'. 27 February. Retrieved 22 March 2020 from <https://www.statista.com/statistics/1081454dead-yellow-vests-movement-protests-france/>.

Gavin, N. 2018. 'Media Definitely Do Matter: Brexit, Immigration, Climate Change and Beyond', *British Journal of Politics and International Relations* 20(4): 827–45. <https://doi.org/10.1177%2F1369148118799260>.

Gehring, T. 1994. *Dynamic International Regimes: Institutions for International Environmental Governance*. Frankfurt a.M.: Peter Lang.

Genschel, P., and Seelkopf, L. 2016. 'Winners and Losers of Tax Competition', in P. Dietsch and T. Rixen (eds), *Global Tax Governance: What is Wrong with it and How to Fix it*. Colchester: ECPR Press, 55–76.

Genschel, P., and Schwarz, P. 2011. 'Tax Competition: A Literature Review', *Socio-Economic Review* 9(2): 339–70. <https://doi.org/10.1093/ser/mwr004>.

Gerber, A. S., and Green, D. P. 2012. *Field Experiments: Design, Analysis, and Interpretation*. New York: W. W. Norton.

Gertler, P. J., Martinez, S., Premand, P., Rawlings, L. B., and Vermeersch, C. M. J. 2016. *Impact Evaluation in Practice*. Washington, DC: World Bank.

Gilad, S. 2010. 'It Runs in the Family: Meta-Regulation and its Siblings', *Regulation and Governance* 4(4): 485–506. <https://doi.org/10.1111/j.1748-5991.2010.01090.x>.

Gilens, M. 2005. 'Inequality and Democratic Responsiveness', *Public Opinion Quarterly* 69(5): 778–96. <https://doi.org/10.1093/poq/nfi058>.

Gilens, M. 2015. 'Descriptive Representation, Money, and Political Inequality in the United States', *Swiss Political Science Review* 21(2): 222–8. <https://doi.org/10.1111/spsr.12164>.

Gingrich, J. 2011. *Making Markets in the Welfare State: The Politics of Varying Market Reforms*. Cambridge: Cambridge University Press.

Glennerster, R., and Takavarasha, K. 2013. *Running Randomized Evaluations: A Practical Guide*. Princeton and Oxford: Princeton University Press.

Global Witness. 2020. 'Europe's Golden Doors'. 27 March. Retrieved 8 March 2021 from <https://www.globalwitness.org/en/campaigns/corruption-and-money-laundering/europes-golden-doors/>.

Gneezy, U., and Rustichini, A. 2000. 'A Fine is a Price', *Journal of Legal Studies* 29(1): 1–17.

Gofen, A. 2012. 'Entrepreneurial Exit Response to Dissatisfaction with Public Services', *Public Administration* 90(4): 1088–1106. <https://doi.org/10.1111/j.1467-9299.2011.02021.x>.

Gofen, A., and Golan, E. 2020. 'Laboratories of Design: A Catalog of Policy Innovation Labs in Europe'. Available at SSRN 3822821, <https://papers.ssrn.com/sol3/papers.cfm?abstract_id=3822821>. <http://dx.doi.org/10.2139/ssrn.3684515>.

Gofen, A., and Needham, C. E. 2015. 'Service Personalization as a Response to Noncompliance with Routine Childhood Vaccination', *Governance* 28(3): 269–83. <https://doi.org/10.1111/gove.12082>.

Golden, M., and Min, B. 2013. 'Distributive Politics around the World', *Annual Review of Political Science* 16: 73–99. <https://doi.org/10.1146/annurev-polisci-052209-121553>.

Golden, M. A., and Picci, L. 2008. 'Pork-Barrel Politics in Postwar Italy, 1953–94', *American Journal of Political Science* 52(2): 268–89.

Goo, J. J., and Heo, J.-Y. 2020. 'The Impact of the Regulatory Sandbox on the Fintech Industry, with a Discussion on the Relation between Regulatory Sandboxes and Open Innovation', *Journal of Open Innovation: Technology, Market, and Complexity* 6(2): 43. <https://doi.org/10.3390/joitmc6020043>.

Gorvett, J. 2021. 'China at the Heart of Rising Nile River Conflict. China-Financed Grand Ethiopian Renaissance Dam is Africa's Largest and Most Divisive Development Project', *Asia Times*, 19 January. Retrieved 8 May 2021 from <https://asiatimes.com/2021/01/china-at-the-heart-of-rising-nile-river-conflict/>.

Graf, L. 2018. 'Combined Modes of Gradual Change: The Case of Academic Upgrading and Declining Collectivism in German Skill Formation', *Socio-Economic Review* 16(1): 185–205. <https://doi.org/10.1093/ser/mww044>.

Greenhouse, S. 2013. 'Major Retailers Join Bangladesh Safety Plan', *New York Times*, 13 May. Retrieved 21 May 2021 from <https://www.nytimes.com/2013/05/14/business/global/hm-agrees-to-bangladesh-safety-plan.html?_r=0>.

Groll, S. 2019. 'Coal Commission Final Report—Assessment'. Heinrich-Böll-Stiftung. 18 February. Retrieved 8 March 2021 from <https://www.boell.de/en/2019/02/18/coal-commission-final-report-assessment>.

Grossmann, M. 2012. *The Not-So-Special Interests: Interest Groups, Public Representation and American Governance*. Stanford, CA: Stanford University Press.

Grove, J. 2020. 'Coronavirus: USS Pensions could Become "Much Less Generous"', Times Higher Education, 23 March. Retrieved 8 March 2021 from <https://www.timeshighereducation.com/news/coronavirus-uss-pensions-could-become-much-less-generous>.

Gunningham, N. 2010. 'Enforcement and Compliance Strategies', in R. Baldwin, M. Cave, and M. Lodge (eds), *The Oxford Handbook of Regulation*. Oxford: Oxford University Press, 120–45.

Haas, P. M. 1992. 'Introduction: Epistemic Communities and International Policy Coordination', *International Organization* 46(1): 1–35. <https://doi.org/10.1017/S0020818300001442>.

Haas, P. M. 2016. *Epistemic Communities, Constructivism, and International Environmental Politics*. London and New York: Routledge.

Hacker, J. S., Pierson, P., and Thelen, K. 2015. 'Drift and Conversion: Hidden Faces of Institutional Change', in J. Mahoney and K. Thelen (eds), *Advances in Comparative-Historical Analysis*. Cambridge: Cambridge University Press, 180–208.

Haeder, S. F., and Weimer, D. L. 2013. 'You can't Make me Do it: State Implementation of Insurance Exchanges under the Affordable Care Act', *Public Administration Review* 73(1): 34–47. <https://doi.org/10.1111/puar.12065>.

Hall, P. A. 1993. 'Policy Paradigms, Social Learning, and the State: The Case of Economic Policymaking in Britain', *Comparative Politics* 25(3): 275–96. <http://www.jstor.org/stable/422246?origin=JSTOR-pdf>.

Hall, P. A., and Soskice, D. W. 2001. 'An Introduction to Varieties of Capitalism', in P. A. Hall and D. W. Soskice (eds), *Varieties of Capitalism: The Institutional Foundations of Comparative Advantage*. Oxford and New York: Oxford University Press, 1–68.

Hallsworth, M., and Kirkman, E. 2020. *Behavioral Insights*. Cambridge, MA: MIT Press.

Halpern, D., and Mason, D. 2015. 'Radical Incrementalism', *Evaluation* 21(2): 143–9. <https://doi.org/10.1177/1356389015578895>.

Halpin, D. 2014. *The Organization of Political Interest Groups: Designing Advocacy*. London and New York: Routledge.

Halpin, D., and Jordan, A. G. eds. 2012. *The Scale of Interest Organization in Democratic Politics: Data and Research Methods*. Basingstoke: Palgrave Macmillan.

Hardin, G. 1968. 'The Tragedy of the Commons', *Science* 162: 1243–8.

Harris, J. L., Frazier, W., Romo-Palafox, M. A., Hyary, M., Fleming-Milici, F., and Haraghey, K. 2017. *FACTS 2017 Food Industry Self-Regulation After Ten Years: Progress and Opportunities to Improve Food Advertising to Children*. Hartford, CT: University of Connecticut Rudd Center for Food Policy and Obesity.

Hartz, P. 2002. Moderne Dienstleistungen am Arbeitsmarkt. Bericht der Kommission (Broschüre A 306 des Bundesministeriums für Arbeit und Sozialordnung). Berlin: Bundesministerium für Arbeit und Soziales.

Harvard Law Review. 2015. 'New York Statewide Coalition of Hispanic Chambers of Commerce v. New York City Department of Health and Mental Hygiene: New York Court of Appeals Affirms Invalidation of Soda-Portion Cap'. 10 March. Retrieved 11 May 2021 from <https://harvardlawreview.org/2015/03/new-york-statewide-coalition-of-hispanic-chambers-of-commerce-v-new-york-city-department-of-health-and-mental-hygiene/>.

Hassel, A., and Palier, B. 2021. 'Tracking the Transformation of Growth Regimes in Advanced Capitalist Economies', in A. Hassel and B. Palier (eds), *Growth and Welfare in Advanced Capitalist Economies: How Have Growth Regimes Evolved?* Oxford: Oxford University Press, 3–55.

Hassel, A., and Schiller, C. 2010. *Der Fall Hartz IV: Wie es zur Agenda 2010 kam und wie es weiter geht*. Frankfurt a.M.: Campus Verlag.

Hatzopoulos, V. 2007. 'Why the Open Method of Coordination is Bad for You: A Letter to the EU', *European Law Journal* 13(3): 309–42. <https://doi.org/10.1111/j.1468-0386.2007.00368.x>.

Heclo, H. 1974. *Modern Social Politics in Britain and Sweden*. New Haven, CT: Yale University Press.

Heclo, H. 1978. 'Issue Networks and the Executive Establishment', in A. King (ed.), *The New American Political System*. Washington, DC: American Enterprise Institute, 87–124.

Heclo, H. H. 1972. 'Policy Analysis', *British Journal of Political Science* 2(1): 83–108.

Heider, C. 2016. 'What Comes After the Evaluation is Completed? Five Tips to Make your Evaluation More Influential'. Independent Evaluation Group. 21 June. Retrieved 11 May 2021 from <https://ieg.worldbankgroup.org/blog/what-comes-after-evaluation-completed>.

Heimlich, R. 2019. 'Interview mit Renate Mayntz "Ich wollte unbedingt in die Forschung"', *Kölner Stadtanzeiger*, 26 April. Retrieved 8 May 2021 from <https://www.ksta.de/koeln/interview-mit-renate-mayntz—ich-wollte-unbedingt-in-die-forschung—32433182?cb=1620220364807>.

Heims, E. 2019. 'Why Cooperation between Agencies is (Sometimes) Possible: Turf Protection as Enabler of Regulatory Cooperation in the European Union', in T. Bach and K. Wegrich (eds), *The Blind Spots of Public Bureaucracy and the Politics of Non-Coordination*. Cham: Palgrave Macmillan, 113–31.

Heineman, R. A., Bluhm, W. T., Peterson, S. A., and Kearny, E. N. 1990. *The World of the Policy Analyst: Rationality, Values, and Politics*. Chatham, NJ: Chatham House.

Herd, P., and Moynihan, D. P. 2019. *Administrative Burden: Policymaking by Other Means*. New York: Russell Sage Foundation.

Héritier, A. 1999. *Policy-Making and Diversity in Europe: Escape from Deadlock*. Cambridge: Cambridge University Press.

Hern, A. 2020. 'Facebook Says it may Quit Europe over Ban on Sharing Data with US', *The Guardian*, 22 September. Retrieved 8 March 2021 from <https://www.theguardian.com/technology/2020/sep/22/facebook-says-it-may-quit-europe-over-ban-on-sharing-data-with-us>.

Herrera, V., and Post, A. E. 2019. 'The Case for Public Policy Expertise in Political Science', *PS: Political Science and Politics* 52(3): 476–80.

Hinton, E. 2016. *From the War on Poverty to the War on Crime: The Making of Mass Incarceration in America*. Cambridge, MA: Harvard University Press.

Hogwood, B. W., and Peters, B. G. 1982. 'The Dynamics of Policy Change: Policy Succession', *Policy Sciences* 14(3): 225–45. <https://doi.org/10.1007/BF00136398>.

Hogwood, B. W., and Peters, B. G. 1983. *Policy Dynamics*. Brighton: Wheatsheaf Books.

Holland, A. C. 2017. *Forbearance as Redistribution: The Politics of Informal Welfare in Latin America*. Cambridge: Cambridge University Press.

Hood, C. 1983. *The Tools of Government*. London: Macmillan.

Hood, C. 1991. 'A Public Management for All Seasons?', *Public Administration* 69(1): 3–19.

Hood, C. 2006. 'Gaming in Targetworld: The Targets Approach to Managing British Public Services', *Public Administration Review* 66(4): 515–21. <https://doi.org/10.1111/j.1540-6210.2006.00612.x>.

Hood, C. 2011. *The Blame Game: Spin, Bureaucracy, and Self-Preservation in Government*. Princeton: Princeton University Press.

Hood, C. 2012. 'Public Management by Numbers as a Performance-Enhancing Drug: Two Hypotheses', *Public Administration Review* 72(1): 85–92. <https://doi.org/10.1111/j.1540-6210.2012.02634.x>.

Hood, C., and Lodge, M. 2006. *The Politics of Public Service Bargains: Reward, Competency, Loyalty and Blame*. Oxford: Oxford University Press.

Hopfenbeck, T. N., Lenkeit, J., El Masri, Y., Cantrell, K., Ryan, J., and Baird, J. 2018. 'Lessons Learned from PISA: A Systematic Review of Peer-Reviewed Articles on the Programme for International Student Assessment', *Scandinavian Journal of Educational Research* 62(3): 333–53. <https://doi.org/10.1080/00313831.2016.1258726>.

Hovland, I. 2005 *Successful Communication: A Toolkit for Researchers and Civil Society Organisations*. London: Overseas Development Institute.

Howlett, M. 2019. *Designing Public Policies: Principles and Instruments*. Abingdon, Oxon, and New York: Routledge.

Howlett, M., and Goetz, K. H. 2014. 'Introduction: Time, Temporality and Timescapes in Administration and Policy', *International Review of Administrative Sciences* 80(3): 477–92. <https://doi.org/10.1177/0020852314543210>.

Howlett, M., and Tosun, J. 2021. *The Routledge Handbook of Policy Styles*. London and New York: Routledge.

Howlett, M., Ramesh, M., and Perl, A. 2020. *Studying Public Policy. Principles and Processes*. Oxford: Oxford University Press.

Htun, M., and Jensenius, F. R. 2020. 'Aspirational Laws as Weak Institutions. The Politics of Institutional Weakness in Latin America', in D. M. Brinks, S. Levitsky, and M. V. Murillo (eds), *The Politics of Institutional Weakness in Latin America*. Cambridge: Cambridge University Press, 141–60.

Hucke, J., and Bohne, E. 1980. 'Bürokratische Reaktionsmuster bei regulativer Politik und ihre Folgen', in H. Wollmann (ed.), *Politik im Dickicht der Bürokratie*. Leviathan Sonderheft 3/1979, Opladen: Westdeutscher Verlag, 180–97.

Human Rights Campaign. 2014. 'Business Coalition for Workplace Fairness'. Retrieved 1 March 2021 from <https://assets2.hrc.org/files/assets/resources/Business_Coalition_for_Workplace_Fairness_4.17.2014.pdf>.

Human Rights Campaign. n.d. 'Business Coalition for Equality'. Retrieved 2 March 2021 from <https://www.hrc.org/resources/business-coalition-for-equality>.

Human Rights Watch. 2020. 'Sparkling Jewels, Opaque Supply Chains. Jewelry Companies, Changing Sourcing Practices, and Covid-19'. 24 November. Retrieved 2 March 2021 from <https://www.hrw.org/report/2020/11/24/sparkling-jewels-opaque-supply-chains/jewelry-companies-changing-sourcing>.

Human Rights Watch. n.d. 'Our Research Methodology'. Retrieved 20 April 2021 from <https://www.hrw.org/our-research-methodology>.

Huntington, S. P. 1968. *Political Order in Changing Societies*. New Haven, CT: Yale University Press.

Hupe, P., and Hill, M. 2014. 'Delivery Capacity', in M. Lodge and K. Wegrich (eds), *The Problem-Solving Capacity of the Modern State: Governance Challenges and Administrative Capacities*. Oxford: Oxford University Press, 25–40.

Huskisson, S., Ma, J., Ntim, Z., and Vides, G. 2020. 'Back to the Picket Lines: Cambridge's Three Waves of Strikes in Three Years', Varsity, 28 February. Retrieved 11 May 2021 from <https://www.varsity.co.uk/news/18846>.

Hustedt, T., and Danken, T. 2017. 'Institutional Logics in Inter-Departmental Coordination: Why Actors Agree on a Joint Policy Output', *Public Administration* 95(3): 730–43. <https://doi.org/10.1111/padm.12331>.

Hustedt, T., Kolltveit, K., and Salomonsen, H. H. 2017. 'Ministerial Advisers in Executive Government: Out from the Dark and into the Limelight', *Public Administration* 95(2): 299–311. <https://doi.org/10.1111/padm.12329>.

Hustedt, T., and Seyfried, M. 2016. 'Co-ordination across Internal Organizational Boundaries: How the EU Commission Co-ordinates Climate Policies', *Journal of European Public Policy* 23(6): 888–905. <https://doi.org/10.1080/13501763.2015.1074605>.

ICANN. 1999. 'Memorandum of Understanding between the U.S. Department of Commerce and Internet Corporation for Assigned Names and Numbers'. Retrieved 20 April

2021 from <https://www.icann.org/resources/unthemed-pages/icann-mou-1998-11-25-en>.

ICANN. 2019. 'Bylaws for Internet Corporation for Assigned Names and Numbers: A California Nonprofit Public-Benefit Corporation'. 28 November. Retrieved 20 April 2021 from <https://www.icann.org/resources/pages/governance/bylaws-en>.

Ifimes. 2020. 'Egypt—Ethiopia 2020: Will the Grand GERD Dam Trigger a War between Egypt and Ethiopia?' 25 June. Retrieved 2 March 2021 from <https://www.ifimes.org/en/9839>.

Immenkeppel, G. 2020. '"Yes to Confetti—No to Coma": Campaign Against Binge Drinking during Carnival in Bonn', *General-Anzeiger*, 11 February. Retrieved 8 May 2021 from <https://ga.de/ga-english/news/campaign-against-binge-drinking-during-carnival-in-bonn_aid-48888541>.

Immergut, E. M. 1992. *Health Politics: Interests and Institutions in Western Europe*. Cambridge: Cambridge University Press.

Immergut, E. M., Anderson, K. M., Devitt, C., and Popic, T. (eds). 2021. *Health Politics in Europe: A Handbook*. Oxford: Oxford University Press.

Iskander, N. 2018. 'Design Thinking is Fundamentally Conservative and Preserves the Status Quo', *Harvard Business Review*, 5 September 2018. Retrieved 8 May 2021 from <https://hbr.org/2018/09/design-thinking-is-fundamentally-conservative-and-preserves-the-status-quo>.

Iversen, T., and Soskice, D. 2006. 'Electoral Institutions and the Politics of Coalitions: Why Some Democracies Redistribute More than Others', *American Political Science Review* 100(2): 165–81. <https://doi.org/10.1017/S0003055406062083>.

Jabbar, H. 2013. 'The Case of "Payment-by-Results": Re-examining the Effects of an Incentive Programme in Nineteenth-Century English Schools', *Journal of Educational Administration and History* 45(3): 220–43. <http://dx.doi.org/10.1080/00220620.2013.796912>.

Jachtenfuchs, M., and Kasack, C. 2017. 'Balancing Sub-Unit Autonomy and Collective Problem-solving by Varying Exit and Voice: An Analytical Framework', *Journal of European Public Policy* 24(4): 598–614. <https://doi.org/10.1080/13501763.2016.1273376>.

Jacobs, A. 2018. 'In Sweeping War on Obesity, Chile Slays Tony the Tiger', *New York Times*, 7 February. Retrieved 8 March 2021 from <https://www.nytimes.com/2018/02/07/health/obesity-chile-sugar-regulations.html>.

Jacobs, A. M. 2011. *Governing for the Long Term: Democracy and the Politics of Investment*. Cambridge: Cambridge University Press.

Jacobs, A. M., and Weaver, R. K. 2015. 'When Policies Undo Themselves: Self-Undermining Feedback as a Source of Policy Change', *Governance* 28(4): 441–57. <https://doi.org/10.1017/S0143814X19000047>.

Jacobs, L. R., and Skocpol, T. 2005. *Inequality and American Democracy: What we Know and What we Need to Learn*. New York: Russell Sage Foundation.

James, O. 2004. 'The UK Core Executive's Use of Public Service Agreements as a Tool of Governance', *Public Administration* 82(2): 397–419. <https://doi.org/10.1111/j.0033-3298.2004.00400.x>.

Jann, W., and Wegrich, K. 2007. 'Theories of the Policy Cycle', in F. Fischer, G. J. Miller, and M. S. Sidney (eds), *Handbook of Public Policy Analysis*. Boca Raton, FL: CRC Press, 43–62.

Jann, W., and Wegrich, K. 2019. 'Generalists and Specialists in Executive Politics: Why Ambitious Meta-Policies So Often Fail', *Public Administration* 97(4): 845–60. <https://doi.org/10.1111/padm.12614>.

Jennings, W., Bevan, S., and John, P. 2011. 'The Agenda of British Government: The Speech from the Throne 1911–2008', *Political Studies Review* 59(1): 74–98. <https://doi.org/10.1111%2Fj.1467-9248.2010.00859.x>.

Jensen, N. M., and Malesky, E. J. 2018. 'Nonstate Actors and Compliance with International Agreements: An Empirical Analysis of the OECD Anti-Bribery Convention', *International Organization* 72(1): 33. <https://doi.org/10.1017/S0020818317000443>.

Jessen, J., Schmitz, S., and Waights, S. 2020. 'Understanding Day Care Enrolment Gaps', *Journal of Public Economics* 190, 104252. <http://dx.doi.org/10.1016/j.jpubeco.2020.104252>.

John, P. 2018. *How far to nudge?: Assessing behavioural public policy*. Cheltenham: Edward Elgar Publishing.

Jones, B. D., and Baumgartner, F. R. 2005. *The Politics of Attention: How Government Prioritizes Problems*. Chicago: University of Chicago Press.

Jordan, A. G. 1981. 'Iron Triangles, Woolly Corporatism and Elastic Nets: Images of the Policy Process', *Journal of Public Policy* 1(1): 95–123. <https://doi.org/10.1017/S0143814X00001379>.

Jordana, J., Fernández-i-marín, X., and Bianculli, A. C. 2018. 'Agency Proliferation and the Globalization of the Regulatory State: Introducing a Data Set on the Institutional Features of Regulatory Agencies', *Regulation and Governance* 12(4): 524–40. <https://doi.org/10.1111/rego.12189>.

Jugl, M. 2020. Country Size and State Performance: How Size Affects Politics, Administration and Governance. Doctoral dissertation, Hertie School, Berlin.

Junginger, S. 2013. 'Design and Innovation in the Public Sector: Matters of Design in Policy-Making and Policy Implementation', *Annual Review of Policy Design* 1(1): 1–11.

Kauko, J. 2019. 'The Finnish Comprehensive School: Conflict, Compromises, and Institutional Robustness', in M. Compton and P. /t Hart (eds), *Great Policy Successes*. Oxford: Oxford University Press, 122–42.

Kavanagh, J., and Rich, M. D. 2018. *Truth Decay: A Threat to Policymaking and Democracy*. Santa Monica, CA: RAND Corporation.

Kenworthy, L. 2010. 'Labour Market Activation', in F. G. Castles, S. Leibfried, J. Lewis, H. Obinger, and C. Pierson (eds), *The Oxford Handbook of the Welfare State*. Oxford: Oxford University Press, 435–47.

Kingdon, J. W. 1995. *Agendas, Alternatives, and Public Policies*. New York: Longman.

Kjellberg, A. 2009. 'The Swedish Ghent System and Trade Unions under Pressure', *Transfer: European Review of Labour and Research* 15(3–4): 481–504. <https://doi.org/10.1177%2F10242589090150031601>.

Klein, G. 2007. 'Performing a Project Premortem', *Harvard Business Review* 85(9): 18–19. <https://hbr.org/2007/09/performing-a-project-premortem>. Last accessed 23 March 2021

Klomp, J., and de Haan, J. 2013. 'Political Budget Cycles and Election Outcomes', *Public Choice* 157(1): 245–67. <https://www.jstor.org/stable/42003201>.

Klüver, H. 2013. *Lobbying in the European Union: Interest Groups, Lobbying Coalitions, and Policy Change*. Oxford: Oxford University Press.

Knill, C. 1999. 'Explaining Cross-National Variance in Administrative Reform: Autonomous Versus Instrumental Bureaucracies', *Journal of Public Policy* 19(2): 113–39. <https://www.jstor.org/stable/4007585>.

Knill, C., and Tosun, J. 2020. *Public Policy: A New Introduction*. London: Red Globe Press.

Kommission 'Wachstum, Strukturwandel und Beschäftigung' 2019. Abschlussbericht. Berlin: Bundesministerium für Wirtschaft und Energie. January.

Retrieved 8 March 2021 from <https://www.bmwi.de/Redaktion/DE/Downloads/A/abschlussbericht-kommission-wachstum-strukturwandel-und-beschaeftigung.pdf?__blob=publicationFile&v=4>.

Koop, C., and Lodge, M. 2014. 'Exploring the Co-ordination of Economic Regulation', *Journal of Public Policy* 21(9): 1311–29. <https://doi.org/10.1080/13501763.2014.923023>.

Kostka, G. 2016. 'Command without Control: The Case of China's Environmental Target System', *Regulation and Governance* 10(1): 58–74. <https://doi.org/10.1111/rego.12082>.

Laín, B. 2019. Report on the Preliminary Results of the B-MINCOME Project (2017–18). Combining a Guaranteed Minimum Income and Active Social Policies in Deprived Urban Areas of Barcelona. Barcelona: Planning and Innovation Department Area of Social Rights, Barcelona City Council.

Lancaster, T. D., and Patterson, W. D. 1990. 'Comparative Pork Barrel Politics: Perceptions from the West German Bundestag', *Comparative Political Studies* 22(4): 458–77. <https://doi.org/10.1177%2F0010414090022004004>.

Lasswell, H. D. 1951. 'The Policy Orientation', in H. D. Lasswell and D. Lerner (eds), *The Policy Sciences*. Stanford, CA: Stanford University Press, 3–15.

Lasswell, H. D. 1956. *The Decision Process: Seven Categories of Functional Analysis*. College Park, MD: University of Maryland Press.

Legislative Observatory of the European Parliament. 2013. 'Resolution on the Sale of EU Citizenship'. 2013/2995(RSP). Retrieved 8 March 2021 from <https://oeil.secure.europarl.europa.eu/oeil/popups/ficheprocedure.do?lang=en&reference=2013/2995(RSP)>.

Le Grand, J. 2007. *The Other Invisible Hand: Delivering Public Services through Choice and Competition*. Princeton: Princeton University Press.

Lehmbruch, G. 1975. 'Consociational Democracy in the International System', *European Journal of Political Research* 3(4): 377–91. <https://doi.org/10.1111/j.1475-6765.1975.tb01252.x>.

Lehtonen, M. 2015. 'Indicators: Tools for Informing, Monitoring or Controlling?', in A. J. Jordan and J. R. Turnpenny (eds), *The Tools of Policy Formulation: Actors, Capacities, Venues and Effects*. Cheltenham: Edward Elgar, 76–99.

Levi, M. 1988. *Of Rule and Revenue*. Berkeley-Los Angeles, CA: University of California Press.

Levi, M. 1997. *Consent, Dissent, and Patriotism*. Cambridge: Cambridge University Press.

Levin, K., Cashore, B., Bernstein, S., and Auld, G. 2012. 'Overcoming the Tragedy of Super Wicked Problems: Constraining our Future Selves to Ameliorate Global Climate Change', *Policy Sciences* 45(2): 123–52.

Levine, R. A. 1970. *The Poor, Ye Need Not Have with You: Lessons from the War on Poverty*. Cambridge, MA: MIT Press.

Levine, R. A., Watts, H., Hollister, R., Williams, W., O'Connor, A., and Widerquist, K. 2005. 'A Retrospective on the Negative Income Tax Experiments: Looking Back at the Most Innovative Field Studies in Social Policy', in K. Widerquist, M. A. Lewis, and S. Pressman (eds), *The Ethics and Economics of the Basic Income Guarantee*. Aldershot: Ashgate, 95–108.

Levitsky, S., and Ziblatt, D. 2018. *How Democracies Die: What History Reveals about our Future*. New York: Crown Publishing.

Lijphart, A. 2012. *Patterns of Democracy: Government Forms and Performance in Thirty-Six Countries*. New Haven: Yale University Press.

Lin, A. C. 2000. *Reform in the Making: The Implementation of Social Policy in Prison.* Princeton: Princeton University Press.

Lindblom, C. E. 1965. *The Intelligence of Democracy: Decision Making through Mutual Adjustment.* New York: Free Press.

Lindblom, C. E., and Cohen, D. K. 1979. *Usable Knowledge: Social Science and Social Problem Solving.* New Haven: Yale University Press.

Lindvall, J. 2017. *Reform Capacity.* Oxford: Oxford University Press.

Lipsky, M. 2010. *Street-Level Bureaucracy: Dilemmas of the Individual in Public Service.* Updated ed. (original edition published 1980). New York: Russell Sage Foundation.

Litman, E. A., Gortmaker, S. L., Ebbeling, C. B., and Ludwig, D. S. (2018). 'Source of Bias in Sugar-Sweetened Beverage Research: A Systematic Review', *Public Health Nutrition* 21(12): 2345–50. <https://doi.org/10.1017/S1368980018000575>.

Lodge, M. 2013. 'Co-ordinating and Controlling Dispersed Systems of Governing'. Unpublished manuscript.

Lodge, M., and Wegrich, K. 2012. *Managing Regulation: Regulatory Analysis, Politics and Policy.* Basingstoke: Palgrave Macmillan.

Lodge, M., and Wegrich, K. (eds). 2014a. *The Problem-Solving Capacity of the Modern State: Governance Challenges and Administrative Capacities.* Oxford: Oxford University Press.

Lodge, M., and Wegrich, K. 2014b. 'Administrative Capacities', in Hertie School of Governance (ed.), *Governance Report 2014.* Oxford: Oxford University Press, 27–48.

Lodge, M., and Wegrich, K. 2016. 'The Rationality Paradox of Nudge: Rational Tools of Government in a World of Bounded Rationality', *Law and Policy* 38(3): 250–67. <https://doi.org/10.1111/lapo.12056>.

Lodge, M., Wegrich, K., and McElroy, G. 2010. 'Dodgy Kebabs Everywhere? Variety of Worldviews and Regulatory Change', *Public Administration* 88(1): 247–66. <https://doi.org/10.1111/j.1467-9299.2010.01811.x>.

Lowi, T. J. 1970. 'Decision Making vs. Policy Making: Toward an Antidote for Technocracy', *Public Administration Review* 30(3): 314–25.

Lowi, T. J. 1972. 'Four Systems of Policy, Politics, and Choice', *Public Administration Review* 32(4): 298–310. <http://links.jstor.org/sici?sici=0033-3352%28197207%2F08%2932%3A4%3C298%3AFSOPPA%3E2.0.CO%3B2-X>.

Lydon, M., and Garcia, A. 2015. *Tactical Urbanism.* Washington, DC: Island Press.

MacKay, D. 2020. 'Government Policy Experiments and the Ethics of Randomization', *Philosophy and Public Affairs* 48(4): 319–52. <https://doi.org/10.1111/papa.12174>.

McAllister, L. K. 2008. *Making Law Matter: Environmental Protection and Legal Institutions in Brazil.* Stanford: Stanford University Press.

McBride, K., Kupi., M., and Bryson, J. J. 2021. 'Untangling Agile Government: On the Dual Necessities of Structure and Agility', in M. Stephens, R. Awamleh, and F. Salem (eds), *Agile Government: Concepts and Practice for Future.* Singapore: World Scientific Publishing.

McConnell, A., and 't Hart, P. 2019. 'Inaction and Public Policy: Understanding Why Policymakers "Do Nothing"', *Policy Sciences* 52(4): 645–61. <https://doi.org/10.1007/s11077-019-09362-2>.

McGann, J. G., and Whelan, L. C. 2020. *Global Think Tanks Policy Networks and Governance.* Abingdon, Oxon, and New York: Routledge.

McGann, M., Blomkamp, E., and Lewis, J. M. 2018. 'The Rise of Public Sector Innovation Labs: Experiments in Design Thinking for Policy', *Policy Sciences* 51(3): 249–67. <https://doi.org/10.1007/s11077-018-9315-7>.

Mahoney, J., and Thelen, K. 2009. 'A Theory of Gradual Institutional Change', in J. Mahoney and K. Thelen (eds), *Explaining Institutional Change: Ambiguity, Agency, and Power*. Cambridge: Cambridge University Press, 1–37.

Mahoney, J., and Thelen, K. (eds). 2015. *Advances in Comparative-Historical Analysis*. Cambridge: Cambridge University Press.

Mair, D., Smillie, L., La Placa, G., Schwendinger, F., Raykovska, M., Pasztor, Z., and van Bavel, R. 2019. *Understanding our Political Nature: How to Put Knowledge and Reason at the Heart of Political Decision-making*. EU Science HUB. Luxembourg: Publications Office of the European Union. <https://doi.org/10.2760/910822>.

Majone, G. 1989. *Evidence, Argument, and Persuasion in the Policy Process*. New Haven: Yale University Press.

Majone, G. 2001. 'Nonmajoritarian Institutions and the Limits of Democratic Governance: A Political Transaction-Cost Approach', *Journal of Institutional and Theoretical Economics* 157(1): 57–78. <https://www.jstor.org/stable/40752249>.

March, J. G., and Olsen, J. P. 2006. 'The Logic of Appropriateness', in M. Moran, M. Rein, and R. E. Goodin (eds), *The Oxford Handbook of Public Policy*. Oxford: Oxford University Press, 689–708.

Marron, D., Gearing, M., and Iselin, J. 2015. *Should we Tax Unhealthy Foods and Drinks?* Washington, DC: Tax Policy Center (Urban Institute and Brookings Institution).

Matthews, D. 2017. 'A Political Scientist Explains the Real Reason Obamacare Repeal is So Hard', Vox, 28 July. Retrieved 8 March 2021 from <https://www.ox.com/2017/3/24/14953202/obamacare-repeal-ryan-trump-paul-pierson-retrenchment>.

Mayntz, R. 1983. 'The Conditions of Effective Public Policy: A New Challenge for Policy Analysis', *Policy and Politics* 11(2): 123–43. <https://doi.org/10.1332/030557383782718779>.

Mayntz, R., Derlien, H.-U., Bohne, E., Hesse, B., Hucke, J., and Müller, A. 1976. *Vollzugsprobleme der Umweltpolitik: Empirische Untersuchung der Implementation von Gesetzen im Bereich der Luftreinhaltung und des Gewässerschutzes*. Stuttgart: Kohlhammer.

Mayntz, R., and Scharpf, F. W. 1975. *Policy-Making in the German Federal Bureaucracy*. Amsterdam: Elsevier.

Mayntz, R., and Scharpf, F. W. 1995. *Gesellschaftliche Selbstregelung und politische Steuerung*. Frankfurt a.M.: Campus.

Meadows, D. H. 1972. *The Limits to Growth: A Report for the Club of Rome's Project on the Predicament of Mankind*. New York: Universe Books.

Meckling, J., Kelsey, N., Biber, E., and Zysman, J. 2015. 'Winning Coalitions for Climate Policy', *Science* 349(6253): 1170–1. <https://doi.org/10.1126/science.aab1336>.

Meckling, J., Sterner, T., and Wagner, G. 2017. 'Policy Sequencing toward Decarbonization', *Nature Energy* 2: 918–22. <https://doi.org/10.1038/s41560-017-0025-8>.

Meier, H. E., and García, B. 2015. 'Protecting Private Transnational Authority Against Public Intervention: FIFA's Power over National Governments', *Public Administration* 93(4): 890–906. <https://doi.org/10.1111/padm.12208>.

Meijer, A., and Wessels, M. 2019. 'Predictive Policing: Review of Benefits and Drawbacks', *International Journal of Public Administration* 42(12): 1031–9. <https://doi.org/10.1080/01900692.2019.1575664>.

Melo, M. A., and Pereira, C. 2012. *Making Brazil Work: Checking the President in a Multiparty System*. New York: Palgrave Macmillan.

Mergel, I., Ganapati, S., and Whitford, A. B. 2020. 'Agile: A New Way of Governing', *Public Administration Review* 81(1): 161–5. <https://doi.org/10.1111/puar.13202>.

Metcalfe, L. 1994. 'International Policy Co-ordination and Public Management Reform', *International Review of Administrative Sciences* 60(2): 271–90. <https://doi.org/10.1177%2F002085239406000208>.

Mettler, S. 2011. *The Submerged State: How Invisible Government Policies Undermine American Democracy*. Chicago: University of Chicago Press.

Milmanda, B. F., and Garay, C. 2020. 'The Multilevel Politics of Enforcement: Environmental Institutions in Argentina', *Politics and Society* 48(1): 3–26. <https://doi.org/10.1177%2F0032329219894074>.

Ministerio de Salud. 2017. *Informe de Evaluación de la Implentación de la ley sobre composición nutricional de los alimentos y su publicidad enero*. Subsecretaría de Salud. Pública División de Políticas Públicas Saludables y Promoción. Santiago de Chile: Departamento de Nutrición y Alimentos. Retrieved 8 May 2021 from <https://www.minsal.cl/wp-content/uploads/2017/05/Informe-evaluaci%C3%B3n-implementaci%C3%B3n-Ley-20606-Enero-2017.pdf>.

Minx, J. 2018. 'How Can Climate Policy Stay on Top of a Growing Mountain of Data?' *The Guardian Science Blog*, 12 June. Retrieved 8 May 2021 from <https: //www.theguardian.com/science/political-science/2018/jun/12/how-can-climate-policy-stay-on-top-of-a-growing-mountain-of-data>.

Moe, T. M. 2012. 'Delegation, Control, and the Study of Public Bureaucracy', in R. Gibbons and J. Roberts (eds), *The Handbook of Organizational Economics*. Princeton: Princeton University Press, 1148–1182.

Morris, C. 2020. 'Brexit Deal: What is in it?' BBC News, 28 December. Retrieved 8 May 2021 from <https://www.bbc.com/news/55252388>.

Moynihan, D. P. 2012. 'Extra-Network Organizational Reputation and Blame Avoidance in Networks: The Hurricane Katrina Example', *Governance* 25(4): 567–88. <https://doi.org/10.1111/j.1468-0491.2012.01593.x>.

Mukum Mbaku, J. 2020. 'The Controversy over the Grand Ethiopian Renaissance Dam', Brookings blog, 5 August. Retrieved 8 March 2021 From <https://www.brookings.edu/blog/africa-in-focus/2020/08/05the-controversy-over-the-grand-ethiopian-renaissance-dam/>.

Müller, T., and Schulten, T. 2020. *The European Minimum Wage on the Doorstep*. ETUI Policy Brief. Retrieved 8 May 2021 from <https://www.etui.org/publications/policy-briefs/european-economic-employment-and-social-policy/the-european-minimum-wage-on-the-doorstep>.

Müller-Hoff, C. 2018. 'The OECD Complaint Mechanism: Remedy or Complicity?' Business and Human Rights Resource Centre, 23 April. Retrieved 2 March 2021 from <https://www.business-humanrights.org/en/blog/the-oecd-complaint-mechanism-remedy-or-complicity/>.

Muller, J. Z. 2018. *The Tyranny of Metrics*. Princeton: Princeton University Press.

Mungiu-Pippidi, A. 2015. *The Quest for Good Governance: How Societies Develop Control of Corruption*. Cambridge: Cambridge University Press.

Muralidharan, K., and Sundararaman, V. 2011. 'Teacher Performance Pay: Experimental Evidence from India', *Journal of Political Economy* 119(1): 39–77. <http://dx.doi.org/10.1086/659655>.

Naczyk, M., and Hassel, A. 2019. 'Insuring Individuals ... and Politicians: Financial Services Providers, Stock Market Risk and the Politics of Private Pension Guarantees in Germany', in A. Hassel and T. Wiss (eds), *The Political Economy of Pension Financialisation: Public Policy Responses to the Crisis*, special issue of the Journal of European Public Policy, 579–98.

Nakamura, R., Mirelman, A. J., Cuadrado, C., Silva-Illanes, N., Dunstan, J., and Suhrcke, M. 2018. 'Evaluating the 2014 Sugar-Sweetened Beverage Tax in Chile: An Observational Study in Urban Areas', *PLoS Medicine* 15(7): 22. <https://doi.org/10.1371/journal.pmed.1002596>.

Nelson, R. R. 1977. *The Moon and the Ghetto: An Essay on Public Policy Analysis*. New York: Norton.

Nicholson-Crotty, S., Nicholson-Crotty, J., and Fernandez, S. 2017. 'Will More Black Cops Matter? Officer Race and Police-Involved Homicides of Black Citizens', *Public Administration Review* 77(2): 206–16. <https://doi.org/10.1111/puar.12734>.

North, D. C. 1991. 'Institutions', *Journal of Economic Perspectives* 5(1): 97–112. <https://doi.org/10.1257/jep.5.1.97>.

Nutt, P. 2002. *Why Decisions Fail: Avoiding the Blunders and Traps that Lead to Debacles*. San Francisco: Berrett-Koehler Publishers.

Obama, B. 2020. 'President Obama—Police Reform & The Impact of Slogans. The Daily Social Distancing Show', *The Daily Show with Trevor Noah*, Youtube video, 15 December. Retrieved 8 May 2021 from <https://www.youtube.com/watch?v=ky7hpzBfh54>.

Ocasio-Cortez, A. 2020. 'The thing that critics of activists don't get is that they tried playing the "polite language" policy game and all it did was make them easier to ignore. It wasn't until they made folks uncomfortable that there was traction to do ANYTHING even if it wasn't their full demands.' 2 December. Retrieved 8 May 2021. [@AOC]. <https://twitter.com/aoc/status/1334182970337464321?lang=de>.

Odermatt, J. 2017. 'Brexit and International Law: Disentangling Legal Orders', *International Law Review* 31: 1051–75.

OECD. 2011. *OECD Guidelines for Multinational Enterprises*. Paris: OECD Publishing.

OECD. 2012. *Recommendation of the Council on Regulatory Policy and Governance*. Paris: OECD Publishing.

OECD. 2015. *Implementing the OECD Guidelines for Multinational Enterprises: The National Contact Points from 2000 to 2015*. Paris: OECD Publishing.

OECD. 2017a. *Chile. A Healthier Tomorrow. OECD Reviews of Public Health. Assessment and Recommendations*. Paris: OECD Publishing.

OECD. 2017b. *Preventing Policy Capture: Integrity in Public Decision Making*. OECD Public Governance Reviews. Paris: OECD Publishing. <https://doi.org/10.1787/9789264065239-en>.

OECD. 2018. 'OECD Guidelines for Multinational Enterprises'. Retrieved 2 March 2021 from <https://mneguidelines.oecd.org/guidelines/>.

OECD. 2019a. *Pensions at a Glance 2019: OECD and G20 Indicators*. Paris: OECD Publishing.

OECD. 2019b. *Enforcement of the Anti-Bribery Convention Investigations, Proceedings, and Sanctions*. OECD Working Group on Bribery. Retrieved 8 March 2021 from <http://www.oecd.org/daf/anti-bribery/OECD-Anti-Bribery-Convention-Enforcement-Data-2019.pdf>.

OECD. 2019c. 'Carbon Dioxide Emissions Embodied in International Trade'. Retrieved 2 March 2021 from <https://www.oecd.org/sti/ind/carbondioxideemissionsembodiedininternationaltrade.htm>.

OECD. 2020. 'How Can Governments Leverage Policy Evaluation to Improve Evidence Informed Policy Making Highlights from an OECD Comparative Study'. Retrieved 8 May 2021 from <https://www.oecd.org/gov/policy-evaluation-comparative-study-highlights.pdf>.

OECD Watch. n.d. 'How to File a Complaint'. Retrieved 2 March 2021 from <https://www.oecdwatch.org/how-to-file-a-complaint/other-filing-considerations/>.

Offe, C. 2014. 'Nudges, Norms, and Policy Relevant Behavior'. Unpublished manuscript, Hertie School of Governance, Berlin.

Oreskes, N., and Conway, E. M. 2010. *Merchants of Doubt: How a Handful of Scientists Obscured the Truth on Issues from Tobacco Smoke to Global Warming.* New York: Bloomsbury Press.

Organizational Research Services. 2004. 'Theory of Change: A Practical Tool for Action, Results and Learning'. Baltimore: Annie E. Casey Foundation. Retrieved 8 May 2021 from <https://www.aecf.org/resources/theory-of-change/>.

Ostrom, E. 1990. *Governing the Commons: The Evolution of Institutions for Collective Action.* Cambridge: Cambridge University Press.

Ostrom, E. 1996. 'Crossing the Great Divide: Coproduction, Synergy, and Development', *World Development* 24(6): 1073–87. <https://doi.org/10.1016/0305-750X(96)00023-X>.

Our World in Data. n.d. 'CO2 Emissions'. Retrieved 21 March 2021 from <https://ourworldindata.org/co2-emissions>.

Page, E. C., and Jenkins B. 2005. *Policy Bureaucracy: Government with a Cast of Thousands.* Oxford: Oxford University Press.

Pahle, M., Burtraw, D., Flachsland, C., Kelsey, N., Biber, E., Meckling, J., Edenhofer, O., and Zysman, J. 2018. 'Sequencing to Ratchet up Climate Policy Stringency', *Nature Climate Change* 8: 861–7. <https://doi.org/10.1038/s41558-018-0287-6>.

Paiva, L. H., Cotta, T. C., and Barrientos, A. 2019. 'Brazil's Bolsa Família Programme', in M. Compton and P. ʹt Hart (ed.), *Great Policy Successes.* Oxford: Oxford University Press, 21–41.

Palthe, J. 2014. 'Regulative, Normative, and Cognitive Elements of Organizations: Implications for Managing Change', *Management and Organizational Studies* 1(2): 59–66. <https://doi.org/10.5430/mos.v1n2p59>.

Parkhurst, J. 2017. *The Politics of Evidence: From Evidence-Based Policy to the Good Governance of Evidence.* London and New York: Routledge.

Patton, M. Q. 2008. *Utilization-Focused Evaluation: The New Century Text.* Thousand Oaks, CA: SAGE.

Patton, M. Q. 2012. *Essentials of Utilization-Focused Evaluation.* Thousand Oaks: SAGE.

Paul, E., Steptoe, A., and Fancourt, D. 2020. 'Attitudes towards Vaccines and Intention to Vaccinate Against COVID-19: Implications for Public Health Communications', *The Lancet Regional Health—Europe* 1 (26 December). <doi.org/10.1016/j.lanepe.2020.100012>.

Paul, K. 2021. 'What Facebook's Australia News Ban Could Mean for its Future in the US', *The Guardian,* 27 February. Retrieved 8 May 2021 from <https://www.theguardian.com/technology/2021/feb/27/facebook-australia-news-ban-us-legislation>.

Pavolini, E., and Van Lancker, W. 2018. 'The Matthew Effect in Childcare Use: A Matter of Policies or Preferences?', *Journal of European Public Policy* 25(6): 878–93. <https://doi.org/10.1080/13501763.2017.1401108>.

Pawson, R., and Tilley, N. 1997. *Realistic Evaluation.* London: SAGE.

Pencheva, I., Esteve, M., and Mikhaylov, S. J. 2020. 'Big Data and AI: A Transformational Shift for Government: So, What Next for Research?', *Public Policy and Administration* 35(1): 24–44. <https://doi.org/10.1177%2F0952076718780537>.

Perkiö, J. 2020. 'From Rights to Activation: The Evolution of the Idea of Basic Income in the Finnish Political Debate, 1980–2016', *Journal of Social Policy* 49(1): 103–24. <https://doi.org/10.1017/S0047279418000867>.

Peters, B. G. 1998. 'Managing Horizontal Government: The Politics of Coordination', *Public Administration* 76(2): 295–311.

Peters, B. G. 2015. *Pursuing Horizontal Management: The Politics of Public Sector Coordination*. Lawrence, KS: University Press of Kansas.

Peters, B. G. 2018. 'The Challenge of Policy Coordination', *Policy Design and Practice* 1(1): 1–11. <https://doi.org/10.1080/25741292.2018.1437946>.

Piereson, J., and Riley, N. S. 2013. 'The Problem with Public Policy Schools', Washington Post, 6 December. Retrieved 8 May 2021 from <https://www.washingtonpost.com/opinions/the-problem-with-public-policy-schools/2013/12/06/40d13c10-57ba-11e3-835d-e7173847c7cc_story.html>.

Pierson, P. 1993. 'When Effect Becomes Cause: Policy Feedback and Political Change', *World Politics* 45(5): 595–628. <https://doi.org/10.2307/2950710>.

Pierson, P. 2000. 'Increasing Returns, Path Dependence, and the Study of Politics', *American Political Science Review* 94(2): 251–67. <https://doi.org/10.2307/2586011>.

Pierson, P. 2015. 'Power and Path Dependence', in J. Mahoney and K. Thelen (eds), *Advances in Comparative-historical Analysis*,. Cambridge: Cambridge University Press, 123–46.

Pollitt, C. 2008. *Time, Policy, Management: Governing with the Past*. Oxford: Oxford University Press.

Polski, M. M., and Ostrom, E. 1999. 'An Institutional Framework for Policy Analysis and Design', presented at the Workshop in Political Theory and Policy Analysis, Bloomington, Indiana University.

Potter, R. A. 2019. *Bending the Rules: Procedural Politicking in the Bureaucracy*. Chicago: University of Chicago Press.

Pressman, J. L., and Wildavsky, A. B. 1973. *Implementation: How Great Expectations in Washington are Dashed in Oakland; Or, Why it's Amazing that Federal Programs Work at All, This Being a Saga of the Economic Development Administration as Told by Two Sympathetic Observers Who Seek to Build Morals on a Foundation*. Berkeley-Los Angeles and London: University of California Press.

Prpic, M. 2014. *The Open Method of Coordination*. Brussels: European Parliamentary Research Service. Retrieved 8 May 2021 from <https://www.europarl.europa.eu/EPRS/EPRS-AaG-542142-Open-Method-of-Coordination-FINAL.pdf>.

Pryser Libell, H., and Bryson Taylor, D. 2020. 'Norway's Supreme Court Makes Way for More Arctic Drilling', *New York Times*, 22 December. Retrieved 8 March 2021 from <https://www.nytimes.com/2020/12/22/world/europe/norway-supreme-court-oil-climate-change.html>.

Quittkat, C. 2011. 'The European Commission's Online Consultations: A Success Story', *Journal of Common Market Studies* 49(3): 653–74. <https://doi.org/10.1111/j.1468-5965.2010.02147.x>.

Radin, B. A. 2013. *Beyond Macchiavelli: Policy Analysis Reaches Midlife*. Washington, DC: Georgetown University Press.

Radin, B. A. 2018. 'The Evolution of the Policy Analysis Profession in the United States', in J. A. Hird (ed.), *Policy Analysis in the United States*. Bristol: Policy Press, 31–54.

Rao, N. D., van Ruijven, B.J., Riahi, K., and Bosetti, V. 2017. 'Improving Poverty and Inequality Modelling in Climate Research', *Nature Climate Change* 7(12): 857–62. <http://dx.doi.org/10.1038/s41558-017-0004-x>.

Rasche, L., and Walter-Franke, M. 2020. *EU-Grenzverfahren: Eindeutig, fair und schnell? Der 'New Pact' im Check*. Policy Brief. Berlin: Jaques Delors Centre, Hertie School. 21 December. Retrieved 8 March 2021 from <https://hertieschool-f4e6.kxcdn.com/fileadmin/2_Research/1_About_our_research/2_Research_centres/6_

Jacques_Delors_Centre/Publications/20201218_Migrations_Pakt_im_Check_Rasche_ Walter_Franke.pdf>.

Reeve, N. 2018. 'Universities Finalise Panel to Scrutinise USS Valuations', IPE Magazine, 25 August. Retrieved 8 March 2021 from <https://www.ipe.com/universities-finalise-panel-to-scrutinise-uss-valuations/10024870.article>.

REF. n.d. 'REF 2021. About the REF'. Retrieved 8 May 2021 from <https://www.ref.ac.uk/about/>.

Reynolds, M. 2018. 'No, Finland isn't Scrapping its Universal Basic Income Experiment', Wired, 26 April. Retrieved 8 May 2021 from <https://www.wired.co.uk/article/finland-universal-basic-income-results-trial-cancelled>.

Rhodes, R. A. W. 2005. 'Everyday Life in a Ministry: Public Administration as Anthropology', American Review of Public Administration 35(1): 3–25. <https://doi.org/10.1177%2F0275074004271716>.

Rhodes, R. A. W. 2011. Everyday Life in British Government. Oxford: Oxford University Press.

Rice-Oxley, M. 2018. 'Grenfell: The Seventy-Two Victims, their Lives, Loves and Losses', The Guardian, 14 May. Retrieved 8 March 2021 from <https://www.theguardian.com/uk-news/2018/may/14/grenfell-the-71-victims-their-lives-loves-and-losses>.

Richardson, J. (ed.). 2013. Policy Styles in Western Europe. Routledge Revivals. Abingdon, Oxon, and New York: Routledge.

Rittel, H. W. J., and Webber, M. M. 1973. 'Dilemmas in a General Theory of Planning', Policy Sciences 4: 155–69. <https://doi.org/10.1007/BF01405730>.

Rivlin, A. M. 1971. Systematic Thinking for Social Action. Washington, DC: Brookings Institution Press.

Roberts, A. 2010. The Logic of Discipline: Global Capitalism and the Architecture of Government. Oxford: Oxford University Press.

Rodrik, D. 2011. The globalization paradox: democracy and the future of the world economy. New York & London: Norton & Company.

Rodrik, D. 2020. 'Why does Globalization Fuel Populism? Economics, Culture, and the Rise of Right-Wing Populism', NBER Working Paper Series. Working Paper 27526. Retrieved 9 May 2021 from <http://www.nber.org/papers/w27526>.

Rogoff, K. 1990. 'Equilibrium Political Budget Cycles'. American Economic Review 80(1): 21–36. <https://www.jstor.org/stable/2006731>.

Römmele, A., and Schober, H. 2013. 'How to Link Citizens and the State: Reasons for— and First Steps Towards—a Participatory Mode of Governance', in A. Römmele and H. Schober (eds), The Governance of Large-Scale Projects. Linking Citizens and the State. Baden-Baden: Nomos, 11–25.

Rosenthal, U., Charles, M. T., and 't Hart, P. 1989. Coping with Crises: The Management of Disasters, Riots and Terrorism. Springfield: Charles C Thomas.

Rothbauer, P. 2008. 'Triangulation', in L. Given (ed.), The SAGE Encyclopedia of Qualitative Research Methods. Thousand Oaks, CA: SAGE, 892–4.

Rothstein, B. 2005. Social Traps and the Problem of Trust. Cambridge: Cambridge University Press.

Rutkowski, L., and Rutkowski, D. 2016. 'A Call for a More Measured Approach to Reporting and Interpreting PISA Results', Educational Researcher 45(4): 252–7. <https://doi.org/10.3102/0013189X16649961>.

Sabatier P. A., and Weible C. M. 2007. 'The Advocacy Coalition Framework: Innovations and Clarifications', in P.A. Sabatier (ed.), Theories of the Policy Process, Second edition. Boulder, CO: Westview Press, 189–222

Sabatier, P. A., and Weible, C. M. (eds). 2014. *Theories of the Policy Process*. Boulder, CO: Westview Press.

Sabel, C. F., and Zeitlin, J. 2012. 'Experimentalist Governance', in D. Levi-Faur (ed.), *The Oxford Handbook of Governance*. Oxford: Oxford University Press, 169–85.

Sachs, J. D., Schmidt-Traub, G., Mazzucato, M., Messner, D., Nakicenovic, N., and Rockström, J. 2019. 'Six Transformations to Achieve the Sustainable Development Goals', *Nature Sustainability* 2: 805–14. <https://doi.org/10.1038/s41893-019-0352-9>.

Sager, F., and Mavrot, C. 2021. 'Participatory vs Expert Evaluation Styles', in M. Howlett and J. Tosun (eds), *Routledge Handbook of Policy Styles*. Abingdon, Oxon: Routledge, 395–407.

Schäfer, A., Elsässer, L., and Hense, S. 2017. '"Dem Deutschen Volke?": Die ungleiche Responsivität des Bundestags', *Zeitschrift für Politikwissenschaft* 27(2): 161–80. <https://doi.org/10.1007/s41358-017-0097-9>.

Scharpf, F. W. 1972. 'Komplexität als Schranke der politischen Planung', in Deutsche Vereinigung für Politische Wissenschaft (ed.), *Gesellschaftlicher Wandel und politische Innovation*. Wiesbaden: VS Verlag für Sozialwissenschaften, 168–92.

Scharpf, F. W. 1986. 'Policy Failure and Institutional Reform: Why Should Form Follow Function?', *International Social Science Journal* 38(108): 179–89. <https://pure.mpg.de/rest/items/item_2228009/component/file_2228006/content>.

Scharpf, F. W. 1993. 'Coordination in Hierarchies and Networks', in F. W. Scharpf (ed.), *Games in Hierarchies and Networks: Analytical and Empirical Approaches to the Study of Governance Institutions*. Frankfurt a.M. and Boulder, CO: Campus and Westview Press, 125–65.

Scharpf, F. W. 1994. 'Games Real Actors Could Play: Positive and Negative Coordination in Embedded Negotiations', *Journal of Theoretical Politics* 6(1): 27–54. <https://doi.org/10.1177/0951692894006001002>.

Scharpf, F. W. 1997. *Games Real Actors Play: Actor-Centered Institutionalism in Policy Research*. Boulder, CO: Westview Press.

Scharpf, F. W. 1999. *Governing in Europe: Effective and Democratic?* Oxford: Oxford University Press.

Schattschneider, E. E. 1960. *The Semi-Sovereign People*. New York: Holt Rinehart.

Schleicher, A. 2019. *PISA 2018: Insights and Interpretations*. Paris: OECD Publishing.

Schlozman, K. L., Verba, S., and Brady, H. E. 2012. *The Unheavenly Chorus: Unequal Political Voice and the Broken Promise of American Democracy*. Princeton: Princeton University Press.

Schmeer, K. K. 1999. Guidelines for Conducting a Stakeholder Analysis. November. Bethesda, MD: Partnerships for Health Reform, Abt Associates Inc. Retrieved 8 March 2021 from <https://www.who.int/management/partnerships/overall/GuidelinesConductingStakeholderAnalysis.pdf>.

Schneider, A., and Ingram, H. 1990. 'Behavioral Assumptions of Policy Tools', *Journal of Politics* 52(2): 510–29. <https://doi.org/10.2307/2131904>.

Schneider, A., and Ingram, H. 1993. 'Social Construction of Target Populations: Implications for Politics and Policy', *American Political Science Review* 87(2): 334–47. <https://doi.org/10.2307/2939044>.

Schon, D. A. 1983. *The Reflective Practitioner: How Professionals Think in Action*. New York: Basic Books.

Schulewirtschaft Deutschland. n.d. 'Zukunft in Partnerschaft gestalten'. Retrieved 2 March 2021 from <https://www.schulewirtschaft.de/kontakt/>.

Scott, W. R. 2014. *Institutions and Organizations: Ideas, Interests, and Identities*. 4th ed. Thousand Oaks, CA: SAGE.

Searchinger, T., Beringer, T., Holtsmark, B., Kammen, D., Lambin, E., Lucht, W., Raven, P., and Van Ypersele, J. 2018. 'Europe's Renewable Energy Directive Poised to Harm Global Forests', *Nature Communications* 9(1). <https://doi.org/10.1038/s41467-018-06175-4>.

Sebenius, J. K. 1983. 'Negotiation Arithmetic: Adding and Subtracting Issues and Parties', *International Organization* 37(2): 281–316. <doi:10.1017/S002081830003438X>.

Sellar, S., and Lingard, B. 2014. 'The OECD and the Expansion of PISA: New Global Modes of Governance in Education', *British Educational Research Journal* 40(6): 917–36. <https://doi.org/10.1002/berj.3120>.

Senatsverwaltung für Bildung, Jugend und Familie. 2015. 'Testbetrieb des elektronischen Klassenbuchs am OSZ Kraftfahrzeugtechnik'. Evaluationsbericht 2015.

Senatsverwaltung für Bildung, Jugend und Familie. 2017. 'Antwort auf die Schriftliche Anfrage Nr. 10/12023 vom 10. August 2017 über Elektronisches Klassenbuch: Ergebnisse Evaluation Erprobungsphase'.

Serhan, A. 2017. 'Interview with UN High Commissioner Mary Robinson', Leadership Solutions. Egon Zehnder Management Consultants. Published 1 January. Retrieved 8 March 2021 from <https://www.egonzehnder.com/what-we-do/leadership-solutions/insights/interview-with-un-high-commissioner-mary-robinson>.

Shaheen, S. 2017. 'The Netherlands and UK Sit at the Heart of the Global Tax Haven Industry', *International Tax Review*, 23 August. Retrieved 8 March 2021 from <https://www.internationaltaxreview.com/article/b1f7n87rh38s0y/the-netherlands-and-uk-sit-at-the-heart-of-the-global-tax-haven-industry>.

Short, J. L. (2019). 'The Politics of Regulatory Enforcement and Compliance: Theorizing and Operationalizing Political Influences', *Regulation and Governance*. <doi.org/10.1111/rego.12291>.

Simola, H. 2005. 'The Finnish Miracle of PISA: Historical and Sociological Remarks on Teaching and Teacher Education', *Comparative Education* 41(4): 455–70. <DOI:10.1080/03050060500317810>.

Simon, F. 2020. 'Warsaw Says "Committed" to EU's Climate Neutrality Goal', Euractiv, 11 September. Retrieved 2 March 2021 from <https://www.euractiv.com/section/energy-environment/news/warsaw-says-committed-to-eus-climate-neutrality-goal/>.

Sklar, K. 2020. 'How to Build Internal Alignment with the Challenge Wheel'. Blogpost. Open Contracting Partnership, 7 February. Retrieved 8 March 2021 from <https://www.open-contracting.org/2020/02/07/how-to-build-internal-alignment-with-the-challenge-wheel/>.

Skocpol, T., and Finegold, K. 1982. 'State Capacity and Economic Intervention in the Early New Deal', *Political Science Quarterly* 97(2): 255–78. <http://www.jstor.org/stable/2149478>.

Solomon, S. 2021. 'US Restoration of Foreign Aid to Ethiopia Signals New Course'. VOA, 25 February. Retrieved 8 March 2021 from <https://www.voanews.com/africa/us-restoration-foreign-aid-ethiopia-signals-new-course>.

Stockmann, D., and Luo, T. 2018. 'Which Social Media Facilitate Online Public Opinion in China?', *Problems of Post-Communism* 64(3–4): 189–202. <https://doi.org/10.1080/10758216.2017.1289818>.

Stone, D. 2013. *Policy Paradox*. New York: W. W. Norton & Co.

Strauss, M., and Biesemans, B. 2020. 'Belgium does Not Have to Shut Engie Nuclear Reactor, Court Rules'. Reuters. Industry, Materials and Utilities, 3 September. Retrieved 8 March 2021 from <https://www.reuters.com/article/belgium-nuclear-idUSL4N2G0214>.

Streeck, W., and Thelen, K. 2005. 'Introduction: Institutional Change in Advanced Political Economies', in W. Streeck and K. Thelen (eds), *Beyond Continuity: Institutional Change in Advanced Political Economies.*. Oxford: Oxford University Press, 1–39.

Svallfors, S., and Tyllström, A. 2019. 'Resilient Privatization: The Puzzling Case of For-Profit Welfare Providers in Sweden', *Socio-Economic Review* 17(3): 745–65. <https://doi.org/10.1093/ser/mwy005>.

Taillie, L., Rivera, J. A., Popkin, B. M., and Batis, C. 2017. 'Do High vs. Low Purchasers Respond Differently to a Nonessential Energy-Dense Food Tax? Two-Year Evaluation of Mexico's 8% Nonessential Food Tax', *Preventive Medicine* 105: 37–42. <doi: 10.1016/j.ypmed.2017.07.009>.

Tawfik, R. 2015. 'The Declaration of Principles on Ethiopia's Renaissance Dam: A Breakthrough or Another Unfair Deal?', Die aktuelle Kolumne, 25 March. Retrieved 8 May 2021 from <https://www.die-gdi.de/die-aktuelle-kolumne/article/the-declaration-of-principles-on-ethiopias-renaissance-dam-a-breakthrough-or-another-unfair-deal/>.

Thaler, R., and Sunstein, C. 2008. *Nudge: Improving Decisions about Health, Wealth, and Happiness*. New York: Penguin Books.

The Economist. 2015. 'A Mucky Business'. 26 September. Retrieved 8 March 2021 from <https://www.economist.com/briefing/2015/09/26/a-mucky-business>.

The Economist. 2019. 'Japan Withdraws from the Treaty that Bans Hunting Whales: Whaling is a Proud Tradition, Supporters Say'. 3 January. Retrieved 8 March 2021 from <https://www.economist.com/asia/2019/01/05/japan-withdraws-from-the-treaty-that-bans-hunting-whales>.

The Economist. 2020. 'America's Supreme Court Protects LGBT Workers Against Discrimination'. 18 June. Retrieved 18 June 2020 from <https://www.economist.com/united-states/2020/06/18/americas-supreme-court-protects-lgbt-workers-against-discrimination>.

The Economist. 2021. 'Why is the Grand Ethiopian Renaissance Dam Contentious?' 11 February. Retrieved 8 March 2021, from <https://www.economist.com/the-economist-explains/2021/02/11/why-is-the-grand-ethiopian-renaissance-dam-contentious>.

The Pressure Group Consultancy. n.d. Advocacy and Campaigning Mini-Guides, <http://thepressuregroup.org/index.php/downloads/advocacy-campaigning-mini-guides/>. Last accessed 21 March 2021.

Thomann, E., van Engen, N. and Tummers, L. 2018. 'The necessity of discretion: A behavioral evaluation of bottom-up implementation theory', *Journal of Public Administration Research and Theory* 28(4): 583–601.

Timeus, K., and Gascó, M. 2018. 'Increasing Innovation Capacity in City Governments: Do Innovation Labs Make a Difference?', *Journal of Urban Affairs* 40(7): 992–1008. <https://doi.org/10.1080/07352166.2018.1431049>.

Torfing, J., Sørensen, E., and Røiseland, A. 2019. 'Transforming the Public Sector into an Arena for Co-Creation: Barriers, Drivers, Benefits, and Ways Forward', *Administration and Society* 51(5): 795–825. <https://doi.org/10.1177/0095399716680057>.

Trampusch, C. 2020. 'The Politics of Shifting Burdens: German Fiscal Welfare Corporatism', in R. Careja, P. Emmenegger, and N. Giger (eds), *The European Social Model under Pressure*. Wiesbaden: Springer VS, 159–76.

Transparency International. 2017. 'Corruption Risks: Mining Approvals in Australia: Mining for Sustainable Development Programme'. Retrieved 8 March 2021 from <https://transparency.org.au/corruption-risks-mining-approvals-in-australia/>.

Transparency International. 2018. 'Golden Visa Programmes in Europe Pose Major Corruption Risk'. 5 March. Retrieved 8 March 2021 from <https://www.transparency.org/en/press/golden-visa-programmes-in-europe-pose-major-corruption-risk>.

Transparency International. 2020a. 'Some Good News: European Commission Wants Bulgaria, Malta and Cyprus to Phase out their #Goldenvisas Schemes Trading in EU Citizenship'. 24 April. Retrieved 8 May 2021 from <https://twitter.com/anticorruption/status/1253656672041656321>.

Transparency International. 2020b. 'Exporting Corruption Progress Report 2020: Assessing Enforcement of the OECD Anti-Bribery Convention'. Retrieved 8 May 2021 from <https://images.transparencycdn.org/images/A-slim-version-of-Exporting-Corruption-2020.pdf>.

Transparency International. n.d. 'European Getaway: Inside the Murky World of Golden Visas'. Retrieved 8 March 2021 from <https://www.transparency.org/en/publications/golden-visas>.

Traxler, C. 2019. 'Behavioural Insights for Health Governance', in Hertie School (ed.), *Governance Report 2019*. Oxford: Oxford University Press, 135–48.

Tsebelis, G. 2002. *Veto Players: How Political Institutions Work*. Princeton: Princeton University Press.

Tummers, L., and Bekkers, V. 2014. 'Policy Implementation, Street-Level Bureaucracy, and the Importance of Discretion', *Public Management Review* 16(4): 527–47. <https://doi.org/10.1080/14719037.2013.841978>.

UN Economic and Social Council. 2015. 'Commission on the Status of Women Political Declaration on the Occasion of the Twentieth Anniversary of the Fourth World Conference on Women, United Nations'. 5 March. Retrieved 8 March 2021 from <https://www.un.org/ga/search/view_doc.asp?symbol=E/CN.6/2015/L.1>.

United Nations. 2015. 'Paris Agreement, United Nations'. Retrieved 8 May 2021 from <https://unfccc.int/sites/default/files/english_paris_agreement.pdf>.

Universities UK. 2018 'Proposal Agreed to Reform USS Pensions'. 23 January. Retrieved 8 May 2021 from https://www.universitiesuk.ac.uk/news/Pages/Proposal-agreed-to-reform-USS-Pensions.aspx.

University of Kent. 2021. 'USS Pension. Background'. Retrieved 8 May 2021 from <https://www.kent.ac.uk/uss-pension/background>.

US Department of Justice. 2015. 'Nine FIFA Officials and Five Corporate Executives Indicted for Racketeering Conspiracy and Corruption'. 27 May. Retrieved 8 May 2021 from https://www.justice.gov/opa/pr/nine-fifa-officials-and-five-corporate-executives-indicted-racketeering-conspiracy-and.

USAID. 2016. 'Environmental Compliance Factsheet. Stakeholder Engagement in the Environmental and Social Impact Assessment (ESIA) Process'. Retrieved 1 March 2021 from <https://www.usaid.gov/sites/default/files/documents/1865/Stakeholder_Engagement_052016.pdf>.

Van Dooren, W., and Noordegraaf, M. 2020. 'Staging Science: Authoritativeness and Fragility of Models and Measurement in the COVID-19 Crisis', *Public Administration Review* 80(4): 610–15. <https://doi.org/10.1111/puar.13219>.

Van Dooren, W., Bouckaert, G., and Halligan, J. 2015. *Performance Management in the Public Sector*. 2nd ed. Abingdon, Oxon: Routledge.

Vanhercke, B. 2019. 'From the Lisbon Strategy to the European Pillar of Social Rights: The Many Lives of the Social Open Method of Coordination', in B. Vanhercke, D. Ghailani, S. Spasova, and P. Pochet (eds), *Social Policy in the European Union 1999–2019: The Long and Winding Road*. Brussels: ETUI, 99–124.

Varone, F., Ingold, K., Jourdain, C., and Schneider, V. 2017. 'Studying Policy Advocacy through Social Network Analysis', *European Political Science* 16(3): 322–36. <https://doi.org/10.1057/eps.2016.16>.

Vedung, E. 2007. 'Evaluation Research', in B. G. Peters and J. Pierre (eds), *Handbook of Public Policy*. London: Sage, 397–416.

VeneKlasen, L. and Miller, V. 2007. *A New Weave of Power, People and Politics: The Action Guide for Advocacy and Citizen Participation*. Rugby, Warwickshire: Practical Action Publishing.

Vogel, D. 1997. 'Trading up and Governing across: Transnational Governance and Environmental Protection', *Journal of European Public Policy* 4(4): 556–71. <https://doi.org/10.1080/135017697344064>.

Wade, R. 2015. 'The Role of Industrial Policy in Developing Countries', in A. Calcagno, S. Dullien, A. M. Márquez-Velázquez, and J. Priewe (eds), *UNCTAD: Rethinking Development Strategies After the Financial Crisis. I. Making the Case for Policy Space. Rethinking Development Strategies After the Financial Crisis*. New York: Geneva United Nations, 67–80.

Waisman, H., et al. 2019. 'A Pathway Design Framework for National Low Greenhouse Gas Emission Development Strategies', *Nature Climate Change* 9(4): 261–8. <https://doi.org/10.1038/s41558-019-0442-8>.

Warner, M. E. 2013. 'Private Finance for Public Goods: Social Impact Bonds'. *Journal of Economic Policy Reform* 16(4): 303–19. <https://doi.org/10.1080/17487870.2013.835727>.

Watts, E. 2018. 'LessThanUThink Campaign Against Binge Drinking Launches on Texas A&M Campus'. Retrieved 13 February 2018 from <https://today.tamu.edu/2018/02/13lessthanuthink-campaign-against-binge-drinking-launches-on-texas-am-campus/>.

Weale, S. 2019. 'Pension Changes will Leave University Staff £240k Worse off—Study', *The Guardian*, 4 September. Retrieved 8 May 2021 from <https://www.theguardian.com/education/2019/sep/04/rising-contributions-reduced-benefits-university-pensions>.

Weaver, R. K. 1986. 'The Politics of Blame Avoidance', *Journal of Public Policy* 6(4): 371–98. <doi:10.1017/S0143814X00004219>.

Weaver, R. K. 2014. 'Compliance Regimes and Barriers to Behavioral Change', *Governance* 27(2): 243–65. <https://doi.org/10.1111/gove.12032>.

Wegrich, K. 2021. 'Policy Instruments and Administrative Capacities', in B. G. Peters and I. Thynne (eds), *Oxford Research Encyclopedia of Politics*. Oxford: Oxford University Press. doi.org/10.1093/acrefore/9780190228637.013.1370

Wegrich, K., and Štimac, V. 2014. 'Coordination Capacity', in M. Lodge and K. Wegrich (eds), *The Problem-Solving Capacity of the Modern State*. Oxford: Oxford University Press, 41–62.

Weiss, C. H. 1979. 'The Many Meanings of Research Utilization', *Public Administration Review* 39(5): 426–31. <https://doi.org/10.2307/3109916>.

Whelan, J., and LaRocca, S. n.d. 'Process Guide: Cutting the Issue'. Retrieved 27 April 2021 from <https://commonslibrary.org/wp-content/uploads/2015-Process-Guide-Cutting-The-Issue.pdf>.

Widerquist, K. 2005. 'A Failure to Communicate: What (if Anything) Can we Learn from the Negative Income Tax Experiments?', *Journal of Socio-Economics* 34(1): 49–81. <https://doi.org/10.1016/j.socec.2004.09.050>.

Widerquist, K. 2019. 'Three Waves of Basic Income Support', in M. Torry (ed.), *The Palgrave International Handbook of Basic Income*. London: Palgrave Macmillan, 31–44.

Wildavsky, A. B. 1964. *Politics of the Budgetary Process*. New York: Little Brown.

Wildavsky, A. 1969. 'Rescuing policy analysis from PPBS'. *Public Administration Review*, 29(2), 189–202. https://www.jstor.org/stable/pdf/973700.pdf?casa_

token=2jbFZru2P0kAAAAA:ZLD0wzv2uKyHHhvojVnqKcYT49_3P4-M8QrL7Y6CIh
u8MRWWKkxnMmvEVX7RQjN9OKDCpI7f5bFQyqrz67djYI9tQKukpOwraIaE3
Z5R_sdoiwFQdcU

Wildavsky, A. 1972. 'The Self-Evaluating Organization'. *Public Administration Review* 32(5): 509–20. <https://doi.org/10.2307/975158>.

Wildavsky, A. B. 1979. *Speaking Truth to Power. The Art and Craft of Policy Analysis*. Boston: Little, Brown.

Williams, W., and Evans, J. W. 1969. 'The Politics of Evaluation: The Case of Head Start', *Annals of the American Academy of Political and Social Science* 385(1): 118–32. <https://doi.org/10.1177/000271626938500111>.

Wilson, J. Q. 1980. 'The Politics of Regulation', in J. Q. Wilson (ed.), *The Politics of Regulation*. New York: Basic Books, 357–94.

Wilson, J. Q. 1989. *Bureaucracy: What Government Agencies Do and Why they Do it*. New York: Basic Books.

Windhoff-Héritier, A., and Czada, R. 1991. 'Introduction', in R. Czada and A. Windhoff-Héritier (eds), *Political Choice: Institutions, Rules, and the Limits of Rationality*. Frankfurt am Main: Campus, 9–23.

Winterton, J., and Winterton, R. 1989. *Coal, Crisis, and Conflict: The 1984–85 Miners' Strike in Yorkshire*. Manchester: Manchester University Press.

Wolff, J. 2015. 'Paying People to Act in their own Interests: Incentives versus Rationalization in Public Health', *Public Health Ethics* 8(1): 27–30. <https://doi.org/10.1093/phe/phu035>.

Wollmann, H. 1983. 'Implementation durch Gegen-Implementation? Das Beispiel der Wohnungspolitik', in R. Mayntz (ed.), *Implementation politischer Programme II: Ansätze zur Theoriebildung*. Opladen: Westdeutscher Verlag, 168–96.

Wollmann, H. 2007. 'Policy Evaluation and Evaluation Research', in F. Fischer, G. J. Miller, and M. S. Sidney (eds), *Handbook of Public Policy Analysis*. Boca Raton, FL: CRC Press, 393–404.

World Bank. 1997. *World Development Report 1997: The State in a Changing World*. New York: Oxford University Press.

World Bank. 2004. *Operationalizing Political Analysis: The Expected Utility Stakeholder Model and Governance Reforms*. Washington, DC: World Bank PremNotes.

World Bank. 2012. *Focus on Results: SIEF—Improving Lives through Evidence-Based Policy-making for Human Development*. Washington, DC: World Bank.

World Bank. 2017. *Doing Business 2018*. Washington, DC: World Bank.

World Bank. 2019. *Doing Business 2020*. Washington, DC: World Bank.

World Health Organization. 2012. *Tobacco Industry Interference: A Global Brief*. Geneva: World Health Organization.

World Health Organization. 2020. 'Obesity and Overweight'. Retrieved 16 April 2021 from <https://www.who.int/en/news-room/fact-sheets/detail/obesity-and-overweight>.

Wright, C. F. 2014. 'How do States Implement Liberal Immigration Policies? Control Signals and Skilled Immigration Reform in Australia', *Governance* 27(3): 397–421. <https://doi.org/10.1111/gove.12043>.

Wright, L. 2018. 'EU Confronts Member States Issuing Citizenship for Money', *DW*, 7 August. Retrieved 8 May 2021 from <https://www.dw.com/en/eu-confronts-member-states-issuing-citizenship-for-money/a-44978389>.

Yackee, S. W. 2019. 'The Politics of Rulemaking in the United States', *Annual Review of Political Science* 22: 37–55. <https://doi.org/10.1146/annurev-polisci-050817-092302>.

Yerkes, M. A., and Javornik, J. 2019. 'Creating Capabilities: Childcare Policies in Comparative Perspective', *Journal of European Social Policy* 29(4): 529–44. <https://doi.org/10.1177/0958928718808421>.

Zacka, B. 2017. *When the State Meets the Street: Public Service and Moral Agency*. Cambridge, MA: Harvard University Press.

Zeitlin, J. 2011. 'Is the Open Method of Coordination an Alternative to the Community Method?', in R. Dehousse (ed.), *The Community Method: Obstinate or Obsolete?* London: Palgrave Macmillan, 135–47.

Zhao, Y. 2020. 'Two Decades of Havoc: A Synthesis of Criticism Against PISA', *Journal of Educational Change* 21: 245–66. <https://doi.org/10.1007/s10833-019-09367-x>.

Zubaşcu, F. 2019. 'JRC Report Says Evidence-Based Policymaking is "Under Attack"', *Science Business*. Retrieved 8 March 2021 from <https://sciencebusiness.net/news/jrc-report-says-evidence-based-policymaking-under-attack>.

Zürn, M. 2018. *A Theory of Global Governance: Authority, Legitimacy, and Contestation*. Oxford: Oxford University Press.

Index